MW01474366

# RESEARCH IN CONSUMER BEHAVIOR

# RESEARCH IN CONSUMER BEHAVIOR

Series Editor: Russell W. Belk

Recent Volumes:

Vols 1–11:   Research in Consumer Behavior

RESEARCH IN CONSUMER BEHAVIOR   VOLUME 12

# RESEARCH IN CONSUMER BEHAVIOR

EDITED BY

## RUSSELL W. BELK

*Schulich School of Business, York University,
Toronto, ON, Canada*

United Kingdom – North America – Japan
India – Malaysia – China

Emerald Group Publishing Limited
Howard House, Wagon Lane, Bingley BD16 1WA, UK

First edition 2010

Copyright © 2010 Emerald Group Publishing Limited

**Reprints and permission service**
Contact: booksandseries@emeraldinsight.com

No part of this book may be reproduced, stored in a retrieval system, transmitted in any form or by any means electronic, mechanical, photocopying, recording or otherwise without either the prior written permission of the publisher or a licence permitting restricted copying issued in the UK by The Copyright Licensing Agency and in the USA by The Copyright Clearance Center. No responsibility is accepted for the accuracy of information contained in the text, illustrations or advertisements. The opinions expressed in these chapters are not necessarily those of the Editor or the publisher.

**British Library Cataloguing in Publication Data**
A catalogue record for this book is available from the British Library

ISBN: 978-0-85724-443-7
ISSN: 0885-2111 (Series)

Emerald Group Publishing Limited, Howard House, Environmental Management System has been certified by ISOQAR to ISO 14001:2004 standards

Awarded in recognition of Emerald's production department's adherence to quality systems and processes when preparing scholarly journals for print

INVESTOR IN PEOPLE

# CONTENTS

LIST OF CONTRIBUTORS ix

INTRODUCTION xi

### SECTION I: RCB REVIEWED PAPERS
#### Part I: Shopping Practices

CONSUMER ATTITUDES TOWARD
ORGANIC FOODS: AN EXPLORATION OF
U.S. MARKET SEGMENTS
  *Julie V. Stanton and Deirdre T. Guion* 5

SHOPPING MATTERS: TAIWANESE YOUNG
TOURISTS' CONSUMER CULTURE IN
ENGLAND
  *Joyce Hsiu-yen Yeh* 43

#### Part II: Consumption Cues

CUE CONGRUENCY AND PRODUCT
INVOLVEMENT EFFECTS ON GENERATION
Y ATTITUDES
  *Timothy Heinze* 75

COUNTRY-OF-MANUFACTURE LABELING
EFFECT ON PRODUCT QUALITY
EVALUATIONS: A MODEL INCORPORATING
CONSUMERS' ATTENTION
  *Pingjun Jiang* 101

## Part III: Material Consumption Phenomena and Processes

**SOCIALIZATION OF ADULT AND YOUNG CONSUMERS INTO MATERIALISM: THE ROLES OF MEDIA AND CHURCH IN PERU**
*Sandra K. Smith Speck and Teri Peterson* — *133*

**MOTIVATION FOR LUXURY CONSUMPTION: EVIDENCE FROM A METROPOLITAN CITY IN CHINA**
*Ying Wang, Shaojing Sun and Yiping Song* — *161*

**CONSUMING COOL: BEHIND THE UNEMOTIONAL MASK**
*Russell W. Belk, Kelly Tian and Heli Paavola* — *183*

## SECTION II: CCT REVIEWED PAPERS

### Part I: Advertising and Branding Practice

**THE STRATEGIC USE OF BRAND BIOGRAPHIES**
*Jill Avery, Neeru Paharia, Anat Keinan and Juliet B. Schor* — *213*

**AUTHENTIC BRAND NARRATIVES: CO-CONSTRUCTED MEDITERRANEANESS FOR L'OCCITANE BRAND**
*Luca Massimiliano Visconti* — *231*

### Part II: Creating Selves

**CONSUMING AUTHENTIC NEIGHBORHOOD: AN AUTOETHNOGRAPHY OF EXPERIENCING A NEIGHBORHOOD'S NEW BEGINNINGS AND ORIGINS WITHIN ITS SERVICESCAPES**
*Michelle Hall* — *263*

BETTER UNDERSTANDING CONSTRUCTION
OF THE SELF IN DAILY CONTINGENCIES:
AN INVESTIGATION OF THE MATERIALITY
OF CONSUMPTION EXPERIENCES IN ONLINE
DISCUSSION FORUMS
 *Alexandre Schwob and Kristine de Valck*   *287*

"PIXELIZE ME!": DIGITAL STORYTELLING AND
THE CREATION OF ARCHETYPAL MYTHS
THROUGH EXPLICIT AND IMPLICIT SELF-BRAND
ASSOCIATION IN FASHION AND LUXURY BLOGS
 *Gachoucha Kretz and Kristine de Valck*   *313*

# LIST OF CONTRIBUTORS

| | |
|---|---|
| *Jill Avery* | Simmons School of Management, Boston, MA, USA |
| *Russell W. Belk* | Schulich School of Business, York University, Toronto, ON, Canada |
| *Deirdre T. Guion* | School of Business, North Carolina Central University, Durham, NC, USA |
| *Michelle Hall* | Institute of Creative Industries and Innovation, Queensland University of Technology, Brisbane, QLD, Australia |
| *Timothy Heinze* | Department of Finance & Marketing, California State University, Chico, CA, USA |
| *Pingjun Jiang* | Department of Marketing, School of Business Administration, La Salle University, Philadelphia, PA, USA |
| *Anat Keinan* | Marketing Unit, Harvard Business School, Boston, MA, USA |
| *Gachoucha Kretz* | Marketing Department, HEC Paris School of Management, Paris, France |
| *Heli Paavola* | Advansis Oy, Tampere, Finland |
| *Neeru Paharia* | Edmond J. Safra Center for Ethics, Harvard University, Cambridge, MA, USA |
| *Teri Peterson* | College of Business, Idaho State University, Pocatello, IO, USA |
| *Juliet B. Schor* | Department of Sociology, Boston College, Chestnut Hill, MA, USA |

| | |
|---|---|
| *Alexandre Schwob* | Marketing Department, HEC Paris School of Management, Paris, France |
| *Yiping Song* | Department of Marketing, School of Management, Fudan University, Shanghai, China |
| *Sandra K. Smith Speck* | College of Business, Idaho State University, Pocatello, ID, USA |
| *Julie V. Stanton* | Department of Business, The Pennsylvania State University, Media, PA, USA |
| *Shaojing Sun* | School of Journalism, Fudan University, Shanghai, China |
| *Kelly Tian* | College of Business, New Mexico State University, Las Cruces, NM, USA |
| *Luca Massimiliano Visconti* | Department of Marketing, Università Bocconi, Milan, Italy |
| *Kristine de Valck* | Marketing Department, HEC Paris School of Management, Paris, France |
| *Ying Wang* | Department of Marketing, Williamson College of Business Administration, Youngstown State University, Youngstown, OH, USA |
| *Joyce Hsiu-yen Yeh* | Department of Ethnic Relations & Cultures, National Dong Hwa University, Hualien, Taiwan |

# INTRODUCTION

Together, the chapters included in this volume represent a cross-section of cutting-edge consumer research. There are two main sections of chapters. The first seven chapters have come through the normal RCB review process, while the last six chapters were first competitively reviewed and accepted into the 2010 Consumer Culture Theory Conference held in Madison, WI. The latter chapters were then selected for publication from the much larger set of papers presented at the conference, by cochairs David Crockett, Markus Giesler, and Craig Thompson. In addition to this division the chapters cohere around a set of five substantive themes:

1. Shopping Practices
2. Consumption Cues
3. Material Consumption Phenomena and Processes
4. Advertising and Branding Practice
5. Creating Selves

These contributions constitute a partial, but quite well-rounded view of the factors involved in consumption: psychological and sociological, online and physical environments, culture and cohorts, institutions and media, luxury and coolness, advertising and brands. Moreover, the focus of the chapters varies from the micro level of meaning cues and the self to the macro level of material discourse and myth. There is a good geographic range found in the volume as well, with data from North America, South America, Europe, and Asia. In bringing in culture, the chapters invoke cultural comparison, cultural mobility, and cultural inferences. The result is a stimulating cornucopia of ideas and perspectives. The open-minded reader should find that the diverse perspectives presented here mutually inform, challenge, and interrogate one another.

Russell W. Belk
*Editor*

# SECTION I
# RCB REVIEWED PAPERS

# Part I
# Shopping Practices

# CONSUMER ATTITUDES TOWARD ORGANIC FOODS: AN EXPLORATION OF U.S. MARKET SEGMENTS

Julie V. Stanton and Deirdre T. Guion

### ABSTRACT

Purpose – *This study explores U.S. consumer attitudes toward organic foods in order to demonstrate that multiple and meaningful segments can be identified based on attitudes and beliefs rather than demographics and that a more targeted marketing strategy could likely create a better fit with consumer wants and needs.*

Methodology – *Q-methodology is employed, in part to demonstrate its usefulness for segmentation purposes.*

Findings – *Six meaningful segments of consumers are generated based on attitudes toward organic foods: Health Enthusiasts, Organic Idealists, Hoban's Hogwashers, Unengaged Shoppers, Bargain Shoppers, and Cynical/Distrustfuls. These groups vary in attitudes toward organic food, and despite conventional wisdom, exhibit a reasonable match between attitude and purchase behavior. Segments are also generated for viewpoints toward conventionally grown foods, revealing that consumers do not simply hold binary positions (pro-organic, anticonventional), but* instead consider each food type on its respective merits. Positioning and media choice strategies are considered for each organic food segment.

Originality – This chapter distinguishes between different types of consumers of organic food by using Q-methodology, with the result being a rich, detailed description of the values and preferences of each group. With these descriptions, the organic food industry can better align its marketing efforts with the priorities of individual consumer groups, rather than their simplistic demographics as are commonly utilized. The chapter also offers a unique perspective on the attitude–behavior gap, revealing that when the attitude is understood in greater detail, the gap appears to disappear.

# INTRODUCTION

In the past few decades the U.S. market for organic foods has grown rapidly; sales in 1980, for example, were $78 million compared to nearly $14 billion in 2005 (Dimitri & Greene, 2002; Organic Trade Association [OTA], 2006a). By the end of 2009, sales reached $24.8 billion (OTA. 2006b). Despite this growth, the market share of organic foods is still small, just 3.7% of all retail food sales in 2009 (OTA, 2006b). For organic food sales to remotely approximate the size of the conventional food industry, both supply and demand initiatives must be addressed.

The Organic Trade Association has called for greater federal investment in facilitating an increase in organic agricultural production (OTA, 2006c). They point to, among other things, the need for more market data to guide the sector in its choices each season. As consumers continue to show interest in organic foods, more precise information about their needs and preferences will aid in that seasonal planning.

As described in Hughner, McDonagh, Prothero, Shultz, and Stanton (2007), studies of organic food consumers abound, but only a relatively small number are empirical and focused on consumers' beliefs. A select few attempt to identify segments of consumers within a given country, but most offer more overarching descriptions. Therefore, while studies have concluded that concern about health and wellness, awareness of environmental issues, perceptions of taste and freshness, and resistance to genetically modified (GM) foods are linked to organic food consumption, there has been little suggestion of differing priorities for such motives. In contrast, consumer confusion about what the "organic" label means, particularly given the proliferation of similar labels such as "all natural," "no artificial ingredients," "GMO-free," "cage-free," and "dolphin-safe," is a common theme. In addition, a wide array of new retail outlets – from the stereotypical local food cooperative to mainstream grocery stores – has created new consumption opportunities. Together, these trends have shaped a consumption environment where consumers vary in demographics, motives, lifestyles, and beliefs about food. Yet, we – marketers, the food industry, academics – know surprisingly little about how consumers identify themselves around organic foods. Indeed, without a more thorough understanding of what motivates consumers, the industry is unlikely to do much more than capitalize on a general momentum in favor of organic foods, rather than effectively position their products by offering meaningful options to multiple interested consumer segments.

In this study, we address the need for a more holistic profile of consumer attitudes toward organic foods, one which reveals the multiple schools of thought to which consumers adhere and which moves away from simplistic, single-dimensional descriptions. Armed with such knowledge, retailers can anticipate growth segments and develop marketing and merchandising strategies to suit them. Growers can plan for increased volume and niche demands. Manufacturers can decide how to enter this market with existing products lines or through brand acquisitions. Policymakers too can benefit by developing a more comprehensive and meaningful set of guidelines for what is labeled "organic" through the National Organic Standard and thereby better serve consumers and industry alike. To date, unfortunately, no study has attempted to generate such an understanding of U.S. consumer attitudes toward organic foods (see Thompson, 1998 for a review of earlier studies).

More specifically, this study demonstrates the potential for generating that richer understanding through Q-methodology. With our data, we are able to: one, identify meaningful consumer segments regarding organic foods and compare the attitudes and beliefs they hold; two, demonstrate the suitability of Q-methodology – rooted in allowing respondents to identify with certain attitudes and beliefs more than others – for constructing those segments; and three, show the organic food industry that different (potential) consumer segments could be communicated to or engaged with better understanding of what matters most to them. Recognizably, this study is exploratory and is not designed to answer all questions that may arise about consumer attitudes toward organic foods. We purposefully seek in-depth understanding of the variety of perspectives regarding organic foods rather than provide an exhaustive schema. Considering that as many as 66% of consumers have purchased organic foods at some point (Dimitri & Greene, 2002), it is imperative that this first step toward developing a broader understanding of the organic food consumer be taken.

In the next section, the literature pertaining to organic food consumers is briefly reviewed. The methodologies previously employed to identify segments of food consumers are then examined. We contend that the most useful segments will be those based on attitudes and beliefs. Details of Q-methodology are then discussed and findings are presented. A discussion of marketing implications concludes.

## LITERATURE ON ORGANIC CONSUMERS

A search for literature about consumers of organic food yields hundreds of citations since 1985, although only a small minority can be classified as empirical studies of consumer purchasing motives, beliefs, and behaviors toward organic foods. As Hughner et al. (2007) indicate the studies vary widely in their methodologies, geographic focus, and conclusions. However, together they demonstrate the potentially great differences in values consumers place on individual attributes of the "organic" concept.

For example, while several studies have found that environmental concern rates highly in encouraging purchase of organic foods (e.g., Hill & Lynchehaun, 2002; Squires, Juric, & Cornwell, 2001; Wandel & Buggel, 1997; Roddy, Cowan, & Hutchinson, 1996), others have found perceptions of healthfulness, taste, and nutrients to outweigh concern for the environment (e.g., Magnusson, Arvola, Hursti, Aberg, & Sjoden, 2003; Zanoli & Naspetti, 2002; Schifferstein & Oude Ophuis (1998)).

On the possible health attributes of organic foods, some studies have concluded that consumers perceive organic foods as healthier because of the requirement that they not be produced with pesticides and other chemicals (e.g., Wilkins & Hillers, 1994; Jolly, 1991; Misra, Huang, & Ott, 1991). Yet according to other studies, some consumers believe organic food is also more nutritious (e.g., Hill & Lynchehaun, 2002), despite little scientific evidence to support that notion.

Studies also demonstrate that consumer motives for purchasing organic foods can stem from taste preferences, food safety concerns, interest in animal welfare, desire to support the local economy, and other sentimental, nostalgia-oriented factors (Hill & Lynchehaun, 2002; Schifferstein & Oude Ophuis, 1998; Roddy et al., 1996). This wide variety of notions and attitudes is viewed by many studies as a principal source of consumer confusion about the term "organic."

This suggests that an effort to segment consumers about organic foods will yield more meaningful descriptions, particularly when membership in a segment is assigned by the consumer and is based on attitudes and beliefs held by the consumers. Yet few of the studies mentioned above actually attempt to segment consumers; those that do will be discussed below. None attempt to segment U.S. consumers regarding organic food. Most studies, through focus groups, interviews, mail surveys, and the like, offer more general conclusions about either organic consumers as a whole or attitudes in the general population about organic foods, leaving a richer understanding of organic food consumer segments undeveloped. Showing that consumers do align themselves in different segments is a principal aim of this study.

In order to demonstrate the strength of Q-methodology to provide a more holistic profile of organic food consumption segments, a review of studies that utilize other segmentation bases is needed.

## METHODS OF SEGMENTING FOOD CONSUMERS

Among the usual textbook bases for segmentation are demographics, behavior, benefits, situation of use, and psychographics, and studies that segment food consumers have used one or more of those methods. While each has the ability to shed light on consumer behavior, the methods vary in their ability to offer marketers tools with which to better communicate or persuade consumers.

Among the more common methods is segmentation based on consumer perceptions of product benefits. For example, Funk and Phillips (1990) segment the Ontario, Canada, table egg market using a combination of benefits and beliefs. Clusters of consumers are identified based on 15 statements such as "I like the taste of eggs" and "Eggs are convenient to use and easy to serve." Similarly, Honkanen, Olsen, and Myrland (2004) segment Norwegian teenagers according to their food preferences, where preferences are identified through "liking" or "taste" for some 20 different at-home meals. Respondents in each case indicate their level of agreement with each statement on Likert scales. Interestingly, the authors use a host of additional questions covering lifestyle, health attitudes, and shopping behavior to describe the resulting clusters, but do not use that information to help form the clusters. Hence, the segments identified do not reflect anything more general about the consumers' beliefs.

Demographic variables have also been a long-time staple of segmentation studies. In one study of Italian consumers, Chinnici, D'Amico, and Pecorino (2002) used socioeconomic variables such as age, gender, and income along with general shopping practices associated with organic foods to segment consumers. While the four resulting segments are partially described on the basis of frequency of purchase of organic foods and where they shop for them, the descriptions rely largely on demographic variables, offering little understanding about the underlying motives for purchase.

In some cases, segmentation studies do not focus on consumers but on the product itself. For example, in a study of Japanese fruit snacking, Gehrt and Shim (2003) use situational factors to segment snacks. For eight situations, respondents rated 18 snacks on a 5-point frequency scale (from "never" to "frequently"). Four product clusters were produced that distinguish between snacks based on most common consumption occasion. However, since consumer benefits, motives, etc. are not reflected in these clusters, they are less valuable to marketers in contextualizing consumer motives and in developing positioning strategies.

Consumer attitudes, beliefs, and motives do serve as the basis for segmentation in several studies. Moschis, Curasi, and Bellenger (2004) examine the motives employed by older U.S. consumers in their decisions to patronize individual food stores, and conclude that four "gerontographic" segments – based on life circumstances and the processes of aging – exist that help explain varying shopping behaviors. Similarly, Verdurme and Viaene (2003) segment Belgian consumers regarding GM foods, using a variety of attitudes and beliefs (e.g., "GM food is artificial"). Roddy et al. (1996) segment the Irish market based on attitudes toward organic foods (e.g., "Organic foods are usually healthier to eat than foods normally available") and find nine distinct segments. Fotopoulos and Krystallis (2002) examine the Greek market using statements about health attributes of food, ethical views, and what constitutes quality of a food.

In each case, however, these attitude-based studies rely on respondent ratings of individual statements, usually by means of Likert scales. Such scales implicitly assume that individual perspectives toward the items reflected in the statements can be represented by a single continuum (the scale), and that the importance of any one item can be captured by the single scale rather than in the context of all statements together. This is a loss in richness that is lamentable and avoided with Q-methodology.

Most segmentation studies offer little toward developing product marketing and positioning strategies as evidenced by how infrequently such strategies are mentioned. Studies that utilize respondent motives and beliefs make the connection most frequently. For example, Moschis et al. (2004) take great care to offer target marketing strategies based on each specific gerontographic group (e.g., offer price-reduction promotions to "ailing outgoers" but avoid senior discounts that carry the stigma of being for "old" consumers). Similarly, in their study of attitudes toward GM foods, Verdurme and Viaene (2003) are very specific as to how the characteristics of each consumer segment would relate to both the communication approach and the most trusted sources of information. For example, to reach the "green opponents" the recommended objective is to provide two-sided factual information to allow the segment to test the validity of their own arguments, while the objective for reaching "enthusiasts" is to make sure they are supporters of GM food for appropriate reasons. Each recommendation is based on specific attitudes held by each group, a result not possible with studies based on demographics or other segmentation bases.

Therefore, despite gathering some information about consumer motives, many food segmentation studies rely on variables that offer little assistance in understanding the complexity of consumer choices around organic foods, their collective attitudes, and subsequent behavior. Additionally, these studies fall short in devising positioning strategies. Further, despite the vast literature on organic food, few studies have actually attempted to segment organic food consumers, none for the U.S. market. Organic food sales have grown rapidly in recent years, but overall the market is still rather small. A careful approach to segmenting U.S. consumers is clearly needed, with a corresponding examination of the marketing implications. Because knowledge about the motives for purchasing organic foods is likely to be a key component to an effective segmented marketing strategy, the approach must adequately incorporate consumer attitudes and beliefs. Q-methodology offers a promising method for capturing those beliefs in meaningful ways.

## METHODOLOGY

### Theoretical Considerations

The study of organic food consumers has been approached from a number of theoretical perspectives. In some instances, focus groups, and in-person and mailed surveys have generated information that describes the organic food consumer, but the empirical work does not appear to be guided by any strain of consumer theory. Collection of demographic and shopping pattern variables is typical and consumer segments, if identified, are based on those variables (see, e.g., Chinnici et al., 2002). While attitudes and beliefs are therefore generally absent from these studies, they do offer an insight into the way organic foods are viewed in the marketplace.

Another relevant strain of literature relies on the economic theory of the consumer, particularly on the Random Utility Model (McFadden, 1973). In this approach, rational consumers will choose from among consumption alternatives such that they maximize their own utility. Utility has both observable and unobservable ("random") components and is usually expressed as a function of exogenous factors including product attributes, the consumer's sociodemographic characteristics, and other relevant attitudes and beliefs. Studies that employ this approach include Larue, West, Gendron, and Lambert (2004) who examine consumer response to functional attributes of organic, conventional, and GM foods. While their inclusion of attitudes is limited to two health properties, they nonetheless demonstrate that consumers have beliefs about these claims and are willing to pay for them. However, little real detail of consumer motivations is generated by this approach.

A third prominent strain of the organic food consumption literature relies on Ajzen's (1991) Theory of Planned Behavior. In this theory, it is argued that a person's salient beliefs are what influence his/her intentions most, and that those beliefs are generally behavioral, normative, or control beliefs. Behavioral beliefs lead to attitudes through an evaluation of desirable versus undesirable consequences of each behavior, such that an individual will have a favorable attitude toward products with desirable attributes, etc. Normative beliefs capture the individual's sense of how "important persons" would view the behavior, for example, a parent, a spouse, a minister. Depending on how important the individual considers those views to be, normative beliefs can affect purchase intention. Control beliefs refer to the individual's sense of how likely it is that the purchase can be made. Affordability, availability, and opportunity would influence control beliefs. In this view of behavioral intentions, segments based on means other than attitudes and beliefs would be expected to have little meaning for marketing strategy.

Verdurme and Viaene (2003) develop a model to link attitudes and purchase intention for GM foods, based in part on Ajzen's work. Their model incorporates the influence that branding has on purchase intention specifically that attitudes toward the particular product develop after the initial purchase that was made based on the brand. For generic products, the

Theory of Planned Behavior and its corollaries hold. Their conclusion: "knowledge, general attitudes, and especially beliefs, attitudes and purchase intentions are the core elements of the hypothetical model intentions related to GM food, and therefore, questions regarding these topics should not be lacking the questionnaire" (p. 94).

Other cognitive approaches to establishing the link between attitude and behavior intentions include that of Zanoli and Naspetti (2002). Their study of organic consumers in Italy uses a means-end chain model, an approach that exploits a "network of links" developed in a consumer's mind when the person considers a specific product. These links reflect an individual's view of how product attributes have consequences, positive or negative, for the individual and the greater world. Those views influence the individual's motivation toward purchasing the product. The authors use an interview-based laddering process to create hierarchical value maps, but the first step in the process is a carefully planned elicitation of product characteristics that are most important to the individual – the individual's attitudes and beliefs regarding the product. This step coincides neatly with Q-methodology.

Other scholars have pointed to the limitations associated with studying consumer values outside of their cultural context (e.g., Thompson & Troester, 2002). Without attention to the underlying cultural influences, little direct link can be drawn between consumers' values and their specific attitudes and behaviors. In reality, consumer attitudes are a product of their culture-based interpretations of consumption experiences and thus a meaningful evaluation of those attitudes must allow for such interpretations.

Q-methodology, as described below, offers a tool for both assessing attitudes and beliefs and viewing them in the consumer's cultural frame of reference. The emphasis is on respondent subjectivity, preserving the individualized meaning placed on product and market attributes, and on collecting an interpretable narrative of those meanings. As such, it offers a structural approach to describing the myriad of consumer attitudes and avoids the simplistic employment of demographic descriptors alone. It allows for statistical confidence in generating meaningful distinctions in consumer attitudes while simultaneously situating those attitudes in the broader context of the consumers' lifestyles.

*Q-Methodology*

Q-methodology was developed by William Stephenson, a British physicist-psychologist in the 1930s as a tool that permits the systematic study of subjectivity (Valenta & Wigger, 1997). Because subjectivity is inherently an individual concept, the method hinges on preserving each individual's frame of reference (McKeown & Thomas, 1988). Toward that end the method is a unique combination of qualitative and quantitative research techniques that have been applied to a broad range of disciplines including psychology, medicine, nursing, communications, and political science. For example, Brodt et al. (2004) identified three distinct farm-management styles among almond and winegrape growers in California, and evaluated each group's adoption decisions regarding biologically integrated farming practices. Their three segments demonstrate varying decisions about environmentally benign production practices, an important input into policy planning, and a corollary to our goal of helping guide marketing strategies.

Popovich and Popovich (2000) created a strategic plan for a small hospital and were able to identify priorities among the various stakeholders, identify three distinct views, and develop a new strategic plan that more accurately reflected the consensus. With a Likert scale–based approach, it is less likely that they would have identified the top priorities for each group and hence what a strategic plan should include.

Al-Makaty, Van Tubergen, Whitlow, and Boyd (1996) identified three segments of Saudi men in terms of their attitudes toward television advertising. With one group ardently opposed to western influences through advertising, a second group seeing economic benefits if still concerned about cultural effects, and a third supportive of cultural modernization, the authors are able to advise international marketers on more suitable and culturally sensitive strategies.

In Q-methodology, each statement that respondents are asked to evaluate is allowed to be interpreted by the individual, and the evaluation of those statements is made in relation to each other, not in isolation. This is in contrast to the studies described above that use Likert scales for each statement. The advantage of the Q approach is that individuals will reveal the statements that are most and least similar to their viewpoints, by sorting them into a discrete quasinormal distribution (ranging from "least characteristic of my viewpoint" to "most characteristic of my viewpoint"). Such a sorting identifies the statements that could most accurately describe the individual, while still allowing his/her other viewpoints to be captured. It is argued here that marketing strategies would be better served by segments that can be described by what is of most value, least value, etc. to the consumers therein.

During the actual Q-sort, the respondent is given a set of cards, each with a statement to be evaluated. A template is prepared on the table in front of the respondent, with markers ranging from −5 to +5 ("least ..." to "most ..."). Since the respondent's subjectivity is central to Q-methodology, the researcher is not involved in the sort itself. After the respondent finishes with the sorting process, the locations of statements in the quasinormal distribution are recorded for statistical evaluation. The sort is followed by an often lengthy semistructured interview during which the respondent is asked for his/her interpretations of characteristic statements and the lifestyle issues that influenced their placement in the continuum. It is not uncommon for a single sort and interview to take one hour or more to complete. In the case of multiple sorts for each respondent, the time allotted should be increased accordingly. This two-step process is not unlike that proposed by Thompson and Troester (2002) in which a two-phase interview is conducted and respondents are free to interpret the focal attributes according to their personal experiences. The second phase interview explores the cultural context of such interpretations.

The statements ("Q-sample") that respondents sort are purposely designed to capture as broad an array as possible of viewpoints on the matter at hand. They may derive from focus groups or interviews, or from review of published literature on the topic. The more representative the statements are of the universe of views on the subject, the more likely the researcher will find a comprehensive set of segments.

An important consequence of the Q-methodology approach is that it is not dependent on large numbers of respondents. Indeed, as McKeown and Thomas argue:

> The major concern of Q methodology is not with how many people believe such-and-such, but with why and how they believe what they do ... (S)mall numbers of respondents, including single cases, are psychometrically acceptable since the observational perspective is the respondent's own. (p. 45)

For market segmentation purposes, what does carry importance is that the set of respondents include a diverse group of people in the context of the research question: a purposive selection of individuals who appear on the surface to have differing views on the value of organic food, for example. If too little attention is paid to that variety of views, the results are not likely to demonstrate the variety of consumer types relevant to the topic at hand.

Q-methodology utilizes factor analysis (with individual respondents forming columns) to identify groupings of like-minded people. In determining the number of factors to rotate, Q-methodology is potentially subject to guidelines typically found in R-method applications such as choosing factors with eigenvalues greater than 1. However, Q-methodology is more interested in identifying factors of theoretical interest than limiting analysis to those that explain high portions of the variance (McKeown & Thomas, 1988). As such, "the importance of a factor cannot be determined by statistical criteria alone, but must take into account the social and political setting to which the factor is organically connected" (p. 51). A parallel situation in which contextual (cultural) elements are emphasized is offered by Thompson and Troester (2002) in their identification of natural health microcultures within the greater consumer system.

Q-methodology offers an avenue of exploration and study not available in more traditional methods, and hence is worthy of trial in this context. In addition, given the literature on behavioral intention and the importance of such for the success of marketing efforts, it seems imperative that a true and useful segmentation of consumers will be based on their attitudes and beliefs. Q-methodology appears to offer an elegant and effective way to not only capture attitudes and beliefs but really distinguish them based on what matters most to each respondent. For these reasons, we use Q-methodology in this study of consumer attitudes toward organic foods.

## DATA COLLECTION

The use of Q-methodology for our study involved several steps. First, the Q-sample, or set of statements, was developed using a careful review of existing literature (see Hughner et al., 2007). Emergent themes served as the basis for our Q-sample. For each theme, statements were then developed that capture different points of view and thereby preserve the intent of the "least characteristic ..." to "most characteristic ..." sorting continuum. In all, 67 statements were developed for use in the Q-sorts. These are reported in Table 1.

Second, the P-sample, or set of respondents, was developed in a purposive manner. As McKeown and Thomas (1988) argue, the P-sample can be chosen by using a factorial design or simply by taking advantage of someone's availability. Factorial design is often chosen when there are types of people of theoretical interest to the researchers. In many cases, however, the principal purpose of the study is to find out what types of people exist in the context of the matter under study, and hence a factorial design would add little meaning. In this study, we first developed a four-factor matrix based on age, education, household income, and presence of small children in the home. These demographic indicators were only meant to serve as general targets so as to avoid a sample heavily concentrated in wealthy

Table 1. Statements in the Q-Sample: "Organic Food ..." or "Conventional Food ...".

| | | |
|---|---|---|
| Belongs in specialty shops rather than conventional supermarkets | Is fashionable | Is spiritual |
| Borders on Frankenfood | Is fresh | Is sufficiently promoted and merchandized |
| Disregards welfare of animals | Is good for my family | Is suspect |
| Does not contain preservatives | Is good for my family's health | Is the same as "cage-free" and "free-range" food |
| Does not include additives | Is of good quality | Is the same as "natural" food |
| Employs preservation practices in production | Is grown without the use of hormones | Is typically blemished or bruised |
| Exposes the food supply to acts of terrorism | Is grown without the use of pesticides | Is unimaginative |
| Feeds everyone | Is harmful to the environment | Is visually appealing |
| Fosters confidence in the food industry | Is highly regulated | Is wholesome |
| Has a harmful effect on humanity | Is morally wrong | Is worrisome |
| Has a positive effect on humanity | Is nonconformist | Is worth a premium price |
| Has hidden health costs | Is not regulated enough | Reflects rejection of time-proven practices |
| Is a way for retailers to charge more | Is overblown | Relies on chemical inputs |
| Is associated with big business | Is part of a healthful diet | Reminds me of the past |
| Is compatible with my lifestyle | Is part of an alternative lifestyle | Supports preventative health care |
| Is consistent with my value system | Is produced as cheaply as possible | Supports smaller, family-owned farms |
| Is consistent with vegetarianism | Is produced in an environmentally friendly manner | Supports the local economy |
| Is conveniently located on store shelves | Is produced through humane treatment of animals | Tastes bland |
| Is costly to produce | Is pure | Tastes different |
| Is difficult to find | Is real, genuine food | Tastes good |
| Is easy to compare to other foods | Is safe from acts of terrorism | Uses chemical inputs in a responsible way |
| Is essential for children | Is safe to eat | |
| Is expensive | Is satisfactory for my needs | |

households, for example. Respondents were then chosen based on our view of their potential to offer a different viewpoint on organic foods compared to others in the sample, a more important criterion than demographics. In the end, we conducted Q-sorts with 31 individuals, who also happen to offer a reasonable distribution of the demographic indicators. There are also three ethnic groups represented in the sample. A participant profile is offered in Table 2.

Finally, as part of the research plan, it was decided to ask respondents to conduct the Q-sort in relation to not only organic foods but also separately to conventional foods. Since this study was intended in part as a test of the power of Q-methodology to segment consumers, it seemed appropriate to also let Q-methodology show that it could yield meaningful groups for different topics by using the same set of statements. That is, if instead respondents grouped together such that the same statements were emphasized regardless of whether referring to organic or conventional foods, then those segments may have little to do with either food category and would be less meaningful. If the statements that a consumer identifies with differ when applied to organic food compared to conventional food, then respondents would demonstrate distinct attitudes about each type of food. Resulting segments would be more meaningful.

## RESULTS

### Q-Sorts on Organic Food

Factor analysis of the Q-sorts on organic food produced six meaningful and distinct segments of consumers, distinguished by their attitudes and beliefs. Together the six segments explain approximately 69% of the total variance. The groups were named based on characteristics that described those statements around which participants positively coalesced: Health Enthusiasts, Organic Idealists, Unengaged Shoppers, Hoban's Hogwashers, Bargain Shoppers, and Cynical/Distrustfuls. Both characteristic and "distinguishing" statements – those placed in locations along the opinion continuum that are statistically significant from other groups – are summarized in Table 3.

*The Health Enthusiasts*
*Health Enthusiasts* are motivated to purchase organic foods based on their assessment that consuming them will lead to better health. Statements that organic food contributes to preventative health care and family health

***Table 2.*** Profile of Participants.

| Pseudonym | Age | Education | Household Income Level | Small Children? | Ethnicity |
|---|---|---|---|---|---|
| Aileen | 45–64 | High school degree | $25,000 to $49,999 | None | Caucasian |
| Ann | 45–64 | Some college | $50,000 to $74,999 | None | African American |
| Barb | 35–44 | College degree | Over $100,000 | 2, ages 8 and 10 | Caucasian |
| Bridget | 25–44 | Graduate degree | $25,000 to $49,999 | None | Caucasian |
| Callie | 35–44 | Graduate degree | $75,000 to $99,999 | 1, age 14 | African American |
| Carlos | 25–34 | Graduate degree | Over $100,000 | 2, ages 1 and 3 | Hispanic |
| Colleen | 45–64 | Graduate degree | Over $100,000 | None | Caucasian |
| Daniel | 35–44 | Graduate degree | Over $100,000 | None | Caucasian |
| Dennis | 35–44 | Graduate degree | $75,000 to $99,999 | 1, age 11 | Caucasian |
| Doug | 35–44 | Some college | Over $100,000 | 1, age 7 months | African American |
| Dreama | 65 or older | Graduate degree | $25,000 to $49,999 | None | African American |
| Eleanor | 18–24 | College degree | Less than $25,000 | None | Hispanic |
| Elise | 35–44 | College degree | $50,000 to $74,999 | 1, age 8 | Caucasian |
| Ernie | 18–24 | College degree | Less than $25,000 | None | Caucasian |
| George | 25–34 | Some college | $50,000 to $74,999 | None | Caucasian |
| Jack | 18–24 | College degree | Under $25,000 | None | Caucasian |
| Janet | 35–44 | College degree | Over $100,000 | 2, ages 4 and 7 | Caucasian |
| Kate | 45–64 | Some college | $50,000 to $74,999 | 1, age 14 | Caucasian |
| Leanne | 35–44 | College degree | $25,000 to $49,999 | 2, ages 7 and 10 | Caucasian |
| Lori | 35–44 | Graduate degree | Over $100,000 | 1, age 7 months | African American |
| Mabel | 65 or older | High school degree | $25,000 to $49,999 | None | Caucasian |
| Mark | 25–34 | Some college | $25,000 to $49,999 | 1, age 3 | Caucasian |
| Millie | 35–44 | Graduate degree | Over $100,000 | 2, ages 2 and 4 | Caucasian |
| Molly | 35–44 | Graduate degree | Over $100,000 | 3, ages 4, 7 and 9 | Caucasian |
| Nadia | 18–24 | College degree | Under $25,000 | None | Caucasian |
| Pam | 45–64 | High school degree | $25,000 to $49,999 | None | Caucasian |
| Rachel | 35–44 | High school degree | $50,000 to $74,999 | 2, ages 4 and 8 | Caucasian |
| Sarah | 45–64 | Graduate degree | $75,000 to $99,999 | None | Caucasian |
| Sophie | 35–44 | College degree | $50,000 to $74,999 | None | Caucasian |
| Tina | 35–44 | Graduate degree | Over $100,000 | 2, ages 3 and 10 | African American |
| Tom | 45–64 | College degree | $25,000 to $49,999 | 1, age 14 | Caucasian |

*Table 3.* Characteristic and Distinguishing Statements Regarding Organic Food.

| Health Enthusiasts | | Organic Idealists | | The Unengaged Shoppers | |
|---|---|---|---|---|---|
| Score | Statement: "organic food …" | Score | Statement: "organic food …" | Score | Statement: "organic food …" |
| *Characteristic statements* | | | | | |
| +5 | Is consistent with my value system** | +5 | Is fresh | +5 | Is expensive |
| +5 | Is good for my family's health | +5 | Is good for my family | +5 | Is good for my family |
| +5 | Is grown without the use of hormones | +5 | Is good for my family's health | +5 | Is grown w/o use of pesticides |
| +5 | Supports preventative healthcare** | +5 | Is safe to eat | +5 | Is wholesome |
| +4 | Has a positive effect on humanity** | +4 | Does not include additives | +4 | Is good for my family's health |
| +4 | Is good for my family | +4 | Is part of a healthful diet | +4 | Is good quality |
| +4 | Is real, genuine food | +4 | Is real, genuine food | +4 | Is grown w/o use of hormones |
| +4 | Is worth a premium price | +4 | Is wholesome | +4 | Is produced in environmentally friendly manner |
| −4 | Has hidden health costs | −4 | Belongs in specialty shops | −4 | Is difficult to find |
| −4 | Is worrisome | −4 | Disregards the welfare of animals | −4 | Is nonconformist** |
| −4 | Relies on chemical inputs | −4 | Exposes the food supply to acts of terrorism | −4 | Is safe from acts of terrorism |
| −4 | Tastes bland | −4 | Is associated with big business | −4 | Tastes different |
| −5 | Has a harmful effect on humanity | −5 | Has a harmful effect on humanity | −5 | Has a harmful effect on humanity |
| −5 | Is harmful to the environment | −5 | Is harmful to the environment | −5 | Is unimaginative** |
| −5 | Is morally wrong | −5 | Is morally wrong | −5 | Is worrisome* |
| −5 | Is overblown** | −5 | Is suspect** | −5 | Tastes bland |
| *Other "distinguishing" statements* | | | | | |
| +1 | Is expensive** | 0 | Is worth a premium price** | +3 | Fosters confidence in the food industry* |
| | | −2 | Is spiritual* | +1 | Feeds everyone* |
| | | | | 0 | Supports local economy* |

# Consumer Attitudes toward Organic Foods

| Hoban's Hogwashers | | Bargain Shoppers | | Cynical/Distrustfuls | |
|---|---|---|---|---|---|
| Score | Statement: "organic food …" | Score | Statement: "organic food …" | Score | Statement: "organic food …" |
| *Characteristic statements* | | | | | |
| +5 | Is costly to produce | +5 | Is expensive | +5 | Is a way for retailers to charge more |
| +5 | Is expensive | +5 | Is grown without use of hormones | +5 | Is expensive |
| +5 | Is fashionable** | +5 | Is safe to eat | +5 | Is not regulated enough** |
| +5 | Is visually appealing** | +5 | Is produced in an environmentally friendly manner* | +5 | Is essential for children |
| +4 | Is a way for retailers to charge more | +4 | Is grown without the use of pesticides | +4 | Employs preservation practices in production* |
| +4 | Is conveniently located on store shelves* | +4 | Is part of an alternative lifestyle | +4 | Exposes the food supply to acts of terrorism** |
| +4 | Is safe to eat | +4 | Is typically blemished or bruised** | +4 | Tastes good |
| +4 | Is wholesome | +4 | Supports smaller, family-owned farms | | |
| −4 | Exposes the food supply to acts of terrorism | −4 | Disregards the welfare of animals | −4 | Feeds everyone |
| −4 | Has a harmful effect on humanity | −4 | Has a harmful effect on humanity | −4 | Is easy to compare to other foods |
| −4 | Is harmful to environment | −4 | Is conveniently located on store shelves | −4 | Is safe from acts of terrorism |
| −4 | Is unimaginative | −4 | Is satisfactory for my needs** | −4 | Reminds me of the past* |
| −5 | Borders on Frankenfood | −5 | Is compatible with my lifestyle** | −5 | Is highly regulated** |
| −5 | Feeds everyone | −5 | Is harmful to the environment | −5 | Tastes bland |
| −5 | Is morally wrong | −5 | Is produced as cheaply as possible* | −5 | Is spiritual |
| −5 | Is spiritual | −5 | Relies on chemical inputs | −5 | Is produced in an environmentally friendly manner** |
| *Other "distinguishing" statements* | | | | | |
| +3 | Is overblown* | −2 | Is good for my family** | +3 | Is suspect** |
| +1 | Is not regulated enough** | −3 | Is visually appealing** | −1 | Has a harmful effect on humanity* |
| 0 | Is produce in an environ.-friendly manner* | | | −2 | Supports smaller, family-owned farms** |
| −1 | Is satisfactory for my needs* | | | −3 | Fosters confidence in the food industry* |
| −1 | Employs preserv. practices in production* | | | −3 | Uses chemical inputs in a responsible way** |
| | | | | −3 | Supports the local economy** |

**Indicates statement is "distinguishing" at $p < .01$; *indicates significance of $p < .05$.

ranked high with this group and they disagreed strongly that organic food had hidden health costs or harmful effects on humanity. Organics are also seen as consistent with their value system – emphasizing connections between health and spirit – and hence worthy of premium prices. This group disagreed strongly that organic food is harmful to the environment, however, so did most of the groups.

The connections between food and health as well as between food and spirituality are evident in the participants' comments:

> Organic food *is* "spiritual." What you put in your body should be as important as who you are. The way you live your life reflects how you want others to live. If you feel good about how you eat, then you feel good about who you are. (George)

> Organic food is necessary for human and environmental sustainability. It is spiritual because you're connected to the natural rhythms of the earth. (Daniel)

The shopping behavior reported by this group (in a written survey) demonstrates their commitment to organic foods. Consumers in this segment dedicate nearly half of their grocery dollars to organic foods, and purchase organic versions in most food categories, especially milk (68%), other dairy products (55%), and fruits and vegetables (53%). Indeed, the *Health Enthusiasts* are the most optimistic about organic food availability, especially if they are located within urban areas. They rely on conventional grocers for less than half of their purchases, otherwise shopping at specialty retailers, natural grocers, and farmers' markets.

*The Organic Idealists*
This group holds a generally positive attitude toward organic foods but also reaches the rather practical conclusion that they cannot participate as organic consumers. While they recognize organic food's general characteristics of environmental friendliness, wholesomeness, and healthfulness, particularly for children, they also remain uncommitted to its inclusion in their lifestyles or its premium prices. (That is, they neither agree nor disagree that organic food is consistent with their lifestyles or worth a premium price.) There is a high overall correlation (.77) between this group and the *Health Enthusiasts*, but the *Organic Idealists* neither assign preventative health care attributes to organic food nor emphasize spiritual connections. Part of their sentiment derives from a relatively weak attitude: the Q-sort exercise was the first real occasion on which most of these consumers had given much concentrated thought to organic food.

The positive evaluation of organic foods is reflected in their comments:

> Organic food is healthier than the stuff I buy. Organic *means* healthier. It doesn't have chemicals processed in it. I believe that's what's better for kids. Our health problems today – for example, allergies – are probably due to our processed foods. (Dennis)

> I think organic food is "real, genuine" food. It's not processed. It reminds me of "what Jesus would eat." It's "the God diet." (Leanne)

The limitations they perceive as preventing their adoption of organic foods include convenience, expense, and information.

> Organic food isn't compatible with my lifestyle because we live in a fast-paced environment where there's no time to put energy into shopping for it. (Dennis)

> It's not a price issue for me. I just don't know enough about it to make me reach for it. Since I'm not sure exactly what it is, I don't think it is sufficiently promoted. I'm not even sure I'm 60 percent right. (Rachel)

> I don't buy organic food. I know it's better for my family, but I don't do it on purpose. Expense is a real issue. It's also about convenience. I'm not going to go to a special section of the store to look for it. (Barb)

The shopping behavior of this group supports their sentiment that organic food is not generally in their consideration set, even though they hold positive views on it. While they average less than 14% of grocery dollars on organic food, only three of the eight participants purchase any organic foods, principally milk and fruits & vegetables. This largely reflects the spending of one mother who purchases organic foods for her child. This group is "mainstream" in its shopping, spending 75% of their food dollars in conventional grocery stores. Consistent with their emphasis on convenience, this group perceives organic food to be harder to obtain through conventional supermarkets and that serious effort to patronize a variety of stores is probably required to find a full selection.

## *The Unengaged Shoppers*

A third group of consumers, the *Unengaged Shoppers*, exhibit a profound disinterest in product differentiation and in the overall shopping experience. We discuss them now because their Q-sorts have moderately high correlation with *the Health Enthusiasts* (.62) and *the Organic Idealists* (.69). That is, similar to the earlier two groups, these consumers agree with statements about organic food being good for family health, wholesome, produced in an environmentally friendly manner, and grown without the use of pesticides. They too disagree that it has a harmful effect on humanity.

They differ on accuracy of terminology, confusing "organic" with "cage-free," "free-range," and "natural." They also differ in trust in the food system: they do not feel that organic food is safe from acts of terrorism, but they do not feel it lacks regulation or is worrisome. They have confidence in the food industry, but also feel retailers are just trying to charge more money when they sell organic food.

The disengagement demonstrated by this group is reflected in their apparent misuse or misunderstanding of terms, or alternatively, their lack of interest in the difference.

> Organic food is "real, genuine" food because it doesn't have blemishes on it like you'd find on stuff in the field. It also doesn't have sugar in it. Most processed foods have added sugars. (Tom)

> I don't see much point in differentiating between organic and non-organic foods. I'm looking for simpler, healthier foods, not necessarily organic. (Carlos)

This group exhibits shopping behavior that is both consistent with their positive evaluation of organic foods (as correlated with the previous two groups) and their unwillingness to expend cognitive effort to differentiate products. Overall, they average less than 9% of their grocery spending on organic foods, all of which is spent for milk (30%), grains (17%), and fruits and vegetables (27%). They are influenced by the presence of small children in the household and by vague notions that organic food may be safer to eat, but do not carry either motive into committed organic consumption. This group, which spends nearly 80% of its food dollars in supermarkets, was unanimous in assessing organic food as available in mainstream grocers but only for certain product categories.

*Hoban's Hogwashers*

In contrast to the groups just discussed, *Hoban's Hogwashers* (named in reference to Thomas Hoban's, 1996 work on consumer attitudes toward GM foods), has clear negative opinions about organic food. Distinguishing statements for this segment indicate that these consumers see little merit in the organic food sector, judging it as fashionable, overblown, and not regulated enough. While they do not find organic food production morally wrong, they generally relegate it to alternative lifestyles, particularly those associated with vegetarianism. Organic foods are merely a trend category with little substance or value. Consumers in this group doubt the veracity of environmental and animal welfare claims made about organic foods as well.

Unlike any of the other groups identified in this study, *Hoban's Hogwashers* do have some demographic similarities: all are women, most are 45 years and older and none have small children at home. This is somewhat consistent with empirical studies of organic consumers: those who are younger and have small children are more likely to hold positive attitudes toward organic foods (Magnusson, Arvola, Hursti, Aberg, & Sjoden 2001; Hill & Lynchehaun, 2002). However, demographic indicators do not appear to be associated with membership in our groups more generally.

Members of this group indicate that they are highly unlikely to switch to organic foods.

> I don't see any difference between organic and non-organic foods in the food itself. Organic foods are just overblown. In fact, they might be more dangerous than people want to believe. If they are not treated with preservatives then what's to protect them during food handling? (Colleen)

> Organic food isn't spiritual. That's silly. It's just a trend and it's baloney to say it's essential for children. (Kate)

> Organic foods are just a trend. Right now, we're in the 'certified organic' cycle; we'll find another one in a few years. It just doesn't carry much weight with me. I'm not sure anyone is living up to the actual rules of production. And it doesn't help prevent health care problems. Please! What proof do they have of that? It's just a way for retailers to charge more. (Sarah)

*Hoban's Hogwashers* demonstrates a fairly conventional shopping pattern. Organic food is purchased by only one of the seven respondents who sorted into this group – a mother whose purchases are strongly influenced by her teenage son (an "important person" in Ajzen's normative beliefs). Her purchases are so minimal that the overall average for the segment is less than 1.5% of food dollars. With our relatively small groups, few statistically significant differences are expected, but there is some evidence ($p = .054$) that the percentage of food expenditures going to organic foods differ between *the Health Enthusiasts* and *Hoban's Hogwashers*. This group relies on conventional supermarkets more than most groups, spending 81% of their food dollars there. Interestingly, this group is much more optimistic about the availability of organic foods than other groups, reflecting both a willingness to evaluate organic foods and an awareness of their presence in the market. Both aspects are consistent with studies on attitude accessibility (Fazio, Powell, & Williams, 1989) and attitude strength (Priester, Nayakankuppam, Fleming, & Godek, 2004), according to which attitude strength is influenced by attitude accessibility and accessibility is influenced by prior evaluation of the product choices. It is clear that *Hoban's Hogwashers* have given much thought to the merits of organic food and have strong attitudes, even if they conclude that organic foods have no merit. Demographic data also suggest that this group is the most educated of all groups.

*The Bargain Shoppers*

The fifth group in our sample is termed *the Bargain Shoppers* due to their strong emphasis on price as a determining factor in food choices. Distinguishing statements for this group indicate a general dissatisfaction with what organic foods offer the consumer. This is in contrast to *the Organic Idealists* who were also concerned about price but otherwise saw organic food as positively differentiated from conventional food. While *Bargain Shoppers* are aware of definitional aspects of the term and acknowledge some positive aspects (safe to eat, mindful of animal welfare and the environment), they relegate organic foods to alternative lifestyles and fads. Health does not enter their evaluation of organic foods at all. However, price does. The relative expense of organic foods leaves them out of the consumer's consideration set altogether; any purchases are made on other grounds, such as freshness or support of a local farm stand. Respondents in this group also find organic food to be typically bruised or blemished, inconvenient to locate in stores, and generally not satisfying for their needs.

Unlike most other groups, *Bargain Shoppers* also expresses some conflict about the value of organic foods – their midscale (0) ranking of "organic food is overblown" contrasts with more extreme agreement or disagreement in other groups. Similarly, while the other groups each disagree strongly with "organic food is morally wrong," the *Bargain Shopper* is not as emphatic in its disagreement (factor score of $-1$). In fact, this group believes that conventional foods offer much of the same value as organic food, if not more. Finding a balanced, healthy diet with plenty of fruits and vegetables is a more important objective. Unlike the *Unengaged Shoppers*, however, this perspective is based on active consideration of their alternatives.

Their judgment of organic foods as not offering anything superior to conventional foods is reflected in their comments.

> Organic food may be good, but there is nothing wrong with conventional foods. Generations have grown up on pop tarts and frosted flakes and have turned out fine. Everything needs to be eaten in moderation. I'm not going to be one of these "controlling" parents. Fresh fruits are important to the health of my children and I make sure they have fruit around. Our food supply is good, conventional grocery stores are convenient, carry all that any consumer could possibly want, and the large national brands have high quality standards of food. (Janet)
>
> Organic food is not compatible with my lifestyle primarily because it's too expensive. When you look at fresh fruits and vegetables, I can't really tell whether it's organic or

not. If I buy something because it looks fresh and then find out it's also organic, that'd be okay with me. But I'm just not going to buy it for the label "organic." I'd rather buy something to help our local farmers. (Elise)

With this perspective, consumers in *the Bargain Shoppers* segment rely almost exclusively on conventional grocery stores and farmers' markets, and purchase organic foods only accidentally (0.7% of food expenses). Indeed, we find statistical significance ($p = .036$) in comparing this group to *the Health Enthusiasts*. They have clearly taken note of organic foods while shopping, but do not see any value in paying the higher prices usually asked.

*The Cynical/Distrustfuls*
The last of our segments on attitudes toward organic foods is characterized by a strong sense of mystery and conspiracy around big business and government, resulting in their serious doubts about the credibility of any government or business claim. We have termed them the *Cynical/Distrustfuls* to reflect this overwhelming trait. Unlike *Hoban's Hogwashers*, this group is not entirely against the idea of organic food; they simply do not trust the "organic" label to be meaningful. Accordingly, their distinguishing statements reflect skepticism about retailer motives, insufficient regulation of the industry, exposure of the food supply to terrorism, and a general "suspect" evaluation of organic food. Unlike other groups, the *Cynical/Distrustfuls* do not agree that organic food production uses chemical inputs in a responsible way, fosters confidence in the food industry, or supports the local economy. In fact, this group is unique in strongly disagreeing ($-5$) that organic food is produced in an environmentally friendly manner.

The nature of their skepticism is such that they distrust government and business alike, assigning blame to greed and poor regulatory oversight.

Organic food is shrouded in mystery. There's so much black market stuff going on. Anyone can throw a "this is organic" label on. Money is the bottom line. Regulations, from start to finish, are not followed through with. Theoretically, organic food is wholesome and great for children health-wise, but you don't know what's in them, in any food really. It seems something must be going on to keep it shippable, some practice we don't know about. It's all mysterious. (Nadia)

Expenditures by *Cynical/Distrustfuls* on organic foods are a small percentage of overall food dollars, averaging 11%. The group leans toward distrusting the organic label, yet purchase organic foods anyway. While we did not measure strength of attitude, it was clear that respondents in this group wanted to believe in organic foods even if their more general problems with government and big business gave them doubts.

## Q-Sorts on Conventional Food

As indicated earlier, a key goal of this chapter was to demonstrate that Q-methodology can reveal meaningful segments of consumers based on their attitudes toward organic foods. An interesting avenue for exploring this power is to have respondents sort the same Q-sample for a different context: conventional foods. As respondents reveal different views and indeed fall into different segments, we obtain not only an insight into what Q-methodology offers, but also a different appreciation, in this case, for what influences consumers to purchase organic foods or not.

Factor analysis of the Q-sorts on conventional food produced three meaningful and distinct segments of consumers, which together explained 59% of the total variance. We termed these segments Satisfied Shoppers, Farm Traditionalists, and Ardent Opponents. Characteristic and distinguishing statements for these groups are summarized in Table 4.

### The Satisfied Shoppers

Consumers in one segment – *the Satisfied Shoppers* – are distinguished by their clear satisfaction with conventional foods. Conventional food is compatible with their lifestyles, satisfactory for their needs, safe to eat, and good for their families. These consumers look at buying conventional food as the normal thing to do, choosing foods that their parents did and viewing them as part of a healthful diet. They are not overly concerned about regulatory or terrorism issues, nor about the environmental impacts. Most statements about hidden health costs, animal welfare, and environmental impact are ranked about midscale (around 0), although this group is well aware that conventional foods are produced using pesticides and preservatives.

Accordingly, this group averages less than 3% of its food expenses on organic foods. Their comments reflect this exclusivity to conventional foods, but also a desire to avoid the cognitive effort to evaluate conventional foods against organics.

> It suits me just fine. I don't look into it (organic v. conventional) and take for granted that if it's there in the store, then it's ok. I trust the supermarket. I just have to believe that the food industry is highly regulated because I'm not looking into it any further. If I believed there were hidden health costs, then I couldn't feed it to my family. I just can't go there. (Rachel)

> Of course it's real, genuine food. It's the food we all grew up on. There weren't a lot of choices; that's why it's real. If your mom bought this, then you're going to. (Barb)

**Table 4.** Characteristic and Distinguishing Statements Regarding Conventional Food.

| Satisfied Shoppers | | Farm Traditionalists | | Ardent Opponents | |
|---|---|---|---|---|---|
| Score | Statement: "conventional food ..." | Score | Statement: "conventional food ..." | Score | Statement: "conventional food ..." |
| *Characteristic statements* | | | | | |
| +5 | Is fresh | +5 | Feeds everyone* | +5 | Is associated with big business |
| +5 | Is good for my family** | +5 | Is compatible with my lifestyle | +5 | Is conveniently located on store shelves |
| +5 | Is satisfactory for my needs** | +5 | Is conveniently located on store shelves | +5 | Is harmful to the environment |
| +5 | Is suffic. promoted and merchandized | +5 | Tastes good | +5 | Relies on chemical inputs** |
| +4 | Is compatible with my lifestyle | +4 | Is associated with big business | +4 | Has hidden health costs |
| +4 | Is part of a healthful diet | +4 | Is expensive | +4 | Disregards the welfare of animals |
| +4 | Is safe to eat | +4 | Is good quality | +4 | Is suffic. promoted and merchandized |
| +4 | Tastes good | +4 | Is part of a healthful diet | +4 | Is suspect |
| −4 | Does not contain preservatives | −4 | Is difficult to find | −4 | Does not include additives |
| −4 | Does not include additives | −4 | Has a harmful effect on humanity | −4 | Is difficult to find |
| −4 | Is part of an alternative lifestyle | −4 | Is overblown | −4 | Uses chemicals in a responsible way |
| −4 | Is typically blemished or bruised* | −4 | Exposes the food supply to acts of terrorism* | −4 | Is produced in an environmentally friendly manner* |
| −5 | Belongs in specialty shops | −5 | Is consistent with vegetarianism | −5 | Does not contain preservatives |
| −5 | Is difficult to find | −5 | Is morally wrong | −5 | Is grown w/o the use of hormones** |
| −5 | Is grown without use of pesticides | −5 | Is spiritual | −5 | Is grown w/o the use of pesticides |
| −5 | Is morally wrong | −5 | Supports preventative health care | −5 | Is produced through humane treatment of animals |
| *Other "distinguishing" statements* | | | | | |
| +3 | Is consistent with my value system* | +3 | Is produced in an environmentally friendly manner* | 0 | Is fresh* |
| +2 | Is highly regulated** | +2 | Is same as "natural"** | −2 | Is part of a healthful diet** |
| −1 | Exposes the food supply to acts of terrorism* | 0 | Does not include additives* | −3 | Is good for my family's health* |
| −2 | Is worrisome* | | | | |

**Indicates statement is "distinguishing" at $p < .01$; *indicates significance of $p < .05$.

Logically, this group consists of all of *the Bargain Shoppers* and most of *Hoban's Hogwashers* from the organic food sort. Some *Organic Idealists* also fall into this group, consistent with both their weak positive attitudes toward organic foods and the exclusion of organic foods from their consideration set, as we indicated. No member of *the Health Enthusiasts, Cynical/Distrustfuls,* or *Unengaged Shoppers* sorted into this group.

*The Farm Traditionalists*
A second group emerging from the sorts on conventional foods was termed *the Farm Traditionalists* because of their strong connection to the traditions of agriculture. To this group, "conventional" food is just today's farming, a good, honest profession from which good, safe food is obtained. These consumers just appreciated food in the general sense. Conventional food production "feeds everyone" with food that "tastes good," "is of good quality," and "part of a healthful diet." While these consumers strongly agree that conventional foods are compatible with their lifestyles, they also lament high prices, a sentiment usually expressed about organic foods in this study.

The views of this group did correlate highly with *the Supermarket Shoppers* (.72) but this group de-emphasizes any differences between organic and conventional foods, unique in their agreement that conventional food is the same as "natural" food. In addition, these consumers do not view conventional foods as supporting preventative health care. Food itself is to be appreciated, according to this group.

> When I go shopping, I'm thinking about meals worth presenting to my family. I find the ingredients I need, whether it's chicken, rice or soy milk. I don't think about organic foods in that sense. Pesticide residues don't weigh on my mind. It's important to choose foods carefully, but I'm not convinced that there's any truth that certain foods help prevent poor health. (Sarah)

> Conventional food is not spiritual; it's just the food you stuff your mouth with. It's "natural" because it tastes good and no different from something "organic." (Tom)

Membership in this group spanned three of the organic food groups: *the Organic Idealists, Hoban's Hogwashers,* and *the Unengaged Shoppers,* suggesting that this view toward conventional foods is largely independent of their position on organic foods.

*The Ardent Opponents*
Distinguishing statements for consumers in *the Ardent Opponents* reflect a more ethical evaluation of conventional food production and include

a litany of complaints. These consumers believe conventional food production to be harmful to the environment, harmful to humanity, indifferent to the welfare of animals, full of hidden health costs, irresponsible about use of chemicals, morally wrong, and generally unsafe to eat. They also associate conventional foods with the greed of big businesses where profit margins are maximized at the cost of responsibility toward nature and human welfare.

Statements made by this group indicate the furtiveness of their beliefs, particularly about health concerns.

> There's some good food and some stuff that shouldn't be called food, like cheese in a can. Nothing is truly "real" unless you picked it from the tree. (Nadia)

> Conventional food is Frankenfood, genetically engineered. That's the reason why kids are 8 feet tall today; they're maturing at a younger age. There's not enough testing done. We grow up thinking that it's safe for consumption but having airplanes spread chemicals around can't be good. There are long-term effects on your health. We should look at how we treat our bodies and at how we treat the land too. (George)

> Conventional food is definitely not good for my family's health. All the additives, preservatives – you have to see the connection between that and cancer. Standards are just not high enough. The FDA lets a certain percent of whatever go through just to make it grade A food. And big businesses can be lazy when the FDA isn't looking. Look at partially hydrogenated fats: they're bad for you yet they're everywhere. (Mark)

> The conventional food industry is not safe from acts of terrorism and not necessarily safe to eat. I've seen contamination during production and not everyone working in the industry is focusing on quality. (Carlos)

Membership in this group draws from the *Health Enthusiasts*, the *Cynical/Distrustfuls*, the *Unengaged Shoppers*, and an *Organic Idealist*. The origins of their negative perceptions thus vary, but collectively present a segment that would like a safe and reliable alternative to our current production methods.

### Contrast between Conventional and Organic Food Sorts

A comparison of the segments produced for conventional foods with those for organic foods yields several interesting points. First, Q-methodology clearly can reveal different segmentations of consumers based on different contexts. Our Q-sample was appropriate to capture opinions for one type of food as distinct from the other, rather than reveal segments about food or another construct more generally.

Second, the segments that were produced for conventional foods reveal another side of the consumer thought process as it relates to organic foods. For example, some consumers do not simply feel that organic foods are healthy choices, as any fruit or vegetable might be; they also feel that conventional foods are unhealthy choices. In that sense, the motives for some consumers are to move away from conventional foods. For others, there is little relation between their judgment of organic foods and that of conventional foods. They see no difference, so their motives are not based on the comparison.

Third, comparing where individual respondents fell in the two sets of segments also reveals more about the individuals. Some respondents are both *Organic Idealists* and *Farm Traditionalists* – liking the organic ideal but also very positive about the value of today's conventional farming. Similarly, an *Unengaged Shopper* also comes through as an *Ardent Opponent* to conventional foods – not spending much effort in distinguishing between foods but also skeptical of the quality of today's conventional foods.

Together, these last two points suggest that the messages designed to target individual consumer segments should place more emphasis on the positive traits each group associates with organic foods (if any) than on comparisons to conventional foods, as their views on conventional foods differ substantially.

## IMPLICATIONS

### *What Sells Organic Foods?*

An interesting result of our analysis of organic foods was that all segments but one disagree strongly that organic foods are harmful to the environment. This is a fairly strong indication that the environmental message about organic food production methods has been widely heard – and that it does not make much difference for most consumers.

Instead, a variety of other factors are pointed to as relevant motivators including healthfulness, concern for animal welfare, and food safety. Perceptions of healthfulness are linked to family health, disease prevention, and wholesomeness. Concern for animal welfare is tied to the somewhat competing concepts of general treatment of captive animals and the vegetarian lifestyle. Food safety stems from less chemical use, localized production (less handling), and less big-business greed. All are aspects of the broader notion of "organic" food and may thus be useful in promotional efforts.

In addition, a variety of detractors to greater acceptance of organic foods is noted. Price and availability are chief among them, but so are appearance (e.g., blemishes, wilt), regulatory failures, and perceptions of its greater suitability for niche interests and alternative lifestyles. These issues are largely ones of the public image of organic foods, and as such deserve an across-the-board effort to improve. While retailers also influence price and availability, this finding really speaks to the challenges ahead for the grower and food manufacturer, whether small and dedicated to organic foods or large and experimenting with them as a Kraft or General Mills might.

## Marketing Strategies

Addressing the unique marketing challenges associated with each segment clearly requires distinct campaigns. As Brodt et al. (2004) note for the context of biologically integrated farming practices, it will be insufficient to just widely disseminate definitional characteristics of organic food. Instead, information that is more tailored for individual goals and values may be needed to get consumers to operationalize it, to understand and act upon it. It is, therefore, important to examine the media use by and appropriate positioning strategies for our organic food segments.

Through our brief survey, it is clear from our respondents that television, newspapers, and mainstream magazines are of only moderate importance as sources of guidance on food choices for their families. While the *Bargain Shoppers* are the exception in ranking all three highly, the Internet, books, lifestyle magazines (e.g., Organic Style, Mother Jones), public service circulars such as those found in natural grocers and doctors' offices, and "word of mouth" are of greater importance for most of our groups. For example, *Organic Idealists* will consult mainstream magazines, but public service circulars and "word of mouth" rank higher than any other media type. The *Cynical/Distrustfuls* have a similar pattern of interest although they would prefer lifestyle magazines over more mainstream versions. *Hoban's Hogwashers*, in contrast, use the Internet and books in addition to television. An implication for such variations is that marketing and advertising messages designed to appeal to each group would necessarily be delivered via distinctly targeted media strategies as well (Tseng & Lii, 2006).

Moreover, depending on the specific segment and their degree of satisfaction with conventional food sources, marketing efforts may need to be more subtle, general educational efforts rather than typical advertising promotions. For instance, efforts to increase awareness of what impacts overall health, disease prevention, or disease onset (such as links between pesticides and some cancers) might tip *Organic Idealists* over the edge or give *Hoban's Hogwashers* a new perspective on the value of organic foods. A similar strategy could be used regarding environmental considerations. To attract the *Cynical/Distrustfuls*, attention to government and big business credibility problems is needed – perhaps by demonstrating openness to regulatory inspections or promoting community supported agricultures (CSAs). Similarly, informative analysis of food safety, food system terrorism risks, etc., while serving to alert conventional food regulators to improve that safety, can also provide a reason to differentiate sources of organic foods, a concern raised by those who value locally grown produce (e.g., *Bargain Shoppers*). Whether any of these educational efforts would be considered controversial is perhaps a matter of opinion, but it is clear that only with greater understanding of the structure of the U.S. food system might some consumers be sufficiently informed to make a different choice.

More conventional advertising methods still have a role to play in communicating with consumers. The *Health Enthusiasts* are seasoned consumers of organic foods and can thus be targeted with print ads that differentiate among products and brands. Misconceptions about the meaning of "organic" – as expressed by *Organic Idealists* and *Unengaged Shoppers*, for example – can also be addressed by using advertisements. However, alternative communication strategies such as viral marketing ("word of mouth") and development of informative brochures should be considered as well, particularly for the *Cynical/Distrustfuls* who would doubt the veracity of any corporate claim. Whether these strategies need to extol the benefits of consuming organic foods or dispel myths and negative stereotypes depends on the targeted segment. What is clear is that the segments of consumers we have identified hold highly differentiated views on organic foods and the industry's effort to communicate with each must both reflect those differences and improve on its information flow performance to date.

*Policy Implications*

In developing the National Organic Standard – the specific regulations for what can be labeled "organic" – the U.S. government attempted to incorporate a wide range of ideas as to what it should capture. Indeed, during the development period, the government received over 275,000 comments on its proposal and subsequently made significant modifications before issuing the final rule (Gutman, 1999). In the end, the rule represented a general view of what organic farming should entail – no synthetic inputs, growth hormones, sewage sludge, or bioengineered elements – but was missing traits that many held in great importance.

The consumer segments identified in this study suggest that indeed there may be some disagreement about what the term "organic" should mean. For example, members of several segments mentioned their concerns about animal welfare, in both conventional and organic food production. According to the NOS, animals used to generate organic food products must be given "access" to the outdoors, but this does not mean that the animals are free to roam the outdoors. Some consumers, particularly vegetarians, appear to have great concern about whether organic food production is sufficiently humane to animals.

Other consumers mentioned their concerns that organic food production was becoming a "big business" industry – greedy and unlikely to have consumer interests as a priority. Clearly the NOS does not distinguish between scale of farming, and yet the "organic" ideal appears to resonate with those consumers who are concerned about local communities, consumer protection, etc. Whether this or other desired traits of "organic" food can be adequately addressed in a national standard is up for debate.

### The Attitude–Behavior Gap

Because a key purpose of our study is to uncover strategies that will best match marketing efforts to individual segments, it is important to address the potential for attitude–behavior gaps. The relationship between attitudes and beliefs, on the one hand, and purchase intention or behavior, on the other, has been well analyzed. Priester et al. (2004) offer a perspective that relates directly to our study. They conclude that a consumer's consideration of a product mediates the connection between attitudes and behavior. A strongly held positive attitude increases the likelihood that the product enters the consumer's consideration set, which subsequently influences purchase behavior. In contrast, a weakly held positive attitude may be insufficient to place the product in the consumer's consideration set and hence that product is not purchased. This association between relative strength of attitude and the purchase behavior is seen in a comparison of our *Health Enthusiasts* and *Organic Idealists*. The *Health Enthusiasts* held strong positive attitudes toward organic foods and averaged nearly half of their food dollars on them. The *Organic Idealists*, in contrast, held rather weak positive attitudes and were open about not including organic foods in their consideration sets (and hence few purchases were made).

Similarly, Fazio et al. (1989) focus on how accessibility of attitude from memory serves as a "critical determinant" of whether attitude will lead to corresponding behavior. A highly accessible attitude – easily retrieved from memory – is more likely to lead to the associated behavior than is an attitude that is based only on immediate perceptions. An accessible attitude will have been created by previous evaluation of the object or product. In our case, at least three of the groups demonstrated clearly that their attitudes were easily accessible, if not always positive. Through their Q-sorts and the subsequent interviews, the positive attitude of the *Health Enthusiasts*, the negative attitude of *Hoban's Hogwashers*, and the cynical views of the *Cynical/Distrustfuls* were revealed swiftly and directly. In contrast, the *Organic Idealists*, *Bargain Shoppers*, and the *Unengaged Shoppers* were slower in the mechanics of the Q-sort and less certain of their accuracy vis-à-vis accepted terminology. Since the attitude held by both the *Organic Idealists* and the *Unengaged Shoppers* could be described as positive toward organic foods, the low accessibility of the attitude may partially explain their lack of purchase intention.

These patterns notwithstanding, there is a distinction worth making between a single-dimensional notion of attitude and the more comprehensive depiction of attitude that is revealed via Q-methodology. Our respondents are grouped into consumer segments based on their ranking of 67 statements about organic foods. The collective description of consumer attitude afforded by a large number of statements offers a richer, deeper understanding of how consumers evaluate organic foods than would be afforded by simpler approaches. For example, if attitude were based solely on evaluation of the physical product, on its taste, appearance, freshness, etc., one could say that the *Health Enthusiasts*, the *Organic Idealists*, the *Unengaged Shoppers*, and even the *Cynical/Distrustfuls* all have positive attitudes toward organic foods. In that case, we would easily conclude that each group demonstrates a substantial attitude–behavior gap given their low expenditure share on organic foods.

In contrast, when we expand the concept of attitude to include an evaluation of price, availability, safety, regulatory effectiveness, healthfulness, etc. regarding organic foods, it is no longer appropriate to describe those attitudes as simply "positive" or "negative." They are complex reflections of the consumer's beliefs regarding organic foods and the system through which they reach consumers, as Ajzen's behavioral, normative, and control beliefs would suggest. Viewed this way, we no longer see great evidence of an attitude–behavior gap. *Organic Idealists* may find organic foods environmentally friendly, wholesome, and healthful, but also inconvenient to find, too pricey, and too hard to understand. Such an attitude (even so simplified) does not sound like it will lead to purchase of organic foods. Likewise, the *Unengaged Shoppers* relate to similar positive attributes while also evaluating organic foods as not safe from terrorism, a way for retailers to charge more, and not worthy of their cognitive energies. One would not anticipate purchases from this group. A similar argument can be made regarding the *Cynical/Distrustfuls*. Therefore, for none of these three segments would we conclude that there is an attitude–behavior gap, and one would question marketing strategies designed solely to elicit positive evaluation of the product's physical attributes.

While the relatively negative attitudes exhibited by *Hoban's Hogwashers* and the *Bargain Shoppers* mean that no attitude–behavior gap would be expected there either, we must consider the presence of a gap for the sixth group, the *Health Enthusiasts*. Organic foods enjoy an overwhelmingly positive evaluation by this group, but receive only about 46% of their food budgets, suggestive of an attitude–behavior gap. However, what Q-methodology reveals is that these consumers also evaluate organic foods as insufficiently promoted, not produced as cheaply as possible, somewhat expensive, and possibly difficult to find. Indeed, the challenge of incorporating organic foods into busy family lifestyles, heavily dependent on convenience foods, was a theme of the postsort interviews with this group, as were income constraints. Viewed in this more comprehensive way, it is not convincing that a gap between attitude and behavior exists even for this group. This is a valuable contribution of Q-methodology to the understanding of consumers and their motivations, and a useful lesson for marketing strategies as well.

### *"Organic" as a Reflection of Cultural Values*

As argued by Thompson and Troester (2002), consumer interpretations of product attributes depend to no small extent on the cultural context in which they are experienced. In the case of organic foods, the importance of cultural factors in determining both consumer attitudes and their purchase intentions is clear. How consumers identify themselves around organic foods reflects their greater cultural context. Is food worth the effort to fully investigate? Does the consumer's lifestyle demand certain levels of convenience, value (price), and simplicity? Is food safety or terrorism of great concern to consumers? Is the consumer driven by a food–health linkage? Does the consumer trust in labels such as "certified organic" or in government regulatory power more generally?

Indeed, one can argue that "certified organic" holds the potential for mimicking a brand in the minds of consumers, but has yet to capitalize on it due to the industry's current approach to understanding its consumers. Our respondents were almost unanimous in understanding "organic" to mean "not harmful to the environment" – suggesting that a marker of the brand has been partially filled (Holt, 2004) – but did not otherwise share a common experience. Further, the separate views held about organic are not typically strong, an indication that the degree to which the brand story has been established varies. However, subthemes found among our respondents do suggest that "organic" as linked to alternative lifestyles (e.g., environmentalists, vegetarians) may be associated with an identity myth: the desire for a better balance between consumer lifestyles and its impacts on nature. As such, "organic" may have the potential to become an "iconic brand" (Holt) and to capitalize on that myth. It is clear, however, that to do so, the organic food industry must reflect on the greater cultural context from which consumers derive meaning to the "organic" term.

## CONCLUSIONS AND LIMITATIONS

This study has demonstrated that there are distinct sets of motivations that shape consumer attitudes toward organic foods, and that Q-methodology can be an effective tool for developing meaningful descriptions of those motivations. Further, it is clear from this research that marketing efforts will require a multipronged strategy, with variations on positioning as well as media outlets used.

With regard to attitudes toward organic food, we identified six segments: the *Health Enthusiasts* who emphasize health, environmental, and spiritual attributes of organic food; the *Organic Idealists* who hold positive views on organic food but do not see it as consistent with their lifestyles; the *Unengaged Shoppers* who assign positive traits to organic foods, but also confuse terminology and appear disinterested in the cognitive effort of untangling them; *Hoban's Hogwashers* who judge organic foods as an overblown trend and undifferentiated from conventional foods; the *Bargain Shoppers* who do not appear satisfied with organic foods as a whole and make shopping decisions largely on price; and the *Cynical/Distrustfuls* who associate organic foods with mystery and conspiracy on the part of big business and governments. Q-methodology revealed rich, meaningful descriptions for each, with corresponding appropriate shopping behavior and no apparent gap between attitude and behavior. Further, a contrast with respondent views on conventional foods (which yielded the *Satisfied Shoppers*, *Farm Traditionalists*, and the *Ardent Opponents*) demonstrated that these descriptions of consumer attitudes toward organic foods do not reflect attitudes toward food more generally, but are specific to organic foods. An appropriately designed set of positioning strategies would thus be expected to assist the industry in expanding interest in organic foods.

This study does have its limitations. By design, it was exploratory and considered a small sample of consumers. This is not a serious limitation for Q-methodology in which a single consumer is studied, but a larger sample may produce more refined segments that would offer even greater insight into consumer motivations. As such, more research is needed to generate those data.

In addition, a study like this does not address the size of any segment of consumers. We cannot say that a certain percentage of the population falls into the *Health Enthusiasts* segment, for example. That is left to future research that could build on the knowledge gained in this study. It is one of the strengths of Q-methodology that considerable insight can be achieved without focusing on distribution of segments in the greater population.

Finally, it is likely that additional research could reveal variations in segments and/or their distribution in the population if conducted in multiple locales, particularly cross-culturally. Our results pertain to the U.S. market only and to the locations of the co-authors. It is intriguing to consider the greater understanding that could be achieved by expanding geographic attributes and comparing cultural influences.

## ACKNOWLEDGMENT

The authors thank Renee Shaw Hughner for her contribution to the early stages of the research, and two anonymous referees for their valuable insights.

## REFERENCES

Ajzen, I. (1991). The theory of planned behavior. *Organizational Behavior and Human Decision Processes*, 50, 179–211.

Al-Makaty, S., Van Tubergen, G. N., Whitlow, S. S., & Boyd, D. A. (1996). Attitudes toward advertising in Islam. *Journal of Advertising Research* (May/June), 16–26.

Brodt, S., Klonsky, K., Tourte, L., Duncan, R., Hendricks, L., Ohmart, C., & Verdegaal, P. (2004). Influence of farm management style on adoption of biologically integrated farming practices in California. *Renewable Agriculture and Food Systems, 19*(4), 237–247.

Chinnici, G., D'Amico, M., & Pecorino, B. (2002). A multivariate statistical analysis on the consumers of organic products. *British Food Journal, 104*(3–5), 187–199.

Dimitri, C., & Greene, C. (2002). *Recent growth patterns in the U.S. organic foods market.* U.S. Department of Agriculture, Economic Research Service, Agricultural Information Bulletin Number 777.

Fazio, R. H., Powell, M. C., & Williams, C. J. (1989). The role of attitude accessibility in the attitude-to-behavior process. *Journal of Consumer Research, 16*(December), 280–288.

Fotopoulos, C., & Krystallis, A. (2002). Organic product avoidance: Reasons for rejection and potential buyers' identification in a countrywide survey. *British Food Journal, 104*(3–5), 233–260.

Funk, T. F., & Phillips, W. (1990). Segmentation of the market for table eggs in Ontario. *Agribusiness, 6*(4), 309–327.

Gehrt, K. C., & Shim, S. (2003). Situational segmentation in the international marketplace: The Japanese snack market. *International Marketing Review, 20*(2), 180–194.

Gutman, B. N. (1999). Ethical eating: Applying the Kosher food regulatory regime to organic food. *The Yale Law Journal, 108*, 2351–2384.

Hill, H., & Lynchehaun, F. (2002). Organic milk: Attitudes and consumption patterns. *British Food Journal, 104*(7), 526–542.

Hoban, T. (1996). Trends in consumer acceptance and awareness of biotechnology. *Journal of Food Distribution Research, 27*(1), 1–10.

Holt, D. B. (2004). *How brands become icons, the principles of cultural branding.* Boston, MA: Harvard Business School Press.

Honkanen, P., Olsen, S. O., & Myrland, O. (2004). Preference-based segmentation: A study of meal preferences among Norwegian teenagers. *Journal of Consumer Behaviour, 3*(3), 235–250.

Hughner, R., McDonagh, P., Prothero, A., Shultz II, C. J., & Stanton, J. (2007). Who are organic food consumers?: A compilation and review of why people purchase organic food. *Journal of Consumer Behaviour, 6*(2/3), 94–110.

Jolly, D. A. (1991). Determinants of organic horticultural products consumption based on a sample of California consumers. *Acta Horticultura, 295*, 41–48.

Larue, B., West, G. E., Gendron, C., & Lambert, R. (2004). Consumer response to functional foods produced by conventional, organic or genetic manipulation. *Agribusiness, 20*(2), 155–166.

Magnusson, M. K., Arvola, A., Hursti, U.-K., Aberg, L., & Sjoden, P.-O. (2001). Attitudes toward organic foods among Swedish consumers. *British Food Journal, 103*(3), 209–227.

Magnusson, M. K., Arvola, A., Hursti, U.-K., Aberg, L., & Sjoden, P.-O. (2003). Choice of organic foods is related to perceived consequences for human health and to environmentally friendly behavior. *Appetite, 40*(2), 109–117.

McFadden, D. (1973). Conditional logit analysis of qualitative choice behavior. In: P. Zarembka (Ed.), *Frontiers in economics.* New York: Academic Press.

McKeown, B., & Thomas, D. (1988). *Q methodology.* Newbury Park, CA: Sage Publications.

Misra, S., Huang, C. L., & Ott, S. L. (1991). Georgia consumers' preference for organically grown fresh produce. *Journal of Agribusiness, 9*(2), 53–63.

Moschis, G., Curasi, C., & Bellenger, D. (2004). Patronage motives of mature consumers in the selection of food and grocery stores. *Journal of Consumer Marketing, 21*(2), 123–133.

Organic Trade Association. (2006a). Organic sales continue to grow at a steady pace. Press Release dated May 7. Available at http://www.organicnewsroom.com

Organic Trade Association. (2006b). U.S. organic product sales reach $26.6 billion in 2009. Available at http://www.organicnewsroom.com. Press Release dated April 22.

Organic Trade Association. (2006c). Organic trade association seeks to advance organic agriculture in next farm bill. Press Release dated October 17. Available at http://www.organicnewsroom.com

Popovich, K., & Popovich, M. (2000). Use of Q methodology for hospital strategic planning: A case study. *Journal of Healthcare Management*, 45(6), 405–414.

Priester, J. R., Nayakankuppam, D., Fleming, M. A., & Godek, J. (2004). The $A^2SC^2$ model: The influence of attitudes and attitude strength on consideration and choice. *Journal of Consumer Research*, 30(March), 574–587.

Roddy, G., Cowan, C. A., & Hutchinson, G. (1996). Consumer attitudes and behaviour to organic foods in Ireland. *Journal of International Consumer Marketing*, 9(2), 41–63.

Schifferstein, H. N. J., & Oude Ophuis, P. A. M. (1998). Health-related determinants of organic food consumption in the Netherlands. *Food Quality and Preference*, 9(3), 119–133.

Squires, L., Juric, B., & Cornwell, T. B. (2001). Level of market development and intensity of organic food consumption: Cross-cultural study of Danish and New Zealand Consumers. *Journal of Consumer Marketing*, 18(5), 392–409.

Thompson, C. J., & Troester, M. (2002). Consumer value systems in the age of postmodern fragmentation: The case of the natural health microculture. *Journal of Consumer Research*, 28(4), 550–571.

Thompson, G. D. (1998). Consumer demand for organic foods: What we know and what we need to know. *American Journal of Agricultural Economics*, 80(5), 1113–1118.

Tseng, L. P. D., & Lii, Y. (2006). The role of attribute order and number effects in consumers' multiattribute preferential decisions. *Research in Consumer Behavior*, 10, 165–184.

Valenta, A. L., & Wigger, U. (1997). Q-methodology: Definition and application in health care informatics. *Journal of the American Medical Informatics Association*, 4(6), 501–510.

Verdurme, A., & Viaene, J. (2003). Consumer beliefs and attitude toward genetically modified food: Basis for segmentation and implications for communication. *Agribusiness*, 19(1), 91–113.

Wandel, M., & Buggel, A. (1997). Environmental concern in consumer evaluation of food quality. *Food Quality and Preference*, 8(1), 19–26.

Wilkins, J. L., & Hillers, V. N. (1994). Influences of pesticide residue and environmental concerns on organic food preference among food cooperative members and non-members in Washington state. *Journal of Nutrition Education*, 26(1), 26–33.

Zanoli, R., & Naspetti, S. (2002). Consumer motivations in the purchase of organic food. *British Food Journal*, 104(8), 643–653.

# SHOPPING MATTERS: TAIWANESE YOUNG TOURISTS' CONSUMER CULTURE IN ENGLAND

Joyce Hsiu-yen Yeh

## ABSTRACT

Purpose – *This study examines the meaning of shopping for Taiwanese students visiting England. It asks how this activity takes place, what purposes it serves for the students, and how the resulting purchases make meaning for the students once they return to Taiwan.*

Methodology/approach – *The study is ethnographic, involving observation and interviews in England as well as visual elicitation and interviews with the students once they returned to Taiwan and also some time later.*

Findings – *Shopping for souvenirs in England is found to be part of the process by which young Taiwanese tourists come to understand cultural differences. It is also a part of the process by which these students fulfill social obligations to those family members who have largely funded their trips. It is also a way of engaging with locals through the medium and excuse of shopping. Both the items selected and the memories they encode form the somewhat stereotypical condensations of the experience of going abroad to "The West."*

Research limitations/implications (if applicable) – *Those studied represent a young group with limited prior travel experience. Their retrospective recollections are subject to some distortion, although this is a part of the normal process of remembering.*

Practical implications (if applicable) – *For those planning foreign educational exchange programs, the critical role of shopping in this process should not be neglected.*

Originality/value of paper – *The researcher accompanied the students on their trip to England and also followed up with them once they returned home to Taiwan. This produced a rare insight into the process of tourist meaning-making during and after their trip abroad.*

This is a defence of shopping.

(Mary Douglas, 1997, p. 15)

# INTRODUCTION

This chapter concentrates on examining the role and meaning of shopping in cross-border travels, particularly from an Asian perspective, drawing on a great deal of empirical research. I focus on the accounts of young Taiwanese tourists' cross-border shopping in the host society, and of meaning-making through objects that they bought in England. The findings are based on fieldwork observations in Cambridge and London from 1997 and 1999–2002, and post-tour interviews in Taiwan in 2001 and 2004. Using tourists' own narratives of their perspectives on shopping while also examining the objects that they purchased and brought home, I expose veiled realities of consuming English culture and seek to examine study tourists' discourses of shopping and the sociocultural meanings of "English" souvenirs that they bought during their tours in England. The study illustrates the need for an understanding of the complex meanings of tourism-related shopping activities, the socialism of things, and how these material objects contribute to an understanding and analysis of consumer culture. I argue that cross-border shopping has multiple economic, social, and cultural roles, which offer a way to analyze the relationship between local tourism practices and global consumer culture through the consumption of objects. In addition, border-crossing shopping practices have often been linked to wider local–global connections in which the dialectical relations between the global framework and local reality can be examined.

## GO BYE-BYE TO BUY BUY[1]

According to a survey conducted in 1999, college and vocational-school students in Taiwan are not very "adventurous" during their summer holidays, "with 57 percent preferring to stay indoors rather than venture out" (*The Taipei Times*, 1999). The survey also indicates that Taiwanese students prioritized window-shopping as their outdoor activity and listening to music or the radio as their favored indoor activity. This survey report is chosen as the point of departure for this chapter because of the connections between shopping and certain forms of leisure pursuits such as tourism. The report illustrates how important window-shopping is in the leisure time of Taiwanese youths. It is no surprise that this local and cultural phenomenon bears a relation to how they act in different settings. It is important to emphasize here the relevance of Bourdieu's (1984) concept of the "habitus" to illustrate the physical embodiment of cultural practice. Most obviously, this survey report provides an explanation of why window-shopping is still Taiwanese young tourists' favorite leisure activity when they travel abroad. For them, window-shopping and actual shopping are still the most familiar leisure activities that they repeat in England as part of their Taiwanese cultural repertoire, although the purposes and their notions of shopping are varied and multiple (Yeh, 2003, 2009a, 2009b).

In the case of Taiwanese study tours,[2] I am interested in making sense of the local practices of leisure activity within the context of global processes. How does mass-produced culture circulate and how do young Taiwanese tourists consume global products? How do they reflect upon and evaluate their shopping experiences? Another way of posing these questions would be to ask the reasons why study tourists go shopping, and what role souvenirs play in producing their intercultural experiences in England. How are the meanings of these material objects translated and transferred from one culture to another?

Chouliaraki and Fairclough's explanations point out that:

> Any practice is a practice of production – people in particular social relations applying technologies to materials. Also any practice has a reflective element – representations of a practice are generated as a part of the practice. (Chouliaraki & Fairclough, 1999, p. 37)

Such production cannot be viewed in isolation. Traveling, indeed, is not only about experiencing differences and seeing new things; it can also be about the repetition of sameness and seeking familiarities in the form of food and other leisure activities. Travel, to some tourists, can be understood as a journey of learning about "differences" (MacCannell, 1976;

Pearce & Moscardo, 1986; Redfoot, 1984). Yet travel can also be a process of continuity in daily routines or of bringing excitement to the familiar routine. A full account of a tourist's experiences should acknowledge different practices and at the same time bring together certain crucially linked practices that are rooted in each individual's everyday life. At the same time, these practices are mobilized in the movement from the "local" to the "global." It is related to carrying out everyday lives and bringing one's own cultural experiences and "old" habits to "new" places. There is a sense of continuing familiar activities within a new living environment. Thus, Taiwanese study tourists are keen to repeat their experiences of shopping in new and unfamiliar sites in England.

In a focus group from the study tour of summer 2000, 14 members shared their views with me. In responding to my questions about what they did most of the time in England, 10 out of 14 said that they went window-shopping. One 27-year old female study tourist said:

> I don't pretend to be different from who I am in Taiwan. I like window-shopping. I do that in Taiwan most of the time so I do the same thing in England ... Although I have to say that I have to rush to look and try things on here as the shops are closed so early.[3] (August 2, 2000)

For Taiwanese study tourists, their shopping practices have a link with the performance of their local habitus. Their shopping act, I will show later, also involves the desire to search for English material and cultural symbols. The phenomenon of "Bye-Buy" seems to indicate that such practices of leisure activity are not only "a practice of production," as Chouliaraki and Fairclough (1999) point out, but also a practice of individual capacity of consumption of world commodities (Douglas & Isherwood, 1979; Shields, 1991; Brown, 1992; McIntosh & Prentice, 1999), which for many of them is central to the experience of travel to England.

## DISCOURSES OF SHOPPING

We have seen an explosion, in studies of consumer culture, of various key issues such as lifestyles, identity, embodiment, and representation.[4] The body of literature on consumption has made a significant contribution to our understanding of consumerism, everyday life, and the shaping of global culture in contemporary societies. Many of these works are invaluable, and yet not enough empirical research has been done to understand the connections between tourism and consumerism. Little of this research provides empirical evidence on the consumer activities involved in tourist cultural practices. The current study is useful in providing such evidence. One important point that needs to be raised here is that, although my investigations will focus on the functions of shopping and the meanings of the objects, to portray the study tour as a type of what East European researchers called shopping tourism[5] is to misrepresent it. I will demonstrate that shopping for Taiwanese study tourists is more than simply acquiring material objects.

Shopping in some respects is the dominating motivation for travel (see Jansen-Verbeke, 1990; Timothy & Butler, 1995). For example, Jansen-Verbeke (1990) has found that leisure shopping is a tourism resource and a tourist attraction, while Timothy and Butler (1995) provide a North-American example by investigating the role of shopping as a generator of tourism. It may be true that shopping is the tourist imperative performance in which shopping becomes an important element in taking trips. In contemporary society, consumption is an activity that matters. Shopping is not only an activity of mundane routine, but also a set of activities of social relations (see Gordon, 1986; Belk, 1995; Miller, 1998). This section of the chapter investigates the phenomenon of Taiwanese study tourists' shopping in England and trace what shopping might be for and what functions it might have.

Some study tourists regard the study tour as an opportunity for overseas shopping and have taken advantage of it. Like other package tourists, all Taiwanese study tourists spend considerable time and money in shopping. For them, traveling offers multiple sites for their shopping and being abroad extends the range of their permissible allowance. Adam aged 20 and Betty aged 17 traveled to England with credit cards that their parents gave them. Betty said:

> My parents gave me a credit card to pay for my extra costs such as shopping. With the credit card, I can buy whatever I want and they can pay the bills, which wouldn't have happened if I were in Taiwan. It's great to be abroad although I have to buy many things for my mum. (July 22, 2000)

Adam's parents are running a family business. His clothing resembles that worn by many study tourists in his group. He typically dresses in loose jeans and cotton T-shirts with Nike or New Balance trainers. Adam explained why his parents gave him a credit card:

> My parents lost their money and traveller's cheques when they travelled to the USA so they think it's better for me to have a credit card with me when I come to England. I have one but the one I've got only allows me to spend NT$ 10,000[6] which is not enough at all. My dad applied for a new visa card with which we both hold different cards but

can use them at the same time in different places. My dad is the one who pays the credit card bills. Of course, he warned me that I could only use the card when I'm in trouble or run out of money here. (July 12, 2000)

Although these might be two extreme cases, I found that parents or grandparents and other relatives of study tourists are the major sponsors of the trip to England. They not only pay the cost of the study tour, which is about NT$ 100,000 (approximately 3,000 US dollars – the exchange rate between NT dollar American is subject to change) for four weeks,[7] but also their other traveling expenses. "Liberation" from the limited allowances in Taiwan is exactly what is claimed by some study tourists as a right of their foreign travel and yet it also brings some obligations. Because of this financial sponsorship and their web of social relationships, shopping for others is another crucial feature that emerges from study tourists' discourse of "obligatory shopping."

Study tourists view traveling as a way of fulfilling their anticipatory consumption (Jansen-Verbeke, 1990). It is clear that purchasing certain material goods from England has assumed importance in many study tourists' preparations for their tour in England. Some study tourists came with a long list of shopping that they wanted to do in England for themselves and for their families and friends. Not completing their list of shopping before returning to Taiwan was a cause for anxiety among study tourists. They used the last moment at the airport to "grasp" souvenirs to take home for themselves and others. The phenomenon of "Bye-Buy" seems to be a common scene at international airports. They travel to collect and to enjoy the pleasure of the consumption of English culture. They are tourists who shop and collect foreign souvenirs. In this sense, shopping is not just an adjunct of foreign travel; it is what gives such travel its meaning. Through shopping – "I am tourist, therefore I shop!"– they consume English culture and bring it home to establish and demonstrate their sense of identities of being "bloody tourists" and "global customers." This leads to a discussion of three distinctive features of Taiwanese study tourists shopping in England, which I hope would raise consumer researchers' interest in these tourists. Understandably, in practice, these features often merge with another; yet such acts of shopping are important means for understanding how a sense of Taiwaneseness is displayed and how Taiwanese tourists performed their consumer behaviors in England.

*Shopping as a Collective Experience*

Shopping is a shared collective experience for Taiwanese study tourists. They go window-shopping and shopping with their group members or their friends. Study tourists told me that it is always more fun to go shopping with friends who are able to share their needs, interests, and opinions and to influence each other's choices. My fieldwork observations in Cambridge and London for three summers also showed that many of their shopping activities are conducted in groups; thus, the coordination of efforts and companionship are at issue. All the study tourists emphasize the notion of fun, and shopping with friends is a medium of providing entertainment for these students in England. It is a means of spending quality time together and enjoying each other's company. Nearly all the study tourists I interviewed are not too shy to admit that they do take their shopping companions' opinions seriously and are influenced by their friends' attitudes toward the objects of their affection. Seventeen-year-old high school student Jane says:

> I don't like to go shopping by myself. It's boring and pathetic to go shopping alone. Jessica, Sylvia and I always do things together and of course we go shopping together. We can talk about the things that interest us and can discuss them. We help each other out. They are very useful to help me make decisions or prevent me spending too much money. For example, I wanted to buy another Teddy Bear T-shirt, but Sylvia thought I shouldn't do so as I've already bought too much Teddy Bear stuff. I find her advice extremely helpful. (July 21, 2000)

Companions are valued as they can offer their opinions and encourage or discourage the shopper's decision. Some study tourists suggest that shopping serves a particular function in furthering or intensifying friendships. One year after his study tour, Adam, age 21, records his memories of shopping experiences in England:

> I always went window-shopping with Diana [another study tourist] and sometimes we invited others to join us. She helped me to make decisions and I offered my opinions to her as well. If we liked the same thing, we both bought it ... Diana is the same height as my sister so I used her as "model" to try things that I wanted to buy for my sister ... But, it's more than just buying things as sometimes we didn't buy anything. I think it's the social time and looking at things together that I enjoyed most. Moreover, shopping allows me to explore other "English" spaces freely and get some sense of their lifestyles. I especially like the open market in Cambridge ... We got lost several times but we had fun. (August 21, 2001)

There are many interesting points in Adam's accounts. First, window-shopping and shopping are about social relationships. Adam uses shopping as an arena for constructing or deepening his friendship with Diana. Second, shopping is also a resource to get gifts for his sister who does not travel with him. By so doing Adam is able to maintain the intimacy or strengthen affiliations with those left behind. Third, window-shopping and shopping are forms of visual consumption and offer a range of "ways of seeing" and "knowing" English culture. Shopping evokes a feeling of apprehension and appreciation of objects. Through the "collective gaze" (Urry, 1990, 2002) of the objects certain forms of visual aesthetic values are shared. Fourth, shopping is also another form of discovery and adventure. Shopping with companions overcomes boredom and provides a safe way to explore unknown areas, making the experience more fun and exciting. Accordingly, with companions, these processes of shopping become collective activities, experiences, and memories in which various social relationships are established as the case of Adam and Diana has shown.

Indeed, shopping as a collective experience reflects what Miller (1998) concludes from his ethnographic evidence of everyday shopping in London. Miller points out that shopping "is not just approached as a thing in itself. It is found to be a means to uncover, through the close observation of people's practices, something about their relationships" (Miller, 1998, p. 4). Miller goes on to argue that shopping is a social process that creates intimate relationships with loved ones or others. It is true in the present case, as Miller suggests, that shopping is more than getting things done and is interpersonal in specific ways rather than just personal. The findings from Taiwanese study tourists' shopping experiences in London and Cambridge also manifest that shopping is done with others and is a way of forming and sustaining relationships.

Although collective shopping experience is acknowledged, it is important to recognize that there is an ambiguous feeling in shopping with a big party. The shopping experience with companions, for some tourists, is not always an enjoyable experience. One of the most common complaints is that waiting for companions wastes time. Andy, who is now a 19-year-old college student, says:

> It was really a pain to go shopping with a big group. It wastes so much time waiting for people. It's also quite embarrassing as we are big group so we are very loud. We make a lot of noise, laughing or joking with each other at the shops ... Of course, this only happened in the first few days. After a while we went with our own small groups and that really makes shopping a lot of fun as we became friends not just a group of strangers. (August 3, 2000)

Since shopping is a collective experience it can serve as a way to articulate the relations of "friends" or "strangers" and the practices of shopping together can mark out the differences of interpersonal interactions. As Andy recalls, it is only when he and some group members had become friends that he began to enjoy shopping more with a small group.

Shopping with companions who have different interests or tastes can also be a painful experience. This is particularly likely to happen at the beginning when study tourists arrive in England from Taiwan and need someone to keep them company while they familiarize themselves with the new environment. Jack, a 25-year-old university student, says:

> I don't like some group members who always followed me wherever I went in the first week. They said my English is better and I'm a man so I can protect them which is nonsense, of course. Although I've been to other countries, my spoken English is not better than theirs. The things that I want to see are different from those young girls. They seem only to care about shopping for clothes while I am interested in outdoor equipment. I don't want to waste time with them. Fortunately, they left me alone this week. At least, I don't have to offer my opinions on things which I have no idea about. (July 25, 2000)

As a consequence of this unpleasant feeling about being "followed" and "consulted," Jack dissociated himself and left behind this collective group doing their shopping. In Jack's second week in Cambridge, rather than go shopping with young female study tourists, he made an effort to visit the main library in Cambridge University and got a two-day pass which he thought was the most valuable "authentic English" souvenir that he got from his study tour. I will return to analyze this theme in more detail in the final part of this chapter.

### Shopping as an Intercultural Interaction

In many ways it is misleading to suggest that study tourists only shop for pleasure rather than learning when they are abroad. Some study tourists think and use shopping in different ways (see Yeh, 2003, 2009b). Shopping in the tourism context not only is an act of consumption, but also has implications for understanding and experiencing other aspects of cultural life, as suggested by Adam earlier when he used shopping *"to explore other 'English' space freely and get some sense of their lifestyles."* To some extent tourist shopping is an intercultural interaction, through which tourists can develop detailed knowledge about other ways of life. Alice and Beth, both 17-year-olds, comment:

*Alice*: The reason that I joined in the study tour is because I want to be a "global citizen" [in English] and I want to learn English better. But after two weeks in Cambridge I got bored and here in London, the lessons are even worse. So I don't want to waste my time sitting in the classroom. There are so many things to see and to do in London. ... I really want to use my time to see everything before I leave London even though I feel sorry for Toby. [Their English teacher. Both Alice and Beth skipped classes after their first week of language lessons.]

*Beth*: Well, I agree with Alice. We go "shopping" [in English] and it is great fun even though I didn't buy anything. ... When we go shopping we can talk with the shop owners or the assistants. It's very interesting to talk to them. I have a problem understanding their accent sometimes, but it's getting better now. ... Anyhow, I feel I've learned more things through "shopping" [in English] than in the classroom.

*Joyce*: So what kinds of things have you learned from window-shopping?

*Beth*: Many things ... Such as, things are so expensive in Britain although the Body Shop is really much cheaper than Taiwan. Real contact with people or just observing strangers passing by. ... Well, I don't know, but I think my English is getting better as I can use my "broken English" to talk to people here.

Indeed, shopping is about social interaction that is as essential as other forms of cultural tourism practices. Shopping provides what Pratt calls a "contact zone"[8] in which tourists are enabled to see life in various ways; it also provides a place where diverse people can meet and communicate. As shoppers, tourists have the prerogative to enter someone's "private" space freely and go in and out of public spaces with a sense of legitimacy or purpose. Shopping allows tourists to participate in the bodily experiences of certain spaces that are provided to engage in the atmosphere designed to encourage consumption, to try products for free and for fun, and to receive services and make choices. In this sense, shopping is a medium of cultural "comprehension" and a form of communication. It is clear that both Alice and Beth understand shopping as a positive force, which offers them chances to use their English to interact with people and which helps them make sense of English daily reality and culture.

From a sociolinguistic point of view, shopping "involves extensive communicative interaction" (Chouliaraki & Fairclough, 1999, p. 86). This view of shopping echoes what Boorstin regards as the significant meaning of shopping for tourists. He writes:

> It [shopping] is a chink in that wall of prearrangements which separates [the tourist] from the country he visits. No wonder he finds it exciting. When he shops he actually encounters natives, negotiates in their strange language, and discovers their local business etiquette. (Boorstin, 1987, p. 92)

Boorstin recognizes that considerable social interaction and intercultural communication take place during tourist shopping. Shopping is a mundane everyday life activity but it certainly is one of the imperative features of tourists' consumption of other cultures and is a means of social engagement. The experience of shopping was a way for the Taiwanese study tourists to gather information and develop their understanding of English culture, both through people and material objects. In the case of both Alice and Beth, their notion of shopping has demonstrated that shopping is a form of learning. They shop for "enlightenment."

Alice's and Beth's discourse of shopping can be regarded as an antistereotype to popular negative associations of shopping as superficial, wasteful, trivial, and irrational, especially in the context of tourist shopping activity. Their view is, indeed, parallel to Mary Douglas's arguments in her article, "In Defence of Shopping" (1997). Douglas makes an explicit claim that shoppers, especially female shoppers, are on the contrary, coherent and rational beings. According to Douglas, shopping is a conscious and rational activity as the choices involve a reasonable calculation and sociocultural interaction. It is on the strength of such positive beliefs about shopping that Beth and Alice presented themselves. They viewed shopping as a way to increase their understanding of English culture and their confidence in their English language abilities.

## Shopping as Accumulating Guilt

There is also a discourse that shopping is linked to "misguided desire" or "moral weakness" and is therefore "unacceptable" in the eyes of others. Many study tourists approach shopping with mixed feelings. In some cases, this ambivalent view of shopping was not associated with respectability as argued by Pratt (1992) and Douglas (1997). Shopping is essentially about spending money and especially for some young study tourists the money is not their own but their parents', which makes shopping guilt-ridden and inappropriate. Those who are financially dependent on their parents face a hard time justifying their own shopping. One informant wrote in her diary:

> I bought more clothes today. I spent 18 pounds for a long-sleeve T-shirt with Cambridge University's logo on it. I need it and I thought it's not very expensive but I know Mum would be angry if she knew I spent money on buying clothes again ... I've spent so much money in one week. Both Jane and I spent 8 pounds to get the same Teddy bear T-shirt on Tuesday. I'm afraid that I'll be scorned by my parents due to all my shopping here when I return home. I feel I'm the "terminator" of my family wealth.
> 
> (Jessica, aged 16, high school student; July 25, 2000)

Jessica's sense of guilt is exactly the other paradoxical dilemma of shopping, which Beth and Alice have left out in their reflections. Jessica not only has to convince herself that she indeed needs a long sleeved T-shirt (to keep herself warm, as she wrote in another part of her diary), but has to rationalize that the "inexpensive" clothing is worth buying.

It is not, of course, just financial dependence that makes study tourists guilty about their shopping. Another variant of the sense of guilt involves shopping too much for oneself instead of for others. The concern of being selfish evokes a sense of guilt in the study tourists as well. Anna, a 20-year-old university student, explains:

> I feel guilty that I didn't buy anything for my dad. I really don't know what I should get him from England. He seems to have everything and I also have no idea about his taste. I thought of getting him a T-shirt from Cambridge but I think for a 50-something man to wear a t-shirt with a Cambridge logo might look funny. However, I bought 3 T-shirts for myself – one short-sleeve, another long one and the one with a hood. I think I'm very selfish to buy so much for myself and nothing for my dad. (August 12, 2000)

The quote above displays that Anna is explicitly aware that the self and the Other are linked in shopping activities. The celebration of "freedom" to travel has a price. The anxiety to find a "right" gift for the Other who remains at home is the price that one who has the time and freedom to travel has to pay. If they fail to do so, as in the case of Anna for her father, a sense of guilt is accumulated. The guilt Anna feels, however, derives also from the consequences that she feels from having bought too many things for herself.

In sum, at one level, a part of shopping serves as collective entertainment and provides formative and enjoyable experiences of enacting, mingling, and socializing. It is leisure activity with educative functions that are constitutive of experiences. It is equally clear that there is a seduction which brings a sense of guilt that Jessica has been dealing with as a result of spending more on herself rather than on her father. Jessica's ambivalence shows that she was well aware of her parents' perspective, but the T-shirt with a Cambridge logo had practical function and sign value that met her needs and, therefore, it was hard to resist the temptation of buying new clothes.

Obviously, these discourses present quite disparate observations of tourists shopping and imply a degree of complexity in notions of shopping. Nevertheless, most study tourists waver between "positive" and "negative" attitudes toward their acts of shopping, and their narratives suggest that they use shopping as a way of meeting people, making friends, and forming relationships. Some deal with this dialectic by creating a sense of the necessity of getting the objects/souvenirs in order to emphasize implications that extend beyond the act of shopping. Accounts like this allow the study tourists to engage in shopping with less guilt. Shopping becomes for them not an act of indulgence but a performance to ally objects with subjects, self with Other, and local with global.

I will now turn to a discussion of the meanings of tourist souvenirs and examine how and why individual study tourists use objects as ways to demonstrate their desired identity, build up social relationships, and collect and present their sense of English culture.

## MATERIAL CULTURES OF SOUVENIRS

Shopping is more than buying things and the examples chosen demonstrate that shopping provides one central site where intercultural encounters and communication take place. This does not mean, however, that the meanings of things and objects are not in need of further elucidation. On the contrary, material objects and tourist souvenirs are "sites" that must be examined in order to understand tourist experiences and to study consumer culture. Although shopping and the meanings of objects have been discussed separately in this chapter, they are not independent of each other. Nor am I suggesting that they are always interdependent, as some material objects that tourists take home with them are excluded from the act of shopping since they involve cultural imagination and memories, such as a falling leaf that a study tourist picks up from the park or a painting that was drawn by the children in the host family.

My concern about the relationship between objects and meanings is not new. Anthropologists, for example, have provided evidence to indicate the dynamic aspects of goods as communication. Mary Douglas has summarized that

> Man needs goods for communicating with others and for making sense of what is going on around him. The two needs are but one, for communication can only be formed in a structured system of meanings. (Douglas & Isherwood, 1979, p. 95)

Douglas locates her ethnographic research in her concern with goods and their functions as forms of communication and ways of cultural understanding.

In his classic study of youth subcultures, Dick Hebdige (1979) is directly concerned with the uses of material objects by youth subcultures to mark out their distinctive identities. Although Hebdige's analysis does not focus on tourist objects, his consideration of style and youth identity helps to clarify how fashion is experienced and practiced by young tourists' through the consumption of certain global objects. In *Consumer Culture* (1996), one of the powerful accounts that Celia Lury gives us is seeing that "things have social lives" (1996, p. 18), in which things have not only use values, but also sign values that can mean something else. In other words, things are open to multiple interpretations. This analysis enables us to see that objects may be bought for specific purposes to express and communicate certain aspects of life or traveling experiences. It follows that if the meanings of objects are expressive or communicative, then they must contain certain significant meanings that are able to be identified and understood.

In his account, Gordon Brown suggests that goods can "act as social tools" (1992, p. 58). He implies that goods enable the consumer to construct social relations and symbolize the expression of self-identity. Tim Dant (1999) also considers the significant meaning of objects in everyday life. The object "is a vehicle through which social value is expressed as a trace of the people, occasions and cultural contexts that inscribed value in the object" (Dant, 1999, p. 24). According to Dant, material objects are given meanings by being embedded in social practices. They make social relations visible and tangible and they place values on the commodities and add to their social meanings. The implications of objects as mediums of expression, therefore, invite a further investigation of objects, stressing both their material value and their social and discursive construction.

Objects, including the material and cultural, have many functions in social life as well as in tourist intercultural encounters. They provide sustenance, comfort, safety, pleasure, besides serving as signs of one's identity and lifestyle. Things displayed in the markets suggest an everyday reality and they also feed a tourist's perceptions of what others' culture should be. If goods and objects are ways for people to communicate with others, express their notions of cultural values, and make sense of the world, it is necessary to decode what messages and meanings they carry and how meanings are transformed in different cultural settings. We must therefore ask how the meanings of objects are to be comprehended. In order to examine materialities of Taiwanese English culture I focus on two objects, postcards and T-shirts, because they are widely purchased by Taiwanese study tourists.

First, take the postcard. Of the many types of souvenirs, postcards are surely easy to justify as the original function of a postcard is to communicate between tourists and those who remain at home or elsewhere. Yet in both participant interviews and post-tour interviews I found that Taiwanese study tourists use postcards as particular types of souvenirs invested with varied meanings. A postcard from Cambridge is more than a message saying "Wish you were here" – it also functions as a memory object to record the sender's experiences in Cambridge. The act of choosing and purchasing postcards from Cambridge or London can be regarded as the embodiment of global culture, and buying postcards is one of the universal things that many tourists do.

*Jack*: What did I buy? Well, postcards, of course. I have a whole list of friends to send postcards to back home. Some of them are not my real close friends but I sent postcards to them as I think it would be so special to get a card from Cambridge. I've spent a lot of money on them. Anyway, they are beautiful so why not? One of my shy female classmates also asked me to send her a postcard when she knew I was coming to Cambridge. I don't think I've ever talked to her in the past 3 years.

*Diana*: The first thing I bought is postcards. Postcards here are so beautiful. I bought them for myself but I think I will send one or two to my friends. I want to keep them for myself. They are my memories. I also bought a t-shirt for myself and my brother. Different colours, though.

*Alice*: Postcards! I bought lots and lots of postcards. I haven't sent them, but I will. Some of my friends will be surprised that I'm in England this summer, as I didn't tell them. I'm so busy. No time to write cards, really! Perhaps I can give the unwritten postcards to my friends as gifts when I return to Taiwan. I bought them from Cambridge so it means a lot!

*Adam*: Postcards. I don't trust my photography skills so I think postcards would be a good idea to record my summer trip. I will put the postcards into the photo album together with the photographs I took. They help me remember how beautiful the places are that I visited!

The above statements suggest that the study tourists bought postcards to send home in order to demonstrate their experience of "being there." They also imply that postcards are mnemonic objects for them as after the tour those postcards bring back their memories and the sense of "Englishness" that they have taken home. Postcards are constructed into significant cultural objects only through the process of the purchasing act by the tourists. In other words, tourists attach meanings and add their personal values to postcards themselves.

The other popular souvenir item is the long sleeve T-shirt. The reason given by study tourists for these purchases is that the weather in England keeps on changing and they did not have enough clothing to protect them against the "cold" weather. Long sleeve T-shirts serve as a practical function in keeping them warm in England and they can justify spending their own or their parents' money, as Jessica suggested earlier. When study tourists return home, T-shirts have new meanings in that they are cultural products expressing their owners' experience of having traveled to England. Sue joined a study tour when she was 23; she is now a 26-year-old staff member who works in an organization that helps Taiwanese to apply to study in Britain. She said after her tour:

> I dress quite smartly *[when I go to]* to my office as I want to look professional to show my "authority." T-shirts are too casual in my office but my Cambridge and Oxford T-shirts are different. They empower me and many students who come to our office show their respect to me more as they know I have travelled to England so I know more. ... So far, I've collected many famous universities' T-shirts from the USA and Britain. (September 15, 2001)

Although the tone is humorous, the sense of power is not out of place. Sue is well enough aware of the symbolic power of her souvenir T-shirt collection. Obviously, in this way, a T-shirt has the effect of a speech act. For Sue, a T-shirt is more than something to cover her body; it also shows her traveling experiences, and gives her authority to confirm her status as an "expert" licensed to provide information about studies in Britain.

A further reason for getting T-shirts with famous universities' logos on them is that they are sign-makers that can be mediated and translated into meaningful symbols. While many Western tourists use their tanned skin as evidence of their holidays abroad, many Taiwanese study tourists use the T-shirt as a symbol of their traveling experience. Of course, many other tourists from different cultural backgrounds get T-shirts for the same reason and it is inappropriate to suggest that this is a Taiwanese phenomenon only. T-shirts with famous university logos are the most popular cultural products among the study tourists and these T-shirts reflect their views about the hierarchy of educational fields. The T-shirt becomes a cultural object that marks out their traveling experiences, expressing their tourist experiences for them–"Been there, done that, got the T-shirt!" (see Fig. 1).

Rather than the meanings of souvenirs inherent in the objects themselves, they are constructed in the layers of meaning that tourists attach to them. Tourist souvenirs are important cultural objects for the tourists themselves and for others as well. Shopping for others is an excuse that legitimizes

Fig. 1. T-Shirt: Embodiment of "Being English"?

shopping as necessary in order to bring cultural objects home. The transformation is continuous and the meanings of things are varied. Susan Stewart, in *On Longing* (1993), analyses the way in which everyday objects are narrated through discourses to present certain versions of worldview. Stewart investigates two devices for the objectification of desire, the "souvenir" and the "collection" and takes into account the temporality of souvenirs in order to circulate their meanings and functions. Souvenirs, according to Stewart, are "magic objects because of this transformation" (1993, p. 151) in time and space. This transformation makes it possible for new meanings and discursive formations to follow. Objects that Taiwanese tourists buy have sign values that convey their experiences of being and consuming both the English and global cultures.

The study tourists' traveling stories are inseparable from the souvenirs in which their experiences and the meanings of these experiences are embedded. Both traveling stories and souvenirs are modes of representing and collecting Otherness through integration. Tourists have perhaps always wanted to tell others at home about what they saw on their travels and souvenirs, along with photographs, are ways to collect and share their travelling experiences. Such practices and the discourses that surround them reveal the important part that physical experience plays in mediating the meanings of the objects.

Stewart (1993) also points out the differences between the souvenir and the collection. She writes:

> In contrast to the souvenir, the collection offers example rather than sample, metaphor rather than metonymy. The collection does not displace attention to the past; rather, the past is at the service of the collection, for whereas the souvenir lends authenticity to the past, the past lends authenticity to the collection. (Stewart, 1993, p. 151)

Stewart's comment raises significant issues for the debate about "authenticity" in the discussion of souvenirs. How do Taiwanese interpret the "authentic Englishness" as inherent in souvenirs that they get from England? What sense of authenticity is constructed and represented, and how? In the following section, these questions are explored.

## COLLECTING "AUTHENTIC" ENGLISHNESS?

Understanding the sociocultural meanings of souvenirs cannot be taken for granted. It requires a further exploration of issues such as authenticity and representation. Although my discussions are generated from observations and evidence from study tourists' collections, they originate in the bodies of literature of cultural sociology and tourism. From tourism, in particular, I draw on the debate surrounding the issue of authenticity.[9] The question of authenticity in tourism studies is, of course, complex as the question itself involves complex temporal and spatial practices. Authenticity should not be thought of as an absolutely distinct concept, but as one which is able to translate and transform new meanings so that it is usable in different societies. The passage of time and different geographical locations always enrich the values of so-called "authenticity" and yet, as Urry argues, the notion of authenticity always involves "accommodation and reinterpretation" (Urry, 1990, pp. 104–134, 2002, p. 123). I have no wish to exhaust the debates of this issue here, but my emphasis derives from tourists' own narrations and perceptions of authenticity. Hence, like identity, "authentic Englishness" in my research is an open concept, and subject to change.

It varies, flows, and is relational. In this sense, the definition of "Englishness" is constantly being invented and contested. Such openness invites us to focus on the experiences of individuals, yet I suggest that those experiences are still shaped by a collective process of identification of social and cultural notions of "Englishness." On the one hand, individual tourist discourse stands in its own right and deserves respect as such. On the other hand, relations of cultural crossbreeding are also involved. Such discourses are useful in pointing out that the sense of "authenticity" is the outcome of the embodiment and practices of consumption.

For Taiwanese study tourists, the experience of English culture is a primary motive for their travel to England, and their desire for "authentic Englishness" is supposed to be identifiable and attainable. Without doubt, "Englishness" is a mixture of a wide range of different cultures of very different historical formations. However, in contemporary culture and everyday life, "Englishness" as such is no longer sufficient in itself but has to be thought with and through each individual experience of social encounters and cultural practices. The terms "authenticity" and "Englishness" are closely interwoven in study tourists' accounts, to the extent that it has become increasingly difficult to separate these two notions. They are both a means of marking and defining their understandings of English experiences and culture. Thus, it is more appropriate to examine the ways in which Taiwanese study tourists approach and accomplish their English experiences rather than to locate factors that correlate with these practices.

Taiwanese study tourists above all want "authentic English" objects. "Authentic" is, more than anything else, an expression of a taste culture that is applied to the selection of souvenirs to take home. Things that Taiwanese study tourists buy have to be considered "very English," objects that can be also recognized as such by those who remain at home and by travel companions. For these tourists the "authentic Englishness" that they desire implies that they are non-Taiwanese, or has to do with the construction of uniqueness with which the object is associated. Not only the content of the objects but also the wrapping papers or the shopping bags from the stores and gift shops are indicators of "authentic Englishness." Kristy, a 27-year-old female elementary school teacher, said:

> I threw away some of the bags that I got from my shopping. But I do take care of the paper and plastic bags that I got from Harrods's. The special green bags are lovely and useful when I put the gifts to my friends in them. When they saw the colour and the mark of Harrods, they would have known that the gifts come from England. Something you can't get from Taiwan. And I think that's very important; otherwise why bother to shop in foreign countries, when you can get almost everything in Taiwan? (August 5, 2000)

Indeed, what counts is not only the objects that one brings home, but also the specifics of a location of originality. The place of Englishness or the location of culture not only is an important arena for consuming souvenirs, but also serves as a cultural resource for understanding and reshaping conceptions of material culture in everyday life. Gordon summarizes:

> People feel the need to bring things home with them from a sacred, extraordinary time and space, for home is equated with ordinary, mundane time and space. ... When it is taken away and brought into a living room setting, however, it becomes transformed into a significant icon. It becomes sacralized in the new context and is imbued with all the power of associations made with its original environment. (Gordon, 1986, pp. 136–142)

Gordon's comment addresses an important issue between place, space, and "authentic" culture with which objects can be associated. In this sense, objects create different meanings and become multiple sites for intercultural encounters and representations of these experiences of connections to the others of this world. Once "English" souvenirs are taken from England to Taiwan, Taiwanese tourists constitute and invest these souvenirs with sociocultural meanings in specific ways. The discursive practices that produce Englishness are embedded in spatial practices. These various meanings are situated in a complex network of relationships to "here" and "there"; they interfere with one another and reshuffle themselves to construct new cultural and social meanings of these mobile souvenirs.

Not surprisingly, the place where the objects are made is one of the crucial considerations for Taiwanese study tourists. On several occasions when I was invited to go shopping with the study tourists, I observed them checking the label carefully and if the objects were made in Taiwan, they put them aside. Beth, who is a 17-year-old, says, *"I have to look at objects carefully as I don't want to buy things that have 'Made in Taiwan or China' labels on them."* This is not an easy task as many souvenirs are made in either Taiwan or China! Importantly, the "authenticity" that these tourists desire becomes label hunting, as they search for objects "Made in the UK or England," suggesting that "authenticity" is not free-floating but sticks with certain things. Consequently, labels become the most authentic signifiers of the place of English culture and are constitutive of what counts as "authentic Englishness" in the form of commodities for Taiwanese tourists. As Beth further comments:

> I want something with the label of "Made in England or the UK." Occasionally I still got something that was made in Taiwan and I was upset by my carelessness. It's nothing to do with hating Taiwan or whatever; it's just so ridiculous to travel thousands of miles to get stuff that is made in our own country. I also don't want to become a laughing

stock among my family and friends. It seems only illiterate people who don't know English would make such a mistake! (July 25, 2000)

Beth's statement exemplifies many of the Taiwanese study tourists' perceptions and interpretations of their sense of "authentic Englishness." Many of the Taiwanese study tourists make a similar claim that implies making "authentic Englishness" visible. This is the reason why the labels, marks, or logos are so important to Taiwanese study tourists.

As the comments indicate, study tourists reveal that they have some knowledge of global brands as well as famous British shops. Somewhat to my surprise, many of the study tourists came to England with a competent knowledge of world goods and famous logos of global products, along with a set of shopping-abroad experiences, both of which shape these understandings and structure their choices of "authentic" souvenirs. Nineteen-year-old Anita, who made her study tour to England in 2001, recalls:

> I did some "market research" before I went to England this summer. I already knew many global famous goods such as Burberry, Armani and CD, and Calvin Klein, etc. I know that some things are definitely cheaper in England than in Taiwan, such as Dr. Martens and the Body Shop stuff. In order to make sure that I wouldn't get the wrong things, I went to the department stores several times and checked out the prices beforehand. I wrote the prices down in my notebooks so I wouldn't buy the wrong goods. (September 25, 2001)

For Anita getting the "right" things back to Taiwan is an enactment of her knowledge of global consumer culture. She possesses knowledge of goods that are not bound by her cultural and geographical location. She knows what is worth buying from England and her world knowledge about goods enables her to shop confidently in England. In fact she has achieved what she set out to accomplish in her trip to England and her trip seems to have lived up to her expectations. Her familiarity with "world cultures" is the result of the flow of objects and cultures from different locations and is, indeed, a phenomenon of so-called "globalization" (Robertson, 1992; Waters, 1995). By consuming the "cheaper" global commodities in England, Anita actively and self-consciously heightens her individual sense of connectedness to the global. The implicit claim is both her competency to distinguish the "world" from the local and her greater understanding and insight of consumption of global products that England is able to provide. The constitution of her sense of "authentic Englishness," therefore, operates through the process of the consumption of western products and labels such as Burberry, Christian Dior, Giorgio Armani, and Calvin Klein and of course, "very English" and cheap Body Shop products.

During the post-tour interviews (2001 and 2004) with study tourists, I discussed their souvenirs and their reasons for getting them. Study tourists frequently highlighted the price differences and the importance of connections built with Taiwan/local and England/global that reflect upon their own travels. For them, if the objects can be bought in Taiwan, the price that they paid in England should be cheaper and if they are pricey items since they are hard to get in Taiwan, they are worth taking home. For these tourists, the less paid, the more "authentic" or the more paid, the more "authentic;" whatever the case, the amount of money young study tourists spend to acquire "authentic Englishness" is astonishing.[10]

If English culture and sense of Englishness can be recognized and translated through objects, this suggests that there is a recognizable and agreed thing that we might call English authenticity, which can be commoditized and reproduced. It is apparent that tourist souvenir shops contribute to the representation, promotion, and circulation of such common English culture. Tourist souvenir shops embedded in and dependent on "authentic culture" play an important role in the circulation of these English cultural signifiers. Diana said:

> I wanted to buy some English tea to take back to Taiwan. I wanted to get some beautiful fruit & flower tea but the staff in the tea shop told me that Earl Grey is considered to be very English so I bought 4 packs of Earl Grey. I did buy some flower tea at the end for myself but I gave Earl Grey to my friends as I was told that it is more English. (September 28, 2001)

As might reasonably be predicted from Diana's process of choosing "English" tea, the staff uses his/her professional expertise and knowledge to influence and construct Diana's sense of English culture as well as to reinforce Diana's consumption of English culture. In their brief encounter, although in a commercial setting, a certain degree of intercultural communication is established. In this sense, both the staff and Diana shared a common understanding in which participants use souvenir objects specifically to portray and enact "Englishness," sometimes to sell, but most often to take home.

In a similar case, Tony, a 19-year-old university student, relates his final choice of a pair of Dr. (Doc) Martens boots, coming out in a long conversation that he had with a female staff at Covent Garden in London. The female staff member drew Tony's attention to an item that he might not have otherwise considered. As Tony said, he *"wouldn't expect to spend almost 100 pounds on a pair a boots,"* but the staff member encouraged him to get the latest model to show his "Englishness," boots that he "*couldn't find in Taiwan.*" In order to be "authentically English," rather than like other study tourists who get "special offer" of Dr. Martens, which are about one-third or half of the price in Taiwan, Tony managed to pay the extra cost for "authentic" and "unique" English boots. Although there are five authorized shops that sell Dr. Martens in Taiwan, Tony believes that particular style – particularly the 14 holes boots – and the location in which he got them have "authentic Englishness." Tony described his response to acquiring the boots in the post-tour interview in 2001:

> It's definitely a cool decision. It's almost two years now but every time I wear the boots, my friends would like to know where I got them. I was happy and felt superior as my Martens were from England and especially as I bought it from the Dr. Martens Department Store at Covent Garden in London ... At the same time, the boots also remind me of the sweet English girl who encouraged me to buy them. She also showed me how to use the different shoelaces to have a punk-look! (September 12, 2001)

The place of English culture conveys a position of superiority and helps Tony to win admiration from others who do not have the time or money to travel and to consume. It is a distinction measured partly in fashionable terms and obviously Tony has chosen to use Dr. Martens as a mark to single out his "English culture" in Taiwan.

Tony's "cool" consumption of Dr. Martens also brings our focus to the social interaction between tourists and the locals. Clearly, those people who provide services for gift shops and in tourism play essential roles in the construction and circulation of "authentic" culture for their customers. As in the example of Diana's tea shopping, the staff help to shape and reshape tourists' understanding of the locals' outlook and act, in part, to establish their roles as cultural brokers. They monitor their understanding of tourists' needs and show tourists "authentic" souvenirs to take home. But it is not easy to tell if the staff's opinions are mediated through their knowledge about tourist demands of cultural authenticity or from their own business interests, while at the same time it is hard to measure tourists' attempts to bring their cultural understanding back home or to forge cultural stereotypes through purchasing the souvenirs.

Using a pair of work boots/shoes as a "national" and cultural symbol sounds strange, and yet the power of popular culture and the mobility of objects must be recognized on different grounds. Nevertheless, the link between global material objects and cultural identity is a primary concern. Such symbols or signs are of course translated and contested in time and space and with different social groups. Dr. Martens boots/shoes represent English identity and authenticity that Taiwanese young tourists take home with them. There were 29 participants in my research study tour in 1999 and more than half of the group members (16) bought at least one pair of Dr. Martens to take back to Taiwan.[11] Andrew Calcutt (2000) defines the role of Dr. Martens as a "symbol of British style" (2000, p. 163), whereas the result of my research indicates that Dr. Martens are the "authentic" souvenir for the Taiwanese study tourists, a symbol and evidence of their way of consuming and representing their knowledge of English culture through their consumer behaviors and shopping practices.

Although most Taiwanese study tourists do not show much interest in the history of Dr. Martens, they attach considerable importance to being "cool," stylish, "a rebel," "wild," and "very English," the core meaning with which Dr. Martens are identified. Many of the buyers of Dr. Martens also told me that trainers such as Nike or New Balance[12] are now considered to be very "common" and "normal" among Taiwanese youth, but possessing a pair of Dr. Martens boots is still "distinctive." These young tourists reflect the tremendous emphasis on collecting the "cool" brands and the right objects within youth culture.

Some of the study tourists I interviewed associate Dr. Martens with British subcultures of Skinheads or Punks. Sam, a 20-year-old university student, says: "*I always wanted to have a pair of Dr. Martens since I saw some Punks on the TV when I was an elementary school student. I don't like their hair but I want the cool boots that they were wearing.*" Some associate Dr. Martens with pop singers, such as Sting or Madonna. Ann, a 19-year-old university student, says:

> You know Sting? He's one of my favourite male singers. He's English and I think he's really cool! I went to his concert in Taipei a few years ago and my friend told me that Sting wears a pair of Dr. Martens. That was the first time I heard about Dr. Martens. There's a Dr. Martens shop in Tien-Mu [in Taipei], but they're so expensive. This time in England I have bought two pairs of Dr. Martens, one for myself and the other for my boyfriend who is also a fan of Sting. (July 21, 2000)

At the same time, John, an 18-year-old college student, comments: "*I know Madonna is an American but every time I think of Dr. Martens I think of Madonna. Perhaps it is because of MTV.*" This suggests that mass media and cultural industries such as MTV and advertising encourage Taiwanese study tourists to think about and collect certain objects. They have helped to fracture some of the belief systems and cultural values of consuming and collecting in order to influence study tourists' understanding of English cultures and the global brands.

The Dr. Martens brand has spilled over into a kind of general popular cultural icon of English culture for Taiwanese young tourists. By consuming a pair of shoes/boots, they share imaginatively the values of the English world and use these objects to articulate their sense of Englishness and the connections with the western world. In contemporary culture, although global products are traveling across national boundaries, the links between the sense of "authenticity" and hierarchy of places are still apparent for Taiwanese study tourists. The study tourists neither question the influence of Western cultural imperialism nor formulate the complexities of global commoditization that are involved in their shopping activities. Instead they are responding to travel as a rite of passage that allows them to experience global Western culture as part of their travel. If they do not return to Taiwan with "authentic" trophies they would have wasted their journeys to England. While I do not accept their accounts without some skepticism, I believe the phenomenon serves to make the point that Taiwanese study tourists are "trained" by the consequences of commercial globalization and have learned how to celebrate their capacity to consume capitalistic material culture. For them, in traveling and shopping abroad they exercise their knowledge about world goods and global brands to immerse themselves in consuming other cultures. By doing so, their knowledge and competence in interpreting the meanings those global objects convey are displayed in their consumption of contemporary material culture. Such commoditization involving global products, I argue, is itself increasingly commoditized through their journeys to the West.

## CONCLUSION

In this chapter, I have explored the ways in which border-crossing shopping constitutes both a site and a resource for Taiwanese tourists' construction of their sense of Englishness. The manner and the social meanings of shopping in touristic activities and the sociocultural meanings of the souvenirs they bring home can be conceptualized as a framework within which Taiwanese study tourists perceive and understand cultural differences. This chapter has examined the question of what sorts of relationships exist between tourists and their shopping practices. Shopping can be seen as an indicator of local cultural practices, traveling memories, and collecting of a sense of "being there" as well as building closer relations with others. In most cases, these young Taiwanese tourists claimed that their act of shopping had multiple functions and meanings: practicing their English, a pleasure-seeking activity, a means of social interaction or of creating an intimate bond with group members, another way of making sense of English life and culture, or an imperative duty to shop for others. These motives reveal their discourses of "acknowledging consumption" (Miller, 1995) in which they represent what they perceive in the act of shopping in their touristic experiences.

I have also demonstrated that study tourists use souvenirs as an arena for constructing accounts of "authentic Englishness." I have argued that the phenomenon of the study tours is not only a means of accumulating linguistic capital for young Taiwanese people, but also a performance of global customers who have competent knowledge of global brands and are able to take them home to verify their journey to England. Thus the crucial point here is that: shopping matters to Taiwanese study tourists, as the act itself is the route to gain cultural knowledge and experience. They use shopping, which is their most familiar leisure activity, to situate themselves within the strange but familiar environment. Cultural objects from England that are bought by Taiwanese study tourists to represent their traveling and cultural experiences are at the same time means for them to link up with globalization. To them, shopping is not merely buying souvenirs, but also an act of developing a detailed knowledge of global culture and consuming the sense of the Englishness that the global objects signify. Tourist souvenirs are deeply implicated with the meanings of a place, and places are self-referential entities (Appadurai, 1986). Moreover, they are overlaid by elaborate meanings. Souvenirs are contexts of cultural objects of Otherness, which produce and embody various meanings. They are never limited to a single meaning, but reveal a multiplicity of meanings in their exhibition – for instance what souvenirs are about, their place of origin and of purchase.

Shopping matters to Taiwanese study tourists as it provides a shared collective experience for producing their accounts of the embodiment of Englishness. Moreover, shopping matters as it emerges in the dialectical relations between the self–other and local–global. Shopping involves how we look at ourselves and how the world shapes what we view, how we act, and the forms of activity in which we engage. A pair of Dr. Martens boots is not only a fashion or style, but is also a medium for Taiwanese youth to connect with a sense of English culture that is globally recognized. Global objects also imply a self-definition that Taiwanese study tourists desire to achieve. They are ways in which Taiwanese youth construct their understandings of the world and ways they define themselves within it. The multilayered notions of shopping and multiple functions of souvenirs are ways in which tourists express, not only their values, ideas, and experiences, but also their identities. The choice of souvenirs and their meaning-making therefore matter in consumer research and in the sociology of consumption.

# NOTES

1. "Go Bye-Bye to Buy Buy" is based primarily on personal observation during a number of travels with Taiwanese study tours in 1997, 1999, and 2000. I use this phrase to indicate the phenomenon of Taiwanese study tourists' cross-boundary shopping experiences, particularly at international airports.

2. The concept of the study tour in Taiwan originally comes from the idea of language study courses. Such language courses provide Taiwanese students with chances to travel and study abroad for a short period of time and live with host families. It is a tour to study and to play. It is a holiday experience with a win-win position that attracts both young people who participate in the tour and the older generation who pay the cost of the tour. Study tours can be categorized as educational or cultural tourism. For more detailed analysis see Yeh (2003).

3. Most shops and department stores close at 10 pm and are open seven days a week in Taiwan.

4. For an overview of consumption and the theory of shopping see Miller (1987, 1998) and Slater (1997). For understanding the experience of shopping see Falk and Campbell (1997). For consumption and lifestyles see Bocock and Thompson (1992). For lifestyle shopping and the meanings of cultural objects see Shields (1992) and Lury (1996). For a brief history and literature of research on shopping see Hewer and Campbell (1997, pp. 186–206).

5. Anna Wessely defines shopping tourism as "travel abroad with the explicit aim to buy goods that are unavailable or difficult to find in one's country" (Wessely, 2002, p. 6). This is however not the case of the study tour. For Taiwanese study tourists those objects are neither difficult nor unavailable to get in Taiwan. Moreover, unlike some other package tourists, study tourists seldom resell goods that they get from England for commercial purposes.

6. The exchange rate was about NT$33 for one US dollar in the year 2000.

7. The study tour package is varied and therefore the price is subject to change. The one mentioned here is the so-called standard package that includes international flights, 4-week language school fees, food and accommodation, one excursion during the weekend. For more details see Yeh (2003).

8. Mary Louise Pratt in *Imperial Eyes* (1992) describes the contact zone as the "social spaces where disparate cultures meet, clash, and grapple with each other, often in highly asymmetrical relations of domination and subordination – like colonialism, slavery, or their aftermaths as they are lived out across the globe today" (Pratt, 1992, p. 4). Although her notion of "contact zone" refers to the power relationship between colonizers and slaves, the use of "contact zone" in this chapter is employed as a loose term to indicate encounters between the tourists and the locals.

9. For detailed discussions see Yeh (2003).

10. I did not ask the question directly of how much money study tourists spent on shopping. In a 4-week period they spent between 400 and 4000 British pounds, not including food and accommodation.

11. One study tourist bought six pairs – three for the study tourist himself, one for his girlfriend, and the other two for his siblings.

12. Certain Nike basketball shoes are still associated with a "cool" image as they are limited productions and promoted by the NBA basketball stars such as Jordan. Nike's "Just-Do-It" commercials and these advertisements are still popular among the Taiwanese youth. New Balance is advertised in Taiwan as American late President Clinton's running shoes.

# REFERENCES

Appadurai, A. (Ed.) (1986). *The social life of things: Commodities in cultural perspective.* Cambridge: Cambridge University Press.
Belk, R. (1995). *Collecting in a consumer society.* London: Routledge.
Bocock, R., & Thompson, K. (1992). *Social and cultural forms of modernity.* Oxford: Polity Press.
Boorstin, D. (1987). *The image: A guide to pseudo-events in America.* New York: Harper & Row.
Bourdieu, P. (1984). *Distinction: A social critique of the judgement of taste.* London: Routledge.
Brown, G. (1992). Tourism and symbolic consumption. In: P. Johnson & B. Thomas (Eds), *Choice and demand in tourism* (pp. 57–71). London: Mansell.
Calcutt, A. (2000). *Brit cult: An A–Z British Pop culture.* London: Prion.
Chouliaraki, L., & Fairclough, N. (1999). *Discourse in late modernity: Rethinking critical discourse analysis.* Edinburgh: Edinburgh University Press.
Dant, T. (1999). *Material culture in the social world.* Buckingham: Open University.
Douglas, M. (1997). A defence of shopping. In: P. Falk & C. Campbell (Eds), *The shopping experience* (pp. 13–30). London: Sage.
Douglas, M., & Isherwood, B. (1979). *The world of goods: Towards an anthropology of consumption.* New York: Norton.
Falk, P., & Campbell, C. (Eds). (1997). *The shopping experience.* London: Sage.
Gordon, B. (1986). The souvenir: Messenger of the extraordinary. *Journal of Popular Culture, 20,* 135–146.
Hebdige, D. (1979). *Subculture: The meaning of style.* London: Routledge.
Hewer, P., & Campbell, C. (1997). Appendix: Research on shopping – a brief history and selected literature. In: P. Falk & C. Campbell (Eds), *The shopping experience* (pp. 186–206). London: Sage.
Jansen-Verbeke, M. C. (1990). Leisure and shopping: Tourism produce mix. In: G. Ashworth & B. Goodall (Eds), *Marketing tourism places* (pp. 128–135). London: Sage.
Lury, C. (1996). *Consumer culture.* Cambridge: Polity Press.
MacCannell, D. (1976). *The tourist: A new theory of the leisure class.* Berkeley: University of California Press.
McIntosh, A., & Prentice, R. (1999). Affirming authenticity: Consuming cultural heritage. *Annals of Tourism Research, 26*(3), 589–612.
Miller, D. (1987). *Material culture and mass consumption.* Oxford: Blackwell.

Miller, D. (Ed.) (1995). *Acknowledging consumption: A review of new studies.* London: Routledge.
Miller, D. (1998). *A theory of shopping.* Cambridge: Polity.
Pearce, P. L., & Moscardo, G. (1986). The concept of authenticity in tourist experiences. *Australian and New Zealand Journal of Sociology, 22*(1), 121–132.
Pratt, M. L. (1992). *Imperial eyes: Travel writing and trasnsculturation.* London: Routledge.
Redfoot, D. (1984). Touristic authenticity, touristic angst, and modern reality. *Qualitative Sociology, 7*(4), 291–309.
Robertson, R. (1992). *Globalization: Social theory and global culture.* London: Sage.
Shields, R. (1991). *Places on the margin.* London: Routledge.
Shields, R. (1992). *Lifestyle shopping.* London: Routledge.
Slater, D. (1997). *Consumer culture & modernity.* Cambridge: Polity Press.
Stewart, S. (1993). *On longing: Narratives of the miniature, the gigantic, the souvenir, the collection.* Durham: Duke University Press.
*The Taipei Times.* (1999). What did you do this summer? *The Taipei Times,* August 19.
Timothy, D., & Butler, R. (1995). Cross-border shopping: A North American perspective. *Annals of Tourism Research, 22*(1), 16–34.
Urry, J. (1990). *The tourist gaze: Leisure and travel in contemporary societies.* London: Sage.
Urry, J. (2002). *The tourist gaze* (2nd ed.). London: Sage.
Waters, M. (1995). *Globalization.* London: Routledge.
Wessely, A. (2002). Travelling people, travelling objects. *Cultural Studies, 16*(1), 3–15.
Yeh, J. H. (2003). *Travelling, learning and consuming Englishness.* PhD thesis, University of Lancaster, Lancaster.
Yeh, J. H. (2009a). Still vision and mobile youth: Tourist photos, travel narratives and taiwanese modernity. In: T. Winter, et al. (Eds), *Asia on tour: Exploring the rise of Asian tourism* (pp. 302–314). London: Routledge.
Yeh, J. H. (2009b). Embodiment of sociability through the tourist camera. In: M. Robinson & D. Picard (Eds), *The framed world: Tourism, tourist and photography* (pp. 199–216). Surrey: Ashgate.

# Part II
# Consumption Cues

# CUE CONGRUENCY AND PRODUCT INVOLVEMENT EFFECTS ON GENERATION Y ATTITUDES

Timothy Heinze

## ABSTRACT

Purpose – To better understand the general marketing sensitivities of Generation Y and the manner in which Congruency Theory and the Elaboration Likelihood Model (ELM) may apply.

Design/methodology/approach – A quantitative two-factor (peripheral cue congruency and relative product involvement) between-subjects design was used to determine the attitudinal impact associated with the use of congruous peripheral cues in high- and low-involvement product situations.

Findings – Generation Y's attitudinal responses to peripheral cues both align with and vary from the general predictions of the ELM. Relative product involvement is more important than peripheral cue congruency in the formation of attitudes toward an advertisement.

Originality/value – Generation Y is a powerful social and economic consumer group whose attitudinal responses to marketing appeals have not been extensively studied. The current study furthers understanding within this important arena.

Research implications/limitations – *The use of congruent peripheral cues is not sufficient to generate positive attitudes in both high- and low-involvement product scenarios. Effective marketing must move beyond cue congruency to include an involved "lifestyle fit" that will effectively generate positive attitudes. Limitations include the sole review of print advertisements and a sole reliance on college-attending members of Generation Y. Future research should examine the impact of congruency on advertisements whose strategic intent focuses on awareness or action rather than on mere attitude change.*

## INTRODUCTION

Marketing managers are keenly interested in effective marketing strategies used to attract and retain today's burgeoning Generation Y market segment (Cui, Trent, Sullivan, & Matiru, 2003). Generally defined as including individuals born between 1977 and 1994 (Paul, 2001), Generation Y represents a large portion of the population in Europe, Canada, and the United States. In the United States alone, Generation Y's 80 million people comprise nearly a quarter of the population. Since the operational frameworks of many marketers are heavily influenced by generational sensitivities (Strauss & Howe, 2006), and since Generation Y is demonstrating substantive divergence from the orientations of prior generations (Wolburg & Pokryzwczynski, 2001), marketers must re-examine the marketing paradigms and tactics directed toward Generation Y. Despite Generation Y's economic and social importance, the research directed toward Generation Y's marketing sensitivities has been largely scattered and organizationally unfocused. A better understanding of Generation Y's response to the marketing efforts of today's organizations is needed (Yeqing & Shao, 2002). The purpose of the current study is to further that understanding through reviewing the attitudinal effects associated with advertising cue congruency for high- and low-involvement products.

### Cue Congruency

The notion of cue congruency builds on the old adage that "birds of a feather flock together." If the elements of a marketing appeal are similar to the lifestyle, aspirations, or self-perceptions of a given individual, the individual is more likely to relate to the appeal and possibly align future behaviors with appeal recommendations. Though the original arguments for congruency theory (Osgood & Tannenbaum, 1955) are logical and frequently illustrated by myriad marketing campaigns, marketers are still left with confusing questions, especially when considering appeals directed to new audiences. Not all consumers want to "flock together." Being "out" is often "in." And as today's young consumers become increasingly savvy (Wolburg & Pokryzwczynski, 2001), transparent attempts to congruently "fit" a marketing appeal to a given lifestyle might backfire, especially if the attempt is viewed as a mere token. Marketers are faced with the strategic questions of if, how, and what kind of congruency should be utilized in an appeal. These questions are magnified when approaching a group, such as Generation Y, whose marketing sensitivities have not been comprehensively studied and whose underlying orientations differ markedly from prior generations (Wolburg & Pokryzwczynski, 2001).

Though important, cue congruency does not exist in a situational vacuum. The relative level of operative product involvement must also be considered. Petty and Cacioppo's (1981) elaboration likelihood model (ELM) suggests that peripheral cues are typically less important in high-involvement situations and more important in low-involvement situations. However, involvement can and does balance the relative impact of cue congruency on consumer attitudes toward the product.

Because Generation Y has shown substantive variation from prior generations (Wolburg & Pokryzwczynski, 2001), we cannot assume that cue congruency and product involvement will affect it in the same manner as past generations. The purpose of the current research is to determine whether or not cue congruency and product involvement affect members of Generation Y in the traditional manner. Results could provide academicians and practitioners with a better understanding of Generation Y's advertising sensitivities and with a specific set of guidelines for developing effective advertising campaigns directed toward members of Generation Y.

# LITERATURE REVIEW AND CONCEPTUAL BACKGROUND

*Generation Y Background and Research*

*Background*
Now entering the U.S. economy en masse, the almost 80 million members of Generation Y are beginning to make an enormous economic impact

(Eisner, 2005; Paul, 2001). The generation enjoys relatively greater wealth than the Baby Boom generation (Morton, 2002), possesses technological savvy (Newberger & Curry, 2000), and is highly educated (Newberger & Curry, 2000). The college-attending segment of Generation Y is sizeable and wields considerable social/economic impact (Maciejewski, 2004). The Internet is a top media choice and is used both as a means of socialization and entertainment (Morton, 2002).

As opposed to members of Generation X, members of Generation Y are more traditional (Stapinski, 1999), and the value structures of the generation closely resemble the value frameworks of Baby Boomers (Maciejewski, 2004). From a relational perspective, Generation Y is more likely to view intimacy from a technological perspective (Syrett & Lammiman, 2004). Relationships are often initiated and maintained via the Internet or other technological conduits. The utilization of the Internet to build and develop relationships has enabled Generation Y to become adept at multitasking. Simultaneously interacting via multiple communication formats is normative, and Generation Y is perhaps better able to multitask than any prior generation (Cheng, 1999). However, multitasking does not indicate a divided focus that values only surface relationships or interactions. Members of Generation Y value authenticity. Transparent hype or shallow showmanship are not generally appreciated (Cordiner, 2001). Nevertheless, Generation Y is often excited by self-generated, "viral" hype and within this context, the Generation's tastes are particularly fickle and easily transition from one trend to the next (Merrill, 1999).

*Generation Y Advertising Research Overview*
Advertising research directed toward Generation Y has primarily reviewed the (1) social or personal effects of advertising (Braverman & Aaro, 2004; Fox, 1995; Pechmann, Levine, Loughlin, & Leslie, 2005; Ritson & Elliott, 1999; Saffer & Chaloupka, 2000), (2) preferences for and utilization of various advertising and media formats (Clark, Martin, & Bush, 2001; Grant, 2005; Gronbach, 2000; La Ferle, Edwards, & Lee, 2000; Morton, 2002), and (3) relative effectiveness of various types of advertising appeals and the evaluative tools used to analyze those appeals (Andrews & Lysonski, 1991; Cui et al., 2003; Higby & Mascarenhas, 1993; Keillor, Parker, & Schaefer, 1996; Maciejewski, 2004; Martin & Bush, 2000; Mangleburg & Bristol, 1998; Mehta, 1999; Yeqing & Shao, 2002; Wolburg & Pokryzwczynski, 2001).

## Advertising Appeals

Advertising appeals, the focus of the current study, were first reviewed by Goldberg (1990) in an analysis of whether or not advertising affected the awareness and actions of Generation Y children toward certain advertised products. Though not specifically focused on Generation Y, the study was one of the first to utilize Generation Y children. Results indicated that advertising substantively affected both awareness and purchase behavior. However, the study did not review the particular characteristics of the examined advertisements that may have affected awareness and buyer behavior. Fox (1995) conducted a qualitative version of Goldberg's (1990) quantitative study and also suggested that advertising influences both attitudes and actions. However, similar to Goldberg (1990), Fox (1995) only addressed the generic issue of advertising rather than examining specific advertising appeals or approaches. Marney (1996) provided a helpful degree of specificity by suggesting that members of Generation Y are particularly impressed by advertisements that are honest, humorous, clear, and original. However, Marney (1996) did not review whether impressive advertisements influence attitudes or generate buyer behavior.

Martin and Bush (2000) attempted to address this shortcoming by examining whether or not the utilization of role models substantively influences purchase intentions (PI) and behavior. Parents were found to be the most important role models shaping the buying behavior of Generation Y, but athletes and entertainers were also found to exert significant impact. The study suggested that advertising effectiveness can be enhanced through creatively utilizing role models within an advertisement or as a reinforcement of a particular advertising message. In addition to older role models, peer influences are also important and can exert substantive impact on brand purchase choices (Keillor et al., 1996).

Yeqing and Shao (2002) addressed the importance of determining whether or not the utilization of a unique selling proposition can impact the effectiveness of a given advertisement in terms of attitudinal change. Results indicated that uniqueness is valued by members of Generation Y. However, Pechmann and Knight's (2002) review of stimulus advertising indicated that the desire for uniqueness does not exclude members of Generation Y from susceptibility to group influences that can be either reinforced or minimized via effective advertising. Finally, Cui et al., (2003) illustrated that cause-related appeals can be an effective way to influence certain segments of the Generation Y market. Assuming the influenced segments are populated by peer leaders, cause-related appeals can then substantively influence the market via the effective use of buzz marketing techniques (Henry, 2003).

*Advertising Appeal Evaluation Frameworks*
To better understand the evaluative frameworks utilized to process advertising appeals, a final group of studies have addressed the unique ways members of Generation Y evaluate specific advertising appeals. Andrews and Lysonski (1991) first addressed the matter by building on prior research that sought to uncover how young people evaluate specific advertisements and associated appeals. Andrews and Lysonski (1991) particularly reviewed the manner in which United States and international adolescents evaluate advertising, and they suggested that evaluations are heavily dependent upon the political and cultural climate surrounding young people. Higby and Mascarenhas (1993) refined the understanding of evaluation by determining that members of Generation Y can evaluate advertising appeals from either an informative or normative perspective. The idea of informative and normative evaluative perspectives was expanded by Mangleburg and Bristol (1998) who utilized the perspectives as a basis for understanding whether or not members of Generation Y evaluate advertising with a skeptical eye. Results indicated that peer influences lead to normative evaluative techniques that are moderated by the impact of parents and macroexposure to mass media and popular culture. The results mirror those associated with complementary studies involving the manner in which role models and other socializing influences affect not only the evaluative criteria employed by members of Generation Y, but also the resultant attitude and action effects (Clark et al., 2001; Martin & Bush, 2000).

Wolburg and Pokryzwczynski (2001) specifically reviewed several microevaluative criteria employed by members of Generation Y and uncovered that evaluation of advertisements is often based on the degree to which the advertisement relates to an individual's life. In particular, "hard sells" are not appreciated since these approaches do not mirror the lifestyle characteristics of Generation Y. However, the study did not present additional recommendations by which an advertiser could determine the relative congruency of a given advertising approach or appeal. To address this deficiency, Maciejewski (2004) reviewed the issue of sexual and fear advertising appeals. Results indicated that moral frameworks and gender orientations can significantly affect how members of Generation Y evaluate the utilization of sexual or fear appeals within a given advertisement.

In summary, several studies have addressed the macro issue of evaluative frameworks, but relatively few studies have explored how members of

Generation Y positively or negatively evaluate specific advertising appeals or formats. Evaluative influences are generally understood, but the manner in which these influences affect the evaluation of a specific advertising appeal or message has not been extensively explored. In light of the large number of gaps, it is easier to review the research that has been accomplished rather than the holes that remain to be filled.

Goldberg (1990) illustrated that advertising generically affects the attitudes and purchase behaviors of young members of Generation Y, but the specific factors that drive these effects were not identified or studied. Other studies have started to offer precision by reviewing the effects of advertising appeals that utilize humor, honesty, clarity, originality, nonconformity, role models, lifestyle descriptions, congruency, and activism (Cui et al., 2003; Keillor et al., 1996; Marney, 1996; Martin & Bush, 2000; Mehta, 1999; Morton, 2002; Yeqing & Shao, 2002). However, the list is observably incomplete and leaves room for a large number of new and confirmatory studies.

In relation to the analysis of advertising and Generation Y, the arena of advertising effectiveness (defined in terms of attitudinal and behavioral alteration) offers the greatest opportunity for further research and substantive advance. To this end, the current study reviews whether congruent peripheral cues, in the form of peer or nonpeer models, within high- and low-involvement product advertisements affect attitudes.

## Consumer Involvement

Zaichkowsky's (1985) classic definition suggests that involvement is the personal relevance of an object and is driven by an individual's needs, values, and interests. Zaichkowsky (1985) developed a Personal Involvement Inventory (PII) that offered a means to test the relative involvement of a product or category on a low-involvement/high-involvement scale. Gordon, McKeage, and Fox (1998) attempted to expand this bidimensional understanding of involvement through suggesting that involvement includes the affectations, cognitions, and behavioral responses that comprise a consumer's views regarding a specific product or category. These dimensions were modeled in a multidimensional consumer involvement profile that included ten levels of involvement. However, attempts to compare these levels with the information processing responses of consumers are nonexistent (Cochran & Quester, 2004).

The bidimensional approach has enjoyed greater review, thanks in part to its alignment with Petty and Cacioppo's (1981) ELM.

The ELM proposes two basic paths to attitude change. If individuals are highly involved with a message and have the ability to process message-specific arguments, the *central* path to attitude alteration is taken. If involvement and/or processing ability are low, the *peripheral* path is usually followed. The variables leading to attitude change under the central and peripheral routes are called *central* and *peripheral cues*, respectively. Examples of central cues within advertising messages include product superiority or differentiation claims (Lord, Lee, & Sauer, 1995; Petty, Cacioppo, & Schuman, 1983) and the utilization of rational appeals that demonstrate the utility of a product (Areni, 2003; MacInnis & Stayman, 1993). When the central route is taken, resulting attitudes are usually stronger, more resilient to counter-persuasion, easier to recall, and better at predicting behavior (Krosnick & Petty, 1995; Sengupta, Goodstein, & Boninger, 1997).

Peripheral cues involve the physical manner in which a message is conveyed. Peripheral cues are utilized to form simple, inference-based attitudes. These cues are generally believed to influence attitudes in low-involvement scenarios. Usually, they are not influential in high-involvement situations. Examples of peripheral cues include spokespersons, celebrity endorsers, or seals of approval (Kimery & McCord, 2002; Petty et al., 1983). Though minor alterations to the model have been suggested (Morris, Woo, & Singh, 2005), the ELM has largely stood the test of time and offers insights into the effects of cue congruency in high- and low-involvement situations.

*Congruency*

The notion of congruency was originally recognized by Osgood and Tannenbaum (1955), whose congruity theory sought to determine the evaluative effects associated with a decrease or increase in the congruency between a given appeal and a given subject's referent orientations. Results indicated that congruency is positively associated with attitudinal receptivity to external appeals. The theory predicts that as congruency between elements of an appeal and a subject's own frame of reference increases, attitudinal change is positively affected. Conversely, as congruency decreases, positive reception declines.

Although utilized within multiple disciplines, congruity theory has provided a specifically applicable foundation for marketing research. Hong and Zinkhan (1995) utilized the theory as a basis for reviewing the impact that congruency between advertising appeals and subjects' self-concepts had on brand recall, brand preferences, and PI. The resulting model indicated that as an advertisement's congruency with an individual's self-concept increases, attitudinal responses and PI are positively affected. This relationship was strengthened when a person's ideal self-concept was substituted for actual self-concept. The ability to see one's actual or desired self in an advertisement generates positive attitudes and PI. The positive relationship between congruency and attitudes was confirmed by both Bennett (1996) and Mehta (1999). However, explicit reviews of the interactions between congruency and product involvement were not conducted. Likewise, differences between central and peripheral cues were not specifically highlighted. Since involvement can affect the relative emphasis given to central or peripheral cues, attention should be given to whether congruous central or peripheral cues are relatively more important for a given product. Additionally, relative involvement might render either central or peripheral cue congruency ineffective if the cue is incorrectly aligned with the product's relative involvement levels.

Congruity theory was first utilized in relation to Generation Y by Wolburg and Pokryzwczynski (2001). Their study considered the manner in which members of Generation Y assess advertising *informativeness* based upon the congruency between various advertising appeals and target market characteristics. The study examined both psychographic and demographic characteristics and identified both demographic and psychographic congruency as legitimate arenas for review. The study, along with Yeqing and Shao's (2002) review of Generation Y's nonconformity advertising preferences, highlighted the uniqueness of Generation Y and called for further reviews of the relationship between advertising congruency and Generation Y.

## *Attitudes and Advertising Effectiveness*

Hierarchy-of-effects models were popularized in marketing when Lavidge and Steiner (1961) proposed a method by which to measure advertising effectiveness. The approach split advertising effectiveness into reviews of sales and communication effectiveness. Attitudes were considered an appropriate means by which to measure communication effectiveness, which in turn presumably forecast sales effectiveness. Ajen and Fishbein (1980, p. 64) defined an attitude as indexing "the degree to which a person likes or dislikes an object" Ghingold's (1981) consistency theory suggested that attitudes could be assessed via affective, cognitive, and conative measurements. Fishbein's model (Fishbein & Ajzen, 1975) and the resulting theory of reasoned action (TRA) supported the notion and have provided the theoretical underpinnings for studying attitudes and utilizing them to predict behaviors. Baker and Churchill's (1977) scale used all three attitudinal components (affective, cognitive, and conative) to measure advertising effectiveness in terms of communication effectiveness and impact. Subsequent researchers have differentiated attitudes toward the advertisement (Aad) and attitudes toward the product or brand (Mitchell & Olson, 1981). Aad and cognitive product beliefs influence attitudes toward the product and/or brand (Batra & Ray, 1986; Mitchell, 1986). Attitude toward the brand (Ab) is often coupled with PI to offer a means by which to forecast sales effectiveness (Burton & Lichtenstein, 1988; Morwitz & Schmittlein, 1992; Mostafa, 2005). However, whether or not Ab and PI are empirically distinct constructs has been debated (Spears & Singh, 2004).

## HYPOTHESES

In light of the above discussion, the current study confined advertising effectiveness to the realm of communication effectiveness and measured this effectiveness through examining affective, cognitive, and conative responses. Since peripheral cues are generally easier to specifically manipulate, congruency was measured in terms of peripheral cue congruency. Congruent peripheral cues were expected to have a favorable effect on attitudes in low product involvement situations, while having a minimal effect in high product involvement situations (Petty et al., 1983). Therefore, since cue congruency can generate favorable attitudinal responses (Hong & Zinkhan, 1995), the use of congruent peripheral cues in an advertisement should generate favorable affective, cognitive, and conative responses in low-involvement product situations. It was hypothesized that:

**H1.** Generation Y college students will rate an advertisement for a high-involvement product higher on the attitudinal advertising effectiveness scale than they will rate an advertisement for a low-involvement product.

Although the ELM predicts a null effect for the use of peripheral cue congruency in high-involvement product situations, recent research has indicated that (1) peripheral cues can affect evaluations of high-involvement product advertisements, and (2) high levels of relative product involvement can favorably influence attitudinal responses to advertisements (Cochran & Quester, 2004). Therefore, it was also hypothesized that:

**H2a.** For low-involvement products, Generation Y college students will rate an advertisement that uses peripheral cue congruency higher on the attitudinal advertising effectiveness scale than they will rate an advertisement that does not use peripheral cue congruency.

**H2b.** For high-involvement products, Generation Y college students will rate an advertisement that uses peripheral cue congruency higher on the attitudinal advertising effectiveness scale than they will rate an advertisement that does not use peripheral cue congruency.

# METHODOLOGY

The study used a $3 \times 2$ two-factor between-subjects design in which the independent research variables involved the type of peripheral cues (three levels) utilized within a given advertisement and the degree of relative product involvement (two levels). Dependent research variables included the affective, cognitive, and conative components of an attitude. A questionnaire measuring attitudes and demographics was administered to participants after they were exposed to one of six advertisements that utilized congruous, noncongruous, or neutral peripheral cues for a relatively high- or low-involvement product. GLM Multivariate analysis was used to develop a two-way fixed-effects model with interaction.

Two experiments preceded the main study to determine appropriate involvement products and peripheral cue types. Generation Y college students ($n = 118$) at schools in Pennsylvania and California completed surveys to determine product type and peripheral cues. The involvement survey borrowed from Zaichkowsky's (1994) approach for measuring product involvement. A 7-point Likert scale (1 = strongly disagree, 7 = strongly agree) was used to test involvement for a range of products primarily drawn from Zaichkowsky's (1985) PII. The list was supplemented with products from more recent studies (Cochran & Quester, 2004), and the final selection was based on an independent sample $t$-tests and comparisons with Mitchell's (1986) product choice guidelines. The final chosen products were a laptop (M:5.81) and USB drive (M:2.92). Levels of involvement were significantly different ($t(55) = 7.17$, $p < 0.001$).

An important peripheral cue involves the demographic congruity between the spokesperson or model used in an advertisement and the characteristics of the target market (Wolburg & Pokryzwczynski, 2001). Pictures of demographically congruent models and noncongruent models were used as the peripheral cue. A neutral (no human model) ad was also developed. The two human models in the treatment advertisements were chosen after conducting a field test in which the researcher showed 34 Generation Y college students 16 pictures of individuals. Students voluntarily rank ordered the pictures based on the degree to which the students considered the pictured individuals representative of the students' peer group. The four pictures with the highest congruency rankings and the four pictures with the highest noncongruency ranking were then included in a survey administered to another sample of 29 students. The survey utilized a 7-point Likert scale based on Gotleib and Sarel's (1991) pretested instrument. Scale items asked participants to indicate their agreement or disagreement with statements such as "I consider the individual pictured in the advertisement to be one of my peers." The two illustrations with the highest mean congruous and noncongruous ranking spreads were then selected and used as the peripheral cue manipulations for the final study. A manipulation check indicated that the manipulations were successful ($f = 61.93$, $p < 0.001$). The mean response for the congruous advertisement was 4.76, while the mean response for the noncongruous advertisement was 2.09.

The study's final advertisements were based on formats used in prior print advertisement studies and included identical headlines, brand names, product names, product pictures, and copy for the six treatment cells (Cline, Altsech, & Kellaris, 2003; Cline & Kellaris, 1999; Heckler & Childers, 1992). Only illustrations were manipulated. To control for the impact of pre-existing attitudes toward known product brands, fictitious names were used for the advertised product and brand (Lafferty, Goldsmith, & Newell, 2002). Finally, the advertisements were reviewed by a graphic designer to ensure a relative degree of attractiveness.

## Participants

The study's population was members of Generation Y who are attending college. The study's sampling frame, from which a sample of 432 students in randomly selected courses was drawn, was full time Generation Y students above the age of 18 at two four-year universities in Pennsylvania and California. A 3 × 2 between-subjects design was used where the first factor (peripheral cue congruency) included three levels (congruous, noncongruous, and neutral) and the second factor (product involvement) included two levels (high and low). Students were randomly assigned to one of six treatment cells that were developed via manipulating factor levels (congruous/high, noncongruous/high, neutral/high, congruous/low, noncongruous/low, and neutral/low).

## Procedure

Treatment packets were created for each cell and included a cover letter, manipulated advertisement, and questionnaire. The cover letter highlighted the voluntary nature of the study, provided brief instructions, and thanked students for participation. Students were instructed to read the letter, examine the advertisement at their own speed, and then complete the questionnaire. Although student overlap was not expected, a survey question asked students whether or not they had taken the survey in a different class. Five surveys were discarded due to overlap. The various treatment packets were distributed to the students via the use of a systematic random sampling process. Students were counted off as either "1," "2," "3," "4," "5," or "6," and all "1s" received the first treatment packet, while all "2s" received the second packet and so forth. After the researcher read the cover letter, students completed and submitted the survey packet. A short debriefing was conducted once all packets were returned.

## Independent Variables

The study's independent variables included product involvement and the congruency of peripheral cues within advertisements. Advertisements showed either a fictional laptop or USB drive, an identical headline ("As extraordinary as you"), and copy highlighting several generic, yet pertinent, competitive features of the product. Peripheral cue illustrations utilized a male college student, male middle-aged businessperson, or a neutral cue (no human picture).

## Dependent Variables

Baker and Churchill's (1977) attitudinal scale for measuring advertising communication effectiveness was used. The scale, utilized in other recent advertising effectiveness studies (Cochran & Quester, 2004), measures the affective, cognitive, and conative components of an attitude toward an advertisement. The 7-point semantic differential scale measures the affective component through using item adjectives such as *interesting, appealing, impressive, attractive,* and *eye catching.* The cognitive component is measured by several items anchored by words such as *believable* and *clear,* and the conative component is measured via *try product, buy product, seek product,* and *compare product.* Cronbach's alpha was 0.832, substantially above the 0.70 mark (Cronback, 1951; Nunnally, 1978). Confirmatory factor analysis with Varimax rotation indicated that the questionnaire's items properly loaded on the factors of interest. The Kaiser–Meyer–Olkin measure of sampling adequacy was a healthy 0.885. Apart from an item termed *informativeness* (which was dropped from the study), all terms loaded on their proper factors.

*Manipulation Checks*

Similar to the trial study, manipulation checks were successful for both factors. Analysis of variance indicated that perceptions of peripheral cue congruity differed among the groups ($p<0.001$) with respective means of 4.62 (congruous) and 2.13 (noncongruous). Likewise, perceptions of the relative degree of product involvement, tested by an independent sample $t$-test, indicated that students viewed laptops as being high-involvement products and USB drives as being low-involvement products ($t(432) = 14.06$, $p<0.001$). Respective means were 6.37 and 3.16.

# RESULTS

Hypotheses were tested via GLM Multivariate analysis. Dependent variables included affective, cognitive, and conative components of respondents' attitudes toward an advertisement. Independent variables were level of peripheral cue congruency (congruous, noncongruous, neutral) and type of product involvement (high or low). Model assumptions (error independence, constant dependent variable covariance, and multivariate normal distribution of errors across dependent variables) were tested via Box's M test and Levene's test. Both tests indicated that model assumptions were met (Box's M $f= 1.40$, $p = 0.136$; Levene's $f = 1.54$, $p = 0.176$; Levene's PI $f = 1.362$, $p = 0.237$).

Table 1 includes treatment cell descriptive statistics. A review of cell means indicates possible involvement effects. The use of congruous peripheral cues for low-involvement products resulted in affective and cognitive responses that were more favorable than those associated with the use of noncongruous cues. In high-involvement product situations, peripheral cue congruity appeared to have a minimal effect. Apart from involvement and congruency effects, gender effects were also examined and were found to be insignificant.

Test results (see Table 2) confirm that congruency is not a significant main effect. Pillai's trace (0.009 value) and Wilks' Lamda (0.9891) indicate the minimal effect of peripheral cue congruency on the overall model ($f = 0.627$; $p = 0.709$). Relative product involvement, on the other hand, is significant with $f = 21.79$ and $p < 0.001$ (Pillai's trace = 0.133, Wilks' Lambda = 0.867). There were no significant factor interaction effects

*Table 1.* Means and Standard Deviations for Scaled Dependent Measures.

|  | n | Affective | Cognitive | Conative |
|---|---|---|---|---|
| Congruous/high involvement | 75 | 19.85 (6.22) | 6.68 (2.21) | 17.55 (3.76) |
| Noncongruous/high involvement | 75 | 20.41 (5.07) | 6.37 (2.08) | 17.55 (4.32) |
| Neutral/high involvement | 75 | 20.39 (5.84) | 6.97 (2.21) | 17.91 (4.51) |
| Congruous/low involvement | 67 | 22.60 (5.14) | 5.88 (2.14) | 17.25 (4.66) |
| Noncongruous/low involvement | 68 | 24.69 (6.30) | 6.47 (2.55) | 18.56 (5.32) |
| Neutral/low involvement | 72 | 23.99 (5.82) | 5.99 (2.82) | 18.11 (4.66) |
| Total/high involvement | 225 | 20.22 (5.71) | 6.68 (2.17) | 17.67 (4.19) |
| Total/low involvement | 207 | 23.77 (5.81) | 6.11 (2.53) | 17.98 (4.89) |

*Note:* Mean scores represent summations of individual scale items that comprise each attitudinal component. Lower numbers indicate a favorable response. Standard deviations are in parentheses.

*Table 2.* GLM Results.

| Effect | Multivariate | | | F | p | Univariate F | | |
|---|---|---|---|---|---|---|---|---|
| | Pillai's trace | Wilkes' $\lambda$ | df | | | Af | Cog | Con |
| Congruency | 0.009 | 0.991 | 4 | 0.627 | 0.709 | 1.81 | 0.224 | 0.772 |
| Involvement | 0.133 | 0.867 | 2 | 21.79 | 0.000 | 41.96* | 5.92* | 0.619 |
| Interaction | 0.013 | 0.987 | 4 | 0.912 | 0.485 | 0.587 | 2.21 | 0.709 |

*$p < 0.001$.
*Note:* Af, Affective; Cog, Cognitive; Con, Conative.

($f = 0.912$; $p = 0.485$). Univariate analysis indicated a main effect of relative product involvement on the affective ($f = 41.96$; $p = 0.000$) and cognitive ($f = 5.921$; $p = 0.015$) components of attitudes, but not on the conative component ($f = 0.619$; $p = 0.432$). There were no significant congruency or interaction effects.

H1 was partially supported. Relative product involvement appears to influence affective and cognitive responses. Generation Y college students rate an advertisement for a high-involvement product higher on the affective and cognitive components of the attitudinal advertising effectiveness scale than they rate an advertisement for a low-involvement product.

Results indicated that H2a was not supported. For low-involvement products, Generation Y college students do not rate an advertisement that uses peripheral cue congruency higher on the attitudinal advertising effectiveness scale than they rate an advertisement that does not use peripheral cue congruency. Likewise, H2b was rejected, indicating that for high-involvement products, Generation Y college students do not rate an advertisement that uses peripheral cue congruency higher on the attitudinal advertising effectiveness scale than they rate an advertisement that does not use peripheral cue congruency.

## Discussion

The study's results align with prior findings in some areas while diverging in others. Generation Y is clearly different from prior generations and is beginning to demonstrate a level of advertising sophistication that is more developed than that of prior generations.

The study's conclusion regarding the ineffectiveness of peripheral cue congruency both agrees and disagrees with prior product involvement research. Although the study confirmed the ELM's (Petty & Cacioppo, 1981) forecasts regarding the relative ineffectiveness of peripheral cues in high-involvement scenarios, the study indicated that the ELM's assertions regarding peripheral cues in low-involvement scenarios might not fully apply to Generation Y.

Music, pictures, spokespersons, and other peripheral cues have traditionally influenced attitudes in low-involvement product situations (Petty et al., 1983), but peripheral cues did not significantly affect Generation Y's attitudes toward a low-involvement product advertisement. This finding supports the contention that the marketing sensitivities of Generation Y differ from those of prior generations (Beard, 2003;

Howe, Strauss, & Matson, 2000; Morton, 2002; Wolburg & Pokryzwczynski, 2001). Emotional connectivity in both high- and low-involvement scenarios appears to play a subordinate role to rational value propositions, and effective marketers must rely on deeper structural and content propositions to influence attitudes in both high- and low-involvement settings. The simple attempt to connect with Generation Y through the use of congruent peripheral cues is not sufficient to overcome a product appeal that does not offer comprehensive value in the eyes of the target market. In fact, the scheme could backfire if it is perceived as insinuating that a company feels it can circumvent a weak value proposition through attempting to *affectively* identify with Generation Y. This suggestion supports the notion that member of Generation Y are savvy, sophisticated consumers who are discerning processors of advertising and associated promotional claims (La Ferle et al., 2000; Morton, 2002).

However, the current study's results do not comprehensively deny the applicability of congruency theory for Generation Y. Rather, the study only asserts that a certain form of peripheral cue congruency (i.e., model/spokesperson demographic congruency) fails to affect attitudinal responses to products advertised via print media.

Similar to another recent study utilizing Generation Y college students (Cochran & Quester, 2004), the current study found that relative product involvement influences affective and cognitive evaluations of an advertisement. The ELM contends that messages associated with high-involvement products are centrally processed. Examples of centrally processed cues within advertising messages include product superiority or differentiation claims (Lord et al., 1995; Petty et al., 1983) and the utilization of rational appeals that demonstrate the utility of a product (Areni, 2003; MacInnis & Stayman, 1993). Both the high- and low-involvement product advertisements in the current study used peripheral (pictures) and central (competitive features) cues. High-involvement product messages are centrally processed while low-involvement product messages are peripherally processed (Petty et al., 1983). Hence, the favorable affective and cognitive responses for the high-involvement product were presumably influenced by the advertisement's central cues. However, since central cues are not involved in low-involvement situations and the peripheral cues were not able to favorably influence attitudes (see H1), the attitudes toward the low-involvement product advertisements were less favorable than attitudes toward the high-involvement product advertisements.

The question that remains is whether peripheral cues are entirely ineffective for low-involvement products. Although the current study's findings could indicate that peripheral cues and cue congruency are irrelevant to college-attending members of Generation Y, the assertion cannot be made with certainty. Peripheral cues do appear to be irrelevant in high-involvement situations, but their lack of relevance for low-involvement products could be the result of the individual ineffectiveness of the unique peripheral cues that were studied (e.g., model congruency).

*Recommendations*

The sole utilization of congruent peripheral cues within print advertisements is not sufficient to guarantee positive attitudinal change among college-attending members of Generation Y. Peripheral cues do not significantly affect attitudes, even in situations where the cues enjoy considerable congruency with the target market. Rather, marketers must develop strategies and campaigns that rely on more than simple demographic congruency.

The notion of "lifestyle fit" is an important component of advertising directed toward Generation Y. Noble, Haytko, and Phillips (2009) highlighted the need for strategic lifestyle fit in the areas of value, trust, and personality. Generation Y is increasingly value conscious, and effective appeals should align with the Generation's requirements for price/quality and long-term reliability. Trust provides a means to reduce uncertainty in today's rapidly changing consumer climate. It also enables a believable foundation for value propositions.

Finally, value and trust must be combined and presented in a manner that aligns with consumer personalities. Peripheral cue congruency (in low-involvement situations) often provided this alignment for past generations, but the current study indicates that peripheral cue congruency is not sufficient to ensure product and consumer personality congruence for Generation Y. Discovery and experience are important to Generation Y (Tapscott, 2008), and effective marketers will foster personality congruence by moving beyond simple peripheral cue representations of the market.

To move past peripheral cue representations, marketers should allow Generation Y-ers to "co-develop" campaigns and appeals. This approach enables a level of congruence that extends beyond mere depiction. Involvement should replace observation. The experience economy is increasingly requiring that marketers offer an involving experience, starting with initial exposure and concluding with purchase and use. As indicated by the current study's findings, involvement is a key factor to drive attitudinal change. Behavioral involvement transforms initial appeal exposure from a simple observational activity to a launching pad for personal inspiration. Inspiration uses central processing and thereby develops attitudes and intentions that are generally stronger, more positive, and less resistant to change. Therefore, the current study indicates that although cue congruency is not as important for Generation Y as it was for past generations, the need for overall involvement congruency is still present. The congruency requirements of Generation Y are more sophisticated, and the unidimensional attempts of bygone years are no longer sufficient to generate positive attitudinal change.

*Limitations*

Yeqing and Shao (2002) illustrated that the attitudinal responses of college-age members of Generation Y are not affected in the same manner as their awareness or product trial responses. The fact that the current study failed to show a linkage between congruency and attitudinal responses does not indicate that the same linkage is also nonexistent for awareness or sales responses.

Second, varying forms of congruency exist (Wolburg & Pokryzwczynski, 2001), and the study's findings regarding model/spokesperson demographic congruence do not necessarily mean that other forms of congruency are not applicable for Generation Y. Three considerations support this caution. First, Keillor et al. (1996) illustrated that members of Generation Y are heavily influenced by their peers when developing product preferences. Second, Omelia (1998) demonstrated that members of Generation Y demand advertising to be unique and propositionally compelling. Third, lifestyles are very important to Echo Boomers (Bennett & Lachowetz, 2004; Maciejewski, 2004; Morton, 2002; Stone, Stanton, Kirkham, & Pyne, 2001; Weiss, 2003). With these considerations in mind, it can be posited that congruency may be effective if it can be elevated from mere demographic congruency to lifestyle congruency and combined with a uniquely compelling advertising proposition.

The study only reviewed the attitudinal effects associated with peripheral cue congruency within a print advertisement. Although attitudinal effects are a legitimate area for review when attempting to assess the relative effectiveness of a given advertising method or tactic (Baker, Honea, & Russell, 2004; Batra & Stayman, 1990), attitudinal effects are not the sole means by which to assess advertising effectiveness. Researchers have also used awareness and action methodologies to assess effectiveness

(Bendixem, 1993; Coffin, 1963; Fritz, 1979; Kruegel, 1988; Martin, Bhimy, & Ageec, 2002; Weiss & Windal, 1980), and the current study's results should not be assumed to include awareness or action effects.

The study's findings can only be generalized to college-attending members of Generation Y and should not be assumed to apply to the entire generation. However, since approximately half of Generation Y has or will attend college (Newberger & Curry, 2000) and Generation Y college graduates are trendsetters expected to exert a tremendous economic and social impact influence (Paul, 2001; Weiss, 2003), it is legitimate to study collegiate members of Generation Y rather than the entire population (Wolburg & Pokryzwczynski, 2001; Yeqing & Shao, 2002).

### Future Research

A significant amount of research is still required to attain a comprehensive understanding of the optimal manner by which to advertise to Generation Y. Three specific recommendations for future research are suggested.

First, minority groups within the college-attending Generation Y population should be studied. The current study, along with other studies examining Generation Y's response to congruency (Wolburg & Pokryzwczynski, 2001), underrepresented minority students. Since Generation Y is the most ethnically diverse generation on record (Morton, 2002), research should be conducted for specific minority segments within the generation.

Second, the current study only reviewed peripheral cue congruency in relation to print advertisements. Since lifestyle congruency is a recommended avenue by which to advertise to Generation Y (Bennett & Lachowetz, 2004), advertising mediums that offer richer lifestyle depiction opportunities (e.g., television) should be examined.

Third, since certain advertising methodologies affect awareness, attitudes, and actions differently (Yeqing & Shao, 2002), the ineffectiveness of peripheral cue congruency for generating attitudinal change cannot be assumed to influence awareness or action responses in a similar manner. Further research should examine the impact of congruency on advertisements whose strategic intent focuses on awareness or action rather than on mere attitude change.

## CONCLUSION

Members of Generation Y are savvy, sophisticated consumers who are discerning processors of advertising and associated promotional claims. The simple attempt to emotionally connect with members of Generation Y through the use of congruent peripheral cues is not uniformly sufficient in high- or low-involvement product scenarios to overcome product appeals that do not offer comprehensive value.

However, relative product involvement does influence the affective and cognitive components of attitudes. Marketers must understand and use relative product involvement when developing marketing messages. Additionally, marketers must strive for connections between perceptions of product involvement and actual behavioral involvement. Behavioral involvement helps transform involvement perceptions from a simple observational activity to an attitude-altering activity. If properly utilized, this involvement will then allow for attitudes that are stronger, more positive, and less resistant to change.

# REFERENCES

Ajzen, I., & Fishbein, M. (1980). *Understanding attitudes and predicting social behavior.* Englewood Cliffs, NJ: Prentice-Hall.

Andrews, J., & Lysonski, S. (1991). Understanding cross-cultural student perceptions of advertising in generation: Implications for advertising educators and practitioners. *Journal of Advertising, 20*(2), 15–37.

Areni, C. S. (2003). The effects of structural and grammatical variables on persuasion: An elaboration likelihood model perspective. *Psychology and Marketing, 20*, 349–375.

Baker, M., & Churchill, G. (1977). The impact of physically attractive models on advertising evaluations. *Journal of Marketing Research, 14*(4), 538–555.

Baker, W., Honea, H., & Russell, C. (2004). Do not wait to reveal the brand name: The effect of brand-name placement on television advertising effectiveness. *Journal of Advertising, 33*(3), 77–87.

Batra, R., & Ray, M. L. (1986). Affective responses mediating acceptance of advertising. *Journal of Consumer Research, 13*, 234–249.

Batra, R., & Stayman, D. (1990). The role of mood in advertising effectiveness. *Journal of Consumer Research, 17*(2), 203–214.

Beard, F. (2003). College student attitudes toward advertising's ethical, economic, and social consequences. *Journal of Business Ethics, 48*(3), 217–226.

Bendixem, M. (1993). Advertising effects and effectiveness. *European Journal of Marketing, 27*(10), 19–32.

Bennett, G., & Lachowetz, T. (2004). Marketing to lifestyles: Action sports and Generation Y. *Sports Marketing Quarterly, 13*(2), 239–243.

Bennett, R. (1996). Effects of horrific fear appeals on public attitudes towards AIDS. *International Journal of Advertising, 15*(3), 183–217.

Braverman, M., & Aaro, L. (2004). Adolescent smoking and exposure to tobacco marketing under a tobacco advertising ban. *American Journal of Public Health, 94*(7), 1230–1238.

Burton, S., & Lichtenstein, D. R. (1988). The effect of ad claims and ad context on attitude toward the advertisement. *Journal of Advertising, 17*, 3–11.

Cheng, K. (1999). Setting their sites on Generation Y. *Adweek, 40*(32), 46–49.
Clark, P., Martin, C., & Bush, A. (2001). The effect of role model influence on adolescents' materialism and marketplace knowledge. *Journal of Marketing Theory and Practice, 9*(4), 27–43.
Cline, T., Altsech, M., & Kellaris, J. (2003). When does humor enhance or inhibit ad responses: The moderating role of the need for humor. *Journal of Advertising, 32*(3), 31–45.
Cline, T., & Kellaris, J. (1999). The joint impact of humor and argument strength in a print advertising context: A case for weaker arguments. *Psychology and Marketing, 16*(1), 69–86.
Cochran, L., & Quester, P. (2004). Product involvement and humor in advertising: An Australian empirical study. *Journal of Asia Pacific Marketing, 3*(1), 68–88.
Coffin, T. (1963). A pioneering experiment in assessing advertising effectiveness. *Journal of Marketing, 27*(3), 1–10.
Cordiner, R. (2001). Generation Y: Tricky for sports. *Sports Marketing, 77*, 8.
Cronback, L. J. (1951). Coefficient alpha and the internal structure of test. *Psychometrika, 17*, 297–334.
Cui, Y., Trent, E., Sullivan, P., & Matiru, G. (2003). Cause-related marketing: How generation Y responds. *International Journal of Retail and Distribution Management, 31*(6/7), 310–321.
Eisner, S. (2005). Managing generation Y. *S.A.M. Advanced Management Journal, 70*(4), 4–15.
Fishbein, M., & Ajzen, I. (1975). *Belief, attitude, intention and behavior: An introduction to theory and research*. Reading, MA: Addison-Wesley.
Fox, R. (1995). Manipulated kids: Teens tell how ads influence them. *Educational Leadership, 53*(1), 77–80.
Fritz, N. (1979). Claim recall and irritation in television commercials: An advertising effectiveness study. *Academy of Marketing Science Journal, 7*(1), 1–13.
Ghingold, M. (1981). Guilt arousing marketing communications: An unexplored variable. In: K. Monroe (Ed.), *Advances in consumer research* (pp. 442–448). Ann Arbor, MI: Association for Consumer Research.
Goldberg, M. (1990). A quasi-experiment assessing the effectiveness of TV advertising directed to children. *Journal of Marketing Research, 27*(4), 445–454.
Gordon, M. E., McKeage, K., & Fox, M. A. (1998). Relationship marketing effectiveness: the role of involvement. *Psychology and Marketing, 15*(5), 443–459.
Gotleib, J., & Sarel, D. (1991). Comparative advertising effectiveness: The role of involvement and source credibility. *Journal of Advertising, 20*(1), 38–45.
Grant, I. (2005). Young peoples' relationships with online marketing practices: An intrusion too far? *Journal of Marketing Management, 21*, 607–623.
Gronbach, K. (2000). Generation Y: Not just kids. *Direct Marketing, 63*(4), 36–39.
Heckler, S., & Childers, T. (1992). The role of expectancy and relevancy in memory for verbal and visual information: What is incongruence?. *Journal of Consumer Research, 18*, 475–492.
Henry, A. (2003). How buzz marketing works for teens. *Advertising and Marketing to Children, 4*(3), 3–10.
Higby, M., & Mascarenhas, O. (1993). Media, parent, and peer influences in teen food shopping. *The Journal of Marketing Management, 3*(2), 45–55.
Hong, J., & Zinkhan, G. (1995). Self-concept and advertising effectiveness: The influence of congruency, conspicuousness, and response mode. *Psychology and Marketing, 12*(1), 53–77.

Howe, N., Strauss, W., & Matson, R. (2000). *Millennials rising: The next great generation.* Great Falls, VA: LifeCourse Associates.

Keillor, B., Parker, R., & Schaefer, A. (1996). Influences on adolescent brand preferences in the United States and Mexico. *Journal of Advertising Research, 36*(3), 47–56.

Kimery, K. M., & McCord, M. (2002). Third-party assurances: Mapping the road to trust in e-retailing. *Journal of Information Technology Theory and Application, 4*(2), 63–83.

Krosnick, J. A., & Petty, R. E. (1995). Attitude strength: An overview. In: R. E. Petty & J. A. Krosnick (Eds), *Attitude strength: Antecedents and consequences.* Mahwah, NJ: Erlbaum.

Kruegel, D. (1988). Television advertising effectiveness and research innovation. *The Journal of Consumer Marketing, 5*(3), 43–51.

La Ferle, C., Edwards, S., & Lee, W. (2000). Teens' use of traditional media and the internet. *Journal of Advertising Research, 40*(3), 55–70.

Lafferty, B., Goldsmith, R., & Newell, S. (2002). The dual credibility model: The influence of corporate and endorser credibility on attitudes and purchase intentions. *Journal of Marketing Theory and Practice, 10*(3), 1–12.

Lavidge, R., & Steiner, G. (1961). A model for predictive measurements of advertising effectiveness. *Journal of Marketing, 25*(6), 59–62.

Lord, K., Lee, M., & Sauer, P. (1995). The combined influence hypothesis: Central and peripheral antecedents of attitude toward the ad. *Journal of Advertising, 24*, 73–85.

Maciejewski, J. (2004). Is the use of sexual and fear appeals ethical: A moral evaluation by Generation Y college students. *Journal of Current Issues and Research in Advertising, 26*(2), 97–105.

MacInnis, D., & Stayman, D. (1993). Focal and emotional integration: Constructs, measures, and preliminary evidence. *Journal of Advertising, 22*, 51–66.

Mangleburg, T., & Bristol, T. (1998). Socialization and adolescents' skepticism toward advertising. *Journal of Advertising, 27*(3), 11–22.

Marney, T. (1996). The wherefores and whys of Generation Y: The younger siblings of the Gen-Xers are now coming into marketers' sites. *Marketing Magazine, 101*(13), 15–17.

Martin, B., Bhimy, A., & Ageec, T. (2002). Infomercials and advertising effectiveness: An empirical study. *The Journal of Consumer Marketing, 19*(6), 468–480.

Martin, C., & Bush, A. (2000). Do role models influence teenagers' purchase intentions and behavior? *Journal of Consumer Marketing, 17*(5), 441–454.

Mehta, A. (1999). Using self-concept to assess advertising effectiveness. *Journal of Advertising Research, 34*(1), 35–53.

Merrill, C. (1999). The ripple effect reaches Gen Y. *American Demographics, 21*(11), 15–17.

Mitchell, A. (1986). The effect of verbal and visual components of advertisements on brand attitudes and attitude toward the advertisement. *Journal of Consumer Research, 13*, 12–24.

Mitchell, A., & Olson, J. (1981). Are the product attributes beliefs the only mediator of advertising effects on brand attitude? *Journal of Marketing Research, 18*(3), 318–332.

Morris, J., Woo, C., & Singh, A. J. (2005). Elaboration likelihood model: A missing intrinsic emotional implication. *Journal of Targeting Measurement and Analysis for Marketing, 14*(1), 79–98.

Morton, L. (2002). Targeting Generation Y. *Public Relations Quarterly, 47*(2), 46–48.

Morwitz, V. G., & Schmittlein, D. (1992). Using segmentation to improve sales forecasts based on purchase intend: Which intenders actually buy. *Journal of Marketing Research, 29*(4), 391–405.

Mostafa, M. M. (2005). An experimental investigation of the Egyptian consumers' attitudes toward surrealism in advertising. *International Journal of Consumer Studies, 29*, 216–231.

Newberger, E., & Curry, A. (2000). *Education attainment in the United States (Update) (PPL-140)*. Washington, DC: U.S. Census Bureau.

Noble, S. M., Haytko, D. L., & Phillips, J. (2009). What drives college-age Generation Y consumers? *Journal of Business Research, 62*(6), 617–628.

Nunnally, J. C. (1978). *Psychometric theory* (2nd ed.). New York: McGraw-Hill.

Omelia, J. (1998). Understanding Generation Y: A look at the next wave of US consumers. *Global Cosmetics Industry, 163*(3), 90–92.

Osgood, C., & Tannenbaum, P. (1955). The principle of congruity in the prediction of attitude change. *Psychological Review, 62*(1), 42–55.

Paul, P. (2001). Getting inside Generation Y. *American Demographics, 23*(9), 42–49.

Pechmann, C., & Knight, S. (2002). An experimental investigation of the joint effects of advertising and peers on adolescents' beliefs and intentions about cigarette consumption. *Journal of Consumer Research, 29*, 5–19.

Pechmann, C., Levine, L., Loughlin, S., & Leslie, F. (2005). Impulsive and self-conscious: Adolescents' vulnerability to advertising and promotion. *Journal of Public Policy and Marketing, 24*(2), 202–221.

Petty, R., & Cacioppo, J. (1981). *Attitudes and persuasions: Classic and contemporary approaches*. Dubuque, IA: William C. Brown.

Petty, R., Cacioppo, J., & Schuman, D. (1983). Central and peripheral routes to advertising effectiveness: The moderating role of involvement. *Journal of Consumer Research, 10*, 135–146.

Ritson, M., & Elliott, R. (1999). The social use of advertising: An ethnographic study of adolescent advertising audiences. *Journal of Consumer Research, 26*(3), 260–277.

Saffer, H., & Chaloupka, F. (2000). The effect of tobacco advertising bans on tobacco consumption. *Journal of Health Economics, 19*, 1117–1137.

Sengupta, J., Goodstein, R. C., & Boninger, D. S. (1997). All cues are not created equal: Obtaining attitude persistence under low-involvement conditions. *Journal of Consumer Research, 23*(4), 351–361.

Spears, N., & Singh, S. N. (2004). Measuring attitude toward the brand and purchase intentions. *Journal of Current Issues and Research in Advertising, 26*(2), 53–66.

Stapinski, H. (1999). Y not love? *American Demographics, 21*(2), 62–69.

Stone, M., Stanton, H., Kirkham, J., & Pyne, W. (2001). The digerati: Generation Y finds its voice: Why cannot brands do the same? *Journal of Targeting, Measurement, and Analysis for Marketing, 10*(2), 158–167.

Strauss, W., & Howe, N. (2006). *Millennials and the pop culture*. Great Falls, VA: LifeCourse Associates.

Syrett, M., & Lammiman, J. (2004). Advertising and millennials. *Young Consumers, 3*, 62–73.

Tapscott, D. (2008). Net Gen transforms marketing. Business Week Online. Available at http://www.businessweek.com. Retrieved on 22 March 2009.

Weiss, D., & Windal, P. (1980). Testing cumulative advertising effects: A comment on methodology. *Journal of Marketing Research, 17*(3), 371–378.

Weiss, M. (2003). To be about to be. *American Demographics, 25*(7), 28–36.
Wolburg, J., & Pokryzwczynski, J. (2001). A psychographic analysis of Generation Y college students. *Journal of Advertising Research, 41*(5), 33–53.
Yeqing, B., & Shao, A. (2002). Nonconformity advertising to teens. *Journal of Advertising Research, 42*(3), 56–66.
Zaichkowsky, J. L. (1985). Measuring the involvement construct. *Journal of Consumer Research, 12,* 341–352.
Zaichkowsky, J. L. (1994). The personal involvement inventory: Reduction, revision, and application to advertising. *Journal of Advertising, 23*(4), 59–69.

# COUNTRY-OF-MANUFACTURE LABELING EFFECT ON PRODUCT QUALITY EVALUATIONS: A MODEL INCORPORATING CONSUMERS' ATTENTION

Pingjun Jiang

### ABSTRACT

Purpose – *The marketing literature does not provide a satisfactory explanation for the role of consumer's attention in the process of how Country-of-Manufacture (COM) information influences consumer product evaluations. The research contributes to an improved understanding of this process by integrating the construct of "attention to Country-of-Manufacture" into the model and examining its relationship with the influence of COM.*

Design/methodology/approach – *Survey data are collected from American consumers aged 18 years and above. To test the research hypotheses, MANOVA and canonical correlation analysis are performed in analyzing the data.*

Findings – *COM has more influence on the attentive group (consumers consciously paying attention to the COM information on a product label), on their evaluations of abstract product attributes such as* durability and reliability than it does on the inattentive group (consumers not paying conscious attention to such information). In contrast, COM's influences on evaluating concrete product attributes such as style, model, availability, and quality are all significantly related to involvement with COM, but not to attention.

Research limitations/implications – *The product assessments sought from respondents are generally on "foreign" products. Future research needs to obtain product-specific evaluations within each product category in testing the model and see how the results may differ or not differ across product categories.*

Practical implications – *Marketers selling products with high performance in abstract attributes such as durability and reliability should increase consumers' attention to the COM through effective product labeling.*

Originality/value – *This research identifies and empirically investigates the difference of COM effects on consumers' product judgment between consumers who are attentive and the ones who are inattentive to COM information.*

# INTRODUCTION

A growing globalization has increasingly exposed consumers in markets worldwide to a wider range of foreign products (Douglas & Craig, 1995; Cateora & Graham, 2005). As a result of this change, there has been rising interest among marketers and researchers on the perceived image variable associated with the Country-of-Origin and its effects on consumers' attitudes, preferences, and behavior (Verlegh & Steenkamp, 1999; Parameswaran & Pisharodi, 1994). Johansson, Douglas, and Nonaka (1985) defined Country-of-Origin as the country where the headquarters of the company that manufactures and markets the product or brand is located. This definition presents the nature of Country-of-Origin construct with multiple dimensions, among which the widely studied are Country-of-Brand Origin and Country-of-Manufacture. For instance, a number of studies made comparisons on the relative salience of country of manufacture and brand effects on product evaluations (e.g., Tse & Gorn, 1993; Nebenzahl & Jaffe, 1996; Lee & Ganesh, 1999; Hui & Zhou, 2001). A criticism, from these researchers, early studies on the subject centering on the treatment of Country-of-Origin as a single construct, as opposed to the multiple dimensions of which is composed (Bilkey & Nes, 1982; Peterson & Jolibert, 1995), may have produced confounding effect from Country-of-Manufacture and Brand Origin. Therefore, this chapter will use the more specialized term *Country-of-Manufacture*.

Country of manufacture, from this point on referred as "COM," refers to the information on where a product is made. COM image has been defined as "the overall perception consumers form of products from a particular country, based on their prior perceptions of the country's production and marketing strengths and weaknesses" (Roth & Romeo, 1992; Iyer & Kalita, 1997). Since Schooler's (1965) ground-breaking study, it has been broadly acknowledged that COM image affects consumer's perception of the features and consequent overall evaluation of the product (Cattin, Jolibert, & Lohnes, 1982; Alashban, Hayes, Zinkhan, & Balazs, 2002; Audhesh, Shailesh, & Gopala, 2003; Clarke, Owens, & Ford, 2000; Coulter, Price, & Feick, 2003; Dinnie, 2004, 2002; Douglas, Craig, & Nijssen, 2001; Kaynak & Kara, 2002; Lim & O'Cass, 2001; Lin & Kao, 2004; Loeffler, 2002; Lwin, Pecotich, & Thein, 2006; van Mesdag, 2000; Pecotich & Shultz, 2006; Ramsay, 2003; Zafar, Johnson, Chew, Tan, & Ang, 2002). Furthermore, the literature has provided consistent findings showing that consumers are prejudiced against products coming from some developing countries. Similarly, research have found that consumers were most willing to buy products made in developed countries, with a European, Australian, or New Zealand edifying base. Studies on COM effects have since tried to identify the process that may help to explain COM influence.

Regardless of their differences, the theoretical explanations from the sizable past research on COM and product evaluations share the basic assumption that, as long as the COM information is available, consumers will view it as relevant information and deliberately use it in their evaluation of a product. Most researchers contributing to this body of work take the position that the mere presence of COM information on the label (e.g., made in USA; made in China) can spark favorable or unfavorable country stereotypes and may influence purchase decisions even if unintentionally.

Though researchers widely acknowledge today that COM has an impact on product evaluation (Papadopoulos, 1993), and their study results provide converging evidence that COM effects occurred as an unconscious reflex and contributed to product evaluation without the participant's intention or control, there are surveys that repeatedly show that the consumer lacks cognized intention or desire to use COM as a basis for product judgment (e.g., Hugstad & Durr, 1986; Johansson, 1993). In their study of 2,220 respondents from eight countries, Heslop and Papadopoulos (1993, p. 69) acknowledged the contradiction by stating: "There is enough evidence to confirm that origin does matter; but, for reasons we have yet to understand fully, people do not like to admit that it does." On the other hand, the unperceptive connection linking consumer thought and action to COM information may not be direct and self-evident to consumer introspection. However, there is no research in existence about the size of the effect of the presence or absence of consumers' attention to the extrinsic product cues which brings about reliance on the COM.

The mandatory product-labeling policy carried in the United States, Canada, and other countries forces manufacturers to consider the impact of the COM information on consumers. Product labels serve the purposes of exposing such information, regulatory compliance, and product positioning (marketing). Obviously, consumers' positive (or negative) evaluations of foreign products can have a serious impact on various strategic marketing decisions, such as how the COM information needs to be presented on product labels. The first response to the exposure, consumer's attention is an important behavioral component known to influence consumer comprehension process, as well as perceptions, attitudes, and behavior. An improved understanding of how COM information influences consumer product evaluations with an integration of attention will be valuable to marketing practitioners, for whom the formulation of appropriate segmentation and positioning strategies are two important issues. The marketing literature does not provide a satisfactory explanation for the role of consumer's attention in the process. Therefore, to examine and elucidate this construct and understand its relationship with influence of COM contributes to the existing literature.

This chapter aims to make contributions to the current literature by addressing the following major research objectives:

(1) To introduce and conceptualize a new construct "consumer attention to COM."
(2) To identify and empirically investigate the difference of COM effects on consumers' product judgment between consumers who are attentive and the ones who are inattentive to COM information.
(3) To propose a theoretical framework to explain these differences, which relates to researching the influence of COM cue on perceived quality dimensions with an integration of consumers' attention.

Does the same effect of COM on product evaluations occur when the consumer pays or does not pay attention to the COM information on a product label? An answer to this question from this study is of primary importance. For instance, an empirical comparison between attentive and inattentive consumers apparently will address some critical issues such as consumers' indifference to COM information on product labels may reflect the limits of the influence of COM on consumers' product judgment. Conclusions drawn from this study will be of assistance to global corporate directors and policymakers, as well as a tool for further research. For instance, since information focus can be manipulated by marketers via communication programs, these researchers contend that COM evaluations can be manipulated by marketers to a significant extent.

Following this section, the remaining parts are organized as follows:
- First, the extant literature on COM effects is reviewed.
- Second, construct of attention to COM is introduced and conceptualized.
- Third, a theoretical model integrating attention to COM is proposed and hypotheses corresponding to the proposed model are developed.
- Fourth, the methodology adopted in designing and executing the study is explained.
- Fifth, the study findings, with reference to testing each hypothesis, are presented, analyzed, and discussed.
- Finally, several conclusions are drawn and implications are derived while the directions for future research are presented.

## LITERATURE REVIEW

Consumers have different attitudes toward various product categories from a given country, which is the result of the existence of associations/ previous experience with the foreign country, beliefs about its manufacturing system, knowledge about specific brands, etc. (Etzel & Walker, 1974; Kaynak & Cavusgil, 1983; Roth & Romeo, 1992). One view falls within the framework of the Fishbein model, that is, a belief about the product's attributes preceding and influencing attitude towards the product (Fishbein & Ajzen, 1975). According to this view, when consumers engage in product evaluations, they base their evaluations on conjectural and descriptive information cues associated with the product. Such cues can be intrinsic or extrinsic. Intrinsic cues are those that are integral to the product, such as color, smell, design and specifications of a product, consistence, and materials used in fabrication. Extrinsic cues are those that are not a part of the physical essence of product, such as the brand name

(Olson & Jacoby, 1972). Research has shown that consumers often use intangible extrinsic cues as surrogate indicators when there are missing and/or difficult cues.

COM is regarded as an extrinsic cue – an intangible product attribute, which is widely used by consumers, especially when they have only limited familiarity with products of foreign origin (Han, 1988; Hanne, 1996). This is because, in the absence of information about tangible traits of products, consumers tend to rely on extrinsic cues as indirect indicators of quality and risk (Han, 1988; Papadopoulos & Heslop, 1993; Maheswaran, 1994). Hence, COM is not merely a cognitive cue – providing, for example, a signal of product quality, but is also an effective one – with a symbolic and emotional meaning, in the sense that it relates to the identity, pride, and memories of consumers (Batra, Alden, Steenkamp, & Ramachander, 1999).

Researchers have attempted to explain the psychological processes of COM by the use of the halo effect model and the cognitive elaboration model (e.g., Han, 1989; Hong & Wyer, 1989; Knight & Calantone, 2000). For instance, Johansson et al. (1985) noted the existence of a persistent "halo" effect in the ratings of specific product attributes. This tendency was stronger if knowledge or awareness of the attribute was low or inaccurate. In some studies, COM influences belief formation rather than attitude (evaluation), although its effects may not be identical across different product attributes (e.g., Erickson, Johansson, & Chao, 1984) or for all individuals (Johansson et al., 1985). Thus, whatever the mechanism adopted, COM leads to a greater cognitive elaboration about tangible product attributes, thus shaping consumer attitude and intention to purchase (Cordell, 1992; Verlegh & Steenkamp, 1999).

Most research on COM effects focused on studying overall product quality as a dependent variable, and many have sought to identify some dimensions of "country image," as a consumer perception of products from different countries. Garvin (1987) noted that most firms must select those quality dimensions on which they are competitive. The dimensions included in this study are availability, model, reliability, durability, product warranty, price, style, and perceived quality. Lawrence, Marr, and Prendergast (1992) suggest consumers use country stereotyping to simplify the choice process. Johansson, Ronkainen, and Czinkota (1994) point to stereotypes leading to an untrue judgment of a foreign product. Janda and Rao (1997) conceptualized COM effects as resulting from two separate processes: cultural stereotype syndrome and personal beliefs. O'Shaughnessy and O'Shaughnessy (2000) noted that as countries increase their international presence, it seems logical for consumers to associate their posture with country-specific stereotypes.

A product's COM is an extrinsic product cue or an "intangible" product characteristic distinct from physical product characteristics or intrinsic attributes. As such, a COM cue is similar to brand name or retailer reputation in that none of these directly bear on product performance and can be manipulated without changing the physical product. Ideally, empirical studies of COM should manipulate a product on a number of cues and assess the impact of COM alongside the other cues in the overall evaluation of the product. A number of studies test a variety of cues or factors such as price, brand name that may lessen or assuage COM's impact on product evaluations (Pecotich & Rosenthal, 2001; Parameswaran & Pisharodi, 2002; Hui & Zhou, 2002; Lin & Kao 2004). Individual consumer factors such as the level of product involvement have been found to moderate COM effects (Gurhan & Maheswaran, 2000; Lee, Yun, & Lee, 2005). Notably, the nature of the product seems to play an important moderating role in shaping consumer evaluations based on COM information: the greater the degree of involvement in the buying-decision process for a specific product, the more likely it is for the consumer to use COM information in his/her evaluation (Johansson, 1993).

Despite the consensus on the effect of COM on consumers' product evaluation and purchase decisions (Baughn & Yaprak, 1993; Bilkey & Nes, 1982; Liefeld, 1993; Peterson & Jolibert, 1995), insufficient evidence exists to suggest under what conditions COM information is particularly influential to the consumer. Such knowledge is significant since it can enable firms to adopt more effective strategies in sourcing and marketing their products overseas. Samiee (1994) pointed out that one key drawback of current COM studies is the a priori assumption that "customers were typically knowledgeable or sought to acquire country of origin/manufacturing information, and that COM is a primary attribute in their decisions." This assumption clearly biased the effect size because consumers are not all the same in regard to COM influence. The literature has clearly paid little attention to the customers' difference in their attention to and perceived importance of COM (involvement with COM). Consumers are less likely to make inferences about a brand based on its COM when their processing goal guides attention away from COM information. For instance, the lack of statistical significance of the COM effect found in some previous studies (e.g., Erickson et al., 1984; Johansson et al., 1985) may be due to the study subjects' preexisting individual differences in their cognitive predispositions. Knowledge about a product's COM can affect how consumers think about it. Consumers stereotype products based on where they are made. Products labeled "Made in France" are likely to create inferences about elegance and style. Research shows that consumers in developing countries infer higher quality from brands that are perceived as foreign. Many Latin American consumers, for instance, infer that foreign telephone companies offer better service and quality than local companies.

Empirical evidence in the literature also indicates that other variables could moderate the effect of COM. For example, it has been observed that consumer social-economical status may influence the COM effect. Anderson and Cunningham (1972) found that the less educated and politically conservative is more likely to be averse to foreign products. Consumer groups differing by gender, age, and occupation were differentially receptive to foreign products (Johansson et al., 1985; Shimp & Sharma, 1987). Such differences were also observed in consumers from different countries, such as the United Kingdom (Bannister & Saunders, 1978). Such differences lead to suggesting that the COM effect may be influenced by more fundamental consumer differences with respect to a person's willingness and readiness to process information. More recent efforts have begun focusing on individual information-processing perspective (e.g., Han, 1989; Hong & Wyer, 1989; Wall, Liefeld, & Heslop, 1991).

In summary, the written material on COM has made much progress since the early days of single cue studies. However, previous work done in the product quality evaluation and COM areas has not taken into consideration consumers' attention to COM label; this issue needs to be explored. Furthermore, there is lack of conceptual basis for examining how attended and unattended country cues may affect different dimensions of quality. It needs to be studied how the impact of COM on perceived dimension of quality differ between consumers who are attentive to COM information and those who are not. It should be determined how quality dimensions are affected by the consumer's attention to the COM and to what extent, direction, and degree of perception these quality dimensions are affected in the decision-making process. The model thus presented in this research is based on the integration of consumers' attention to COM and also seeks to investigate the influence of such attention in product evaluations. In particular, this study addresses the issue of COM by specifically considering the influence of one intrinsic consumer characteristic on the effect of COM, that is, the individual awareness in the customer's tendency to engage in effortful information processing on COM when evaluating a product.

This approach is relevant since the effect of COM exhibits itself, first and foremost, at the individual level.

# THEORETICAL FRAMEWORK AND RESEARCH HYPOTHESES

## Conceptualization of the "Attention to COM"

Attention process involves selecting a large set of information and ignoring other information. Attention connotes awareness and consciousness and also suggests intensity and arousal. Consumers must be somewhat alert and aroused to consciously attend to something, and their level of alertness influences how intensively they process the information. Attention processes vary along a continuum from a highly automatic, unconscious level called preconscious attention to a controlled, conscious level called focal attention. As a consumer's interpretation processes shift from preconscious attention toward focal attention, greater cognitive capacity is needed, and the consumer gradually becomes more conscious of paying attention to a stimulus. At a focal level, attention is largely controlled by the consumer, who decides which stimuli to attend to and comprehend based on what goals are activated. As attention processes reach focal levels, comprehension begins to involve sense-making processes for constructing meaning. Once consumers are exposed to COM information on a product label, the process of attention to COM begins. To attend to COM information means to be conscious of where the product is made. Consumers attending or not attending to the COM factor will be called, hereafter, attentive or inattentive consumers.

To the extent that inattentive consumers can process information from their peripheral vision even if they are not conscious that they are attending to it – they are engaged in preattentive processing. With preattentive processing, most of their attentional resources are devoted to one thing, leaving very limited resources for attending to something else. As a result, consumers who are inattentive to COM may devote just enough attention to "where the product is made" in peripheral vision when processing information about the product. But because the amount of attention is so limited, they are not conscious that they are attending to and processing information about that COM on the product label. Preattentive processing is a fast, parallel, fairly effortless process; it is not limited by short-term memory capacity and is not under direct participant control. Preattentive processing also involves the spontaneous activation of a set of associations or responses that have been developed through repetitive process in the memory. That is why such processing can be initiated for inattentive consumers by the mere presence of COM cues in the environment. A determining characteristic of automatic processes is their inevitability; they occur despite attempts to bypass or ignore them.

To the extent that attentive consumers can process information via their central routes to persuasion with increased scrutiny as they involve the intentional use of COM information through conscious attention – they are engaged in controlled processing. Controlled processing, as a qualitatively distinctive and independent way in human information processing, has been well established and commonly known in the literature of cognitive science (Posner, 1978; Schneider & Shiffrin, 1977). Contrary to preattentive processing, controlled processing is characterized by a slow, capacity-limited, generally serial, effortful, and participant-regulated processing mode. It is capacity-limited in the sense that interference is strong between tasks to be performed at that processing level. In controlled processing, attentive individuals are able and motivated to engage in extensive issue and argument processing, with conclusions emerging from issue-relevant arguments.

## *Research Hypotheses*

Individual differences between attentive and inattentive consumers on their level of attention to COM information can influence the subsequent process of interpretation, comprehension, and evaluation of product attributes. Specifically, when consumers intentionally focused on the COM, they were more likely to consider the information and elicit more influence on product evaluations. On the other hand, when consumers did not initially focus on the COM but focused instead on other brand attributes or beliefs, COM information was not used strongly in their judgments. In an attempt to explain the cognitive determinants of COM evaluations, Gurhan and Maheswaran (2000) followed an information-processing approach and found motivational intensity, information-processing goals, and product information to impact COM evaluations by affecting the number and depth of COM-related thoughts engendered in individuals on evaluating product attributes. This is theoretically due, in part, to systematic individual differences between these two groups in their desire to engage in issue-relevant thinking when they form their viewpoint (Cacioppo, Chuan, Petty, & Rodriguez, 1986). Consumers' involvement with COM is the antecedent of such desire, the individual's intrinsic enjoyment, and motivation to engage in effortful cognitive information process (Cacioppo & Petty, 1985).

Attentive individuals or intrinsically inclined ones are interested in analyzing and processing distinct pieces of information and are more likely to evaluate products based on the relevance and strength of the product attributes. In contrast, inattentive individuals who would go directly to results rather than considering the analytical process will be more likely to base their evaluation on other apparent extrinsic characteristics. In such cases, consumers may simplify the information processing or employ the heuristic process, as characterized by Wright (1975). For instance, the role of brand name as a surrogate product quality indicator has been widely documented in the literature. Product evaluations by attentive individuals in comparison to inattentive individuals are based more on evaluation of attributes (Fig. 1).

Liu and Johnson (2005) found that "country stereotypes" significantly influence COM evaluations and such stereotypes appear to be spontaneously activated by the mere presence of COM information in the external environment without participants' intentions to use the information when forming product judgments. We recognize the automaticity of country

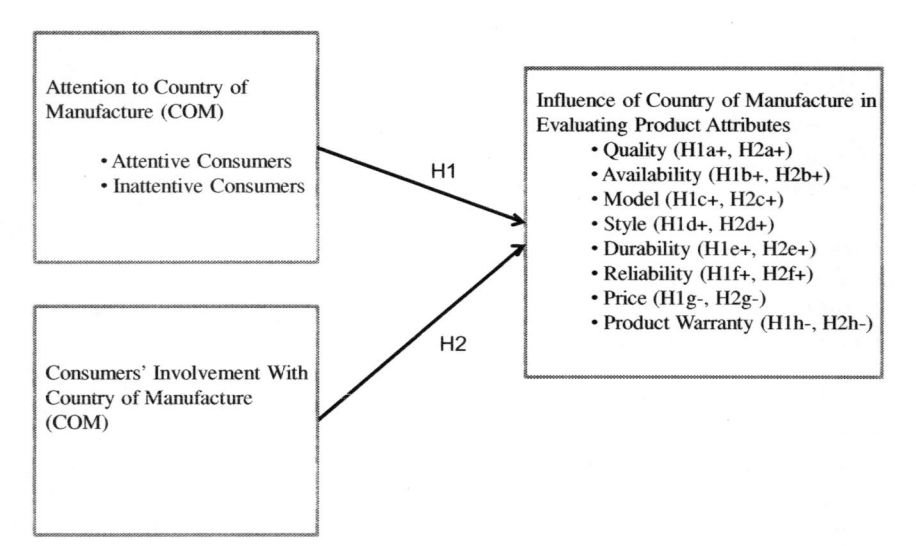

*Fig. 1.* Country-of-Manufacture (COM) Effects on Product Evaluations: A model Integrating Consumers' Attention. H1a–h: Influence of COM on the evaluation of product attributes (attentive vs. inattentive consumers).

stereotypes that they could be activated spontaneously upon exposure to COM cues with or without intention; nevertheless, we argue COM's influence on consumers' product judgment varies by their attention to COM, and more importantly, the attended COM information can be more influential in evaluating products than that in the absence of deliberate attention. The rationale for this argument is that the COM effects may occur more strongly with conscious effort to achieve them, and that they could only be facilitated by information accessed through a controlled process. Attention to COM is the process by which consumers devote mental activity to the COM information on the product label. A certain amount of attention is necessary for information to be perceived – for it to activate consumers' senses. Furthermore, after consumers perceive information, they may pay more attention to it and continue with the higher-order processing activities.

In a situation where COM information on a product label is consciously noticed, attribute information is retrieved and evaluated accordingly. In other words, information processing takes the route through which COM and attribute information is given credibility when the consumer makes a quality judgment. COM's influence on attribute judgment is intentional, and product evaluations on the basis of attended COM follow the controlled process.

In such situations where conscious attention to COM activates country stereotype at the moment of purchase, country stereotype activation is an inevitable result of intentional exposure to COM information. A consumer may learn of and evaluate each particular product attribute under the influence of the activated country stereotype and its product judgment influence over related attributes may be stronger. In other words, the country stereotype may result in a spontaneous a priori hypothesis on which product evaluations are based. Based on this reasoning, the extent to which an activated country stereotype exerts its influence on product judgment depends on the relative accessibility of attribute-related information previously stored in memory. According to Lichtenstein and Srull (1985), consumers would engage in piecemeal, attribute-based recall only when an overall brand evaluation was not available. Subsequent studies show that overall brand evaluation made during advertising encoding is much easier to retrieve from memory than brand attribute information (e.g., Lynch, Marmorstein, & Weigold, 1988). The same holds true for retrieving attribute information, which demands conscious effort through attending to the COM information in the first place.

The first group of hypotheses postulates that the influence of COM on the evaluation of attributes differs between consumers attentive and inattentive to COM information from checking product label. Specifically, H1a–f posits that the consumers attentive to COM are more likely to depend on it for evaluating intrinsic product quality dimensions, such as quality, availability, model, style, durability, and reliability to make a purchase decision compared to those consumers inattentive to COM. H1g and h posits that attentive consumers are less influenced by extrinsic quality cues such as price and product warranty than inattentive consumers.

**H1a–f.** Consumers attentive to the Country of Manufacture (COM) are more influenced by COM on evaluating such attributes as (a) product quality, (b) availability, (c) model, (d) style, (e) durability, and (f) reliability than those who are not attentive to COM information.

**H1g–h.** Consumers attentive to the Country of Manufacture (COM) are less influenced by COM on evaluating such attributes as (g) price and (h) product warranty than those who are not attentive to COM information.

Consumers' involvement with COM can affect the strength of the relationship between COM and product evaluations. COM may present stronger effects on evaluating intrinsic product attributes for highly involved consumers, in whose decision-making process COM plays an important role. However, if consumers place more importance on the extrinsic attribute COM, other extrinsic attributes of price and product warranty will become less important determinants in their purchase decision-making process.

**H2a–f.** Consumers with higher involvement with the Country of Manufacture (COM) are more influenced by COM on evaluating such attributes as (a) product quality, (b) availability, (c) model, (d) style, (e) durability, and (f) reliability than those with lower involvement with COM.

**H2g–h.** Consumers with higher involvement with the Country of Manufacture (COM) are less influenced by COM on evaluating such attributes as (g) price and (h) product warranty than those with lower involvement with COM.

## METHODS

To test the research hypotheses, a survey was conducted in 2006 among consumers residing in the United States, where the mandatory product-labeling policy makes it an excellent basis for COM research, along with two other reasons: (1) a huge market for foreign products, as a result of its relatively large population and high per capita income; and (2) a highly open economy largely depending on external trade from EU, Asia, and South America.

## Sampling Procedures

The target population was American consumers aged 18 years and above, with permanent residency in the United States. Because of the multicultural nature of the local society, and in order to exclude the possibility of bias resulting from differences in nationality (Parameswaran & Pisharodi, 2002), eligible respondents were confined to those having American citizenship or permanent resident status for at least 5 years. A sample of 180 consumers was randomly selected using a systematic stratified procedure, with provision made for the inclusion of two of the country's major cities (namely, New York City and Philadelphia). An attempt was also made to ensure that the gender, age, educational, and income characteristics of the participants in the sample were representative of those of the national population. Central locations were identified in each selected area and consumers were randomly chosen, using a predetermined key. In the case of refusals by certain individuals, the next consumer to fulfill the prescribed demographic criteria was selected.

## Survey Instruments and Measurement

For the purpose of collecting data, a structured questionnaire consisting of three major parts was designed. The first part incorporated questions concerning consumers' usage behavior of different foreign products. Attention to COM was measured on a 5-point scale and recoded into a dichotomous variable using a cutoff point at "3.0," as equal to zero ("I do not pay attention to where the product is made when purchasing a product") and equal to one ("I pay attention to where the product is made when purchasing a product"). In the second part, questions were developed to identify the extent at which consumers would acknowledge the product COM ahead or during purchase in associating with a set of eight specific product attributes, which were extracted after an exhaustive review of the pertinent literature (see Table 1). A 5-point modified Likert scale with endpoints of "not at all" and "entirely" was employed to allow the

**Table 1.** Literature Sources of Country-of-Manufacture on Evaluation of Product Attributes.

| Product Attribute | References |
|---|---|
| Quality | Parameswaran and Yaprak (1987), Knight and Calantone (2000), Martin and Eroglu (1993), Heslop and Papadopoulos (1993), Iyer and Kalita (1997), and Han (1989) |
| Availability | Heslop and Papadopoulos (1993) |
| Model | Parameswaran and Yaprak (1987), Knight and Calantone (2000), and Heslop and Papadopoulos (1993) |
| Style | Parameswaran and Yaprak (1987), Knight and Calantone (2000) |
| Durability | Parameswaran and Yaprak (1987), Knight and Calantone (2000), and Hui and Zhou (2003) |
| Reliability | Heslop and Papadopoulos (1993), Hui and Zhou (2003), and Haubl (1996) |
| Price | Parameswaran and Yaprak (1987), Knight and Calantone (2000), and Iyer and Kalita (1997) |
| Product Warranty | Newly developed in this study |

respondents to rate on the influence of COM on the aforementioned attributes. To measure consumers' involvement with COM, the respondents were also asked a question about the importance of COM in their purchasing process. Specifically, a 5-point Likert scale with endpoints of "strongly disagree" and "strongly agree" was employed to let respondents rate the following statement: "Where the product is made is important to me when I make a purchasing decision." Demographic questions (e.g., gender, age, and education) were included in section three of the questionnaire.

The questionnaire was designed from the findings of a preliminary focus-group interview in order to lend greater validity to the terminology used. The concepts in the framework and the research hypotheses were operationalized in the questionnaire. To improve readability and understanding, the questionnaire was pretested using a judgment sample of actual consumers, and was subsequently revised. Because this research is interested in advancing the general understanding of COM effect rather than obtaining product-specific evaluations, the assessments sought from respondents are generally on "foreign" products. However, consumers' attention to COM may vary across product categories. To gain an exploratory view on the significance of such difference, questions were also asked on if the respondents knew the COM of the various types of products they have recently purchased. Those products include medical, electronic, textile, cosmetic, auto, and fashion products. Cross-tabulations of percentages of respondents who were aware of the COM because they attended to it by product categories were run, and results were included in this research for additional insights.

## Data Collection

Data were collected by means of personal, face-to-face interviews, conducted by six experienced interviewers at preselected central locations (e.g., department stores, supermarkets, and shopping malls). All interviewers had previously undergone rigorous training, during which the study objectives, the respondent selection method, and the questionnaire were fully explained. Rehearsal interviews in a classroom environment were conducted among interviewers to ensure familiarity with the questionnaire and resolve any potential problems. Each interviewer carried out a prespecified number of interviews (around 35). All questionnaires were subsequently edited to ensure that they were properly answered, while data were carefully inserted in SPSS files for statistical analysis.

## Sample Profile

In terms of demographic characteristics, the final sample was more or less equally split between males and females (see Table 2). About 45.3% of the respondents were less than 35 years old, 36.5% were in the 35–54 age group, while the remaining (18.2%) were 55 years old and above. About 12.1% of the participants in the survey had had only secondary education; another 79.3% had graduated from college or with an undergraduate degree; and the remaining 8.6% had had a postgraduate education. In terms of household annual income, two-fifths (41.4%) of the respondents earned $50,000–$100,000, while the remainder (20.7%) had an income exceeding $100,000.

# ANALYSES AND RESULTS

This section analyzes and discusses the results with regard to each of the research hypotheses. In order to carry out the statistical analysis, differences among the means of consumer evaluations on the eight product attributes were compared between the attentive and inattentive groups, as reported in Table 3. The multivariate $F$-ratio of MANOVA is significant at the 0.05

***Table 2.*** Sample Size and Structure ($n = 180$).

| Characteristics | Group | Percentage (%) |
|---|---|---|
| Gender | Male | 55.2 |
| | Female | 44.8 |
| Age | 18–34 | 45.3 |
| | 35–54 | 36.5 |
| | 55+ | 18.2 |
| Education | High school graduate or less | 12.1 |
| | College and undergraduate | 79.3 |
| | Postgraduate | 8.6 |
| Income | Up to $50,000 | 37.9 |
| | $50,000 to $100,000 | 41.4 |
| | $100,000+ | 20.7 |

***Table 3.*** MANOVA Results for Differences in COM's Influence on the Evaluation of Attributes in Purchase Decision Making between Consumers Attending to COM and those not Attending to COM.

| Attributes | F-Ratio | Sig. | Mean (Attentive Group) | Mean (Inattentive Group) |
|---|---|---|---|---|
| Quality | 1.106 | 0.294 | 3.0 | 3.27 |
| Availability | 1.788 | 0.183 | 3.13 | 2.81 |
| Model | 0.650 | 0.421 | 3.0 | 2.83 |
| Style | −0.113 | 0.738 | 3.75 | 3.17 |
| **Durability** | 13.187 | **0.000** | 4.25 | 3.4 |
| **Reliability** | 9.399 | **0.003** | 4.13 | 3.38 |
| Price | 0.838 | 0.361 | 2.88 | 3.1 |
| Product Warranty | 2.358 | 0.127 | 3.13 | 2.75 |

*Note*: Bold terms indicate the attributes that are significantly different between the two groups at the 0.05 level.

level, indicating overall differences between the two groups. However, the subsequent univariate procedures show that at the 0.05 level, the two groups are only statistically different on two of the eight attributes, durability and reliability. COM presents a higher influence of 4.25 on durability for attentive consumers than for inattentive consumers with the average influence of 3.4 on this attribute. COM has a higher influence on evaluating reliability (4.13) for attentive consumers than the average rating of 3.38 for inattentive consumers.

**Table 4.** Canonical Correlation Analysis Relating COM's Influence on Product Evaluations with Attention to COM and Involvement with COM Measures of Overall Model Fit for Canonical Correlation Analysis Univariate $F$-Tests on Each of the Dependent Variables with (2,159) D. F.

| Variable | Sq. Mul. $R$ | Adj. $R^2$ | $F$ | Sig. of $F$ |
|---|---|---|---|---|
| Quality | 0.121 | 0.110 | 10.916 | 0.000 |
| Price | 0.007 | 0.000 | 0.549 | 0.579 |
| Model | 0.091 | 0.080 | 7.976 | 0.001 |
| Style | 0.040 | 0.028 | 3.331 | 0.038 |
| Durability | 0.107 | 0.096 | 9.516 | 0.000 |
| Reliability | 0.069 | 0.057 | 5.859 | 0.004 |
| Availability | 0.042 | 0.030 | 3.524 | 0.032 |
| Warranty | 0.037 | 0.024 | 3.020 | 0.052 |

Multivariate Tests of Significance ($N = 75$)

| Test name | Value | Approx. $F$ | Sig. of $F$ |
|---|---|---|---|
| Pillais | 0.393 | 4.672 | 0.000 |
| Hotellings | 0.495 | 4.671 | 0.000 |
| Wilks | 0.644 | 4.672 | 0.000 |
| Roys | 0.237 | | |

*Note:* $F$ statistic for Wilks' lambda is exact; D. F., degree of freedom.

To obtain a better understanding of the interactive statistical relationships between the attention to and involvement with COM and how they affect COM's influence in evaluating product attributes, an aggregate canonical analysis was performed. These results are reported in Table 4 and suggest that the two predictors explain a significant share of the variance in COM's influence in attribute evaluations. The first statistical significance test is for the canonical correlations of each of the eight dependent variables. All canonical correlations are statistically significant at a 0.05 level except for COM's influence on "price" and "product warranty" (see Table 4). In addition to tests of each dependent variable separately, multivariate tests of all dependent variables simultaneously are also performed. The test statistics employed are Wilks' lambda, Pillai's criterion, Hotelling's trace, and Roy's greatest root. Table 4 also details the multivariate test statistics, all of which indicate that the canonical functions, taken collectively, are statistically significant at the 0.05 level.

The data were further analyzed using separate canonical correlation analyses to test for relationships between the attention to and involvement

**Table 5.** Canonical Regression Analysis for COM's Influence on Each Product Attribute with Attention to and Involvement with COM (Individual Univariate 0.950 Confidence Intervals).

| Dependent Variable | Independent Variable | B | Beta | SE. | t-Value | Sig. of t |
|---|---|---|---|---|---|---|
| Quality | Attention | 0.439 | 0.134 | 0.247 | 1.780 | 0.077 |
| | Involvement | 0.288 | 0.345 | 0.063 | 4.568 | 0.000 |
| Price | Attention | 0.258 | 0.079 | 0.261 | 0.989 | 0.324 |
| | Involvement | 0.034 | 0.041 | 0.067 | 0.517 | 0.606 |
| Model | Attention | −0.110 | −0.044 | 0.192 | −0.570 | 0.570 |
| | Involvement | 0.186 | 0.291 | 0.049 | 3.789 | 0.000 |
| Style | Attention | −0.032 | −0.010 | 0.246 | −0.128 | 0.899 |
| | Involvement | 0.158 | 0.198 | 0.063 | 2.514 | 0.013 |
| Durability | Attention | 0.819 | 0.264 | 0.236 | 3.469 | 0.001 |
| | Involvement | 0.120 | 0.151 | 0.060 | 1.988 | 0.049 |
| Reliability | Attention | 0.755 | 0.237 | 0.248 | 3.042 | 0.003 |
| | Involvement | 0.064 | 0.078 | 0.063 | 1.004 | 0.317 |
| Availability | Attention | −0.249 | −0.083 | 0.237 | −1.052 | 0.294 |
| | Involvement | 0.134 | 0.174 | 0.060 | 2.212 | 0.028 |
| Warranty | Attention | −0.332 | −0.109 | 0.241 | −1.378 | 0.170 |
| | Involvement | 0.108 | 0.139 | 0.062 | 1.758 | 0.081 |

with COM as two predictors and the influence of COM on evaluating each of the eight different product attributes as the criterion variable. Table 5 shows the results of these correlations. The significances of the associations in this study between the two predictor variables and each of the dependent variable were reported. The strengths of the associations between each of the predictor variables and the criterion variable were indicated by the beta values in Table 5.

An inspection of the coefficients for the canonical function (Table 5) indicates that the COM's influence on evaluating durability is significantly related to "attention to COM," and evaluating reliability is significantly related to both "attention to COM" and "involvement with COM," but the magnitudes of betas show attention explains more variation in COM's influence on evaluating reliability than involvement does. COM's influences on evaluating quality, model, style, and availability are all significantly related to involvement with COM, but not to attention. COM's influences on evaluating Price and Product Warranty are not significantly related to either attention to or involvement with COM. Table 5 shows that all the significant relationships between predictor variables and criterion variables are positive. Thus, H1e and f are supported, as evaluations on the two abstract attributes of reliability and durability are related to the attention to COM. In the meantime, H2a–d are supported as evaluations on the four concrete attributes (quality, availability, model, and style) are significantly related to the involvement with COM. Abstract attribute durability does, though both significant, however, appear to have a stronger relationship with attention than it does with involvement. This is evident in the larger beta value derived for the supportive relationships. H2f is supported.

These data further indicate that, as predicted in the rationale for H1g, h and H2g, h, attention to and involvement with COM are not related to the influences of COM in evaluating extrinsic attributes such as Price and Product Warranty. This finding is consistent with previous studies' results regarding intrinsic versus extrinsic attributes. As COM exerts similar halo effects on evaluating product quality attributes like other extrinsic attributes do, consumers relying on other extrinsic attributes will not be influenced by COM (Fig. 2).

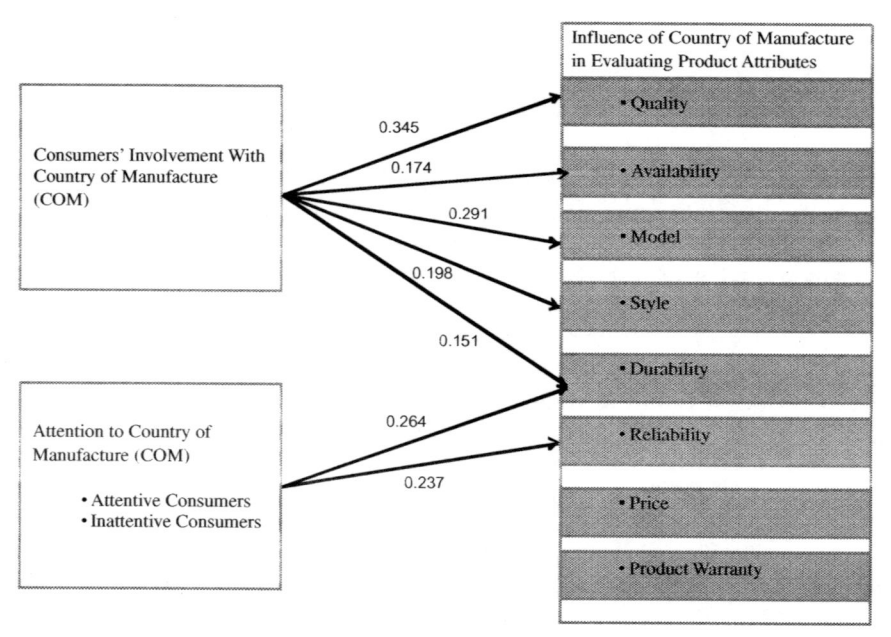

*Fig. 2.* Country-of-Manufacture (COM) Effects on Products Evaluations: A Model Integrating Consumers' Attention.

## DISCUSSIONS, CONCLUSIONS, AND MANAGERIAL IMPLICATIONS

Individual differences in their attention to COM only significantly influence the effect of COM on evaluations of select product attributes. The results indicate that evaluations on durability and reliability are more influenced by the COM information for consumers who consciously attend to COM information. One explanation for these associations is that COM's halo effect addresses consumers' evaluation as part of the knowledge, but such knowledge requires intentional attention to the COM when evaluating the consequences of concrete attributes, that is, abstract attributes, as the latter needs elaborative comprehension to produce thoughts about abstract attributes that ask for focused attention. This explanation is particularly relevant when one considers the high degree of ambiguity typically found in a set of abstract attributes. Furthermore, the significant differentials on the more abstract performance attributes such as Durability and Reliability as perceived by the attentive and inattentive groups of consumers suggest the rationale of benefit segmentation for determining workable positioning and for effectively communicating/ conveying the differential advantages on these two attributes. Products' differential uniqueness on durability and reliability can be communicated successfully to the potential consumers on the basis of benefits sought and their tendency to attend COM information. Marketers selling products with high performance in abstract attributes such as durability and reliability should increase consumers' attention to the COM through effective product labeling.

And consistent with expectations, involvement has a significant, positive effect on consumers' COM's influence on evaluating concrete product attributes. Consumers who perceive a high degree of importance of using COM in product evaluations tend to experience more of its impact on quality, availability, style, and model evaluations. Different from durability and reliability, these four intrinsic attributes are what we may label as "concrete attributes."

The research results of this study are supported by the means-end chain perspective. The specific meanings attached to each product attribute that consumers use COM information to construct depend on the level of comprehension that occurs during the interpretation process of decision making. Consumers paying conscious attention to COM, an antecedent of deep comprehension, experience stronger effects of COM on their evaluations of abstract attributes such as durability and reliability; these two abstract attributes are the functional consequences of product use, supporting that deep comprehension is needed to produce meanings for attributes that represent less tangible, more subjective, and more symbolic concepts. In contrast, nonattentive consumers experience the same, if not stronger, effects of COM on their evaluations of concrete attributes such as model and style, supporting that shallow comprehension produces meanings at a concrete, tangible level, therefore, no need for the focal or conscious attention in the process.

We found that because some consumers feel that some products made in a particular country are of better quality than those made in another country, this does not mean that all consumers pay equal amount of attention to COM. Findings point out that attention to COM has a significantly stronger effect on the use of the COM information in evaluation(s) of product reliability and durability. The effects of attended COM information have greater impact on abstract product attributes whose evaluations are not determined by intuition or impulse. COM, as an extrinsic cue, is more influential in evaluating those attributes when conscious attention incurs a much great deal of deliberate comparisons that facilitate the persuasive attempts of the COM.

These findings have clear implications for vendors. As the attentive consumers seem more sensitive to durability and reliability in associating them with the COM than the inattentive consumers, this suggests that vendors who target an attentive and more discerning consumer could make use of a favorable country image to position a new product on these abstract attributes. On the other hand, an unfavorable product–country image may hamper the success of a new brand aimed at the sensitive segment of the population for positioning on these attributes. For products originating from countries that are viewed favorably, an effective advertising strategy needs to be created to reinforce a memory representation of the brand relating to reliability and durability, such that both controlled recollection of brand attributes and deliberately examined information about country stereotype work in agreement and not in opposition. To maximize the effects of favorable country stereotyping on product reliability and durability, advertising, and packaging should be made to increase the salience of the COM information and the consumers' attention to such information, especially when the message contains little or no supportive attribute information.

The findings go a step beyond previous COM research and demonstrate that the effect can be generalized to a traditional marketing situation involving the unintentional use of COM information. The results are also consistent with the dissociation model of social stereotyping which, when used to explain the findings, suggests that the positive or negative effect associated with COM can be involuntarily conveyed to a brand response situation, even when consumers have no memory of having seen the information through conscious attention and they only comprehend COM information unintentionally. Attended COM information is found having stronger influence on the evaluation of product attributes such as reliability and durability about which an individual does not have enough information to allow for an unbiased judgment. Moreover, the results also offer some preliminary support for the automatic COM effects on product evaluation of other concrete attributes through intrinsic involvement with COM even when no intentional attention is allocated to COM information. In real life, consumers are subject to a constant stream of incoming marketing input, which makes their exposure to COM information quite prevalent. Consumers are in a state of being continuously geared up by COM information, and the extent of its influence is so great that consumers, when facing incomplete knowledge of or missing information about COM, tend to form inferences to "fill in the blanks" based on their schemas of knowledge acquired from past experience. For instance, consumers who are highly knowledgeable about clothing styles may be able to infer the COM and even the designer of a coat or dress merely by noticing a few details. Consumers often use tangible, concrete product attributes as cues in making inferences about more abstract attributes, consequences, and values. In highly familiar situations, these inferences may be made automatically without much conscious awareness. For instance, some consumers draw inferences about the cleaning power of a powdered laundry detergent from its color: blue and white granules seem to connote cleanliness. For products originating from countries associated with unfavorable stereotypes, the priority of positioning should be directed to concrete attributes and benefits that are capable of countering the influence of the COM, as consumers may draw their inference about COM from these attributes that they can physically examine.

As stated earlier, COM research was largely based on the assumption that deliberate cognitive activities and resources of undivided attention are involved in conventional models of information processing. However, these activities may occur involuntarily, with the consumer neither having the intention nor being aware of engaging in such process. Although consumers can process information preattentively, the information will have more impact on abstract attributes when consumers devote full attention to it. In addition, inattentive consumers rated the influence of COM on their evaluation of the two extrinsic attributes, price and product warranty, just as highly as did the consumers consciously attending to COM information. Unlike their intrinsic counterparts, other extrinsic attributes, usually functioning as the surrogate for COM, seem to be immune from the COM's influence in consumers' decision-making process. Future Research – a side note on the descriptive analysis of product categories by consumers' attention to COM.

As regards the recently purchased medical products, 57.1% of the respondents from the attentive group indicated their unawareness of the products' COM, while 76.1% of the inattentive group indicated their unawareness of the products' COM. When it comes to the recently purchased electronic products, 37.5% of the respondents from the attentive group indicated their unawareness of the products' COM, while 46.8% of the inattentive group indicated their unawareness of the COM. Regarding the recently purchased textile products, 71.4% of the respondents from the attentive group indicated their unawareness of the products' COM, while 63.0% of the inattentive group indicated the unawareness of the COM. As regards the recently purchased auto products, 0% of the respondents from the attentive group indicated their unawareness of the products' COM, while 43.5% of the inattentive group indicated the unawareness of the COM. For the recently purchased fashion products, 50.0% of the respondents from the attentive group indicated their unawareness of the products' COM, while 34.8% of the inattentive group indicated the unawareness of the COM. As regards to cosmetic products, 87.5% of the attentive group indicated their unawareness of the products' COM, while 66.0% of the inattentive group indicated the unawareness of the COM.

Conscious attention leads to deep comprehension for electronic, auto, and medical products, from which the part of the outcome is the recall of the purchased item's COM, but such attention seems to have an opposite effect on generating the same memory effects for textile, cosmetic, and fashion products. These three product categories seem to only require preconscious attention for the remembering and interpretation of COM. Future research needs to use each of the aforementioned product categories in testing the model that integrates consumers' attention to COM and see how the results may differ or not differ across product categories.

# REFERENCES

Alashban, A. A., Hayes, L. A., Zinkhan, G. M., & Balazs, A. L. (2002). International brand-name standardization/adaptation: Antecedents and consequences. *Journal of International Marketing, 10*(3), 22.
Anderson, W. T., & Cunningham, W. H. (1972). Gauging foreign product promotion. *Journal of Advertising Research, 12*(1), 29.
Audhesh, K. P., Shailesh, K., & Gopala, G. (2003). Loyalty towards the country, the state and the service brands. *Journal of Brand Management, 10*(3), 233.
Bannister, J. P., & Saunders, J. A. (1978). UK consumers' attitudes towards imports: The measurement of national stereotype image. *European Journal of Marketing, 12*(8), 562.
Batra, R., Alden, D. L., Steenkamp, J. E. M., & Ramachander, S. (1999). Effects of brand local non-local origin on consumer attitudes in developing countries. *Journal of Consumer Psychology, 9*(2), 83–96.
Baughn, C. C., & Yaprak, A. (1993). Mapping country of origin research: Recent developments and emerging avenues. In: N. Papadopoulos & L. Heslop (Eds), *Product-country images: Impact and role in international marketing* (pp. 47–63). New York: International Business Press.
Bilkey, W. J., & Nes, E. (1982). Country of origin effects on product evaluation. *Journal of International Business Studies, 8*(1), 89–99.
Cacioppo, J. T., Chuan, F. K., Petty, R. E., & Rodriguez, R. (1986). Central and peripheral routes to persuasion: An individual difference perspective. *Journal of Personality and Social Psychology, 51*(5), 1032.
Cacioppo, J. T., & Petty, R. E. (1985). Physiological responses and advertising effects: Is the cup half full or half empty? *Psychology and Marketing, 2*(2), 115.
Cateora, P. R., & Graham, J. (2005). *International marketing.* New York: McGraw-Hill/Irwin.
Cattin, P., Jolibert, A., & Lohnes, C. (1982). A cross-cultural study of 'made in' concepts. *Journal of International Business Studies* (Winter), 131–141.
Clarke, I., Owens, M., & Ford, J. B. (2000). Integrating country of origin into global marketing strategy: A review of US marking statutes. *International Marketing Review, 17*(2), 114.
Cordell, V. (1992). Effects of consumer preferences of foreign sourced products. *Journal of International Business Studies, 23*(2), 251–269.
Coulter, R. A., Price, L. L., & Feick, L. (2003). Rethinking the origins of involvement and brand commitment: Insights from postsocialist central Europe. *Journal of Consumer Research, 30*(2), 151.
Dinnie, K. (2002). National image and competitive advantage: The theory and practice of country-of-origin effect. *Journal of Brand Management, 9*(4/5), 396.
Dinnie, K. (2004). Global brand strategy: Unlocking brand potential across countries, cultures and markets. *Journal of Brand Management, 12*(1), 69.
Douglas, S. P., & Craig, C. S. (1995). *Global marketing strategy.* New York: McGraw-Hill.
Douglas, S. P., Craig, C. S., & Nijssen, E. J. (2001). Executive insights: Integrating branding strategy across markets – Building international brand architecture. *Journal of International Marketing, 9*(2), 97.

Erickson, G. M., Johansson, J. K., & Chao, P. (1984). Image variables in multi-attribute product evaluations: Country-of-origin effects. *Journal of Consumer Research, 11*, 694–699.

Etzel, M. J., & Walker, B. J. (1974). Advertising strategy for foreign products. *Journal of Advertising Research, 14*(3), 41–44.

Fishbein, M., & Ajzen, I. (1975). *Belief, attitude, intention, and behavior: An introduction to theory and research* (p. 2). Reading, MA: Addison-Wesley.

Garvin, D. A. (1987). Competing on the eight dimensions of quality. *Harvard Business Review, 65*(November–December), 101–109.

Gurhan, C., & Maheswaran, D. (2000). Determinants of country-of-origin evaluations. *Journal of Consumer Research, 27*(1), 96–108.

Han, C. M. (1988). The role of consumer patriotism in the choice of domestic versus foreign products. *Journal of Advertising Research, 28*, 25–32.

Han, C. M. (1989). Country image: Halo or summary construct? *Journal of Marketing Research, 26*(2), 222–229.

Hanne, N. (1996). Country of origin marketing over the product life cycle: A Danish case study. *European Journal of Marketing, 30*(3), 6–22.

Haubl, G. (1996). A cross-international investigation of the effects of country-of-origin and brand name of the evaluation of a new car. *International Marketing Review, 13*(5), 76–97.

Heslop, L. A., & Papadopoulos, N. (1993). But who knows where or when: Reflections on the images of countries and their products. In: N. Papadopoulos & L. A. Heslop (Eds), *Product-country images: Impact and role in international marketing* (pp. 39–76). New York: International Business Press.

Hong, S. T., & Wyer, R. S. (1989). Effects of country-of-origin and product attribute information on product evaluation: An information processing perspective. *Journal of Consumer Research, 16*(2), 175–187.

Hugstad, P. S., & Durr, M. (1986). A study of manufacturer impact on consumer perceptions. In: N. Malhotra & J. Hawes (Eds), *Developments in marketing science* (Vol. 9, pp. 115–119). Coral Gable, FL: Academy of Marketing.

Hui, M. K., & Zhou, L. X. (2001). Country-of-manufacture effects for known brands. *European Journal of Marketing, 37*(1/2), 133–153.

Hui, M. K., & Zhou, L. X. (2002). Linking product evaluations and purchase intention for country-of-origin effects. *Journal of Global Marketing, 15*(3/4), 95–116.

Hui, M. K., & Zhou, L. X. (2003). Country of manufacture effects for known brands. *European Journal of Marketing, 31*(1/2), 133–153.

Iyer, G. R., & Kalita, J. K. (1997). The impact of country-of-origin and country-of-manufacture cues on consumer perceptions of quality and value. *Journal of Global Marketing, 11*(1), 7–28.

Janda, S., & Rao, C. P. (1997). The effects of country-of-origin related stereotypes and personal beliefs on product evaluation. *Psychology and Marketing, 14*(7), 689–702.

Johansson, J. K. (1993). Missing a strategic opportunity: Managers' denial of country-of-origin effect. In: N. Papadopoulos & L. A. Heslop (Eds), *Product country images: Impact and role in international marketing* (pp. 77–86). New York: International Business Press.

Johansson, J. K., Douglas, S. P., & Nonaka, I. (1985). Assessing the impact of country of origin on product evaluations: A new methodological perspective. *Journal of Marketing Research, XXII*(November), 388–396.

Johansson, J. K., Ronkainen, I. A., & Czinkota, M. R. (1994). Negative country-of-origin effects: The case of the new Russia. *Journal of International Business Studies, 25*(10), 157–176.

Kaynak, E., & Cavusgil, S. T. (1983). Consumer attitudes towards products of foreign origin: Do they vary across product classes? *International Journal of Advertising, 2*(2), 147–157.

Kaynak, E., & Kara, A. (2002). Consumer perceptions of foreign products: An analysis of product country images and ethnocentrism. *European Journal of Marketing, 36*(7/8), 928–949.

Knight, G. A., & Calantone, R. J. (2000). A flexible model of consumer country-of-origin perceptions: A cross-cultural investigation. *International Marketing Review, 17*(2), 127–145.

Lawrence, C., Marr, N. E., & Prendergast, G. P. (1992). Country-of-origin stereotyping: A case study in the New Zealand motor vehicle industry. *European Journal of Marketing, 26*(3), 37–51.

Lee, D., & Ganesh, G. (1999). Effects of partitioned country image in the context of brand image and familiarity. *International Marketing Review, 16*(1), 18–39.

Lee, W. N., Yun, T. W., & Lee, B. K. (2005). The role of involvement in country-of-origin effects on product evaluation: Situational and enduring involvement. *Journal of International Consumer Marketing, 17*(2,3), 51–59.

Lichtenstein, M., & Srull, T. K. (1985). Conceptual and methodological issues in examining the relationship between consumer memory and judgment. In: L. Alwitt & A. A. Mitchell (Eds), *Psychological processes and advertising effects* (pp. 113–128). Hillsdale, NJ: Erlbaum.

Liefeld, J. P. (1993). Experiments on country-of-origin effects: Review and meta-analysis of effect size. In: N. Papadopoulos & L. A. Heslop (Eds), *Product country images*. Binghamton, NY: International Business Press.

Lim, K., & O'Cass, A. (2001). Consumer brand classifications: An assessment of culture-of-origin versus country-of-origin. *The Journal of Product and Brand Management, 10*(2), 120.

Lin, C. H., & Kao, D. T. (2004). The impacts of country-of-origin on brand equity. *Journal of American Academy of Business, Cambridge, 5*(Jan/Feb), 3740.

Liu, S. S., & Johnson, K. F. (2005). The automatic country-of-origin effects on brand judgments. *Journal of Advertising, 34*(1), 87.

Loeffler, M. (2002). A multinational examination of the '(non-) domestic product' effect. *International Marketing Review, 19*(4/5), 482.

Lwin, M., Pecotich, A., & Thein, V. (2006). Myanmar: Foreign brands trickling through. In: A. Pecotich & C. J. Shultz (Eds), *Handbook of markets and economies: East Asia, Southeast Asia, Australia, New Zealand* (pp. 447–476). Armonk, NY: M.E. Sharpe, Inc.

Lynch, J. G., Marmorstein, H., & Weigold, M. F. (1988). Choices from sets including remembered brands: Use of recalled attributes and prior overall evaluations. *Journal of Consumer Research, 15*(2), 169–184.

Maheswaran, D. (1994). Country of origin as a stereotype: Effects of consumer expertise and attribute strength on product evaluations. *Journal of Consumer Research, 21*(2), 354–365.

Martin, I. M., & Eroglu, S. (1993). Measuring a multi-dimensional construct: Country image. *Journal of Business Research*, 28(3), 191–210.

Nebenzahl, I. D., & Jaffe, E. D. (1996). Measuring the joint effect of brand and country image in consumer evaluation of global products. *International Marketing Review, London*, 13(4), 5.

Olson, J. C., & Jacoby, J. (1972). Cue utilization in the quality perception process. In: M. Venkatesan (Ed.), *Proceedings of the third annual conference* (pp. 167–179). Association for Consumer Research.

O'Shaughnessy, J., & O'Shaughnessy, N. J. (2000). Treating the nation as a brand: Some neglected issues. *Journal of Macromarketing*, 20(1), 56–64.

Papadopoulos, N. (1993). What product and country images are and are not. In: N. Papadopoulos & L. A. Heslop (Eds), *Product-country images: Impact and role in international marketing*. Binghampton, NY: The Haworth Press.

Papadopoulos, N., & Heslop, L. A. (1993). *Product-country images: Impact and role in international marketing*. New York: International Business Press.

Parameswaran, R., & Pisharodi, R. M. (1994). Facets of country of origin image: An empirical assessment. *Journal of Advertising*, 23(1), 43–56.

Parameswaran, R., & Pisharodi, R. M. (2002). Assimilation effects in country image research. *International Marketing Review*, 19(3), 259–278.

Parameswaran, R., & Yaprak, A. (1987). A cross-national comparison of consumer research measures. *Journal of International Business Studies*, 18(2), 35–49.

Pecotich, A., & Rosenthal, M. J. (2001). Country of origin, quality, brand and consumer ethnocentrism. *Journal of Global Marketing*, 15(2), 31–41.

Pecotich, A., & Shultz, C. J. (Eds). (2006). *Handbook of markets and economies: East Asia, Southeast Asia, Australia, New Zealand*. Armonk, NY: M.E. Sharpe, Inc.

Peterson, R. A., & Jolibert, A. J. P. (1995). A meta analysis of country-of-origin effects. *Journal of International Business Studies*, 26(4), 883–900.

Posner, M. I. (1978). *Chronometric explorations of mind*. Hillsdale, NJ: Erlbaum.

Ramsay, B. (2003). Whither global branding? The case of food manufacturing. *Journal of Brand Management*, 11(1), 9.

Roth, M. S., & Romeo, J. B. (1992). Matching product category and country image perceptions: A framework for managing country-of-origin effects. *Journal of International Business Studies, Third Quarter*, 477–497.

Samiee, S. (1994). Customer evaluations of products in a global market. *Journal of International Business Studies*, 25(3), 579–604.

Schneider, W., & ShifFrin, R. M. (1977). Controlled and automatic human information processing: Detection, search, and attention. *Psychological Review*, 84(1), 1–66.

Schooler, R. D. (1965). Product bias in the central American common Market. *Journal of Marketing Research* (November), 294–297.

Shimp, T. A., & Sharma, S. (1987). Consumer ethnocentrism: Construction and validation of the CETSCALE. *Journal of Marketing Research*, 24(3), 280.

Tse, D. K., & Gorn, G. J. (1993). An experiment on the salience of country-of-origin in the era of global brands. *Journal of International Marketing*, 1(1), 57–76.

van Mesdag, M. (2000). Culture-sensitive adaptation or global standardization – the duration-of-usage hypothesis. *International Marketing Review*, 17(1), 74.

Verlegh, P. W. J., & Steenkamp, J. E. M. (1999). A review and meta-analysis of country-of-origin research. *Journal of Economic Psychology*, 20(5), 521–546.

Wall, M., Liefeld, J., & Heslop, L. A. (1991). Impact of country-of-origin cues on consumer judgments in multi-cue situations: A covariance analysis. *Journal of the Academy of Marketing Science, 19*(2), 105–113.

Wright, P. (1975). Consumer choice strategies: Simplifying vs. optimizing. *Journal of Marketing Research, 12*(1), 60–67.

Zafar, U. A., Johnson, J. P., Chew, P. L., Tan, W. F., & Ang, K. H. (2002). Country-of-origin and brand effects on consumers evaluations of cruise lines. *International Marketing Review, 19*(2/3), 279.

# Part III
# Material Consumption Phenomena and Processes

# SOCIALIZATION OF ADULT AND YOUNG CONSUMERS INTO MATERIALISM: THE ROLES OF MEDIA AND CHURCH IN PERU

Sandra K. Smith Speck and Teri Peterson

## ABSTRACT

Purpose – *The present research seeks insights into the consumer socialization process of both children and adults in a developing country, Peru. The role played by two socialization agents, media and church, has been explored in terms of how each is related to an important facet of consumer attitudes, level of materialism.*

Methodology/approach – *Male students attending a faith-based high school in Peru, as well as one of their parents, completed a survey in Spanish seeking information on their television viewing, their faith, and their views regarding possessions.*

Findings – *The more traditional socialization institution, church, appears to be less important to younger consumers than to their parents; but it has a greater influence on materialism for youth than their parents. The power of media as a socialization agent for both groups is seen not only via television advertising, but also through television programming.*

*Research implications* – *As one considers how consumers learn to be consumers, both from a purely theoretical standpoint as well as from a strategic marketing perspective, one should take into account both avenues for information transmission. The role played by both seems to change people's lives, both in terms of perceived importance, as well as actual consumer decision making.*

Research on the process of consumer socialization has focused largely on children. Indeed, an early definition of the construct specifically addresses children as the segment being educated in this way: Consumer socialization is "the process by which young people acquire skills, knowledge and attitudes relevant to their functioning as consumers in the marketplace" (Ward, 1974, p. 2). However, Moschis (1987) points out that as people move through their life, they continually learn different things from different sources. Indeed, as one looks at the global marketplace, adults in economically developing countries are learning to be consumers alongside their children, and thus are experiencing the process of consumer socialization later in life. Other than Dholakia (1984), there appears to be little research on such socialization in developing countries.

Developing countries, however, prove to be valuable backdrops for examining consumer socialization because of the rapid rate of change that takes place as the economies of such countries adopt technologies already available to developed economies. This change contributes to an evolution in socializing forces, with the introduction of new agents effecting the socialization of both children and adults. Moschis's (2007) most recent research on life course perspectives in consumer behavior confirms the importance of recognizing the adaptations that take place over a lifetime because of changing sociocultural contexts and circumstances.

The present study attempts to fill the aforementioned void, considering the influence of external socialization forces affecting both children and adults in a Peruvian community. The primary purpose of this study is to seek insights into how the influence of two particular socialization agents, church and the media, affect both children and adults. The institution of church has been a significant socializing force for generations. However, media, for our purposes television, is a relatively recent innovation and, thus, a young socialization force. In the present research, we evaluate the relative effect of each agent on the level of materialism in both groups, focusing on materialism because it is a cultural value affected by consumer socialization as has been stressed by past consumer research. The subsequent discussion will introduce the particular outcome of socialization we are using to illustrate the relative influence of two socialization agents, followed by a description of the key socialization agents we are investigating.

## LITERATURE REVIEW

### Evidence of Consumer Socialization: Materialism

Two major perspectives on the construct of materialism, including both its definition and its measurement are provided by Belk (1985) and Ger and Belk (1996), as well as Richins and Dawson (1992). The former perspective views materialism as "the importance a consumer attaches to worldly possessions" (Belk, 1984, p. 291). Richins and Dawson (1992) view materialism as a value, instrumental or terminal; this perspective views materialism as an enduring belief in acquiring and possessing things as a desirable activity.

The Ger and Belk (1996) materialism research identifies four subscales representing separate aspects of the construct: nongenerosity, possessiveness, envy, and preservation. Nongenerosity is that component of materialism which represents "an unwillingness to give possessions to or share possessions with others" (Belk, 1985, p. 268). Possessiveness is viewed as distinct in this research from nongenerosity, and is defined by Belk (1983) as the desire to control one's possessions. Envy involves a desire for other's possessions and resentment of the owners of those possessions (Belk, 1985). Finally, preservation is a fourth component of materialism identified in Ger and Belk (1996); it involves the conservation of the past, for example, memories, experiences, in the form of material possessions.

The other major perspective on materialism is that provided by Richins and Dawson (1992). These scholars have identified three themes consistently appearing in prior definitions of materialism: acquisition centrality, acquisition as the pursuit of happiness, and possession-defined success. Under this perspective, possessions and their acquisition are viewed to be at the center of the lives of people who are materialistic. Among the reasons for this centrality is the fact that those consumers who are more materialistic see possessions as a key to being satisfied and happy with their lives. In the view of this research, ultimately one's success and that of others is determined by the possessions collected, both in quantity and in quality. Because the present research views materialism as a cultural value, we use this approach to materialism in our study.

Social learning theory (Churchill & Moschis, 1979; Moschis & Smith, 1985) views socialization as the result of environmental forces acting on a person; the individual is viewed as passive in the learning process and development of attitudes comes from interaction with others. According to this theory, agents may be any person, institution, or organization interacting with the individual, for example, family, peers, media, and institutions. In the present research, we focus on two sources of influence, media (i.e., television programming and advertising) and the institution of church, the former a relatively recent agent and the latter having deep roots.

*Media: Television as a Socialization Agent*

The idea of television as a socialization agent with respect to consumption was recognized shortly after its mass distribution in the United States. At that early juncture, Bandura (1969, 1971) determined that television advertisements were a means by which people learn how to attach social meaning to goods. Churchill and Moschis (1979) identify a positive relationship between an increase in the amount of television viewing and a person's motivations for consumption and consumer skills. The strong link between this media-based source of socialization influence and the consumption value of materialism has been documented repeatedly in subsequent research (e.g., Kasser & Ryan, 2001; O'Guinn & Shrum, 1997; Richins, 1987).

In addition to the quantity of television viewed, this more recent research suggests that the content of the programming and advertising also contributes to the socialization process, for example, development of materialism. Television content provides information on how to live, that is, social image formation (Belk & Pollay, 1986). It tells us how we should look and what we should wear by providing a media image standard (Richins, 1991). In addition, Wells (1997) suggests that television programming provides messages about how products are used, the consumption context, and people who use them. Comparison with those who are "better off" may be unavoidable, induced by "television commercials portraying happy, beautiful, and wealthy people" (Goethals, 1986, p. 273). Idealized media images of wealth and beauty reinforce and exacerbate the drive to acquire more of the desired goods or to replicate the ideal look, at least among those consumers who feel that they can move closer to the desired image with effort (Duval, Duval, & Mulilis, 1992).

Cultivation theory has posited that heavy exposure to media and cultural imagery shapes a viewer's concept of reality (Gerbner, Gross, Morgan, & Signorielli, 1980). In addition, O'Guinn and Shrum's (1997) research related to cultivation theory considers the consumerist content of television programming and advertising of central importance, along with the quantity viewed, in the development of materialism.

While the content of the programming and advertising viewed, then, is considered a major factor in the power of media as an instrument of consumer socialization, it has not been considered in most subsequent studies of the relationship between media and materialism. The present research seeks to address this relative void.

From a practical perspective, an important consideration for the current study is the growing number of televisions in Peru. To serve as a socialization agent, televisions must be available in order for its contents to have an effect on people. In 1980, when the adults in this study would have been completing high school, there were about 52 television sets per 1,000 people in Peru; by 1990 that number had grown to 96.30 (Navia & Zweifel, 2006). In 2002, there were over 111 sets per 1,000 people (Goodwin, 2002). Television's potential as a socialization agent, then, has grown a great deal since the adults in this study were their children's age.

In the present study, then, we consider the influence of media as a socialization agent by examining the role of the quantity of television viewed, as well as the content of the television programming and advertising, on the level of materialism (consumer socialization) of a sample of Peruvian adults and their high school-aged sons. In terms of content, we consider images regarding how one should dress and look, as well as the relative standard of living. We have selected this particular content (appearance and standard of living perceptions) because it is specifically addressed in previous materialism literature. We examine this influence for both population samples, ascertaining whether this socialization agent is operative for both older and young consumers. Specifically, we hypothesize,

**H1a.** There is a significant positive relationship between quantity of television viewed and level of materialism.

**H1b.** That relationship will be stronger for the younger respondents than for the adults.

**H2a.** There is a significant positive relationship between comparison to television programming content and level of materialism.

**H2b.** That relationship will be stronger for the younger respondents than for the adults.

**H3a.** There is a significant positive relationship between comparison to television advertising content and level of materialism.

**H3b.** That relationship will be stronger for the younger respondents than for the adults.

*Institutions: Church as a Socialization Agent*

With regard to church as a socialization agent, Hirschman (1983) demonstrates that the religious affiliations of Catholics, Protestants, and Jews significantly shaped their attitudes towards dancing, magazines, restaurants, and political ideas. Anand and Kumar (1982) and Venkatesh and Swamy (1994) indicate that religion has always been and continues to be an important force in India.

In the present study, we examine the role of the institution of church and religiosity in a similar fashion as we have approached media, specifically television programming and advertising – as a socialization agent fostering the development of consumer skills and attitudes, particularly that of materialism. Research evidence confirms that faith-based institutions are associated with the socialization process. For example, Sood and Nasu (1995) document the significant effect of this socialization agent on consumer behavior in general. Mitchell and Al-Mossawi's (1999) findings provide evidence on the importance of religiosity in the communication of brand values.

The particular perspective on the cultural value of interest here, materialism, however may differ depending on the specific religion involved. For example, Vatikiotis (1996), however, finds that some modern-day religious sects view material gain as compatible with spirituality, even seeing material success as a blessing from God. On the other hand, major religions have long criticized excessive materialism as being incompatible with religious fulfillment (Belk, 1983). Criticisms aimed at the excessive pursuit of material goods at the expense of "higher" pursuits comes from many organized religions, for example, Buddhism, Hinduism, Islam, Judaism, and Christianity (for our purposes, specifically Catholicism), all of which condemn concentrating on building excessive material wealth (Pollay, 1986). Each of these faith perspectives concur that one's primary goal should be spiritual, while aiming only at the minimum level of material wealth needed to maintain life (Elgin & Mitchell, 1977). Directly related to the present study, Flouri (1999) confirms that the effect of the institution of church as an economic socialization force is negative, that is to say, religiosity is negatively related to materialism in his research. Most recently, Speck and Roy (2008) include an examination of the effect of religiosity on materialism as part of a larger study of changing cultural values. A sample from Latin American countries is included in this project, so the findings are particularly relevant to our current research. In their study, religiosity is, in fact, negatively related to materialism for the Latin American sample.

Unlike television, which is a relatively new presence in Peru, the institution of church in the form of the Catholic Church has been an integral part of the Peruvian society for a much longer time frame. Religion is a dominant cultural influence, with 81% of the population identifying with that faith (CIA– the World Fact Book, 2009). The Catholic Church has traditionally used its influence to discourage a yearning for worldly goods, as noted above, thus representing a negative socializing influence for materialism.

Because the adults in the present study grew up with the religious influence of the Catholic Church in their lives, it has had significant opportunity to affect their consumer socialization over their lifetime. Their sons will have had fewer years to internalize the tenets of this faith. Given this, we hypothesize that:

**H4a.** There will be a significant negative relationship between level of religiosity and level of materialism.

**H4b.** That relationship will be stronger for the adults than for the children.

## METHODOLOGY

### Sample and Procedure

Data were collected via pencil-and-paper surveys administered to students at a boy's high school in Lima, Peru, as well as to one of the parents of each of these students. This convenience sample was made available to the author because of the relationship between the author's university and the high school. The survey was translated into Spanish to maximize its comprehension by the survey participants. The questionnaire gathered information on the students' and parents' self-reports of quantity of television viewing, perspectives on television programming and advertising content, religiosity, materialistic tendencies, and demographic data. The data were entered into Excel and analyzed using PASW (2009). Separate multiple regression analyses were run for the parents and sons to assess the first hypotheses in each pair. The analyses were run separately since the observations about the parents and sons are neither matched nor independent. Only standardized regression coefficients were reported to correct for differences in scale of the measurements. To assess the second hypothesis in each pair, the strength of the relationships were compared between the parents and sons using a Fisher's $z$ transformation (Zar, 1984).

Fifty-three fathers and sixty-six mothers completed the questionnaire, with 153 male students. The average age for the total sample was 28.01, that of the fathers was 48 (SD of 7.14), that of the mothers 43.88 (SD of 4.55), and 14.37 for the sons (SD of 1.35). In terms of income, overall, the majority of the total sample of participants rated themselves as having a family income that was above average when compared to the average family in their country. The contact at the high school confirmed that many of the student's parents are leaders in the community, and so are not representative of the population in general.

*Measures*

Several measures were used to collect data; these measures are provided in detail in the appendix. A description of the operationalization of each follows.

*Television Viewing*: The television viewing measure was created by finding the mean score of the answers given for: (1) hours of television watched yesterday, (2) hours of television usually watched every day, and (3) average hours of television watched weekly divided by seven (yielding another measure of daily television watching). The questions used for this measure were taken from a measure previously created by Sirgy and colleagues (1998) and each of the three questions were open ended, allowing participants to enter any number they wished to use as a measure of their time spent watching television. For these questions, participants responded with scores ranging from zero to twenty hours. This measure was referred to as TV Amount or TVAmt.

*Television Programming*: The measure evaluated how participant's viewed the impact of television programming content. Specifically, these questions borrowed from Yoon (1995) and Richins (1991) asked participants to rate the role of television programming in providing information on what one should wear and how one should look. A 7-point Likert scale (1 = strongly disagree to 7 = strongly agree) was used for each question. A television programming measure was then created by finding the mean of the seven questions focused on appearance comparison relative to television programming. Higher scores indicated greater agreement with using television programming to provide information on appearance. This measure was referred to as Appearance in Programming or AppProg.

In addition, we included perceived evaluations of their standard of living in comparison to television programming content similar to Sirgy et al.'s (1998) questions related to evaluations of standard of living based on comparisons made with images from television advertising content. Examples of questions include "I am more well off than most people shown on television programs," and "I usually find that I am materially better off than the typical family shown on television programs," measured on a 5-point Likert scale, that is, 1 = strongly disagree to 5 = strongly agree. Three questions were combined to create a measure focused on standard of living comparison relative to television programming. This measure was referred to as Standard of Living in Programming or SLProg.

*Television Advertising*: Similarly, the effect of television advertising content was measured using a modified form of the above-described questions, inserting advertising in place of programming content. The nine items included in this scale were rated via a 7-point Likert scale (1 = strongly disagree to 7 = strongly agree), and the measure was then scored by calculating the mean for each participant. This construct was referred to as Appearance in Advertisements or AppAd. Sirgy et al.'s (1998) questions related to evaluations of standard of living based on comparisons made with images from television advertising were included as well. Examples of questions include "I am better off financially than most people shown on television commercials," and "I usually find that I am materially better off than the typical family shown on television ads," measured on a 5-point Likert scale, that is, 1 = strongly disagree to 5 = strongly agree. Four items were averaged to create this measure. This construct was referred to as Standard of Living in Advertisements or SLAd.

*Importance of Church*: Three questions were used to ascertain the importance of the role that church plays in respondents lives. One question from the religiosity section of the questionnaire was used to measure personal faith. The question "rate the importance of your personal faith to you" (Hadaway & Roof, 1978) was rated with a 5-point Likert scale (1 = not at all important to 5 = extremely important). The other two items asked about membership in a church or synagogue and frequency of church attendance. A single factor of religiosity was calculated using factor analysis.

*Materialism*: The particular perspective on materialism that we are adopting for the present research is that of Richins and Dawson (1992), who describe materialism as a cultural value. Hence, we use the materialism scale they have developed to measure this construct. Each question in the measure was rated with a 5-point Likert scale (1 = strongly disagree to 5 = strongly agree). Richins and Dawson's scale contains three subscales to measure an individual's level of materialism as a measure of success, the centrality of materialism, and materialism as a measure of happiness. These subscales were scored using the sum of all questions included in each subscale.

# RESULTS

## Reliability and Validity Issues

Table 1 summarizes the results of our analyses of the construct measures, including the confirmatory factor analyses and reliability of each of the multiitem measures. Factor analyses were performed on all constructs developed as variables. The factor loadings for the rotated factor matrices for all of the constructs are included in Table 1. In addition, Cronbach's alpha reliabilities are reported for all measures used in the analyses. All alphas were greater than 0.7 except that for religiosity. An alpha greater than 0.7 indicates an adequate or good internal consistency reliability among the items in the construct (Nunnally, 1978). Religiosity is lower than desirable; however, no better scale of religiosity was available at the time these data were collected. In addition, the factor analysis confirmed that the three items on the questionnaire which measured religiosity loaded together as a single factor.

The means and standard deviations of our key constructs are shown in Table 2. One-way analysis of variance was performed on all constructs to test for differences among mothers, fathers and children. Observed significance levels ($p$-values) are reported in Table 2. Tukey's posthoc tests for pairwise comparisons were calculated. There were no significant differences among the mothers and fathers in average scores on all the constructs. Therefore, mothers and fathers were combined into a single group of adults. There were frequently differences between the adults and the children.

*Table 1.* Confirmatory Factor Analysis Factor Loadings.

| Item | Richins–Dawson Scale | TVAmt | AppProg | SLProg | AppAd | SLAd | Religiosity |
|---|---|---|---|---|---|---|---|
| MASUC1 | 0.401 | | | | | | |
| MASUC2 | 0.391 | | | | | | |
| MASUC3 | 0.380 | | | | | | |
| MAHAPP1 | 0.419 | | | | | | |
| MAHAPP2 | 0.611 | | | | | | |
| MAHAPP3 | 0.629 | | | | | | |
| MAHAPP4 | 0.590 | | | | | | |
| MACENT1 | 0.338 | | | | | | |
| MACENT2 | 0.433 | | | | | | |
| MACENT3 | 0.191 | | | | | | |
| TVAMT1 | | 0.761 | | | | | |
| TVAMT2 | | 0.585 | | | | | |
| TVAMT3 | | 0.763 | | | | | |
| APPPROG1 | | | 0.805 | | | | |
| APPPROG2 | | | 0.787 | | | | |
| APPPROG3 | | | 0.539 | | | | |
| APPPROG4 | | | 0.755 | | | | |
| APPPROG5 | | | 0.715 | | | | |
| APPPROG6 | | | 0.744 | | | | |
| APPPROG7 | | | 0.689 | | | | |
| SLPROG1 | | | | 0.807 | | | |
| SLPROG2 | | | | 0.806 | | | |
| SLPROG3 | | | | 0.797 | | | |
| APPAD1 | | | | | 0.829 | | |
| APPAD2 | | | | | 0.782 | | |
| APPAD3 | | | | | 0.741 | | |
| APPAD4 | | | | | 0.823 | | |
| APPAD5 | | | | | 0.761 | | |
| APPAD6 | | | | | 0.750 | | |
| APPAD7 | | | | | 0.771 | | |
| APPAD8 | | | | | 0.766 | | |
| APPAD9 | | | | | 0.579 | | |
| SLAD1 | | | | | | 0.864 | |
| SLAD2 | | | | | | 0.834 | |
| SLAD3 | | | | | | 0.762 | |
| SLAD4 | | | | | | 0.394 | |
| RELIG1 | | | | | | | 0.614 |
| RELIG2 | | | | | | | 0.505 |
| RELIG3 | | | | | | | 0.681 |
| *Reliability* | 0.702 | 0.721 | 0.878 | 0.725 | 0.919 | 0.709 | 0.578 |

Table 2. Means and Standard Deviations of Variables.

| Group[a] | Mean (SD) | | | | | | | | | |
|---|---|---|---|---|---|---|---|---|---|---|
| | RD Total[b] | Success[c] | Happiness[d] | Centrality[e] | TVAmt[f] | AppProg[g] | SLProg[h] | AppAd[i] | SLAd[j] | Religiosity[k] |
| Parents | 24.1 (5.3) | 6.9 (2.1) | 10.2 (3.2) | 7.3 (1.7) | 2.0 (1.3) | 1.9 (1.0) | 3.3 (0.81) | 1.8 (1.0) | 3.2 (0.74) | 0.17 (0.74) |
| Sons | 27.5 (5.2) | 7.4 (2.4) | 11.6 (2.8) | 8.5 (2.2) | 2.8 (1.6) | 2.6 (1.0) | 3.3 (0.86) | 2.3 (1.1) | 3.3 (0.69) | −0.14 (0.83) |
| Total | 26.0 (5.5) | 7.2 (2.3) | 11.0 (3.0) | 7.9 (2.1) | 2.4 (1.5) | 2.3 (1.1) | 3.3 (0.84) | 2.1 (1.1) | 3.2 (0.71) | 0 (0.80) |

[a]Mothers and fathers not significantly different from each other in all variables.
[b]Sum of ten items on a 5-point scale.
[c]Sum of three items on a 5-point scale.
[d]Sum of four items on a 5-point scale.
[e]Sum of three items on a 5-point scale.
[f]Average of three questions measured in hours per day.
[g]Average of seven items on a 7-point scale.
[h]Average of three items on a 5-point scale.
[i]Average of nine items on a 7-point scale.
[j]Average of four items on a 5-point scale.
[k]Factor score constructed from three questions.

The correlation coefficients for all of the constructs for each of the study segments are shown in Table 3. There are no correlations with an absolute value greater than 0.8. In addition, there were no variance inflation factors greater than 3. Therefore, there is not an issue with multicollinearity. The constructs of television programs and television ads did have a correlation greater than 0.7; however, this did not lead to a variance inflation factor greater than 3.

In examining the portion of the correlation matrix containing the correlations between the independent variables and the dependent variables, different patterns are evident for the parents and the children. A significant negative correlation between religiosity and the materialism scales is evident in the sons, and entirely absent in the parents. In the sons, there are only two significant but weak positive correlations between the appearance comparison to television programs or ads and the materialism success subscale. For the parents, however, there is a consistent significant positive relationship between the appearance comparison to television programs or ads and all the materialism scales except centrality. In the standard of living comparison scales there are three weak negative correlations with the materialism subscales for the sons, while the parents have significant negative correlations with the standard of living variables and the total materialism scale, as well as the success and happiness subscales. Two other broad patterns to note are the complete lack of significant correlation between amount of television viewing with any of the materialism scales, and the lack of correlation between the centrality subscale and any of the hypothesized independent variables.

## Regression Results

Multiple regression with backward selection of variables was employed to select constructs that were significant in predicting materialism. Multiple regression enabled us to test the hypotheses concerning all the explanatory variables, while taking the presence of the other explanatory variables into account. The assumption of homoscedasticity was assessed using residual plots and normality was assessed using the Kolmogorov–Smirnov test with the Lilliefors correction. No violations of normality or homoscedasticity were found. The results of the final models are presented in Table 4.

The amount of television watched was not significant in any of the models for either parents or children. Responses by both parents and their sons reveal a significant relationship between their use of television programming

*Table 3.* Correlations and Cronbach Alpha Reliabilities (in Square Brackets).

|  | RD Total | Success | Happ. | Cent. | TVAmt | AppProg | SLProg | AppAd | SLAd | Relig. |
|---|---|---|---|---|---|---|---|---|---|---|
| **RD Total** | | | | | | | | | | |
| Parents | [0.71] | | | | | | | | | |
| Sons | [0.65] | | | | | | | | | |
| **Success** | | | | | | | | | | |
| Parents | 0.73** | [0.37] | | | | | | | | |
| Sons | 0.71** | [0.50] | | | | | | | | |
| **Happiness** | | | | | | | | | | |
| Parents | 0.83** | 0.40** | [0.77] | | | | | | | |
| Sons | 0.79** | 0.38** | [0.59] | | | | | | | |
| **Centrality** | | | | | | | | | | |
| Parents | 0.59** | 0.29** | 0.21* | [0.38] | | | | | | |
| Sons | 0.59** | 0.13 | 0.19* | [0.55] | | | | | | |
| **TVAmt** | | | | | | | | | | |
| Parents | 0.11 | 0.09 | 0.13 | −0.01 | [0.68] | | | | | |
| Sons | 0.01 | 0.10 | −0.02 | −0.05 | [0.70] | | | | | |
| **AppProg** | | | | | | | | | | |
| Parents | 0.30** | 0.30** | 0.23* | 0.09 | 0.04 | [0.90] | | | | |
| Sons | 0.08 | 0.18* | 0.08 | −0.11 | 0.09 | [0.84] | | | | |
| **SLProg** | | | | | | | | | | |
| Parents | −0.26** | −0.18 | −0.23* | −0.12 | −0.05 | −0.27** | [0.67] | | | |
| Sons | −0.14 | −0.17* | −0.18* | 0.09 | −0.06 | −0.28** | [0.77] | | | |
| **AppAd** | | | | | | | | | | |
| Parents | 0.34** | 0.28** | 0.27** | 0.17 | 0.08 | 0.79** | −0.25** | [0.90] | | |
| Sons | 0.09 | 0.20* | 0.08 | −0.10 | 0.11 | 0.79** | −0.23** | [0.91] | | |
| **SLAd** | | | | | | | | | | |
| Parents | −0.30** | −0.20* | −0.33** | −0.03 | −0.10 | −0.26** | 0.71** | −0.25** | [0.68] | |
| Sons | −0.09 | −0.09 | −0.22** | 0.16* | 0.09 | −0.05 | 0.62** | −0.08 | [0.74] | |
| **Religiosity** | | | | | | | | | | |
| Parents | −0.07 | −0.02 | −0.13 | 0.00 | −0.11 | 0.03 | −0.13 | −0.03 | −0.11 | [0.52] |
| Sons | −0.33** | −0.25** | −0.36** | −0.03 | −0.11 | 0.05 | 0.04 | 0.00 | 0.13 | [0.60] |

*Significant at the .05 level
**Significant at the .01 level

content as a comparison and their materialistic tendencies, in particular with respect to the Richins and Dawson's success subscale. Television advertising content as a source of information on appearance was positive and significant for parents in predicting the total materialism score, and for predicting

**Table 4.** Results of Stepwise Regression with Standardized Regression Coefficients and Level of Significance.

|  | RD Total | Success | Happiness | Centrality |
|---|---|---|---|---|
| Parents ($N = 118$) | | | | |
| TVAmt | NS | NS | NS | NS |
| AppProg | NS | 0.260** | NS | NS |
| SLProg | NS | NS | NS | NS |
| AppAd | 0.266** | NS | 0.191* | NS |
| SLAd | −0.247* | −0.169 | −0.325** | NS |
| Religiosity | NS | NS | −0.157 | NS |
| Kids ($N = 123$) | | | | |
| TVAmt | NS | NS | NS | NS |
| AppProg | NS | 0.188* | NS | NS |
| SLProg | NS | NS | NS | NS |
| AppAd | NS | NS | NS | NS |
| SLAd | NS | NS | NS | NS |
| Religiosity | −0.313** | −0.257** | −0.349** | NS |

*Significant at the 0.05 level.
**Significant at the 0.01 level.
No asterisks indicate significant at the 0.10 level.

the happiness subscale. Television advertising as a standard of living comparison was negative and significant in predicting the total materialism score, the success subscale and the happiness subscale. Advertising content, as measured in this study, did not appear to be significantly associated with the sons' materialism. Since the television programming and television advertising scales are strongly correlated, it was consistent that only one of these two scales was significant in the regression analysis.

Religiosity was significant in all models except for that predicting centrality, for the children. In every model, the relationship was negative as hypothesized. However, religiosity was not significant in any of the models for adults.

*Fisher's z Transformation Results*

No differences were found in the strength of the correlations between the amount of television watched and the materialism variables when comparing parents and sons. Therefore, H1b was not supported. No differences were found in the strength of the correlations between the level of comparison to programming variables and the materialism variables, as well as between the level of comparison to advertising variables and the materialism variables,

*Table 5.* Results of Fisher's $z$ Transformation Comparing Strength of Correlation between Parents and Sons.

|  | RD Total | Success | Happiness | Centrality |
|---|---|---|---|---|
| TVAmt | NS[a] | NS | NS | NS |
| AppProg | NS | NS | NS | NS |
| SLProg | NS | NS | NS | NS |
| AppAd | NS | NS | NS | NS |
| SLAd | NS | NS | NS | NS |
| Religiosity | $P<0.05$ | $P<0.05$ | $P<0.05$ | NS |

[a]NS = not significant.

when comparing parents and sons; H2b and 3b were, therefore, not supported. However, there were significant differences between parents and sons in the strength of the correlations between the religiosity and the total materialism scale, the success materialism scale, and the happiness materialism scale. Therefore, H4b was supported (Table 5).

# DISCUSSION

From the above results, one can see that support for the hypothesized relationships was mixed. We will now relate the results to these hypotheses.

### Media: Quantity of Television Viewed

While the high school students in the study watched a significantly larger quantity of television than their parents, the effect of television quantity is not seen in the results of the related hypotheses tested (H1a and b). There was no relationship between the number of hours of television watched on materialism levels reported by either the parents or the sons. Thus, results regarding sheer quantity of television watching do not support the hypothesis that television is the powerful socialization agent suggested by past research, in particular cultivation theory.

### Media: Television Programming and Advertising Content

On the other hand, the results of the additional exploration of the role played by television programming and advertising content does provide significant evidence of the impact of media as a socialization force (H2 and H3 are supported). The strongest relationships between the measures of television programming and advertising content impact and the dependent materialism measures are found in the parent sample. In addition, the coefficients for the appearance comparison variables are positive, while the coefficients for the standard of living comparison variables are negative. Keeping in mind that the respondents in this sample self-report their income as above average, one would not expect to see a positive link between socioeconomic status and materialism. They already have what they see on television programs and advertising in terms of the goods that reflect a higher standard of living. These images, then, would not lead them to be motivated to want or value possessions more.

*Parents*
The results reported above reveal that the adults in the study watch less television on average than their sons. In addition, they report less reliance on television programming and advertising content as a source of information about how they should look and dress, as well as desired lifestyle (standard of living) than their sons. Finally, the parents appear to be less materialistic than their sons based on their responses to the materialism questions. However, what television they do watch appears to be significantly related to their development of consumer attitudes, specifically their adoption of materialistic tendencies. In particular, the regression results indicate a significant positive relationship between their use of television advertising content related to appearance and their score on the overall Richins–Dawson materialism scale. However, the relationship between the standard of living comparison with television advertising content is significant and negative. In terms of the subscales, the aspects of materialism related to the happiness dimension of the Richins and Dawson measure are particularly strong. Their use of the images they see in television advertising is such that it produces a positive outcome, happiness. This may be explained by the fact that the parents who completed this survey were from a higher than average income level (based both on self-reports and information from a school administrator). Hence, they may view themselves in a relatively favorable light when relying on advertising content as a source of information and comparison regarding their appearance. They may already have much acquired the "look" and lifestyle offered by products being advertised; the things they have acquired, inspired by the "buy" messages in television advertising, have brought the happiness material possessions may bring (Richins and Dawson's acquisition-based happiness).

Similarly, the standard of living comparison to television advertising is negatively associated with materialism. This may be a result of their already high standard of living, in that they perceive themselves as having a high standard of living relative to the advertising content. The higher they perceive their standard of living relative to television ads, the lower they report their materialism to be.

While television programming content does not appear to be significantly related to the overall materialism measure, it is associated with the success dimension of materialism. This relationship is limited, however, to content about appearance and not about standard of living. In comparing themselves with many of the characters portrayed in programs they watch, they view themselves as having the "look" that implies success, the success that comes from being able to buy the right clothes and personal care products (Richins and Dawson's possession-defined success).

These results, in total, suggest that this older generation *is* being socialized by the media, in this case, television. They are learning to be consumers from both television advertising and programming, with advertising apparently being the stronger educator.

*Sons*
Though the high school students in the study watch significantly more television and perceive that television has more impact on them in terms of providing information and bases for comparison than their parents (as documented in the construct means for television programming and advertising content), the association of programming and advertising with overall materialism is smaller than that for the parents. Just like their parents, there is a significant relationship between television programming and the success materialism subscale, indicating that at least some aspect of the sons' materialism is related to the impact of the television content, specifically, the relationship between how successful one is (in terms of materialistic measures) and how one looks and dresses. This result, along with those described above, adds further support to the idea that television programming can affect attitudes towards consumption, for example, materialism, just as much (or even more, as in this case) than television advertising content that has as its explicit purpose the forming of consumer attitudes and promotion of purchasing behavior. To overlook the important role played by the programming itself, focusing only on advertising as have most past studies, is to miss a key source of socialization influence. In fact, the advertising and programming constructs are strongly correlated, thus both are related to materialism.

None of the other measures of television programming and advertising content, appearance or standard of living based, were linked to overall materialism or the other subscales for the student sample. This lack of a relationship between the two may be explained by the skepticism that many young people in this generation have regarding advertising, and media in general. They are suspicious of many of the traditional promotional avenues and require different strategies as a target market. It does appear that they are more receptive to materialism's possession-defined messages related to the relationship between appearance and success that come to them via television programming, where the "sell" message is not as strong or direct as with advertising. Through programming then, like their parents, these young people are learning how to think as consumers and to see the benefits that material possessions may bring.

### *Institutions: Church in Terms of Role of Personal Faith*

The hypothesized relationship between faith and materialism, H4, is partially supported by the data, especially in the sons' sample. Given the parents' age and the fact that television is a relatively new socializing influence in their lives, with the institution of church being a significant socialization force since their childhood, one might anticipate that their religiosity would represent a relatively stronger force. However, though the parents report a higher level of personal faith and connection with their church, that church connection does not appear to have the strong relationship to materialism levels that television programming and advertising content have, thus not supporting H4a.

The negative relationship between personal faith and materialism is more strongly evident among sons than their parents, in spite of parent's greater self-perceived importance of personal faith. As with the role of media, we see that subjective perceptions of general importance may not provide a clear assessment of the influence of a factor within a given domain. Even though faith has a lower *mean* level of self-perceived influence among the younger generation, differences in faith among youth are more important for materialism than they are for adults. This may reflect the fact that the *variation* in importance of faith is greater among sons than parents. Some members of the younger generation rate church and religiosity as highly as the older generation, but there are more members of the younger generation who assign it a low level of importance. In other words, religion more strongly differentiates among the students than it does among their more traditional parents. At any rate, it appears to be more strongly associated with their materialistic tendencies than it does for their parents, with that relationship being a very significant negative one. Those students for whom church is very important report very negative responses with regard to materialism. It is not central to their lives, not the focus of their happiness, nor is it the way they define success. Important to note here is that these students are attending a Catholic high school. For some, this may be producing a very strong short-term tie to the Church and its teachings. Given this, it is possible that these students will come to more closely resemble their parents as they graduate from high school, age, and mature. They may continue to rate the church as important, perhaps even more important than they currently rate religiosity (mirroring their parents' higher level of importance), while it simultaneously loses its influence over other aspects of life, such as materialistic aspirations.

Given this we would suggest that their perceived level of materialism will not decline, which is relatively high if one looks at the materialism self-reports means. They have been socialized as consumers and will still continue to value material things. The counterinfluence that the church seems to play in their lives as students may lose its power with time. The self-perceived levels of importance of religiosity and materialism reported by their parents provide evidence supporting this.

Many of the results of this research suggest the importance of taking into account Moschis' (2007) life course perspective when studying consumer behavior. Different cohorts (here the parents and the sons) would have been exposed to different socialization agents, as determined by the sociocultural and historical context and events of their early years. This is important to consider when looking at differences between age segments. One of the central aspects of the life course perspective is the personal changes one makes due to psychological or social events and changes that one may go through during a lifetime (Clausen, 1986). In the present study, perhaps the adult respondents have developed a more ritualistic perspective on their faith. They perceive themselves to be faithful, but that belief does not actively impact the way they view the world as does a relatively new socialization influence, that of television.

# IMPLICATIONS, LIMITATIONS, AND CONCLUSION

## *Implications*

The present research seeks insights into the consumer socialization process of both children and adults. The role played by two socialization agents, media (television programming and advertising) and church, has been explored in terms of how each is related to an important facet of consumer attitudes, level of materialism. The more traditional socialization agent of church or religiosity, as measured in this study, appears to be less important to younger consumers than to their parents; but it has a more significant relationship with materialism for the students than their parents. For parents in the study, religiosity, though more important to them than to their sons, seems to be less effective as a socialization agent than the media in the context of television programming and advertising content.

The power of media as an agent is seen not only via television advertising and how it influences consumers' perspectives on their appearance and standard of living. That power is also realized through television programming, the impact of which has been largely overlooked in previous research. As one considers how consumers learn to be consumers, both from a purely theoretical standpoint as well as from a strategic marketing perspective, one must take into account both avenues for information transmission. In addition, one should identify the different strategies required for different target markets based on age-based cohorts. The present study illustrates the difference in efficacy of television advertising between the adults and the children, representing two different generations with different attitudes towards advertising in general.

An important final point in this discussion has to do with the averages of the perceived importance of both advertising and programming reported by both the parents and their sons. When viewed in isolation, they are very low, considering that the constructs were measured using a 5-point scale; the parents are below 2 on average and the sons are about a 2.5. Compared with related research in the United States, former eastern block European countries, as well as Mexico, the mean importance levels assigned by the entire sample of the present study are much lower for both types of television content. This lower importance level may provide further evidence that both generations are still learning to be consumers and that the impact that television is having on that process is just beginning to have an effect.

*Limitations*

While this study represents a further extension of previous work on consumer socialization, there are limitations to this research. Certainly, other samples in other developing countries, as well as other socioeconomic levels within Peru, should be included in future research to determine the extent to which this study's findings are generalizable in other contexts.

In addition, other aspects of consumer skills/attitudes besides materialism should be examined in future studies, as well as other socialization agents. One important improvement in future studies which could enhance research results would be to be certain that parent and child survey responses are paired, as well as to include daughters as well as sons. While there were no differences between mothers and fathers in the current study, there may be gender effects at the younger ages. In this way, one can explore not only the impact of external institutional socialization agents, but also the relative influence of interpersonal, intergenerational interactions in developing consumer skills, as well as gender effects. This would include not only parent–child transmission of knowledge, but also child–parent interaction.

Using alternative measures for the central constructs should also be an important consideration in future research in this area. Improving upon the scale reliabilities of the measures used here is necessary to improve upon the generalizability of the research, especially those used to measure religiosity and materialism. Past research, especially in the global realm, has often been challenged by problems with existing measures; future replications of the present research will incorporate measures that are currently under development and attempt to better capture cultural values like religiosity and materialism.

*Conclusion*

Consumers of all ages are developing consumer skills and undergoing continual socialization. The institutions that are influencing this socialization are evolving over time. Certainly churches as an institution and the religiosity that they foster have been a central socialization agent for many centuries. In addition, a relatively new institution affecting the socialization process, media, is also playing ever larger roles in that process as it becomes as deeply entrenched in the global culture. Studying the relative importance of these socialization agents in the context of developing countries allows us to understand the changes that are taking place within these cultures and their core cultural values.

# ACKNOWLEDGMENTS

The authors thank Loyola College in Maryland for their support of the original data collection for this research project. In addition, Dr. Speck would like to dedicate this chapter to her father, Clifford L. Smith, a life-long

Wyoming rancher, who through their ongoing discussions about the project, inspired her to continue to pursue an understanding of other cultures.

# REFERENCES

Anand, C., & Kumar, M. (1982). Developing a modernity attitude scale. *Indian Educational Review, 17*(3), 28–41.

Bandura, A. (1969). *Principles of behavior modification*. New York: Holt, Rinehart, and Winston.

Bandura, A. (1971). Modeling Influences on Children. Testimony to the Federal Trade Commission (November).

Belk, R. W. (1983). Worldly possessions: Issues and criticisms. In: R. P. Bagozzi & A. M. Tybout (Eds), *Advances in consumer research* (Vol. 10, pp. 514–519). Ann Arbor, MI: Association for Consumer Research.

Belk, R. W. (1984). Three scales to measure constructs related to materialism: Reliability, validity, and relationships to measures of happiness. In: T. Kinear (Ed.), *Advances in consumer research* (p. 291). Provo, UT: Association of Consumer Research.

Belk, R. W. (1985). Materialism: Trait aspects of living in the material world. *Journal of Consumer Research, 12*(December), 265–280.

Belk, R. W., & Pollay, R. (1986). Images of ourselves: The good life in twentieth century advertising. *Journal of Consumer Research, 11*(March), 887–897.

Churchill, G. A., & Moschis, G. P. (1979). Television and interpersonal influences on adolescent consumer learning. *Journal of Consumer Research, 6*, 23–35.

CIA – the World Fact Book (2009). Available at https://www.cia.gov/library/publications/the-world-factbook/geos/PE.html. Retrieved on July 13, 2009.

Clausen, J. A. (1986). *The life course: A sociological perspective*. Englewood Cliffs, NJ: Prentice Hall.

Dholakia, R. R. (1984). Intergeneration differences in consumer behavior: Some evidence from a developing country. *Journal of Business Research, 12*, 19–34.

Duval, T. S., Duval, V. H., & Mulilis, J. P. (1992). Effects of self-focus, discrepancy between self and standard, and outcome expectancy favorability on the tendency to match self to standard or to withdraw. *Journal of Personality and Social Psychology, 62*, 340–348.

Elgin, D., & Mitchell, A. (1977). Voluntary simplicity. *Co-Evolution Quarterly, 14*(Summer), 4–19.

Flouri, E. (1999). An integrated model of consumer materialism: Can economic socialization and maternal values predict materialistic attitudes in adolescents? *Journal of Socio-Economics, 28*, 707–724.

Ger, G., & Belk, R. W. (1996). Cross-cultural differences in materialism. *Journal of Economic Psychology, 17*(1), 55–77.

Gerbner, G., Gross, L., Morgan, M., & Signorielli, N. (1980). Aging with television: Images on television drama and conceptions of social reality. *Journal of Communication, 30*(Winter), 37–47.

Goethals, G. R. (1986). Social comparison theory: Psychology from the lost and found. *Personality and Social Psychology Bulletin, 12*(September), 261–278.

Goodwin, P. (2002). *Global studies: Latin America, Peru* (10th ed). Storrs, CT: University of Connecticut.

Hadaway, C. K., & Roof, W. C. (1978). Religious commitment and the quality of life in American Society. *Review of Religious Research, 19*(3), 295–307.

Hirschman, E. (1983). Religious affiliation and consumption processes. *Research in marketing* (pp. 131–170). Greenwich, CT: JAI Press.

Kasser, T., & Ryan, R. M. (2001). *Be careful what you wish for: Optimal functioning and the relative attainment of intrinsic and extrinsic goals. Life goals and well-being: Towards a positive psychology of human striving* (pp. 116–131). Goettingen, Germany: Hogrefe & Huber.

Mitchell, P., & Al-Mossawi, M. (1999). Religious commitment related to message contentiousness. *International Journal of Advertising, 18*, 427–443.

Moschis, G. P. (1987). *Consumer socialization: A life-cycle perspective.* Lexington, MA: Lexington Books.

Moschis, G. P. (2007). Life course perspectives on consumer behavior. *Journal of the Academy of Marketing Science, 35*, 295–307.

Moschis, G. P., & Smith, R. B. (1985). Consumer socialization: Origins, trends and directions for future research. In: C. Tiong Tan & J. Sheth (Eds), *Historical perspective in consumer research: National and international perspectives* (pp. 275–281). Singapore: Association for Consumer Research.

Navia, P., & Zweifel, T.D. (2006). I Want MY MTV: Media Freedom of Information and Democracy. Midwest Political Science Association, Chicago, IL, April 20.

Nunnally, T. (1978). *Psychometric theory* (2nd ed.). New York: McGraw-Hill.

O'Guinn, T. C., & Shrum, L. J. (1997). The role of television in the construction of consumer reality. *Journal of Consumer Research, 23*, 278–294.

PASW, T. (2009). *Rel. 18.0.0.* Chicago: SPSS Inc.

Pollay, R. W. (1986). The distorted mirror: Reflections on the unintended consequences of advertising. *Journal of Marketing, 50*(2), 18–36.

Richins, M. (1987). Media, materialism, and human happiness. *Advances in Consumer Research, 14*, 352–357.

Richins, M. (1991). Social comparison and the idealized images of advertising. *Journal of Consumer Research, 18*(June), 71–83.

Richins, M., & Dawson, S. (1992). A consumer values orientation for materialism and its measurement: Scale development and validation. *Journal of Consumer Research, 19*(December), 303–316.

Sirgy, M. J., Lee, D.-J., Kosenko, R., Meadow, H. L., Rahtz, D., Cicic, M., Jin, G. X., Yarsuvat, D., Blenkhorn, D. L., & Wright, N. (1998). Does quantity of television viewing play a role in the perception of quality of life. *Journal of Advertising, 17*, 125–142.

Sood, J., & Nasu, Y. (1995). Religiosity and nationality: An exploratory study of their effect on consumer behavior in Japan and the United States. *Journal of Business Research, 34*, 1–9.

Speck, S. K. S., & Roy, A. (2008). The interrelationship between television viewing, values, and perceived well-being: A global perspective. *The Journal of International Business Studies, 39*(7), 1–23.

Vatikiotis, M. (1996). Material God. *Far East Economic Review, 159*(29), 62–63.

Venkatesh, A., & Swamy, S. (1994). India as an emerging consumer society: A critical perspective. In: *Consumption in marketizing economies* (pp. 193–223). Greenwich, CT: JAI Press.

Ward, S. (1974). Consumer socialization. *Journal of Consumer Research, 1,* 1–14.
Wells, W. D. (1997). *Narratives in consumer research.* Working paper no. 55455 School of Journalism and Mass Communication, University of Minnesota, Minneapolis.
Yoon, K. (1995). Comparison of beliefs about advertising, attitude toward advertising, and materialism held by African Americans and Caucasians. *Psychological Reports, 77,* 455–466.
Zar, J. H. (1984). *Biostatistical analysis* (2nd ed.). Englewood Cliffs, NJ: Prentice Hall.

## APPENDIX. CONSTRUCT MEASURES

*Quantity of TV Viewing [TVVIEW] (Adapted from Sirgy et al., 1998)*

How much time do you usually spend watching television every day?
How much time do you spend watching television yesterday?
How much time do you spend watching television per week?

*Content of TV Programming and Advertising:*
*[APPAD, APPPROG, SLAD, SLPROG]*

*Appearance [Look and Dress]: APAD (Adapted from Yoon (1995) and Richins (1991))*

When I see models in clothing ads on television, I think about how well or how badly I look compared to the models.

When I see television ads for personal care/cosmetic items, I think about how well or how badly I look compared to the models.

Television ads for clothing items make me feel dissatisfied with the way I look.

Television ads for personal care/cosmetics products make me feel dissatisfied with the way I look.

Television ads help me know which products will or will not reflect the sort of person I am.

I have wished I looked more like the models in personal care/cosmetics advertisements.

When buying clothes, I look at television ads to give me ideas about how I should look.

When buying personal care/cosmetics items, I look at television ads to give me ideas about how I should look.

Television ads tell me about fashions and about what to buy to impress others.

*Appearance [Look and Dress]: APPPROG (Adapted from Yoon (1995) and Richins (1991))*

When I see actors in television programs, I think about how well or how badly I dress compared to the actors.

When I see actors in television programs, I think about how well or how badly I look compared to the actors.

Television programs help me know which products will or will not reflect the sort of person I am.

I have wished I looked more like the actors in television programs.

When buying clothes, I look at television programs to give me ideas about how I should look.

When buying personal care/cosmetics items, I look at television programs to give me ideas about how I should look.

Television programs tell me about fashions and about what to buy to impress others.

*Perceived Relative Socioeconomic Status [SLPROG, SLAD]
(Adapted from Sirgy et al., 1998)*

SLPROG (reversed) the average family we see in most television programs has a higher standard of living than my own family. (R)

SLPROG I consider my family to be lower class compared to the typical family they show on television programs. (R)

SLPROG (reversed) I believe that my family's standard of living is below that of the typical family shown in television programs. (R)

SLAD I am better off financially than most people shown on television commercials.

SLAD The average family we see in most television ads has a higher standard of living than my own family. (R)

SLAD I consider my family to be lower class compared to the typical family they show on television ads. (R)

SLAD I believe that my family's standard of living is below that of the typical family shown in television ads. (R)

*Religiosity [RELIG] (Adapted from Hadaway & Roof, 1978)*

Rate the importance of personal faith to you. (1 = Not at all important; 5 = Extremely important)

How frequently do you attend religious services? (1 = Less than once a month; 5 = More than once a week) (O)

How deeply attached are you to your place of worship?

*Materialism [MATER] (Adapted from Richins & Dawson, 1992)*

*Success [MASUC]*

I admire people who own expensive homes, cars, and clothes.

Some of the more important achievements in my life include acquiring material possessions.

I don't place much emphasis on the amount of material objects people own as a sign of success. (R)

I don't pay much attention to the material objects other people own. (R) (O)

*Centrality [MACENT]*

I usually buy only the things that I need. (R)

I try to keep my life simple, as far as my possessions are concerned. (R)

The things I own aren't all that important to me. (R)

I enjoy spending money on things that aren't practical. (O)

*Pursuit of Happiness [MAHAPP]*

I have all the things I really need to enjoy life. (R)

My life would be better if I owned certain things that I don't have.

I'd be happier if I could afford to buy more things.

# MOTIVATION FOR LUXURY CONSUMPTION: EVIDENCE FROM A METROPOLITAN CITY IN CHINA

Ying Wang, Shaojing Sun and Yiping Song

## ABSTRACT

Purpose – *The purpose of this study was to explore Chinese consumers' motivations for purchasing luxury products, and to unravel the interrelationships among individual differences, motives, and luxury consumption.*

Methodology – *Data were collected from general consumers living in a large cosmopolitan city of China. A total of 473 questionnaires provided usable data and were analyzed using SPSS.*

Findings – *Eight motives were identified: self-actualization, product quality, social comparison, others' influence, investment for future, gifting, special occasions, and emotional purchasing. Results showed that personal income, age, the motives of gifting, others' influence, and product quality were significant predictors of luxury spending. Younger consumers, who did not typically make plans before buying, were more likely to buy luxury products out of emotion and less likely to do so for self-actualization or future investment.*

Research limitations – *The conceptualization and operationalization of some concepts used in this study (e.g., luxury brands, luxury consumption, and motives) may not be robust. Social desirability bias could comprise the validity of some research findings.*

Originality – *Despite a large body of research on luxury consumption, to date, most studies have been conducted in Western developed countries. Past research has showed that the symbolic and social values related to luxury consumption are deeply embedded in culture. As such, it is meaningful to investigate luxury consumption in China, whose culture is vastly different from the West.*

## INTRODUCTION

Luxury consumption has long been an important component of the global economy. Apart from functional utilities, luxury products also provide esteem and prestige to the owners (Arghavan & Zaichkowsky, 2000). In this regard, the psychological benefits that luxury consumption affords may outweigh the functional ones (Vigneron & Johnson, 2004). As Nueno and Quelch (1998) stated, luxury brands are those "whose ratio of functional utility to price is low while the ratio of intangible and situational utility to price is high" (p. 61).

Despite a large body of research on luxury consumption, to date, most studies have been conducted in Western developed countries (e.g., Dubois & Duquesne, 1992; Dubois & Laurent, 1994; Vigneron & Johnson, 2004). However, with its large population and surging consumer buying power, China is becoming an attractive market for brand name luxury products (Wong & Ahuvia, 1998). According to Goldman Sachs (as cited in KPMG, 2006), excluding private jets and luxury yachts, the luxury product market in China reached $6 billion in 2004, accounting for 12% of the global market. Between 2006 and 2010, the Chinese luxury product market is predicted to enjoy an annual growth rate of 25%. At this pace, China would surpass Japan to become the world's largest luxury product market.

The symbolic and social values related to luxury consumption are deeply embedded in culture. For instance, prior research has indicated that people in collectivistic cultures may have different motivations for luxury consumption than those in individualistic societies (Dubois, Czellar, & Laurent, 2005; Tidwell & Dubois, 1994; Wong & Ahuvia, 1998). Specifically, Mooij (2005) surveyed expenditures on expensive luxury products by high income groups in Europe and found that results varied enormously across cultures. As such, it is meaningful to investigate luxury consumption in China, whose culture is vastly different from the West.

The present study seeks to achieve two goals: the first is to explore the underlying motivations of luxury consumption among Chinese consumers, and the second is to learn the relationships between individual factors (e.g., age, income, and self-construal), motivation, and luxury consumption in the context of Chinese culture.

The chapter is organized in the following manner: first, the current state of the Chinese luxury market is introduced, and relevant literature on individual factors, motivation, and luxury consumption is reviewed; second, sampling procedure and measurement instruments are described; third, data analysis and results are presented; fourth, significant findings are discussed, and research limitations, as well as future directions, are addressed.

## THEORETICAL RATIONALE AND LITERATURE REVIEW

### Chinese Luxury Market

The growth of luxury consumption is driven by a combination of social forces and business factors (Silverstein & Fiske, 2001). In the past, Chinese people often held deep-rooted stereotypes of luxury and viewed it against the backdrop of corruptions (Tse, Belk, & Zhou, 1989). However, as a result of China's phenomenal economic growth, the number of wealthy people is rising rapidly in China. The trend of globalization also stimulates the desire for a luxury lifestyle in China, and, thus, the affluent are willing to and capable of paying high prices for luxury brands that provide status and prestige. It is not uncommon to see the well-off Chinese shop overseas and eagerly seek out prestigious foreign brands such as Gucci, Louis Vuitton, Prada, among others (KPMG, 2006).

In recent years, luxury consumption has been penetrating different levels of societal communities. Even among those not having much cash in hand, luxury goods are no longer far beyond reach. Trendy views on consumption, such as "spend tomorrow's money" or "spend ahead of income," are gaining popularity in the younger generation (*Trendy Life*, 2006). As Miller (1991) pointed out, the average Chinese income is lower in contrast with developed countries. However, the status consumption is expanding exponentially in China. It is suggested that luxury-brand purchases tend to rise steeply after an average income reaches $2,500. That said, China could soon have as many as 100 million luxury consumers and take over Japan as the most lucrative luxury market in the world (*The Financial Times*, 2005).

The Chinese luxury market has demonstrated unique characteristics as it has evolved. First, young people between 20 and 40 years are the largest buyers of luxury products. In contrast, people aged between 40 and 70 years form the largest segment for luxuries in developed countries (*Trendy Life*, 2006). Such a difference in consumer makeup can be ascribed to the drastic social and economic changes occurring in China. In addition, recent years have witnessed a waning influence of traditional Chinese cultural values, such as modesty and frugality, in younger generations (Lu, 2008). Instead, living in a culture of modernization and globalization, young Chinese people are more susceptible to the impact of Western values and lifestyles. The younger generations, in general, are less cautious about spending money compared with their parents and grandparents (Li, 1998; Masaru, Yasue, & Wen, 1997).

Second, Chinese luxury consumption has manifested an item-driven pattern. Put succinctly, the luxury consumption is concentrated in personal accessories such as cosmetics, perfume, and watches. Comparatively, luxury consumers in developed countries are more likely to seek experiences such as family vacations and time-saving services (KPMG, 2006). Hence, the current study focuses on small luxury items such as apparel and clothing.

In the past, little research has inspected Chinese luxury consumption in depth, particularly from a Chinese cultural perspective. Wong and Ahuvia (1998) explored Singaporean women's consumption of brand name luxury goods in comparison with that of the West. The researchers suggested that Asians' luxury consumption was mainly influenced by factors including Confucian collectivism, individual or group needs, values of being modest and thrifty, among others. Similarly, as a typical collectivistic culture and heavily influenced by Confucianism, Chinese consumers are expected to focus more on external social needs than internal individual needs. As Yang (1981) contended, Chinese are concerned with their images among in-group members. And, thus, Chinese seek the inclusion of a certain social group through owning luxury brands, and hence differentiate themselves from other camps. Wong and Ahuvia (1998) also pointed out that Asians are more likely to place importance on the symbolic value as opposed to the hedonic value of luxuries, at least under conditions of consuming in public. Put differently, Chinese consumers pay close attention to the brand and country of origin of luxury goods, and tend to have preferences for well-known foreign luxury brands with familiar logos.

Counterfeit products are a great concern in the luxury product market. Although the emerging affluent Chinese consumers seek and embrace authentic luxury products, Chinese consumers in general are price-conscious as well. Luxury product sales have been eroded somewhat by the sale of knockoff counterfeit products (KPMG, 2006). However, it is also argued that availability of counterfeit products may help increase the brand awareness of luxury names and thereby make the authentic products more sought after (Nia & Zaichkowsky, 2000).

## A Model of Luxury Consumption in China

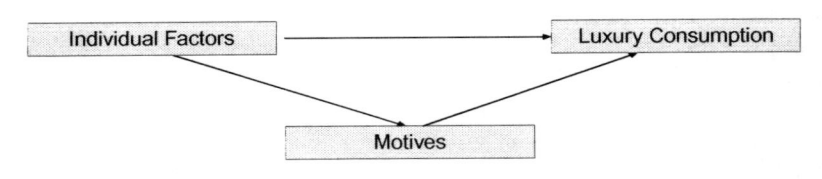

Consumer behavior is greatly influenced and molded by cultural, social, personal, and psychological factors. A review of past research testifies to the link between individual factors, motivation, and consumer behavior (Dubois & Duquesne, 1992; Mooij, 2005; Wong & Ahuvia, 1998). The consumer behavior process begins with consumer's needs and wants. Culture is a strong influencing factor that shapes much of a person's wants and behavior. As discussed earlier, culture plays an important role in people's luxury consumption because of the unique symbolic meaning often associated with luxury brands. As Wong and Ahuvia (1998) stated, "just because many of the products are the same in Asian and Western societies does not mean that consumers buy them for the same reasons" (p. 424).

Based upon prior research, a model of luxury consumption is presented below. Individual factors (a) are believed to influence motives (b) for buying luxury brands, which in turn have an impact on luxury consumption (c). Individual factors also directly impact motives and luxury consumption. The Chinese cultural context exerts a broad and deep influence on all three categories of variables. The following diagram depicts the relationship between these three groups of variables:

A Model of Luxury Consumption in China

Chinese Cultural Context

## Motives for Luxury Consumption

Motivation is an important variable that links individual factors and purchasing behavior. Understanding consumers' motivation for buying luxury goods and services is important to marketers (Danziger, 2002). Specifically, such knowledge may help marketers segment the market, predict consumer behavior, and communicate with the target audience effectively. Danziger (2002) identified a range of purchase motives for buying luxury products including but not limited to improving the quality of life, pleasure, relaxation, entertainment, and emotional satisfaction. Vigneron and Johnson (2004) categorized two types of motivation orientations for luxury consumption: social orientation and personal orientation. The former refers to purchasing luxuries for enhancing self-image in others' eyes (e.g., seeking social status and social comparison, obtaining respect, and differentiating self from others). The latter refers to purchasing luxury goods for one's own benefit or internal needs (e.g., self-indulgence, self-reward, and self-expression).

Past research has indicated that consumers' motives for luxury consumption vary across cultures. Wong and Ahuvia (1998), for example, argued that collectivistic and individualistic self-concepts, to a great extent, accounted for the difference in luxury consumption motivation across Asia and Western societies. Specifically, Asian consumers are more likely to purchase luxury brands for gifting, conforming to social pressure, and status differentiation reasons than westerners.

Previous studies (e.g., Zhou & Belk, 2004; Zhou & Nakamoto, 2000) have suggested that "face," an important collectivistic value, may provide an explanation for Asian consumers' strong appetites for luxuries despite their relatively low income. Face has been defined as "the positive social value a person effectively claims for himself by the line others assume he has taken during a particular contact" (Goffman, 1967, p. 5). Although "face" is a universal concept, its role in Chinese culture is more salient and profound (Ho, 1976). In a recent survey, 87% of Chinese respondents agreed that saving face was an integral part of their lives (*China Youth Daily* cited in Shan, 2005). Hu (1944) classified face into two types, "Lian" and "Mianzi." The former "represents the confidence of society in the integrity of ego's moral character, loss of which makes it impossible for him to function properly within the community," while the latter "stands for the kind of prestige that is emphasized, a reputation achieved through getting on in life, through success and ostentation" (p. 54). Face in China also connotes a group orientation. For example, family face, which refers to family honor or making sure that the family looks good, is an important aspect of Chinese culture (Braxton, 1999). When an individual, for example, becomes successful and wealthy, he/she gains face for not just himself/herself but for the whole family.

The concept of Mianzi is particularly meaningful in the study of Chinese luxury consumption because Mianzi may be obtained either through personal qualities or nonpersonal characteristics such as wealth, social connections, and authority (Ho, 1976). The symbolic values of status and prestige are quite consistent with the consumption of luxury products and may satisfy Chinese consumers' desire to gain Mianzi. In accordance with the national survey, Zhou and Belk (2004) argued that Asian consumers buy luxury products primarily to enhance and maintain their "face." Similarly, Li and Su (2006) compared the influence of "face" on consumer luxury purchasing across the United States and China. The results showed that Chinese consumers were more likely to relate product brands and price to face than did their U.S. counterparts.

Gifting has been identified as another important motive for Chinese luxury product buying. Consuming expensive gifts reflect the social hierarchy as well as maintenance of the balance between group needs and individual needs. Ger and Belk (1996) suggested that it is especially important for Asians to purchase luxury goods for family members and "package" families with luxury brands to show off family wealth and status. Previous research also linked gifting to establishing *guanxi* in the Chinese society. *Guanxi*, conceptualized as interpersonal ties, is a dominant and ubiquitous aspect of Chinese daily life. As a typical collectivistic culture, Chinese society emphasizes harmonious interpersonal relationships. Exchanging gifts and favors plays an important role in maintaining and expanding *guanxi* (Bond, 1991, 1996; Bond & Lee, 1981; Gu, Hung, & Tse, 2008). As a result of an implicit reciprocity norm as well as the motivation of "saving face," receivers are obliged to return favors and thus an interlocking and mutually obligating *guanxi* is developed and maintained over time (Bond, 1991, 1996; Hwang, 1987). Together with "Mianzi," "guanxi" culture makes consumers especially favor luxury products, and purchase luxury brands even beyond their means. Chinese consumers tend to believe that the more expensive the gift is, the more recognition will be gained, the more "Mianzi" they will have and give, and the better relationship they will achieve. In the business world, luxury goods such as Rolex watches are viewed as perfect gifts to establish *guanxi* with other business people and with government officials in China (Ahlstrom, 2009).

A main goal of the current study is to explore Chinese consumers' motivation for luxury consumption. Therefore, the following questions are asked:

RQ1: What are the purchase motives of Chinese consumers for buying luxury products?

RQ2: How do motives relate to Chinese consumers' luxury product purchases?

## Individual Factors

To date, research on luxury consumption has investigated a range of individual demographic and psychographic factors, among which income, age cohort, self-construal, and decision-making style are identified as prominent variables (e.g., Mooij, 2005; Dubois & Duquesne, 1992; Hauck & Stanforth, 2006). Roughly speaking, luxury products are expensive and often conceived to be "trivial" products with little manifest functional edge over nonluxury products. As such, luxury product marketers tend to believe that customers come primarily from upper income classes. Dubois and Duquesne (1992), for example, examined the predictive power of income for luxury market, and found that income was the most powerful predictor of luxury acquisition.

Also, past research has revealed the interconnections between age cohort/generational differences and purchase motives for luxuries. Hauck and Stanforth (2006), for example, examined different motives and perceptions of luxury goods among cohorts in the United States. The study showed that the older cohorts were more likely to buy luxuries for decorating homes while younger ones were more likely to buy on impulse or as a self-gift. As mentioned earlier, a distinctive feature of the Chinese luxury market is that young people constitute the primary market for luxuries (Tu, 1992). Having grown up with China's economic reform and modernization since the late 1970s, young and urban consumers are referred to as Generation X (or Gen X) in China. Compared with older generations, Generation X consumers are mostly better-educated, financially well-off, and prone to Westernized values and spending habits (Dou, Wang, & Zhou, 2006). It would be interesting to see whether differences exist among different age cohorts in terms of luxury consumption among Chinese consumers.

Related to self-concepts, interdependent self-construal is an important factor pertaining to luxury consumption (Wong & Ahuvia, 1998). The independent construal of self, which is dominant in Western cultures, is rooted in the belief that distinct individuals are inherently autonomous and separate. The interdependent construal of self, which is evident in Asian cultures, emphasizes conformity to group needs and respect for others' suggestions. Such a construal difference across cultures could result in varying degrees of susceptibility to others, which further shape one's luxury consumption.

Luxury consumption entails a decision-making process, which speaks of one's decision-making styles, particularly in terms of how much planning is invested in shopping behavior (Cowart & Goldsmith, 2007;

Hafstrom, Chae, & Chung, 1992). For instance, research in the Western markets (e.g., Danziger, 2002) has demonstrated that luxury brand purchase is related to impulsive buying behavior without much planning because luxury items typically carry low functionality/utility value but high symbolic and emotional value. However, the decision-making process may be different in China given the different motives for purchasing luxury brands. Along an impulsive-analytical continuum, Lu (2008) classified Chinese luxury consumers into four groups: Luxury lovers, luxury intellectuals, luxury followers, and luxury laggards. The latter two segments tend to be more impulsive than the former two. It would be interesting to investigate the relationship between consumer planning and luxury consumption.

Based upon the four individual factors discussed above, we propose the following research questions:

RQ3: How do age, income, consumers' planning, and interdependent self-construal affect Chinese consumers' motivation for buying luxuries?

RQ4: How do age, income, consumers' planning, and interdependent self-construal affect Chinese consumers' luxury purchases?

# METHOD

## Procedure and Sampling

To examine the proposed research questions, a survey was developed in Chinese. Major instruments developed in English were translated into Chinese. Back-translation was conducted by bilingual third parties to improve the translation accuracy. Research participants were residents living in a large cosmopolitan city of China. The reason for sampling participants from this city is based on the level of economic development of this region, where more residents are likely to have contact with luxury products.

The questionnaires were administered by a professional business research center residing in China. The response rate was around 35%. Overall, 610 responses were collected and 473 of them were usable. To check nonresponse bias, responses of those who returned the first mailing of a questionnaire were compared to those who returned the second mailing. No statistically significant difference was identified on key variables between the two groups, and thus nonresponse bias is unlikely. Regarding the sample, 203 were male (42.9%) and 270 were female (57.1%). In terms of educational level, about 1.3% of the participants received only middle school education or below; 13.1% with high school education; 23.9% with college education but no degree; 50.6% with a Bachelor's degree; and 11% with graduate education or higher. Participants ranged in age from 17 to 62, with an average age of 31 years.

## Measurement

*Motivation for buying luxury products.* To measure individuals' motivation for buying luxury products, a 26-item scale was derived from previous studies (Danziger, 2002; Vigneron & Johnson, 2004; Wong & Ahuvia, 1998) and focus group discussions. Responses were measured on a 5-point Likert scale ranging from 1 (*strongly disagree*) to 5 (*strongly agree*).

Principal components analysis with varimax rotation was conducted to examine the underlying structure of those 26 items measuring motives for buying luxury. The rules of a minimum eigenvalue of 1.0 and at least two loadings (60/40 loadings) per factor were referenced for extracting factors. Together, 21 items and eight factors were retained and 61.18% of the total variance was explained. Descriptive statistics are presented in Table 1, and factor loadings are presented in Table 2.

Factor 1, *self-actualization* (eigenvalue = 4.76, Cronbach alpha = 0.76). This factor consists of three items and reflects individuals' motivation for buying luxury and realizing one's self-value. Items include "Luxuries are special and wearing them makes me feel different"; "I feel successful when buying luxuries"; "Using luxuries increases my self-confidence." High scores on this factor refer to a strong motivation for buying luxury because it confers a feeling of success.

Factor 2, *product quality* (eigenvalue = 2.42, Cronbach alpha = 0.66). This factor consists of three items and reflects one's perception that luxury products are of good quality. Items include "Luxuries are easy to use"; "Luxuries are detail-oriented and made of good materials"; "Luxuries are high quality and worth the money." High scores on this factor mean that one believes that luxury products are good and useful.

Factor 3, *social comparison* (eigenvalue = 2.17, Cronbach alpha = 0.80). The factor consists of three items and reveals one's motivation for comparing self with others. Items include "I want other people to know that I own expensive luxuries"; "I am satisfied when other people compliment on my luxuries"; "I want people to know the luxury brands I use." High factor scores refer to strong motivation to buy luxury due to social comparison reasons.

***Table 1.*** Descriptive Statistics of Motive Items.

| Item | | M | SD |
|---|---|---|---|
| 1 | I want other people to know that I own expensive luxuries | 2.58 | 1.06 |
| 2 | I am satisfied when other people compliment on my luxuries | 3.05 | 1.12 |
| 3 | I want people to know the luxury brands I use | 2.90 | 1.13 |
| 4 | When I use luxury products, I feel other people's impressions about me have changed | 2.81 | 1.12 |
| 5 | Using luxuries brings me better services | 3.72 | 1.04 |
| 6 | Buying and using luxuries is an exciting experience | 3.00 | 1.22 |
| 7 | I like the connotation of certain luxury brands | 3.94 | 0.93 |
| 8 | Luxuries are easy to use | 3.89 | 0.95 |
| 9 | Luxuries are detail-oriented and made of good materials | 4.35 | 0.69 |
| 10 | Luxuries are fashionable | 3.95 | 0.88 |
| 11 | Luxuries are high quality and worth the money | 3.66 | 1.07 |
| 12 | I often buy luxuries as gifts for others | 2.22 | 1.23 |
| 13 | I purchase many luxury products, but seldom use them myself | 2.16 | 1.14 |
| 14 | Luxuries are special and wearing them makes me feel different | 3.03 | 1.07 |
| 15 | I feel successful when buying luxuries | 3.08 | 1.15 |
| 16 | Using luxuries increases my self-confidence | 3.45 | 1.07 |
| 17 | I have to use luxuries because of my working environment | 2.61 | 1.11 |
| 18 | People around me use luxuries | 2.97 | 1.18 |
| 19 | I can't help buying luxuries when I see others do | 2.57 | 1.40 |
| 20 | I buy luxuries because my family and friends do | 2.95 | 1.19 |
| 21 | I often buy luxuries on impulse | 2.60 | 1.23 |
| 22 | When I am depressed, I buy luxuries to make me feel better | 2.55 | 1.24 |
| 23 | I buy luxuries for holidays | 3.50 | 1.10 |
| 24 | I buy luxuries for special occasions | 3.68 | 1.15 |
| 25 | I buy luxuries because I believe their values will increase in the future | 2.25 | 1.13 |
| 26 | Buying luxuries is a way of investment for me | 2.10 | 1.09 |

Factor 4, *others' influence* (eigenvalue = 1.74, Cronbach alpha = 0.64, China). This factor consists of four items and refers to the others' impact on one's buying behavior. Items include "I have to use luxuries because of my working environment"; "People around me use luxuries"; "I can't help buying luxuries when I see others do"; "I buy luxuries because my family and friends do." High scores indicate a strong motivation for buying luxury because of others' persuasion or influence.

Factor 5, *investment for future* (eigenvalue = 1.42, Cronbach alpha = 0.85). This factor consists of two items and reveals one's belief that buying luxury is a way of investment. Items include "I buy luxuries because I believe their values will increase in the future"; "Buying luxuries is

**Table 2.** Factor Loadings of Motive Items.

| Item | Factor 1 | Factor 2 | Factor 3 | Factor 4 | Factor 5 | Factor 6 | Factor 7 | Factor 8 |
|---|---|---|---|---|---|---|---|---|
| 14 | **0.746** | 0.140 | 0.098 | 0.053 | 0.082 | 0.014 | 0.005 | −0.002 |
| 15 | **0.778** | 0.083 | 0.100 | 0.146 | 0.163 | 0.062 | 0.078 | −0.036 |
| 16 | **0.768** | 0.141 | 0.140 | 0.117 | −0.008 | 0.014 | 0.126 | 0.167 |
| 8 | 0.067 | **0.774** | −0.073 | 0.044 | −0.106 | 0.096 | 0.059 | −0.019 |
| 9 | 0.015 | **0.734** | 0.017 | −0.020 | −0.062 | 0.028 | −0.032 | −0.046 |
| 11 | 0.161 | **0.695** | −0.066 | 0.102 | 0.103 | −0.077 | −0.080 | −0.014 |
| 1 | 0.139 | −0.080 | **0.807** | 0.092 | 0.046 | −0.023 | 0.086 | 0.058 |
| 2 | 0.177 | 0.053 | **0.809** | 0.002 | −0.022 | −0.032 | 0.005 | 0.139 |
| 3 | 0.179 | 0.028 | **0.793** | 0.093 | 0.069 | −0.031 | 0.007 | 0.042 |
| 17 | 0.186 | 0.057 | 0.061 | **0.708** | 0.093 | 0.093 | 0.133 | −0.028 |
| 18 | −0.008 | 0.148 | −0.019 | **0.784** | 0.011 | 0.033 | 0.081 | −0.001 |
| 19 | 0.197 | −0.054 | 0.059 | **0.548** | 0.034 | 0.019 | −0.138 | −0.294 |
| 20 | 0.124 | 0.032 | 0.210 | **0.570** | 0.040 | 0.009 | 0.127 | 0.300 |
| 25 | 0.197 | 0.012 | 0.049 | 0.058 | **0.882** | 0.107 | 0.027 | 0.005 |
| 26 | 0.123 | −0.041 | 0.035 | 0.086 | **0.878** | 0.186 | −0.019 | 0.005 |
| 12 | 0.038 | 0.032 | −0.065 | 0.087 | 0.112 | **0.870** | 0.077 | 0.052 |
| 13 | 0.076 | −0.077 | −0.030 | 0.048 | 0.170 | **0.850** | 0.039 | 0.035 |
| 23 | 0.017 | 0.053 | 0.077 | 0.199 | −0.008 | 0.024 | **0.804** | −0.039 |
| 24 | 0.128 | 0.008 | 0.002 | −0.003 | −0.026 | 0.127 | **0.828** | 0.064 |
| 21 | 0.084 | −0.179 | 0.116 | 0.237 | −0.008 | 0.114 | 0.031 | **0.710** |
| 22 | 0.034 | 0.066 | 0.035 | 0.057 | 0.007 | −0.011 | 0.031 | **0.799** |

a way of investment for me." High scores mean that one's strong motivation for buying luxury is for investment.

Factor 6, *gifting* (eigenvalue = 1.18, Cronbach alpha = 0.75). This factor consists of two items and reveals the motivation that one buys luxury products for others. Items include "I often buy luxuries as gifts for others"; "I purchase many luxury products, but seldom use them myself." High scores mean that there is a high likeliness of buying others luxury brands.

Factor 7, *buying for special occasions* (eigenvalue = 1.16, Cronbach alpha = 0.68). This factor consists of two items and reveals the motivation of buying luxury for special holidays or occasions. Items include "I buy luxuries for holidays"; "I buy luxuries for special occasions." High scores mean that one is strongly motivated to buy luxury products for special times.

Factor 8, *buying out of emotion* (eigenvalue = 1.07, Cronbach alpha = 0.54). This factor consists of two items and reveals one's buying luxury out of emotional reasons. Items include "I often buy luxuries on impulse"; "When I am depressed, I buy luxuries to make me feel better." High scores mean that one is very likely to buy luxury for irrational reasons.

*Consumer behavior.* Consumers' luxury consumption was measured by two items which are "during the past three years, on average, how many luxury products did you purchase each year?" and "during the past three years, how much money did you spend on luxuries?" A standard explanation of luxury was provided to all respondents by the research center during the survey administration.

*Individual Factors.* Respondents were asked to report demographic information such as age, gender, marriage status, education background, profession, and individual annual income. In addition, respondents' degree of planning was assessed by responses to the question "how detailed plan do you make before going shopping?" Response options ranged from 1 (never make plans) to 4 (always make detailed plans) on a Likert scale. Similarly, interdependent self-construal was measured by responses to the question "how much do you care others' view of you?" Response options ranged from 1 (not at all) to 4 (a lot) on a Likert scale.

# RESULTS

Multiple regressions were conducted to examine the relationship between motives and luxury purchases. Results indicated that motivation was a weak predictor of the number of luxury products that customers bought in the past 3 years. However, three motive factors were statistically significant in predicting the amount of money spent on luxury during the past three years ($R = 0.25$, $R^2 = 0.06$, $p < 0.001$). The three motives were gifting ($\beta = 0.17$, $p < 0.001$), buying because of others' impact ($\beta = 0.12$, $p < 0.05$), and product quality ($\beta = 0.10$, $p < 0.05$).

Canonical correlation was conducted to examine the relationship between age, income, planning, interdependent self-construal and the set of motive variables. Three canonical roots were retained, and the results are presented in Table 3. To interpret the substantive meaning of canonical variates, it is advisable to use the correlations rather than the standardized coefficients (Stevens, 2002).

For Root 1 ($R_c = 0.27$, $\lambda = 0.84$, $p < 0.001$), the antecedents set was dominated by age and planning, which were negatively related to each other.

*Table 3.* Results of Canonical Correlation Analysis.

|  | Root 1 | Root 2 | Root 3 |
|---|---|---|---|
|  | Correlation (standardized coefficient) |  |  |
| *Set 1: Individual Difference* |  |  |  |
| Age | −0.626 (−0.636) | −0.304 (−0.442) | −0.484 (−0.274) |
| Income | −0.161 (−0.123) | −0.194 (−0.170) | −0.743 (−0.609) |
| Planning | 0.755 (0.755) | −0.415 (−0.500) | −0.416 (−0.305) |
| Interdependent self-construal | 0.084 (0.136) | 0.711 (0.878) | −0.624 (−0.462) |
| *Set 2: Motives* |  |  |  |
| Self-actualization | −0.496 (−0.380) | −0.352 (−0.224) | 0.149 (−0.179) |
| Product quality | −0.348 (−0.162) | 0.113 (0.132) | −0.157 (−0.105) |
| Social comparison | 0.018 (0.123) | −0.490 (−0.339) | 0.716 (0.805) |
| Others' influence | −0.348 (−0.349) | −0.500 (−0.326) | −0.112 (−0.372) |
| Investment for future | −0.555 (−0.366) | −0.006 (0.259) | 0.380 (0.346) |
| Buying for others | −0.384 (−0.259) | −0.406 (−0.456) | 0.162 (0.103) |
| Buying for special time | −0.044 (0.096) | 0.363 (0.528) | 0.486 (0.505) |
| Buying out of emotion | 0.498 (0.669) | −0.556 (−0.363) | 0.057 (−0.032) |

*Note:* Root 1: $R_c = 0.27$, $R_c^2 = 0.07$, $\lambda = 0.84$, $F(32, 1488) = 2.28$, $p < 0.001$. Root 2: $R_c = 0.21$, $R_c^2 = 0.04$, $\lambda = 0.90$, $F(21, 1161) = 2.01$, $p < 0.01$. Root 3: $R_c = 0.20$, $R_c^2 = 0.04$, $\lambda = 0.94$, $F(12, 810) = 1.97$, $p < 0.05$.

The highest loadings for the motives set were self-actualization, investment for future, and buying out of emotion. Across the two sets, those younger, who did not like making plans before buying, tended to be more likely to buy luxury out of emotion and less likely to buy for reasons including self-actualization and future investment.

For Root 2 ($R_c = 0.21$, $\lambda = 0.90$, $p < 0.01$), interdependent self-construal had the highest loading on the antecedents set. Factors loading highly on the motive set were social comparison, others' influence, and emotional buying. Across the two sets, those who are not susceptible to others' influence were less likely to buy luxury for social comparison and emotional reasons.

For Root 3 ($R_c = 0.20$, $\lambda = 0.94$, $p < 0.05$), income and interdependent self-construal loaded highly on the antecedents set. The highest loadings on the motives set were social comparison and buying for special occasions. Across the two sets, those with low income were more likely to buy luxury for social comparison and special occasions than their counterparts were.

Multiple regressions were conducted to investigate the relationship between individual difference variables and spending on luxury, and the prediction equation was statistically significant ($R = 0.62$, $R^2 = 0.38$, $p < 0.001$). Personal income ($\beta = 0.60$, $p < 0.001$) was a strong predictor of luxury spending. Another statistically significant predictor was age ($\beta = 0.09$, $p<0.05$), which is relatively weak.

## DISCUSSION

In addition to the functional values, luxury brands carry different social values in different cultures. The specific contents of these social values are largely determined by culture. Dubois and Duquesne (1992), for example, proposed that culture, especially the aspects that relates to consumers' self-concept, should be considered an important variable of people's luxury consuming behavior.

The current study explored the motives of Chinese consumers' luxury purchases in order to detect the reasons behind Chinese luxury consumption. We identified eight motives including: self-actualization, product quality, social comparison, others' influence, emotional purchase, gifting, investment for future, and buying for special occasions. The results showed that Chinese consumers bought luxuries for both social and personal reasons, which is similar to Western consumers. However, the hedonic and self-indulgent motives that are often associated with luxury consumption in the Western market are not obvious among Chinese consumers. Instead, social comparison, gifting, and others' influence have emerged as important motives. In addition, gifting and others' influence are significant predictors of luxury consumption. These results are consistent with previous studies. For example, Wong and Ahuvia (1998) suggest that in East Asian societies, luxuries play a predominantly social-symbolic role, and their private meanings and hedonic value are downplayed.

Hofstede's cultural dimension framework may provide explanations for the results. According to Hofstede (2001), in comparison with Western cultures, China is low in individualism and high in power distance. The individualism/collectivism dimension speaks to the dialectical relationship between individuals and groups. People in individualistic cultures are self-oriented, tend to emphasize individual goals, experiences, and individual pleasures. In contrast, collectivistic cultures are other-oriented, emphasizing group goals, social norms, and fitting in with groups (Hofstede, 1984). The collectivistic nature of Chinese culture determines that luxury consumption is not that much an individual behavior, but more for the needs of maintaining group relationships such as family and work (Cheng & Schweitzer, 1996). Logically, Chinese purchase luxuries more for reasons such as social comparison, conformity to group behavior, and gifting. These results are consistent with past research that linked "face" to Asians' luxury consuming behavior. According to Ho (1976), individuals in the Confucius culture are pressured to live under others' expectations to preserve "face." That means they expect others think them rich, generous, and have good taste and so forth, no matter whether they are or not. Through buying and using luxuries, people preserve face, enhance others' opinions about self, and maintain social status (Wong & Ahuvia, 1998). The cultural value emphasizing face definitely promoted the consumption of luxury products in China.

Power distance is another cultural dimension that is relevant. According to Hofstede (1984, 2001), power distance refers to the degree of hierarchical power distribution in a society. Cultures high in power distance tend to emphasize the importance of prestige and wealth in shaping boundaries or vertical relationships between social and economic classes such as rich and poor, and superiors and subordinates (Hofstede, 1984; Inkeles, 1960; Lenski, 1966). Individuals in high-power-distance cultures seek to maintain and increase their power as a source of satisfaction. They are motivated by the need to conform to those in their class or in classes to which they aspire. The conspicuous nature of luxury consumption determines that buying and using luxuries is associated with prestige and social status. Logically, consumers in high-power-distance cultures are more likely to buy luxuries because of social status and affiliation norms. Chinese culture features a high level of power distance and social conformity (Kim, 1994; Markus & Kitayama, 1991). Consequently, Chinese consumers are more likely to buy luxuries for reasons such as seeking social representation and position (Li & Su, 2006).

Gifting is another important factor that merits discussion. Even though gifting is a universal social phenomenon around the globe, it has special implications in Asian culture, particularly for its role in establishing and maintaining social ties. Wong and Ahuvia (1998) noted that Asians often view luxuries as appropriate gifts. Expensive gifts not only show respect for the recipient but also reflect the gift giver's status and capability. Their study further suggested that Asian consumers are more likely to purchase luxury goods for gifting than Western consumers. Findings from the present study lend further support to their conclusion. Simply speaking, among Chinese luxury purchasers, there is a segment of consumers that buy luxuries but do not consume them. This group of people is thrifty about buying goods for themselves but is willing to spend big money on name brand luxuries for gifts to enhance "face."

High quality is also a significant predictor for Chinese luxury consumption. Consumers' expectation of superior quality of luxury brand is rather general across cultures. It is necessary to develop a long-term commitment to product quality in order to establish a luxury brand image. Luxury brands are often viewed as standards of excellence. Consumers may attach high values to a luxury brand because they may assume that it will have a greater brand quality and reassurance (Vigneron & Johnson, 2004).

Past research has linked consumers' motivation to both individual factors and consumer buying behavior (Mackenzie & Spreng, 1992). Our results showed that young Chinese consumers with an impulse shopping style were more likely to buy luxury products out of emotion and less likely to buy for self-actualization and future investment. As discussed earlier, young people make up the primary market segment for luxury products in the Chinese market. Chinese traditional culture emphasizes being thrifty, modest, and cautious. Older, more traditional Chinese are less likely to spend their money on luxuries even if they have a lot of money. In contrast, young Chinese consumers are more influenced by Western values such as enjoying the moment, satisfying their own material and emotional needs, and purchasing name brands. Consequently, they are more likely to buy luxuries out of impulse and emotional reasons.

Results also showed that those who were not susceptible to others' influence were less likely to buy luxury products for social comparison and emotional reasons. Social referencing has long been found to influence luxury consumption. Liebenstein (1950) proposed the "bandwagon effect," referring followers who purchase luxury goods to be identified with a reference group serving as role model. People who are concerned with social acceptance and conformity with affluent reference groups are more likely to buy luxuries to show off and impress others. On the other hand, people who are less concerned with social acceptance and conformity to social norms are less likely to buy luxuries for such reasons.

Personal income was found to be the dominating factor influencing luxury consumption in this study. This result makes sense and is consistent with previous research. Economists have consistently argued that consumers' purchasing power is an essential element in defining the demand for luxuries (Giacalone, 2006). Previous research (Dubois & Duquesne, 1992) also shows that income plays a determining role in luxury buying. Luxury products and services are undoubtedly expensive. Naturally, with limited financial resources, low-income consumers have to limit their luxury purchases to special occasions or to gain acceptance from others.

Culture is a powerful variable for luxury consumption. The findings provide preliminary implications for marketing luxuries in China. A better understanding of why Chinese consumers buy luxuries can help luxury brands understand how Chinese satisfy their in-depth needs and wants though luxury consumption. This study also provides insights into product positioning and marketing communication strategies. Advertising themes and concepts are based on buying motives. The motives used in advertising are culturally bound. Advertising tries to attach meanings to brands and these meanings are interpreted in the light of the target market's motivation and aspirations. Therefore, luxury brands that fit the target market's values and motivations will more likely be successful. Specifically, in marketing luxury brands in China, companies may want to position their products in a way that can satisfy consumers' face-enhancing need. In addition, when crafting their creative messages, managers should take motivation into consideration. Commercials for luxuries could be more other-oriented in the Chinese market, emphasizing gifting, peer approval, and high quality of the products. Creative materials could portray luxuries as the perfect gifts in different settings. Using luxuries helps people gain approval and respect from friends, families, and coworkers. In addition, packaging is extremely important for luxury products. Packaging should be done prestigiously and beautifully to reflect the high quality and high price point of luxury brands.

## LIMITATIONS

Several limitations warrant notice here. First, the conceptualization and operationalization of some concepts used in this study (e.g., luxury brands, luxury consumption, and motives) may not be robust. A more rigorous conceptualization and scale development process is needed to validate the concepts. Second, this study only examined motivations for luxury consumption among Chinese consumers. A cross-cultural study between China and other countries may shed more light on how motivation and luxury consumptions differ across cultures. Third, the quantitative research methodology employed here may not offer satisfying in-depth information about the complexity and delicacy of Chinese consumers' motivation for luxury purchase. A multimethods approach incorporating both quantitative and qualitative perspectives (e.g., focus groups and in-depth interviews) could help accomplish both generalizability and rich implications of research findings. Finally, social desirability bias could comprise the validity of some research findings.

## ACKNOWLEDGMENTS

We gratefully acknowledge the research funds (No. 70602025 and No. 70832001) from the National Natural Science Foundation of China.

# REFERENCES

Ahlstrom, D. (2009). *China's rise and the impact on global business*. Keynote Speech for the AACS 51th Annual Conference, Rollins, FL.

Arghavan, N., & Zaichkowsky, J. (2000). Do counterfeits devalue the ownership of luxury brands? *Journal of Product and Brand Management*, 9(7), 485–497.

Bond, M. (1991). *Beyond the Chinese face*. Hong Kong: Oxford University Press.

Bond, M. (1996). *Handbook of Chinese psychology*. Hong Kong: Oxford University Press.

Bond, M., & Lee, P. W. (1981). Face saving in Chinese culture. In: A. King & R. P. Lee (Eds), *Social life and development in Hong Kong* (pp. 288–305). Hong Kong: Chinese University Press.

Braxton, R. (1999). Culture, family and Chinese and Korean American student achievement: An examination of student factors that affect student outcomes. *College Student Journal*, 33, 250–256.

Cheng, H., & Schweitzer, J. C. (1996). Cultural values reflected in Chinese and U.S. television commercials. *Journal of Advertising Research*, 36, 27–45.

Cowart, K., & Goldsmith, R. (2007). The influence of consumer decision-making styles on online apparel consumption by college students. *International Journal of Consumer Studies*, 31, 639–647.

Danziger, P. N. (2002). *Why people buy things they don't need*. Ithaca, NY: Paramount Market Publishing.

Dou, W., Wang, G., & Zhou, N. (2006). Generational and regional differences in media consumption patterns of Chinese X consumers. *Journal of Advertising*, 35(2), 101–110.

Dubois, B., Czellar, S., & Laurent, G. (2005). Consumer segments based on attitudes toward luxury: Empirical evidence from twenty countries. *Marketing Letters*, 16(2), 115–128.

Dubois, B., & Duquesne, P. (1992). The market for luxury goods: Income versus culture. *European Journal of Marketing*, 27(1), 35–44.

Dubois, B., & Laurent, G. (1994). Attitudes toward the concept of luxury: An exploratory analysis. *Asia-Pacific Advances in Consumer Research*, 1, 273–278.

Ger, G., & Belk, R. W. (1996). Cross-cultural differences in materialism. *Journal of Economic Psychology*, 17, 55–77.

Giacalone, J. A. (2006). Market for luxury goods: The case of the Comite Colbert. *Southern Business Review*, (Fall). Available at http://findarticles.com/p/articles/mi_qa3972/is_200610/ai_n18632447/pg_8/. Retrieved on January 10, 2009.

Goffman, E. (1967). *Interaction ritual: Essays on face to face behavior*. Garden City, NY: Anchor.

Gu, F. F., Hung, K., & Tse, D. (2008). When does Guanxi matter? Issues of capitalization and its dark sides. *Journal of Marketing*, 72, 12–28.

Hafstrom, J. L., Chae, J. C., & Chung, Y. S. (1992). Consumer decision-making styles: Comparison between United States and Korean young consumers. *Journal of Consumer Affairs*, 26(1), 146–158.

Hauck, W. E., & Stanforth, N. (2006). Cohort perception of luxury goods and services. *Journal of Fashion Marketing and Management*, 11(2), 175–188.

Ho, D. Y. (1976). On the concept of face. *American Journal of Sociology*, 81, 867–884.

Hofstede, G. (1984). *Culture's consequences: Comparing values, behaviors, institutions and organizations across nations*. Thousand Oaks, CA: Sage.

Hofstede, G. (2001). *Culture's consequences: Comparing values, behaviors, institutions and organizations across nations* (2nd ed.). Thousand Oaks, CA: Sage.

Hu, H. C. (1944). The Chinese concepts of 'face'. *American Anthropologist*, 46, 45–64.

Hwang, K. (1987). Face and favor: The Chinese power game. *American Journal of Sociology*, *92*(4), 944–974.
Inkeles, A. (1960). Industrial man: The relation of status to experience, perception, and value. *American Journal of Sociology*, *75*, 208–225.
Kim, M. (1994). Cross-cultural comparisons of the perceived importance of conversation constraints. *Human Communication Research*, *21*, 128–151.
KPMG. (2006). Luxury brands in China. Available at http://www.kpmg.com.cn/en/virtual_library/Consumer_markets/CM_Luxury_brand.pdf. Retrieved on January 10, 2009.
Lenski, G. E. (1966). *Power and privilege: A theory of social stratification*. New York: McGraw-Hill.
Li, C. (1998). *China: The consumer revolution*. New York: Wiley.
Li, J. J., & Su, C. (2006). How face influences consumption: A comparative study of American and Chinese consumers. *International Journal of Market Research*, *49*(2), 27–39.
Liebenstein, H. (1950). Bandwagon, Snob and Veblen effects in the theory of consumer's demand. *Quarterly Journal of Economics*, *64*(2), 183–207.
Lu, P. (2008). *Elite China: Luxury consumer behavior in China*. Singapore: Wiley.
Mackenzie, S. B., & Spreng, R. A. (1992). How does motivation moderate the impact of central and peripheral processing on brand attitudes and intentions? *Journal of Consumer Research*, *18*, 519–529.
Markus, H. R., & Kitayama, S. (1991). Culture and the self: Implications for cognition, emotion, and motivation. *Psychological Review*, *81*, 224–253.
Masaru, A., Yasue, M., & Wen, G. (1997). China's Generation III: Viable target segment implications for marketing communications. *Marketing and Research Today*, *25*(1), 17–24.
Miller, C. (1991). Luxury goods still have strong market despite new tax. *Marketing News*, *25*, 1–7.
Mooij, M. (2005). *Global marketing and advertising: Understanding cultural paradoxes* (2nd ed.). Thousand Oaks, CA: Sage.
Nia, A., & Zaichkowsky, J. (2000). Do counterfeits devalue the ownership of luxury brands? *Journal of Product and Brand Management*, *9*(7), 485–497.
Nueno, J. L., & Quelch, J. (1998). The mass marketing of luxury. *Business Horizons* (November–December), 61–68.
Shan, E. (2005, August 8). "*Mianzi*" of Chinese weighs a lot, comes at a price. *China Daily*. Available at www.chinadaily.com.cn/english/doc/2005-08/08/content_467216.htm. Retrieved on October 2009.
Silverstein, M. J., & Fiske, N. (2001). *Trading up*. New York: Penguin.
Stevens, J. (2002). *Applied multivariate statistics for the social sciences* (4th ed.). Mahwah, NJ: Lawrence Erlbaum.
*The Financial Times*. (2005). The future of luxury market lies in rapid spread of new marketing segments. *The Financial Times*, May 18.
Tidwell, P., & Dubois, B. (1994). A cross-cultural comparison of attitudes toward the luxury concept in Australia and France. *Asia Pacific Advances in Consumer Research*, *1*, 273–278.
Trendy Life. (2006). Is luxury consumption in China really rising? Available at http://www.ce.cn/life/clfs/xxbb/200610/24/t20061024_9106457_1.shtml. Retrieved on March 1, 2009.

Tse, D. K., Belk, R., & Zhou, N. (1989). Becoming a consumer society: A longitudinal and cross-cultural content analysis of print ads from Hong Kong, the people's republic of China, and Taiwan. *Journal of Consumer Research, 15*, 457–472.

Tu, W. (1992). The Confucian problematique: An overview. In: W. Tu, M. Hejtmanek & A. Wachman (Eds), *The Confucian world observed: A contemporary discussion of Confucian humanism in East Asia* (pp. 1–13). Honolulu, HI: University of Hawaii Press.

Vigneron, F., & Johnson, L. (2004). Measuring perceptions of brand luxury. *Brand Management, 11*(6), 484–506.

Wong, N., & Ahuvia, A. (1998). Personal taste and family face: Luxury consumption in Confucian and western societies. *Psychology and Marketing, 15*(5), 423–441.

Yang, K. S. (1981). Social orientation and individual modernity among Chinese students in Taiwan. *Journal of Social Psychology, 113*, 159–170.

Zhou, N., & Belk, R. W. (2004). Chinese consumer readings of global and local advertising appeals. *Journal of Advertising, 33*(3), 63–76.

Zhou, Z., & Nakamoto, K. (2000). Price perceptions: A cross-national study between American and Chinese young consumers. *Advances in Consumer Research, 28*, 161–168.

# CONSUMING COOL: BEHIND THE UNEMOTIONAL MASK

Russell W. Belk, Kelly Tian and Heli Paavola

## ABSTRACT

Purpose – We use data from the United States and Finland, a literature review, and historical analysis to understand the concept and role of cool within global consumer culture.

Methodology/approach – This is a conceptual review and qualitative analysis of data from depth interviews, journals, and online discussion groups in two U.S. locations and one Finnish location.

Findings – Cool is a slang word connoting a certain style that involves masking and hiding emotions. As cool diffuses we find that it is both distilled and diluted. The concept itself has also evolved. What was once a low-profile means of survival and later a youthful rebellious alternative to class-based status systems has become commoditized.

Research limitations/implications – The study has been conducted in two cultures with a limited range of ages thought to be most susceptible to the appeal of being cool.

Practical limitations/implications – Marketers may not yet have exploited cool as effectively as they have exploited sex, but mainstream consumers now look for cool in the marketplace more than within themselves. The result is a continuous race to offer the next cool thing.

Originality/value of chapter – *It is argued that coolness is a new status system largely replacing social class, especially among the young.*

Oh to be cool! To have that presence, that magical mask of bored indifference that makes our every movement and glance a pronouncement of what is good, true, and worthy of lust by those who would be cool. We would be loved, admired, and sought after. The people and things we touch would be blessed. For cool is their religion and we would be their gods.

Or so it seems at those points and periods in our lives when we seem cursed by insecurity and feelings of inferiority that exclude us from fraternizing with the really cool people. Our parents love us, but they are far from cool. We know the hierarchy of cool people and we can recognize cool when we see it on the screen. But to actually be cool is something that only a few of us can pull off. For the rest of us, the best we may hope for is to avoid the stigma of being considered totally uncool. In large part we pursue this goal through imitating the consumption of cool people. Even if we do not have the script and stage business just right, if we buy the right props and costumes, at least strangers may mistake us for cool people.

Cool is a particular impression-related verbalized and embodied performance. Like any performance, it requires validation by an audience. The relevant audience may be specific subsets of our classmates, friends, children, neighbors, colleagues, or the social networking site to which we belong. Although cool is not inherently tied to consumption or brands, these props have become increasingly central to the successful performance of cool. More than identity is at stake. Cool has arguably become a chief source of status in consumer culture, especially, but not exclusively, among adolescents.

Cool has been studied, directly and indirectly, from diverse perspectives. One approach interrogates socially constructed images of cool articulated within a particular subset of consumption practices such as fashion (e.g., McRobbie, 1988), music (e.g., Kitwana, 2005), transportation (e.g., Hebdige, 1988), or art (MacAdams, 2001). This is often nested within the study of particular youth subcultures, especially in cultural studies (e.g., Hall & Jefferson, 1985). In this approach, subcultural appropriation and reconfiguration of marketplace meanings is generally seen as an assertion (or discovery) of an identity that is shaped by class, race, and gender politics.

Another approach to the study of cool emerged within African American studies starting in the 1960s and 1970s when emphasis was placed on defining a distinct black aesthetic and tracing its impact on broader cultures (e.g., Gayle, 1971; Osumare, 2005). Music, entertainment, literature, dance, art, poetry, theater, film, language, and sports are all recognized as areas of unique black aesthetic contributions. The term cool has been increasingly applied to characterize this aesthetic. The influence of these cool styles is a focus of much discussion, both critical and celebratory (see Caponi, 1999).

A third cultural approach to the origins, transformations, and consumption of cool focuses on the creation of cool branded objects by commercial institutions including advertising (Frank, 1997), retailing (Zukin, 2004), and media (Arvidsson, 2006). Frank's (1997) analysis focuses on advertising of the 1960s and the cooptation of hippie cool with ad slogans like "Join the Dodge Rebellion." He concludes that the process is more complex than simple cooptation. Nevertheless, the importance of a cool image to sell a product became firmly established in the era in which the hippy counterculture emerged and embraced the concept of cool (Bird & Tapp, 2008; Nancarrow, Nancarrow, & Page, 2002).

The importance of cool has also been indirectly examined within the sociology of fashion which theorizes the importance of emulation and the "trickle down" of fashions (Simmel, 1904) from more to less elite segments of the population (leading the more elite to innovate and propelling the wheel of fashion). Although the origin of cool fashions in marginalized groups like minorities, gays, and countercultures has been labeled as a case of inversion or "status float" (Field, 1970) where styles "float" from the bottom toward the top of the status hierarchy, this may not be the case. If we instead see coolness as having its own status hierarchy as Heath and Potter (2004) suggest, then the movement of style remains from top to bottom. However, just as Davis (1992) criticized the reductionism of a trickle-down theory of fashion focusing solely on social class, we should also recognize that cool conveys more than status.

Research and theorizing on cool has consistently focused on the origins rather than the destinations of cool. In this chapter, we seek to reverse this emphasis and consider what happens to cool as it moves from its largely American minority and countercultural origins to mainstream and world audiences.

## THE PERSISTENCE OF COOL

Some argue that cool originated in Africa several thousand years ago and was refined by slaves as a survival strategy using the cool mask of emotional imperviousness (Majors & Billson, 1992). As cool continues its peregrinations in the United States and throughout the world it undergoes changes in its specific meanings and manifestations, but it seems likely that its general meaning remains largely intact. That meaning is generally thought to originate in certain African American urban locales. Music, television, films, magazines, tourism, and the Internet then tell us who, what, and where is currently cool and help diffuse cool trends.

Although Gioia (2009) argues that cool is now dead and has been replaced by a new earnestness, this judgment remains very premature. Remarkably, in the United States the term "cool" has had subcultural popularity since the 1930s and mainstream cultural currency since the 1950s (Moore, 2004). For any slang term to have such staying power, something more than global media influences must be involved. In order to explain cool's longevity we integrate our empirical findings with a diverse literature and history. We argue that the quest to be cool is now a major driver of global consumer culture.

## CHARACTERISTICS OF COOL

### Emotional Control

Stearns (1994) emphasizes that cool is distinctly American and involves dispassionate control of intense emotions together with an air of disengagement and nonchalance aimed at creating an impression of unflappable superiority. He contrasts this ideal with the former Victorian ideal of pursuing good character through the capacity for deep feelings deployed in appropriate contexts like romantic love, participant sports, grief rituals, and maternal sentimentalism. But Stearns (1994) is more interested in a general cultural history of emotions and gives little attention to the urban African American youth whom most other treatments of cool emphasize as the major source of cool attitudes and styles.

Connor (1995) explains the incentive for cool emotions for African Americans both during slavery and under subsequent racism and discrimination:

> Internalizing emotions became, for many African American males, their only means for survival. It is this internalization process that is the beginning of cool. Anger, love, happiness, hatred – these emotions were all potentially dangerous if expressed. Love meant certain disappointment and it left you emotionally vulnerable. An open display of hatred or even anger meant certain punishment. An open demonstration of happiness might mean the removal or destruction of whatever made you happy. (p. 7)

Suppressing overt displays of emotion remains a way of retaining pride, dignity, and masculine ideals of toughness (Holt & Thompson, 2004; Smith & Beal, 2007). But as Majors and Billson (1992) note, the mask of coolness can also be a pathway to dropping out of school, drug and alcohol abuse, delinquency, gang activity, crime, and imprisonment. As Hooks (2004) contends, because they learn to hide their emotions, cool black men have a difficult time showing love as fathers and mates. Pursuit of cool masculinity is something Fraiman (2003) sees equally in cool white men. Recent studies of male university underachievement attribute this decline to "the Bart Simpson model": "For men, it's just not cool to study" (Lewin, 2006). Thus, coolness may extract a high price for the sense of masculine dignity it enables.

## Cool Style

In Stearns' (1994) view the cool control of emotions and avoidance of excess is a part of the same civilizing process of progressively refined manners that Elias (1978) analyzed in post-medieval Europe. But control of emotions and avoidance of excess are not necessarily the same thing and the two seem to have decoupled in contemporary cool. Suppressing and hiding emotions does not mean avoiding emotion altogether. People can be flamboyant in their clothing, furnishings, and lifestyle and still be cool, so long as they do not appear to be passionate about these things (e.g., see Smith & Beal, 2007). We believe that cool performance is highly emotional and evocative; it is only delivered with a style that appears nonchalant and easy. This style is most strongly articulated by African American males, although females and other minority groups contribute to cool style as well. Cool style is expressed in music, dance, sports like basketball, and distinctive ways of walking, talking, gesturing, dressing, and grooming. Within the mask of indifference and exaggerated masculine bravado, a smirk is permissible, but never a cheerful smile or a painful grimace.

Thanks to film, television, and music videos, currently cool gestures, clothing styles, hairstyles, and vocabulary are now widely known. An earlier style of cool walk was described by Majors and Billson (1992):

> In contrast to the white male's robotlike and mechanical walk, the black walk is slower – more like a stroll. The head is slightly elevated and tipped to one side. One arm swings at the side with the hand slightly cupped. The other hand hangs straight to the side or is slipped into the pocket. (pp. 73–74)

Such performances of cool evolve and change with culture, but the underlying attitude of ironic detachment remains.

### Knowingness

A further element of cool is privileged insider knowingness of what is going on and how to act in a given environment (Lacayo & Bellafante, 1994; Moore, 2004). This involves social competence and mastery of a set of skills enabling survival in the face of risk (Majors & Billson, 1992). It comprises a shared knowledge denied to squares (Pountain & Robins, 2000; Holbrook, 1986). Cool is an attitude of mastery and not merely an appearance. This involves being streetwise or having street cred (credibility).

Lyman, Scott, and Harré (1989) distinguish three types of risk in everyday life toward which a cool person responds in a knowing and detached manner by showing poise under pressure: physical risk (e.g., law enforcers and soldiers), financial risk (e.g., gamblers and captains of industry), and social risk (e.g., those in dating and courtship situations). They suggest keeping cool has become everyone's challenge.

### Other Manifestations of Cool

Elements of cool like emotional control are not exclusive to African Americans. Barthes (1979) and Leland (2004) note the cool *sangfroid* of the real world and film gangster, and Harris (2000) and Leland (2004) observe the *savoir faire* cool of the detective of fiction and film. Barthes' (1979) homage to the "icy mockery" of the gangster is a harbinger of current admiration of gangsta rap.

Both Harris (2000) and Cross (2004) observe that, for male children pursuing cool is a coming of age gesture that rejects seeking parental approval in favor of autonomy, self-control, and the admiration of peers. As Pountain and Robins (2000) emphasize, "Cool is a rebellious attitude, an expression of a belief that the mainstream mores of society have no legitimacy and do not apply to you" (p. 23). Heath and Potter (2004) add that the cool person strives to set himself apart as a nonconforming individualist. This sense of contradicting order and rejecting societal normalcy suggests a trickster figure who introduces the chaos of clever new ideas (Hyde, 1998; Leland, 2004).

The trickster figure (usually male) uses his mischievous intellect to fool and trick superiors and gods. A case in point is the Signifying Monkey trickster of the Yoruba people of Nigeria (Gates, 1989). In numerous tales the Signifying Monkey gets the better of the lion (taken to be the white colonialist) through tricks and language. It is easy to see why the trickster element of cool appeals to oppressed minorities as well as to adolescents struggling to break free of authority and establish their own identities. It is also easy to see how the ritual insults by the signifying monkey, carried to the United States by African American slaves and embellished in the ritual insults of "the dozens," provided a prelude to rap music and especially the rap competitions known as battle rap. In the ritual insults of the dozens, slurs against the other's family and especially his mother are used to try to get the one being attacked to "lose his cool" and respond with anger and violence rather than managing his emotions and returning an even better ritual insult (see Wooten, 2006). This helps build a thick skin to withstand racial prejudice and insults, and was commoditized in the MTV program "Yo Mama."

The originators of cool have always been outsiders including ghetto dwellers, disenfranchised minorities, gangsters, tricksters, revolutionaries, countercultural leaders, Jews, gays and lesbians, transgressive comedians, hackers, obscene misogynistic rappers, juvenile delinquents, and other disempowered groups on the margins of society (Leland, 2004; Pountain & Robins, 2000; Liu, 2004). Not coincidentally, these are also the groups that are the fashion innovators who precipitate new style trends (McCracken, 1986). Cool is a way of substituting a particular cultural capital for economic capital, although with the commodification of cool we shall see that economic capital is also increasingly needed.

## THE EVOLUTION OF COOL

### *Origins*

Majors and Billson (1992) place the origin of cool in Africa in approximately 2000–3000 BCE. Thompson (1966) places the origin of cool with the Ibo and Yoruba people of Nigeria in first half of the 1400s. Coolness was taken to mean "grace under pressure" (Thompson, 1983, p. 16). Major (1994) traces several cool-related jazz words to the Wolof in what is now Senegal. These include the Mandingo *hepi* (to see), *hipi* (to open one's eyes), *jev* (to talk falsely), and *dega* (to understand), which became hep, hip, jive, and dig in jazz and beat argot of the 1940s and 1950s, with meanings close to the eighteenth-century Mandingo words.

Although less well researched, other predecessors of contemporary cool may include Italian courtiers of the Renaissance, the proper English gentleman, Anatolian Turkish merchants, and nineteenth-century romance poets (Pountain & Robins, 2000), Tokyo youth cults (Leland, 2004), aristocrats after the French Revolution (MacAdams, 2001), and Japanese

Samurai (Richie, 2003). But contemporary cool grew first and foremost out of African American culture.

## Blues

African American cool is seen in a succession of musical genres. Recorded blues, then called "race music," started in the 1920s, but related blues, rags, and field hollers go back to slave days. In contrast to African American gospel music, which is steeped in Christianity, the blues were considered the Devil's music and came to be associated with sex, hedonism, unemployment, crime, violence, imprisonment, and prostitution (Oliver, 1990). Pountain and Robins (2000) suggest that while the white suburban middle class teenager and the black Mississippi Delta sharecropper may seem to have little in common, "psychologically they share the same sexually confused passive aggressive tone of the blues" (p. 45).

## Jazz, Basketball, and Hip Hop

Cool style and vocabulary are most heavily associated with jazz. Although Gioia (2009) makes a good case for white jazz cornetist Bix Beiderbecke as the progenitor of cool, black tenor saxophonist Lester Young is generally credited with making jazz cool (Dinnerstein, 1999). He would say "I'm cool" to mean "I'm calm," wore sunglasses on stage, dressed in sartorial splendor, used marijuana and alcohol prodigiously, and introduced a unique expressive sadness in the music he made. His cool style of jazz influenced many others and music differed from the hot jazz of the 1920s by being unhurried, balanced, and imperturbable, both in musical rhythm and in stage presence. As Dinnerstein (1999) puts it, "He [Young] generated excitement without getting excited; he stayed cool" (p. 250).

The cool sounds, mannerisms, and jargon of the black jazz musicians were not mere affectations however. Reacting to a prior era of minstrelsy and entertaining black musicians performing to please white audiences, cool jazz was a political act as well as a musical act. Artists like Lester Young, Miles Davis, and Charlie "Bird" Parker would distance themselves from audiences behind sunglasses and jived up language, would decline to introduce their music to their largely white audiences, and would often turn their backs on the audience (Ellison, 1964). The white would-be hipster audience, often sensed the arrogance, rudeness, and surliness of the musicians, and not only accepted it, but came to expect it as part of the entertainment (Ellison, 1964). These whites were also seeking a rebellious expression of individuality within the frustratingly inhibiting atmosphere of the 1950s. And musicians such as Parker were all the more appealing because of their outlaw image, use of illegal drugs, and isolation from mainstream society. Their cool persona, slow dragged out speech, and suppression of active aggression was also aided by widespread use of heroin among black musicians of the period (Sidran, 1971).

Basketball has been compared to a jazz performance and has been singled out as an example of the black aesthetic (Novak, 1994; Boyd, 1997). Novak (1994) refers to the "cool shaded mask" the player must put on in this game full of disguise, fakery, feints, steals, contrivance, deceptive wiggles, and changes of direction. We can again recognize the traits of the trickster. The slam dunk came out of black street basketball and was initially banned when Kareem Abdul-Jabbar (then Lew Alcindor) began using it at UCLA in 1967 (Caponi, 1999).

Rap music and the hip-hop culture from which it emerged are generally accepted as the latest instantiations of coolness (e.g., Kitwana, 2005). Rap music continues the basic character of cool: it is rebellious; romanticizes the outlaw and trickster; and starts trends in fashions and grooming styles. Even sunglasses continue in rap as part of the cool mask. But rap has also modified cool, as Connor (1995) argues:

> Cool had previously been a method of eventually avoiding violence; once accepted as cool a young man was not challenged every minute of the day. However, beginning in the eighties guns and violence took the place of attitude, style, and simply "proving" oneself. Cool was not being dictated solely by the boys on the block. With the advent of crack and the rise in popularity of rap music, money and the requisite organized crime faction began to prevail in a heretofore unheard-of way in the inner city. (p. 119)

And Hooks' (2004) indictment is even more scathing:

> Though [Todd] Boyd and many of his cronies, like to think that calling themselves "niggas" and basking in the glory of gangsta culture, glamorizing addiction to drugs, pussy, and material things, is liberation, they personify the spiritual zombiehood of today's "cool" black male. (p. 153)

But rap's popularity has spread far beyond black males.

### Stealing Cool

Highly successful white rapper Eminem has been called a "culture bandit" (Kitwana, 2005) and a culprit in the "white theft of black cultural art forms"

(Watkins, 2005). Since rap originated in the heavily black South Bronx and continues to be regarded as a key part of the new black aesthetic, Eminem's ascendance to the top of the music charts is curious. Eminem recalls that while he was growing up he would put on sunglasses and lip-sync to Run-DMC songs while looking in the mirror and dreaming he was Dr. Dre or Ice Cube (Watkins, 2005). For street cred, Eminem draws on his impoverished childhood, much of which was spent in heavily black Detroit, his start in battle raps, and his discovery by Dr. Dre, the legendary black rap producer. Eminem's lyrics share the misogyny, sex, gun play, and obscenity of black rap musicians, but he does not use the "n-word" bandied about by black rappers, nor can he fully draw on some rap themes derived from regular encounters with pimps, drugs, racial discrimination, and crime (Kitwana, 2005).

Paralleling Eminem in rock n' roll was Elvis Presley who is frequently described as "the white boy who stole the blues" (e.g., Leland, 2004). When Elvis recorded Arthur "Big Boy" Crudup's "That's All Right Mama" in Sun Studios in 1954, owner Sam Phillips recognized that "a white singer who could ride the beat and sound like a black singer ... [presented] the perfect opportunity to carry the music ... to a larger and much more lucrative market, young white music buyers" (Watkins, 2005, p. 102).

Elvis Presley was not the first or last to appreciate black culture as a source of cool. Other artists accused of being culture bandits who have exploited black culture include Al Jolson, Mark Twain, Benny Goodman, Irving Berlin, Keith Haring, Tom Waits, and Bob Dylan (Leland, 2004). The beats were more open appropriators of black cool. In the classic work of the beat generation, Jack Kerouac's alter ego, Sal Paradise, says:

> I wished I were ... anything but what I was so drearily, a "white man" disillusioned ... .
> I was only myself, Sal Paradise, sad, strolling in this violet dark, this unbearably sweet night, wishing I could exchange worlds with the happy, true-hearted, ecstatic Negroes of America. (Kerouac, 1957, p. 180)

To be fair, Kerouac, Alan Ginsberg, William S. Burroughs, and other beats also drew on Buddhism, jazz musicians, and drug addicts, but their general identification with the marginal and outcast drew them to blacks as an important source of cool, to which they then added their own outcast cool personna.

## *Other Sources of Cool*

The beats were not defined only or even primarily in terms of borrowed or stolen black cool. This is even more true of other countercultural groups like hippies. Countercultural groups are by definition outsiders and are likely to be looked to as a source of cool for that reason alone. This includes both true revolutionaries and outlaws like Che Guevara, Bonnie and Clyde, and the Black Panthers, as well as with film outlaws like black leather-jacketed Marlon Brando in "The Wild One" and James Dean in "Rebel without a Cause." Cool countercultural examples in art include Andy Warhol and Keith Haring (MacAdams, 2001).

A recent source of cool is cyber cool – not just countercultural hackers, but even some corporate computer gurus (e.g., Leland, 2004; Liu, 2004). This should not be too surprising given the countercultural roots of the personal computer and especially the trickster founders Apple computers, Steven Jobs and Stephen Wozniak (Belk & Tumbat, 2005; Kahney, 2004). The same rebellious and leveling spirit of early computer inventors can be seen in the Internet. For a time, Napster and its successors made it possible to throw a sabot in the corporate music machine and showed the way to carry the rebellion by using the simple act of file sharing (Giesler, 2006). Linux and other open source software suggest that cyber-cool rebellion continues (e.g., Goffman, 2005; Hemetsberger, 2006).

There are other influences on what is cool including Japanese manga (McGray, 2001), Australian surfer culture (Beatie, 2001; Canniford & Shankar, 2007), and American skateboarding (Moon & Kiron, 2002). But in part because of its global media, pop culture, and consumer corporate dominance, the U.S. and especially African Americans are seen as the key source of global cool (Leland, 2004).

## Marketing Cooptation and Creation of Cool

When marketers try to copy cool, the process has been described as cooptation (Frank, 1997). But when an "establishment" company affiliates itself with cool, this should be the kiss of death for the source of coolness and for whatever or whomever it promotes as being cool. As Hebdige (1979) puts it, "As soon as the original innovations which signify 'subculture' are translated into commodities and made generally available, they become 'frozen'" (p. 96). Besides the loss of cool when something becomes mainstream, cool people and cool subcultures and countercultures historically set themselves up as opposing and rebelling against commercialism and the consumer culture it promotes (see Holbrook, 1986). But the Sixties changed cool and made it more commercially mediated, blurring the distinction between authentic counter-cultural cool and inauthentic commercial cool (Frank, 1997).

The marketing research technique of "cool-hunting" is also problematic (e.g., Gladwell, 1997; Kerner & Pressman, 2007; Lopiano-Misdom & de Luca, 1998; Nancarrow & Nancarrow, 2007; Southgate, 2003). Through observation, depth interviews, and focus groups with trend-setting cool kids, cool-hunting research agencies try to find the next cool thing quickly enough for marketers to bring out their own version and capitalize on its coolness by taking it to a larger mass market, which in turn makes it uncool. In an effort to dissipate or negate the cool-killing effects of commercializing and popularizing cool things, several "cool" advertising techniques have arisen. Antiadvertising is based on intertextuality and self-referential awareness. Such advertising mocks its own commercial purposes with a knowing wink (Goldman & Papson, 1998). Antiadvertising was pioneered in the early 1960s by Volkswagon's humorous campaign portraying the car as ugly, unstylish, and funny-looking (Frank, 1997). Such antiadvertising messages seek to be cool by seeming to share a hip knowingness with the consumer. Other advertising techniques in this vein include under-the-radar marketing (Boyd & Kirshenbaum, 1997), peer to peer or viral marketing (Quart, 2003), and product placement (Shrum, 2004). Such techniques show advertisers' urgent attempts to make their commercialization and commoditization of cool appear less obvious.

An alternative to trying to discover and copy the next cool thing is to create it (Kerner & Pressman, 2007). This was the technique followed by MTV in throwing parties at which they hire hip teenagers to dance to the music of an ascendant hip-hop band introducing a new album, all the while filming the party to subsequently be shown on MTV (Goodman, 2003). While Sprite succeeded earlier with an antiadvertising campaign mocking the importance of style (George, 1998), they too have sought to participate in the creation of cool by cosponsoring these MTV soirees.

Sometimes a company gets lucky enough to have their brand become cool with no effort on their part, as with the 1986 rap hit "My Adidas" by Run-DMC (de Longville & Leone, 2006) or when the British skinheads and subsequent youth subcultures adopted Dr. (Doc) Martens boots (Roach, 2003). Klein (2000) reports that brands like Nike, Pony, and Stussy were so anxious to have cool kids and rap musicians wear their clothing that they gave them free clothing and did nothing to stop counterfeiting of their brands. And even by age 10 or 11, children are quite aware of cool and uncool brands (Nair & Griffin, 2007).

Apple is one company that was able to maintain its image of producing cool products through a series of innovative and stylish products including the iPod, iPhone, and iPad. Despite the market success of these products

(Kahney, 2004), the cult-like following and cool reputation of Apple products after Steve Jobs returned to the helm has remained strong. This was helped by several factors, including Apple's own historic reputation as a renegade underdog company fighting against dominant corporations like Microsoft. Consumers in a study by Belk and Tumbat (2005) even believed that buying Apple products was striking a blow against corporate capitalism.

The evolution of cool outlined above has been largely devoid of a consumer focus on what cool means. It has also focused more on cool subcultures and countercultures rather than on more mainstream consumers. In the present research, we sought to examine more mainstream manifestations of cool as well as its global proliferation. We focus on consumers' involvement with cool during their adolescence and young adulthood.

## METHODS

Our grounded theoretical account of cool used multiple methods at multiple sites. We elicited participation of both male and female consumers of various ages, ethnic identities, and national citizenships, collecting data in the United States (in two different Western states) and Finland. They are predominantly middle class white consumers in their teens and twenties. Global and local media are the primary means by which foreign notions of cool reach Finland. Although this allows consideration of how "cool" culture changes as it spreads globally, we do not assume that Finnish cool is the same as cool in other world cultures.

In Finland in addition to interviews, data were collected via Internet chatrooms and (primarily) discussion groups over a period of 10 days. The discussion groups included an intellectual group focused on social issues, religion, and media issues and involving adults aged 16–35, a group setup by a TV-network, a group run by a teenage magazine for girls between 12 and 16, and a discussion group for young women.

## FINDINGS: MEANINGS OF COOL

Two participants in an online discussion of cool in Finland had the following reflections on the nature of cool:

> **Scorpius:** A cool person is cool not only in his attitude but also in his behavior. Coolness is ... [a] street-credible image and certain style of speaking. A cool person has a good

sense of style and a certain kind of an attitude. A relaxed, casual look and informal, unconventional style creates the image of cool. At least Mickey Rourke and Pierce Bronson (as James Bond) fulfill the criteria of cool. There are others, of course; for example poker-face Humphrey Bogart with a cigarette hanging loosely from the side of his mouth in *Casablanca* is one of the icons of cool.

**Acousticus:** Coolness involves insensitivity (or hiding feelings) and strong self-confidence, but being really cool means being "cool, calm and collected" and it presupposes a perfect capability to act fast and correctly ... in the most surprising situations; and it doesn't happen if you are a blundering novice. Being cool requires knowledge, talent and experience ...

Elements of cool seen in this discussion include attitude, performance, style, uniqueness, nonchalance, being streetwise, hiding emotions, and possessing talent and knowingness. The exchange also suggests that American films and actors are a key way of learning about coolness.

Both the U.S. and Finnish informants agreed on many things regarded as cool including rap music, jazz, extreme sports, sunglasses, *The Matrix* (film), trendy clothes, expensive and trendy brands, tattoos, smoking, drugs, and alcohol. There were some local variations in both countries regarding who and what is cool as well as some country-specific differences in regard for certain cool traits. For example, cool rebellion was more appealing to Americans than Finns. Finnish informants recognized rebellion as being part of the mediated image of cool, but they were less apt to report such behavior themselves. They also recognized elements of these mediated images of cool that did not translate well in Finland:

I think in Finland coolness is more quiet, narrow and poorer than in the U.S. Rap-stars with gigantic gold necklaces, exaggerated manners, and silicone blonds who are cool in the States seem ridiculous in Finland. (f29, Fin)

These same images would likely seem strange in many American suburban high schools as well, but our American informants recognized that the exaggerated consumption seen in music videos and MTV programs like "Pimp my Ride" and "Cribs" was not what most of America was like. Nevertheless Americans were far from exempt from media influences. As one 23-year-old woman said, "If Britney Spears is wearing midriff, it must be cool."

The controlled emotions aspect of cool was evident in both countries, but the Finnish informants were more likely to report this in the third person as being evident in other's cool behavior rather than their own:

I think that coolness is connected to the need to protect oneself from the evaluating and criticizing eyes of others. A model on the catwalk does not just represent a perfect figure but also the attitude, disinterest toward others and their criticizing looks. (f21, Fin)

Both Finns and Americans chose many products as being cool that seemed to isolate them from the "criticizing eyes of others" – handheld devices like mobile phones, remote controls, and iPods (all of which give the user a focus that precludes having to meet the gaze of others), as well as sunglasses.

In Finland we also found a focus on bits and pieces of cool that seem to reflect a distilled or essentialized notion of cool.

> The Afro-American walking style (Negro-walk) and the position of the head is very much cool, even without sunglasses. (m23, Fin)

> Neo in the Matrix-movie is cool. I think that all Eastern things are cool. Buddha, ninja or karate-heroes or samurai-warriors are cool. A samurai who is ready to die at any moment is cool. A Zen-monk who totally controls his mind is cool. (m25, Fin)

The first example locates cool close to its African American roots, but the second draws on film representations and Japan. Although not as commonly recognized by our American informants, Japan and especially the *iki* character of Tokugawa era samurai share the mask of emotional control, stylized performance, and knowingness that characterize Western cool, lacking only its trickster spirit (Richie, 2003). These distilled versions of cool can be seen as stereotypes of cool. Because media representations need to communicate quickly, they too rely on exaggeration and stereotypes of cool (e.g., Gray, 2001). As cool travels farther from its roots such mediated stereotypes distill portrayals of cool.

### Cool Vocabulary

We found a buffering phenomenon that may help cool achieve the staying power that it has had across four or five generations. This is the phenomenon of cool synonyms. When we asked informants for words that they currently or previously used in place of cool, we encountered large sets of terms and expressions in both cultures (e.g., butter, da bomb, bitchin', dope, fly, niiice, off da hook, phat, pimp, sweet). Informants also provided cool antonyms, some of which also appeared on the synonym list, including bad, crazy, and shit. This reflects changes over time as well as geographic areas. In Finland, besides the English word cool, some other terms used for the concept include viileä (chilly), kolea (colder weather, usually in autumn), and jäinen (icy). Finns also use phrases like "it was icy stylish," "sure as ice," and "ice cool." In each case ice or icy is taken to mean calm, self-controlled behavior, that is, cool. Here too we can see some distillation of the concept. Similarly, one of the words that American men recalled using to refer to or acknowledge cool people within their microcultures was "dude," a term derived from surfing and skateboarding subcultures. Kiesling (2004) found that this term is used by college-age to convey as shared sense of cool masculinity. But our American informants suggested that dude had also become too widely used and was beginning to signal uncoolness. The wide variety of ever-changing synonyms for cool and uncool, like the ever-changing array of styles, brands, and music considered to be cool, help those who are cool to distinguish their cool knowingness from that of less cool followers.

At the other extreme of mainstream usage from distilled cool are instances where the term means little more than "good," as seen in these comments:

> Unselfish actions are cool. ... Serving other people. ... I think friends are cool, and Grandparents are cool and the Gospel is cool. (f19, US)

> I always thought going to music concerts were so cool, and then my experience living in New York City was so cool. And also marrying my high school dream guy. Spending time in Italy learning about art was also really cool. I think its cool to be independent, and financially self-sufficient. I think graduating from college and working in the field that I studied is cool. (f25, US)

If stereotyping is distilled cool, this mainstreaming is best characterized as diluted cool. When cool is diluted into a bland honorific, it threatens the persistence of the term in edgier cool contexts. It is arguably for this reason that informants suggested that although the concept of cool remained, its synonyms were more commonly used. In fact, to use the term cool rather than a synonym was generally considered to be uncool.

> To be seen as cool, performative style was also important.

> With tattoos, sunglasses, and cool clothes even an uncool person seems a bit cooler (at least until the moment when he opens his mouth and expectations prove him wrong) ... If you don't have the attitude, self-confidence, pride of your body, and calmness, clothes don't make you cool. (f23, Fin)

There was consensus that in an anonymous context someone might appear cool based on having cool possessions and the right tastes, preferences, and knowledge, but that at the peer group level of what Wulff (1995) terms a microculture, cool performance is also required. This is also consistent with findings by Milner (2004) that cool kids must evidence self-confidence, recklessness, effortlessness, and "an air of invincibility" (p. 59).

## Cool Consumption

A telling indicant of the commoditization of cool is that when asked what was cool in clothing fashions, 62% of our American informants provided brand names rather than styles or looks. Based partly on their belief that the truly cool person should evince an ironic detachment, nonchalance, and the appearance of indifference to the opinions of others, informants distinguished the individuating consumption of the cool person and the emulative consumption of others who would be cool. A Finnish informant aptly characterized this difference:

> Then there is coolness that is based on consuming cool things. ... In this sense being cool among teenagers requires identifying and accepting popular things and brands. This sort of coolness is not about standing out, it's more like fitting in. (f23, Fin)

Nevertheless personal emulative attempts to be cool were commonly recalled, as with this American man looking back on his adolescence:

> In the 80's mullets were cool and everyone was wearing spandex. I once myself had a small mullet and I thought that I was so cool. I looked like the guys my oldest sister was dating, and they were in high school, could drive, etc. Man was I cool. (m31, US)

Trivial though they may seem in retrospect, such consumption badges were seen as crucial to social acceptance in adolescence. One 21-year-old man recalled that in junior high school he moved from New Jersey to Illinois. He had been regarded as one of the "cool kids" at his former school but found he was not accepted by the cool kids at his new school until he realized they were all wearing high-top Keds basketball shoes with the laces untied (something that comes from prison culture – de Longville & Leone, 2006). After he convinced his mother to buy him a pair as well as some Colorado leather hiking boots like those the in-group wore in the winter, he recalls that he was embraced as a cool kid. A 26-year-old American man recalled that in junior high school a friend lent him his Girbaud jeans and this allowed him to be accepted by the cool kids. Such brands act as marker goods establishing boundaries of inclusion and exclusion. In one school, two primary groups contending for cool status were called "skaters" and "punks." Affiliation was signified by wearing the mutually exclusive clothing that designated each group. In a survey of college students, Labov (1992) found numerous high school microcultures including jocks, motorheads, flea bags, intellectuals, politicos, rah-rahs, freaks, druggies, toughs, and tree people. Such names also signal cool, uncool, and shades in between.

Sometimes the right attitude and the right marker goods used in the right way (e.g., shoes with laces untied) are still not enough. There is also what Thornton (1996) calls subcultural capital or what we encountered as microcultural capital. This is similar to Bourdieu's cultural capital, but rather than operating within the status systems of social classes, it operates within the cool status system of microcultural groups or cliques (see also Nancarrow & Nancarrow, 2007; Ostberg, 2007). Those studied here described how in some junior high and high school groups, membership depended on knowing about the right musical groups, following or participating in the right sports, or having experience with and knowledge of the right drugs. We can also see here that although the heroic model of the individual cool person anointing things with coolness sometimes applies, mainstream cool is more often socially constructed by the group.

## DISCUSSION

We find that cool has shifted from being disdainful of consumption to celebrating consumption. Bling or bling bling (the ostentatious consumption first popularized by rap musician Brian "Baby Birdman" Williams in 1999) is anything but subtle. High-end brands like Cristal champagne, Gucci, and Mercedes are mentioned with great frequency in rap lyrics (Hip Hop, 2003). Advertisers also borrow bling to lend cool status to their brands (Kerner & Pressman, 2007). For example, an ad for The Game athletic shoes by 310 that appeared in the hip-hop magazine *Vibe* in April 2006 shows the shoes draped around the neck of a heavily tattooed young black male standing with a menacing look in front of a Bentley Continental GT Coupe (see Belk, 2006, p. 85). This too suggests that cool has changed from low key to high key; from subtle to conspicuous; from avoiding envy to provoking envy. These advertising images rely on stereotypes to distill cool for mainstream consumption.

This consumption-driven spread of cool can be seen in the popularity of black rap musicians like 50 Cent among our white American informants. Surveys indicate that 70% of rap music sales are to the white community (Gibbs, 2003). Signs like hip-hop fashions in suburban schools and a rapping Barbie Doll affirm that rap has gained considerable popularity among young middle class Caucasians. Some white fans report that they *want to be* black (Roediger, 1998; Zukin, 2004), while others regard themselves *as actually being* black (Kotlowitz, 1999; Sunderland, 1997). They mimic not only rap musical preferences and fashions, but also language, gestures, and facial expressions seen on programs like *Yo, MTV Raps* (Harris, 2000). Many believe that a key reason that middle class white kids like music derived from the black ghetto is that the hip-hop movement has conflated blackness with coolness (e.g., Kitwana, 2005; Rodriquez, 2006). In hooks (1992) phrase, it is a case of "eating the other" in which "ethnicity becomes spice, seasoning the dull dish that is mainstream white culture" (p. 21). Watkins (2005) sees it as the pursuit of an exotic Otherness filled with perceived iniquity. There is rebellion and seduction in the outlaw mystique here as well as a pursuit of something that seems more authentic and exciting than the suburban shopping mall. But still, there is no direct interaction; only vicarious purchased consumer contact with black cool.

We should expect to find both distillation and dilution in the process of white youth consuming black coolness. Local adaptation also occurs, especially in Europe. Our Finnish sample frequently cited Mr. Lordi as a cool person after the monster-costumed Finnish singer and his group won the 2006 Eurovision song competition. Similarly, the baggy trousers, oversized shirts, and baseball caps worn backwards by American rap groups have been adopted by Polish teens (Antoszek, 2003), but many American rap words and phrases like "the hood," "homies," "the yard," and "yo," translated badly into Polish rap. And although hip-hop culture is also quite popular in the Netherlands, gangsta rap is not, since a lack of inner-city "hoods," gang violence, and guns make it hard to identify with these American gangsta rap themes (Krims, 2002). Instead a new hybrid form of music and culture called Nederhop has arisen (Sansone, 1995). Cool and some of its products may be global, but meanings are locally adapted.

The spread of cool has hardly been limited to North American suburbs and Europe. Youth subcultures in India (Karkaria, 2004), Australia (Martino, 1999), Greenland (Kjeldgaard & Askegaard, 2006), New Zealand (Mitchell, 2001), Japan (Condry, 2001), China (Wang, 2005), and Korea (Morelli, 2001), for example, have also embraced the concept and its associated consumption patterns. In each case, there is also local adaptation – for example with Greenlandic youth coveting cool snowmobiles. This suggests that the status that coolness conveys is not a universal currency that can be used anywhere. Rather, it is a microcultural capital that can only be converted into economic, social, and sexual capital within the peer group to whom one is cool. To gain this sort of cool capital, it is necessary not only to stand out and be different, but also to be, or at least appear to be, indifferent to the opinions of others. Milner (2004, p. 60), notes that such pursuit of power through indifference to worldly sanctions is otherwise reserved for saints or holy men. But unlike saints it involves no renunciation of worldly pleasures; only a seeming indifference toward them. Such indifference may scale up to a jaded consumer culture that truly cannot be satisfied.

The commoditization of cool and this take on the cooling of our pleasure in consumption lead us to a more cynical take on contemporary cool. Connor (1995, p. 137) calls advertisers' use of cool appeals "the bastardization of cool." As we move farther from the putative roots of cool and closer to corporate cooptation of the concept, this charge resonates and converges with other discourses critiquing consumer culture. Lasn (1999) laments:

> "Cool" used to mean unique, spontaneous, compelling. The coolest kid was the one everyone wanted to be like but no one quite could, because her individuality was utterly distinct. Then "cool" changed. Marketers got hold of it and reversed its meaning. Now you're cool if you are *not* unique – if you have the look and feel that bear the unmistakable stamp of America$^{TM}$. Hair by Paul Mitchell. Khakis by The Gap. Car by BMW. Attitude by Nike. Pet phrases by Letterman. Politics by Bill Maher. Cool is the opiate of our time, over a couple of generations we have grown dependent on it to maintain our identities of inclusion. (p. 113)

If Lasn were completely correct in suggesting that the fitting-in consumer conformity of mediated cool has replaced the standing-out nonconformity of earlier versions of cool, it seems doubtful that the concept of cool could survive. A truly cool referent is needed in order to sustain the illusion that mimesis can make us cool. Still, there is a tension between standing-out cool and fitting-in cool. And it is this tension, as imitators eat away at cool differentiation, that drives uniquely cool people to continue to innovate regardless of whether or not the new consumption innovations bring pleasure.

# CONCLUSION

Sex, love, respect, money, friends – they would all be ours if only we were cool. The illusion is alluring. Knowing marketers often try to endow their brands with coolness or at least take advantage of the cool imparted when cool people happen to use their brand. Tommy Hilfiger clothing, Timberland boots (Tims), and Adidas sneakers have all enjoyed cool success for a time as they moved from ghetto-initiated condensed cool to distilled cool to diluted cool. But creating the next cool thing is much more difficult. And it is difficult to research because cool things have few inherently cool characteristics and because today's cool becomes tomorrow's uncool. However, as discussed earlier, clever marketers can create or influence cool, at least for a time. For example, in the May, 2006 issue of *Transworld Skateboarding*, Vans introduced a shoe called the Hosoi SK8-HI (see Belk, 2006, p. 83). A high-energy Dutch angle photo shows the shoe's namesake, Christian Hosoi, catching big air off the side of a swimming pool as he performs a seemingly impossible skateboard trick. The only message is tiny body copy reading "very limited edition" and a photo of a high-top shoe festooned with a prominent red Japanese rising sun referencing Hosoi's Japanese-Hawaiian heritage. Hosoi is cool in skateboarding subcultures, but not just because of his outsider heritage or his considerable skateboarding skills. When the ad ran he had just finished four years in prison for trying to bring a suitcase full of methamphetamines into Hawaii. Skateboarding itself has a cool outlaw image, as chronicled in a 2001 Vans-financed documentary film, *Dogtown and Z-Boys* about the start of skateboard culture in Southern California. Vans is steeped in this image due to its long relationship with skateboarding, its prominence in the cool teen film *Fast Times at Ridgemont High*, and it's sponsorship of a competitive musical/skateboard tour called Vans Triple Crown Series (Moon & Kiron, 2002). Skateboarding cool may be less luxurious than the ostentatious bling celebrated in rap, but it is no less commoditized.

Rather than elite status or sex appeal, the currency that is being coined here is that of cool. Coolness remains a rarity, but its rarity is that of the high-priced limited-edition branded commodity rather than the difficult-to-perform cool persona. At the height of Michael Jordan's athletic and celebrity prominence, in a series of TV ads Gatorade showed MJ's athletic feats and challenged the advertising viewer to "Be like Mike." It followed this challenge with a rather improbable strategy for acquiring Jordan's singular skills, finesse, and coolness: "Drink Gatorade." But such advertising is not invoking logic; it is invoking sympathetic magic (Mauss, 1972). The magician (in this case the cool Michael Jordan) relies on his association with the object (Gatorade) to invest it with cool power in the eyes of the audience. If Jordan could make baggy knee-length basketball shorts cool, why not a sports drink? In the words of the theme song for the commercials, "Sometimes I dream, that he is me." This is not a new formula. What is new is that the *mana* we seek is coolness and the locus is a mass produced branded object. It is an easy dream to dream: Oh to be cool!

# REFERENCES

Antoszek, A. (2003). Hopping on the hype: Double ontology of (contemporary) American rap music. In: P. Boi & S. Broeck (Eds), *CrossRoutes – The meanings of "race" for the 21st century* (pp. 239–253). Munich: Lit Verlag.

Arvidsson, A. (2006). *Brands: Meaning and value in media culture*. London: Routledge.

Barthes, R. (1979). Power and 'cool'. In: R. Barthes (Ed.), *The Eiffel tower and other mythologies* (Richard Howard, Trans.), (pp. 43–45). New York: Farrar, Straus and Giroux.

Beatie, K. (2001). Sick, filthy, and delirious: Surf film and video and the documentary mode. *Continuum: Journal of Media and Cultural Studies, 15*(3), 333–348.

Belk, R. W. (2006). Coola skor, cool identitet. In: A. M. Dahlberg (Ed.), *Skor Ger Mer: Makt Flärd Magi* (pp. 77–90). Stockholm: Swedish Royal Armoury.

Belk, R. W., & Tumbat, G. (2005). The cult of Macintosh. *Consumption, Markets and Culture, 8*(September), 205–217.

Bird, S., & Tapp, A. (2008). Social marketing and the meaning of cool. *Social Marketing Quarterly, 14*(Spring), 18–29.

Boyd, J., & Kirshenbaum, R. (1997). *Under the radar: Talking to today's cynical consumer*. New York: Wiley.

Boyd, T. (1997). *Am I black enough for you? Popular culture from the 'hood and beyond'*. Bloomington, IN: Indiana University Press.

Canniford, R., & Shankar, A. (2007). Marketing the savage: Appropriating tribal tropes. In: B. Cova, R. Kozinets & A. Shankar (Eds), *Consumer tribes* (pp. 35–48). Oxford: Butterworth-Heinemann.

Caponi, G. D. (1999). Introduction: The case for an African American aesthetic. In: G. D. Caponi (Ed.), *Signifyin(g), sanctifyin', and slam dunking* (pp. 1–41). Amherst, MA: University of Massachusetts Press.

Condry, I. (2001). A history of Japanese hip-hop: Street dance, club scene, pop market. In: T. Mitchell (Ed.), *Global noise: Rap and hip-hop outside the USA* (pp. 222–247). Middletown, CT: Wesleyan University Press.

Connor, M. K. (1995). *What is cool? Understanding black manhood in America*. New York: Crown.

Cross, G. (2004). *The cute and the cool: Wondrous innocence and modern American children's culture*. Oxford: Oxford University Press.

Davis, F. (1992). *Fashion, culture, and identity*. Chicago: University of Chicago Press.

Dinnerstein, J. (1999). Lester young and the birth of cool. In: G. D. Caponi (Ed.), *Signifyin(g), sanctifyin', and slam dunking* (pp. 239–276). Amherst, MA: University of Massachusetts Press.

Elias, N. (1978). The civilizing process: The history of manners. In: J. Jephcott (Trans.) *The Civilizing Process: The History of Manners and State Formation and Civilization*. New York: Pantheon.

Ellison, R. (1964). *Shadow and act (On Bird, Bird-Watching, and Jazz, 221–232)*. New York: Random House.

Field, G. A. (1970). The status float phenomenon: The upward diffusion of innovation. *Business Horizons, 13*(August), 45–52.

Fraiman, S. (2003). *Cool men and the second sex*. New York: Columbia University Press.

Frank, T. (1997). *The conquest of cool: Business culture, counterculture, and the rise of hip consumerism*. Chicago: University of Chicago Press.

Gates, H. L. (1989). *The signifying monkey: A theory of African American literary criticism*. New York: Oxford University Press.

Gayle, A. (Ed.) (1971). *The black aesthetic*. New York: Doubleday.

George, N. (1998). *Hip hop America*. New York: Viking.

Gibbs, M. (2003). ThugGods: Spiritual darkness and hip-hop. In: G. Tate (Ed.), *Everything but the burden: What white people are taking from black culture* (pp. 81–98). New York: Broadway Books.

Giesler, M. (2006). Consumer gift system: Netnographic insights from Napster. *Journal of Consumer Research, 33*(September), 283–290.
Gioia, T. (2009). *The birth and death of cool.* Golden, CO: Speck Press.
Gladwell, M. (1997). The coolhunt. *The New Yorker, 73*(March 17), 78–88.
Goffman, K. (2005). *Counterculture through the ages: From Abraham to acid house.* New York: Villard Books.
Goldman, R., & Papson, S. (1998). *Nike culture.* London: Sage.
Goodman, B. (2003). *The merchants of cool.* 60-minute Frontline video. Boston: WGBH/PBS.
Gray (director), F. G. (2001). *Be cool.* Culver City, CA: Metro Golden Mayer.
Hall, S., & Jefferson, T. (Eds). (1985). *Resistance through rituals.* London: Hutchinson.
Harris, D. (2000). *Cute, quaint, hungry and romantic: The aesthetics of consumerism.* New York: Basic Books.
Heath, J., & Potter, A. (2004). *Nation of rebels: Why counterculture became consumer culture.* New York: Harper Business.
Hebdige, D. (1979). *Subculture: The meaning of style.* London: Methuen.
Hebdige, D. (1988). *Hiding in the light.* London: Routledge.
Hemetsberger, A. (2006). When David becomes Goliath: Ideological discourse in new online consumer movements. *Advances in Consumer Research, 33,* 494–500.
Hip Hop. (2003). Product mentions in rap music. Available at http://www.uic.edu/orgs/kbc/hiphop/mentions.htm
Holbrook, M. B. (1986). I'm hip: An autobiographical account of some musical consumption experiences. *Advances in Consumer Research, 13,* 614–618.
Holt, D. B., & Thompson, C. J. (2004). Man-of-action heroes: The pursuit of heroic masculinity in everyday consumption. *Journal of Consumer Research, 31*(September), 425–440.
Hooks, B. (1992). Eating the other: Desire and resistance. In: *Black looks: Race and representation* (pp. 21–39). Boston: South End Press.
Hooks, B. (2004). *We real cool: Black men and masculinity.* New York: Routledge.
Hyde, L. (1998). *Trickster makes this world: Mischief, myth, and art.* New York: Farrar, Straus and Giroux.
Kahney, L. (2004). *The cult of Mac.* San Francisco: No Starch Press.
Karkaria, B. (2004). Hinduism and India cool. *The Times of India,* February 27, online edition.
Kerner, N., & Pressman, G. (2007). *Chasing cool: Standing out in today's cluttered marketplace.* New York: Atria Books.
Kerouac, J. (1957). *On the road.* New York: Viking Press.
Kiesling, S. F. (2004). Dude. *American Speech, 79*(Fall), 281–305.
Kitwana, B. (2005). *Why white kids love hip-hop: Wankstas, wiggers, wannabes, and the new reality of race in America.* New York: Basic Civitas Books.
Kjeldgaard, D., & Askegaard, S. (2006). The globalization of youth culture: The global youth segment as structures of common difference. *Journal of Consumer Research, 33*(September), 231–247.
Klein, N. (2000). *No logo! Taking aim at the brand bullies.* New York: Picador.
Kotlowitz, A. (1999). False connections. In: R. Rosenblatt (Ed.), *Consuming desires: Consumption, culture, and the pursuit of happiness* (pp. 65–72). Washington, DC: Island Press.
Krims, A. (2002). Rap, race, the 'local,' and urban geography in Amsterdam. In: R. Young (Ed.), *Music popular culture identities* (pp. 181–196). Amsterdam: Rodopi.
Labov, T. (1992). Social and language boundaries among adolescents. *American Speech, 67*(Winter), 339–366.

Lacayo, R., & Bellafante, G. (1994). If everyone is hip ... is anyone hip? *Time, 144*(August 8), 48–55.
Lasn, K. (1999). *Culture jam: The uncooling of America.* New York: Eagle Brook.
Leland, J. (2004). *Hip: The history.* New York: Harper Collins.
Lewin, T. (2006). At colleges, women are leaving men in the dust: The new gender divide. *New York Times*, July 9, online edition.
Liu, A. (2004). *The laws of cool: Knowledge work and the culture of information.* University of Chicago Press.
de Longville, T., & Leone (director's), L. (2006). *Just for kicks.* 81-minute DVD. New York: CAID.
Lopiano-Misdom, J., & de Luca, J. (1998). *Street trends: How today's alternative youth cultures are creating tomorrow's mainstream.* New York: Colins.
Lyman, S. M., Scott, M. B., & Harré, R. (1989). *Sociology of the absurd* (2nd ed). Dix Hills, NY: General Hall.
MacAdams, L. (2001). *Birth of the cool.* New York: Free Press.
Major, C. (1994). *Juba to jive: The dictionary of African-American slang.* New York: Viking.
Majors, R., & Billson, J. M. (1992). *Cool pose: The dilemmas of black manhood in America.* New York: Lexington.
Martino, W. (1999). 'Cool boys', 'party animals', 'squids' and 'poofters': Interrogating the dynamics and politics of adolescent masculinities in school. *British Journal of Sociology of Education, 30*(2), 239–263.
Mauss, M. (1972). *A general theory of magic* (original in collaboration with Henri Hubert in *Anné Sociologique*, 1902). London: Routledge.
McCracken, G. (1986). Culture and consumption: A theoretical account of the structure and movement of the cultural meaning of consumer goods. *Journal of Consumer Research, 13*(June), 71–84.
McGray, D. (2001). Japan's gross national cool. *Foreign Policy* (May/June), 44–54.
McRobbie, A. (Ed.) (1988). *Zoot suits and second-hand dresses: An anthology of fashion and music.* Boston: Unwin Hyman.
Milner, M., Jr. (2004). *Freaks, geeks, and cool kids.* New York: Routledge.
Mitchell, T. (2001). Kia kaha! (Be strong!): Maori and Pacific Islander hip-hop in Aotearoa – New Zealand. In: T. Mitchell (Ed.), *Global noise: Rap and hip-hop outside the USA* (pp. 280–305). Middletown, CT: Wesleyan University Press.
Moon, Y., & Kiron, D. (2002). *Vans: Skating on air.* Harvard Business School Case 9-502-077, June 22.
Moore, R. L. (2004). We're cool, mom and dad are swell: Basic slang and generational shifts in values. *American Speech, 79*(Spring), 59–86.
Morelli, S. (2001). 'Who is a dancing hero?' Rap, hip-hop and dance in Korean popular culture. In: T. Mitchell (Ed.), *Global noise: Rap and hip-hop outside the USA* (pp. 248–258). Middletown, CT: Wesleyan University Press.
Nair, A., & Griffin, C. (2007). 'Busted are cool but Barbie's a minger': The role of advertising and brands in everyday lives of junior school children. In: K. M. Ekström & B. Tufte (Eds), *Children, media and consumption: On the front edge* (pp. 195–209). Göteborg, Sweden: Nordicom.
Nancarrow, C., & Nancarrow, P. (2007). Hunting for cool tribes. In: B. Cova, R. Kozinets & A. Shankar (Eds), *Consumer tribes* (pp. 129–143). Oxford: Butterworth-Heinemann.

Nancarrow, C., Nancarrow, P., & Page, J. (2002). An analysis of the concept of *Cool* and its marketing implications. *Journal of Consumer Behaviour*, *1*(4), 311–322.

Novak, M. (1994). *The joy of sports: End zones, bases, baskets, balls, and the consecration of the American spirit*. Lanham, MD: Madison Books.

Oliver, P. (1990). *The blues fell this morning: Meaning in the blues* (2nd ed). Cambridge: Cambridge University Press.

Ostberg, J. (2007). The linking value of subcultural capital: Constructing the Stockholm brat enclave. In: B. Cova, R. Kozinets & A. Shankar (Eds), *Consumer tribes* (pp. 93–106). Oxford: Butterworth-Heinemann.

Osumare, H. (2005). Global hip-hop and the African diaspora. In: H. J. Elam, Jr. & K. Jackson (Eds), *Black cultural traffic: Crossroads in global performance and popular culture* (pp. 266–288). Ann Arbor, MI: University of Michigan Press.

Pountain, D., & Robins, D. (2000). *Cool rules: Anatomy of an attitude*. London: Reaktion.

Quart, A. (2003). *Branded: The buying and selling of teenagers*. New York: Basic Books.

Richie, D. (2003). *The image factory: Fads & fashions in Japan*. London: Reaktion.

Roach, M. (2003). *Dr. Martens: The story of an icon*. London: Chrysalis.

Rodriquez, J. (2006). Color-blind ideology and the cultural appropriation of hip-hop. *Journal of Contemporary Ethnography*, *35*(December), 645–668.

Roediger, D. (1998). What to make of wiggers: A work in progress. In: J. Austin & M. N. Willard (Eds), *Generations of youth: Youth cultures and history in twentieth-century America* (pp. 358–366). New York: New York University Press.

Sansone, L. (1995). The making of a black youth culture: Lower-class young men of Surinamese origin in Amsterdam. In: V. Amit-Taliai & H. Wulff (Eds), *Youth cultures: A cross-cultural perspective* (pp. 114–143). London: Routledge.

Shrum, L. J. (Ed.) (2004). *The psychology of entertainment media: Blurring the lines between entertainment and persuasion*. Mahwah, NJ: Lawrence Erlbaum.

Sidran, B. (1971). *Black talk* (The evolution of the black underground: 1930–1947, pp. 78–115). New York: Holt, Rinehart and Winston.

Simmel, G. (1904). Fashion. *International Quarterly*, *10*, 130–155.

Smith, M. M., & Beal, B. (2007). 'So you can see how the other half lives': MTV 'cribs" use of 'the other' in framing successful athletic masculinities. *Journal of Sport and Social Issues*, *31*(May), 103–127.

Southgate, N. (2003). Coolhunting with Aristotle. *International Journal of Market Research*, *45*(Summer), 167–189.

Stearns, P. (1994). *American cool: Constructing a twentieth-century emotional style*. New York: New York University Press.

Sunderland, P. L. (1997). 'You may not know it, but I'm black': White women's self-identification as black. *Ethnos*, *62*(1–2), 32–58.

Thompson, R. F. (1966). An aesthetic of the cool: West African dance. *African Forum*, *2*(Fall), 35–102.

Thompson, R. F. (1983). *Flash of the spirit*. New York: Random House.

Thornton, S. (1996). *Club cultures: Music, media and subcultural capital*. Hanover, NH: Wesleyan University Press.

Wang, J. (2005). Bourgeois Bohemians in China? Neo-tribes and the urban imaginary. *The China Quarterly*, *183*, 532–548.

Watkins, S. C. (2005). *Hip hop matters: Politics, pop culture, and the struggle for the soul of a movement*. Boston: Beacon Press.

Wooten, D. B. (2006). From labeling possessions to possessing labels: Ridicule and socialization among adolescents. *Journal of Consumer Research, 33*(September), 188–198.

Wulff, H. (1995). Inter-racial friendship: Consuming youth styles, ethnicity, and teenage femininity in South London. In: V. Amit-Talai & H. Wulff (Eds), *Youth cultures: A cross-cultural perspective* (pp. 63–80). New York: Routledge.

Zukin, S. (2004). *Point of purchase: How shopping changed American culture*. New York: Routledge.

# SECTION II
# CCT REVIEWED PAPERS

# Part I
# Advertising and Branding Practice

# THE STRATEGIC USE OF BRAND BIOGRAPHIES

Jill Avery, Neeru Paharia,
Anat Keinan and Juliet B. Schor

## ABSTRACT

Purpose – *We introduce the concept of a brand biography to describe an emerging trend in branding in which firms author a dynamic, historical account of the events that have shaped the brand over time. Using a particular type of brand biography, "the underdog," we empirically show how managers can strategically use brand biographies in brand positioning, in this case to mitigate the curse of success. As brands grow and become successful, they are often marked by the negative stigma associated with size and power, which elicits anticorporate sentiment from consumers. An underdog brand biography can be strategically wielded to prevent or offset anticorporate backlash stemming from consumers' negative perceptions of firms' size and/or market power.*

Methodology/approach – *Lab experiments.*

Findings – *We find an underdog effect: consumers like and prefer brands with underdog brand biographies because they identify with them. We show that an underdog brand biography can mitigate the curse of success by making large firms more attractive to consumers.*

Practical implications – *Firms can use brand biographies to weave compelling narratives about their brands that help protect them from negative consumer attitudes and actions.*

Originality/value of the chapter – *Extant branding theory has a dearth of theoretical constructs and frameworks that allow for the dynamism and evolution of brands over time. Through our observation and study of emerging marketplace branding practices, we have identified a new construct, the brand biography, to complement existing theoretical frameworks for understanding brand meaning.*

Extant branding theory has a dearth of theoretical constructs and frameworks that allow for the dynamism and evolution of brands over time. Contemporary branding practice suggests a new construct that can complement existing brand meaning theory: the brand biography. A brand biography is an unfolding story that chronicles the brand's origins, life experiences, and evolution over time in a selectively told narrative. Brand biography transforms the largely static construct of brand personality into a dynamic and unfolding brand meaning narrative selectively authored by the firm. Brands as diverse as Apple, Oprah Winfrey, Nantucket Nectars, and Stacy's Pita Chips are using brand biographies to enliven their brand positioning. A brand biography reminds consumers of the brand's roots and origins, maintaining the brand consistency for which branding scholars advocate (Aaker, 1991; Kapferer, 1992; Keller, 1998), but allows the brand to develop, grow, and change its brand persona over time to reflect changing market conditions and consumer preferences.

Using a particular type of brand biography, "the underdog," we empirically show how managers can strategically use brand biographies in brand positioning, in this case to mitigate the curse of success. As brands grow and become successful, they are often marked by the negative stigma associated with size and power, which elicits anticorporate sentiment from consumers. An underdog brand biography can be strategically wielded to prevent or offset anticorporate backlash stemming from consumers' negative perceptions of firms' size and/or market power.

# CONCEPTUAL FOUNDATIONS

## *Brand Biographies*

We begin by introducing the concept of *brand biography* to describe an emerging trend in branding where companies author a historical account of the events that have shaped the brand over time. Taking the form of a personal narrative, a brand biography chronicles the brand's origins, life experiences, and evolution. Brand biographies are initially authored by the brand's managers and are, therefore, a story selectively told, constructed and reconstructed as needed to promote the brand to consumers. As such, brand biographies are often delivered to consumers via packaging, advertising, branded websites, and other marketing communications. However, as brands circulate through society, brand biographies become multivocally authored, with consumers and other gatekeepers lending their voices to the story.

Brand biographies are much more than a list of facts about the brand. Rather, brand biographies link facts and events in the life of the brand to the experiences of the brand and its founders, selectively choosing anecdotes and incidents to include to shape a coherent life story for the brand. The rhetoric power of brand biographies lies in their ability to use a narrative format to tell a compelling story. Narrative storytelling has been a mainstay in marketing and researchers have shown that it is an effective advertising device (Puto & Wells, 1984; Mick, 1987; Deighton, Romer, & McQueen, 1989; Stern, 1994). Green and Brock (2000) suggest that narrative transportation is a third route to persuasion beyond the two routes generally accepted as part of the elaboration likelihood model (Petty & Cacioppo, 1981). Brand biographies can transport consumers into the brand's story, making it easier for consumers to personally identify with the brand through multiple entry points and making the brand's claims more persuasive to consumers than functional or emotional product claims. As people become immersed in and transported into a story's setting and plot, they are less likely to critically examine the facts in the story and more likely to accept them as true and be persuaded by them.

The emergence of brand biographies in the marketplace demonstrates the continued anthropomorphism and animism of brands by marketers and consumers that has been discussed by researchers studying brand personality (Aaker, 1997) and consumer–brand relationships (Fournier, 1998; Aggarwal, 2004). Adding another facet to the "brand-as-person" concept, brand biographies allow the brand's story to be told in a dynamic and unfolding fashion over its lifetime. The brand's experiences and travels through its life can reveal its changing character to consumers. While brand personalities are often constructed through associations with fictitious concepts and characters, brand biographies are often based on the stories of real people, typically the brand's founders or employees, giving them a tangibility and believability that makes it easier for consumers to identify with the brand. Brand biographies capture the dynamism of a brand story over the course of a brand's life in a way that makes the brand-as-person more believable.

To some extent, the rising utilization of brand biographies can be explained by larger social factors operating beyond marketing, most importantly the normative practice of "constructing" personal identity through narratives in contemporary self-presentation. Social theorists such as Anthony Giddens (1991), Ulrich Beck (1992), and Zygmunt Bauman (2000) have argued that the decline of traditional society, with its more rigid and defined social roles, has led to a new postmodernity in which individuals create their own biographies. In Giddens, (1991) influential account, in this "reflexive modernity," consumers must construct a "trajectory of the self," an original story about their personal origins, life experiences, defining moments, and future plans. The salience of personal biographies accounts for the current popularity of the memoir and narrative styles in both high and mass culture, television talk shows, and the rise of the self-help genre. Indeed, Eva Illouz' (2003) insightful analysis of Oprah Winfrey argues that Oprah's success is largely attributable to her ability to construct a repeating biographical narrative of failure, struggle, and redemption.

Successful applications of the brand biography strategy will use varying content over time, in order to ensure resonance with the values and messages that are most salient for consumers at the time. These are culturally driven, and change with the larger economic and political landscape (Holt, 2004). We turn now to an example of the underdog brand biography, which is currently an exceptionally powerful narrative.

## *The Underdog Brand Biography*

In a recent article (Paharia, Keinan, Avery, & Schor, forthcoming), we note the rise of the underdog brand biography in contemporary branding practice. Table 1 provides examples of brands using underdog brand biographies.

The brand biographies of products as diverse as airlines, snacks, and technology equipment contain underdog narratives that highlight the companies' humble beginnings, hopes and dreams, and noble struggles against adversaries. The common themes that link these brands' underdog biographies are first, a disadvantaged position in the marketplace versus a "top dog," a well-endowed competitor with superior resources or market dominance, and second, tremendous passion and determination to succeed despite the odds. External disadvantage combined with passion and determination jointly contribute to the story told in an underdog brand

*Table 1.* Contemporary Underdog Brand Biographies.

| | |
|---|---|
| AVIS | We are in the rental car business playing second fiddle to a giant. We're number 2. We try harder |
| FOX FAMILY POTATO CHIPS INC. | Rhett Fox, creator of Fox Family Potato Chips, began producing his mouthwatering potato chips in the late 1990s. *He started out very small – unable to supply the demand, but Fox had a dream.* With encouragement from his father he was determined to build a successful chip company and supply the demand for Fox Family Potato Chips |
| NANTUCKET NECTARS | "We started Nantucket Nectars with only a blender and a dream ..." |
| WHEN PIGS FLY | "... I decide to pursue my passion. *I only needed to persuade my doubting friends and family that starting a bakery was a good idea. It was difficult and scary to break out of my daily work routine to pursue a dream that had an unknown outcome.* The name when pigs fly means: I doubt it's possible and that's why it was the perfect name for my bakery" |
| MADHOUSE MUNCHIES | "... We believe that there is nothing wrong with chips for breakfast. *We believe in underdogs ...*" |
| HP | Hewlett Packard recently bought, and has a whole section on their website dedicated to, the garage in which they started in. It is now a historical landmark |

biography. Through the development of an underdog scale and its use in our studies, we deepen the conceptualization of an underdog and show that that it is much more than "the one expected to lose" that colloquial definitions and prior researchers have offered. An underdog brand is one that has faced or is facing external disadvantage and has shown or is showing passion and determination to succeed in the face of this adversity. An underdog brand biography contains these two dimensions that capture elements of the brand's external environment and its internal characteristics. Underdogs are therefore defined by both their personal characteristics and the situation in which they find themselves. The underdog's external environment is largely negative: as captured in our scale, underdogs start from a disadvantaged position and hit obstacles along the way, making it a more difficult struggle for them than for others. Underdogs perceive themselves as a minority and must fight against discrimination from others. Competing with others who have more resources than they do, underdogs feel as if the odds are against them. The underdog's internal characteristics are largely positive: as captured in our scale, underdogs show perseverance in the face of adversity and are resilient even when they fail, staying focused on their end-goal. Their determination forces them to pick themselves up after they lose to try to win again. They defy others' expectations that they will fail. They are more passionate than others about their goals, which serve a central role in defining the meaning of their lives, and they remain hopeful about achieving them, even when faced with obstacles. They are not quitters, despite the odds being placed against them. This more nuanced conceptualization of underdog brand biographies can help companies refine their existing underdog narratives to include both external disadvantage and passion and determination themes.

Why are underdog brands so prevalent in today's marketing environment, given that the existing literature finds that people prefer to associate themselves with winners? Cialdini's work on self-presentation by association describes a "basking in reflected glory" effect, showing that people strategically manage the strength of association between themselves and brands in order to align themselves with winners. For example, students are more likely to wear branded apparel displaying their university's logo following a football victory than a loss (Cialdini et al., 1976). In a black and white world of winners and losers, the conclusion seems clear: consumers want to avoid losers and align themselves with winners. However, the case of the underdog is more complicated and highlights another dimension to the winner versus loser framework. This is a temporal component where there is a continuous series of losses often followed by a win. The underdog endures loss with the hope and determination that one day he/she may win. Depending on when consumers encounter underdogs they may still be struggling, or have already overcome. It is not the docket of wins or losses with which one identifies, but rather it is with the journey along the way that highlights struggles against the odds and the passion and determination that indicates perseverance.

While underdog narratives have inspired people across contexts, cultures, and time, they may resonate most in American culture. Americans throughout history have embraced the "American Dream," which proclaims that through hard work and perseverance anyone can be successful, regardless of their circumstances of class, caste, religion, race, or ethnicity. The American Dream promises that underdogs can win by pulling themselves up by their own bootstraps. The immigrants that founded and continue to shape the United States were largely plucky underdogs who came to America to escape persecution and/or poor living conditions at home and to make a new prosperous life for themselves. Underdog narratives may also be particularly salient at the current moment in America because these historical opportunities to advance are in jeopardy. In today's world, underdog narratives address real world challenges and anxieties faced by increasing numbers of Americans. Economic challenges and anxieties have intensified due to recession, inflation, and the financial crisis of 2008; the housing market has collapsed; job losses due to technical change and globalization are increasing; costs of health care and education have risen, consumer debt is higher, and it is more difficult to reproduce middle class standards of living from one generation to the next (Mishel, Bernstein, & Allegretto, 2007). For the last three decades, the distributions of income and wealth have grown more unequal and rates of socioeconomic mobility have declined (Mishel et al., 2007; Bowles & Park 2005), and millions of households have had to work longer hours, add additional income earners, and devote more effort to succeed on the job (Schor, 1992; Mishel et al., 2007). A 2004 poll found that only 42% of Americans feel they will be able to achieve their idea of the American Dream; 36% are sure they will not achieve it, while 22% are uncertain. Sixty-two percent of survey respondents claim it is harder for Americans today to achieve the American Dream compared to their parents' generation and 64% claim it is harder to achieve it today than it was 10 years ago (Widmeyer Research and Polling, 2004). A harsher and more uncertain economic climate and the casualties it has exacted among the middle class have become a common theme in both popular and scholarly literature.

Cultural branding theory (Holt, 2004) suggests that brands offering identity myths that address the acute cultural contradictions of the moment will resonate with consumers and be successful in the marketplace. The cultural contradiction facing most people today is that the odds are stacked against them, that success requires more effort and hard work, and is less certain. This of course is the classic underdog narrative. Under these prevailing social, economic, and cultural conditions, underdog brand biographies may be especially compelling to Americans now because they offer hope, inspiration, and the promise that success is possible, a much needed message in challenging economic times. Today's grocery store shelves and brand websites are filled with stories of humble beginnings and noble struggles against overpowering adversaries, seeding underdog identity myths for consumers in a cultural moment in which consumers feel the "American Dream" slipping from their grasp.

Our empirical results (Paharia et al., forthcoming) demonstrate the strength of the underdog brand biography for today's consumers. Through a series of four experiments, we find that consumers identify with underdog narratives and this translates into greater liking and preference for underdog-branded products. We show that the use of underdog brand biographies can positively impact consumers' purchase intentions and real choice. Further, we demonstrate that these positive brand effects are driven by consumers' identification with the brand, given consumers' self-identification as underdogs. The underdog effect is moderated by consumers' self-reported underdog disposition and, thus, is greater for consumers who strongly identify as underdogs. It is also stronger in purchasing situations that are identity relevant, such as purchasing for oneself.

These results suggest that managers can use underdog brand biographies strategically for brand management. Below, we explore how underdog brand biographies can help big brands like Apple emphasize their humble beginnings when they were disadvantaged versus larger competitors and their passion and determination, which can mitigate this "curse of success" and help them maintain a positive image as they grow.

### *Avoiding Anticorporate Consumer Backlash with Underdog Brand Biography*

Consumers have a complicated relationship with brand size and market success. Many large, powerful, and dominant brands such as Disney, Coca-Cola, Budweiser, Toyota, and Nike, enjoy widespread success and consumer loyalty. Economically, size can be construed as a signal of a superior product. However, as brands grow and become successful, they are often marked by the negative stigma associated with size and power, and, in more extreme cases, may become the target of consumer activists (Thompson & Coskuner-Balli, 2007; Schor, Slater, Zukin, & Zelizer, 2010). As Starbucks grew out of its humble roots in the artisanal coffee culture of Seattle and became ubiquitous on every street corner, an anti-Starbucks counterculture began to emerge (Thompson & Arsel, 2004). Work on *schadenfreude*, or taking pleasure in the misfortunes of others, shows that people enjoy seeing successful people fail (Smith et al., 1996; Brigham, Kelso, Jackson, & Smith, 1997; Leach, Spears, Branscombe, & Doosje, 2003). This may translate into the enjoyment of seeing large corporations or brands fail. In recent years, some of the world's largest and most popular brands have been targeted by activists. The most dramatic example of this anticorporate sentiment was the so-called "Battle of Seattle," which took place during a meeting of the World Trade Organization, when protests led to physical attacks on retail locations of transnational brands such as Starbucks. Soon after, Naomi Klein's *No Logo*, became a minisensation with its case against the transnational corporations. As Douglas Holt (2002) argued in an insightful discussion of this phenomenon, brands can "cause trouble." This trouble includes groups such as Adbusters, with their spoof advertising and "culture jamming," performance artists such as the Reverend Billy Talon and the Church of No Shopping, and the campus-based anti-Coke crusade. The current anticorporate rhetoric bears some similarity to earlier movements, chronicled in the field of advertising and marketing by Thomas Frank in his *The Conquest of Cool* (1998). Very recently, the *No Logo* trend has been aided by synergy from the rise of ecological consciousness and activism, some of which is directed at consumer brands, such as automobile companies, mass marketed foodstuffs, and consumer electronics. Bigness itself has come under attack, as movements explicitly favoring small, local businesses have thrived (Thompson, Rindfleisch, & Arsel 2006; Schor, 2007).

In this environment, emphasizing a big brand's underdog roots may be a strategic antidote. An underdog brand biography may be able to prevent or offset anticorporate backlash stemming from consumers' negative perceptions of firm size and/or market power. We propose that making an underdog biography salient allows consumers to identify with a brand's projected passion and struggles rather than their size, and this effect may overpower any negative attributions associated with large size or a firm's top dog status.

## METHODOLOGY

In a different study (Paharia et al., forthcoming) we demonstrate that consumers prefer brands with underdog brand biographies and, hence, brands can benefit from using them. The underdog effect we uncovered was mediated by a process of consumer-brand identification: consumers saw themselves as underdogs, so when firms positioned their brands as underdogs, consumers identified with the brand. This drove positive downstream brand attitudes and behaviors, such as increased liking, purchase interest, and real choice.

Here, we explore how brand biographies can be used strategically to improve the performance of a brand. While positive effects have been shown for underdog brand biographies in general, it is possible that some types of brands may benefit from the underdog effect more than others. One particular case where an underdog brand biography may be especially helpful is to mitigate the "curse of success," where a brand's large size or top dog status triggers negative attributions. We use two studies to explore whether underdog narratives can help top dogs become more likeable. In the first, we use a hypothetical top dog person and in the second, we use a hypothetical top dog brand.

# STUDY 1

In study 1, we examine the impact of an underdog biography on a job candidate who would otherwise be considered a top dog. Narratives of a Harvard Business School MBA student who also went to Yale, and planned to become an investment banker, were either presented with an *underdog* or a *top dog* biography. Consistent with our hypothesis we predict that liking will be higher when John has an *underdog* biography, and this will be mediated through a process of identification.

## Procedure

One hundred and two adult participants were recruited through an online survey service to complete a group of unrelated surveys in exchange for points that could be redeemed for products. Participants were randomly assigned to one of two conditions: *underdog biography* or *top dog biography*. When John was portrayed as an *underdog*, subjects read: "John is a 27-year old student at Harvard Business School. John comes from a working class family. His father is a line worker in an auto plant. John is the first member of his family ever to go to college. He went to Yale as an undergraduate on a full scholarship. John plans to become an investment banker." In the *top dog* condition, subjects read "John is a 27-year old student at Harvard Business School. John comes from a wealthy family. His father is a CEO of an auto company. Like members of his family, John attended Yale as an undergraduate. John plans to become an investment banker." After reading the narratives about John, all subjects then answered questions about their attitudes toward John and the likelihood they would hire John for a job. Participants were also asked whether they identified with John, on a scale of 1–7.

## Findings

A manipulation check was administered by asking "How much of an underdog do you think John is?" This check confirmed that John was seen as more of an underdog in the *underdog* biography condition than in the

# The Strategic Use of Brand Biographies

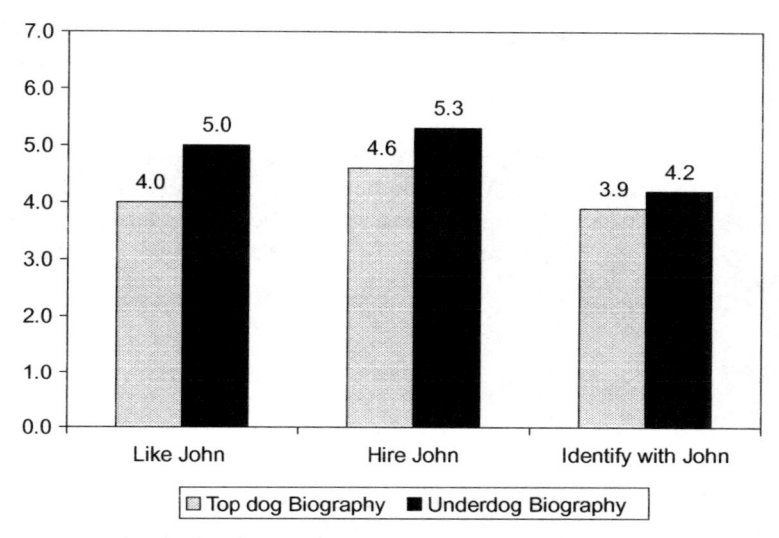

*Fig. 1.* Underdog Biographies Increase Liking for Top Dog People.

*top dog* biography condition ($M = 3.5$ vs. 2.3, $t = 4.14$, $p<0.001$). Participants liked John significantly more when he was described as having an *underdog* biography ($M = 5.0$) than when he had a *top dog* biography ($M = 4.0$) ($t = 3.6$, $p<0.01$), and were significantly more likely to hire him ($M_{underdog} = 5.3$) versus ($M_{top\ dog} = 4.6$; $t = 2.7$, $p<0.01$). These results are graphically represented in Fig. 1.

A mediation analysis indicated that identification with John mediated the effect of communicating an underdog biography on the positive attitudes toward John. The following three conditions for mediation (Baron & Kenny, 1986) were supported: (1) the independent variable (underdog biography) significantly affected the mediator (identification with John, $t = 3.8$, $p<0.001$), (2) the independent variable (underdog biography) significantly affected the dependent variable (liking of John, $t = 3.6$, $p<0.005$), and (3) the mediator affected the dependent variable when the independent variable was also included in the analysis ($t = 8.4$, $p<0.001$), and the effect of the independent variable on the dependent variables was attenuated ($t = 1.3$, n.s.) when the mediator was present.

This study shows that communicating an underdog biography increases liking for top dogs, and that this liking is mediated by identification with the underdog. A job candidate with an underdog biography was more likely to be hired than one with a top dog biography. Furthermore, we showed that an underdog biography could successfully be applied to a job candidate with an Ivy League background who, at first glance, would not appear to be an underdog.

In the next study, we explored whether these positive effects would transfer to top dog brands. Would the identification process highlighted in study 1 transfer to a situation in which the subject of the biography was a company rather than a person? Would consumers be able to identify with underdog company brands?

## STUDY 2

### Procedure

In this study, we investigated whether an underdog brand biography could mitigate some of the negative effects of being a large company. Participants read about a hypothetical company that was described as either small or large, and either had an underdog brand biography or no brand biography. Participants were then asked questions on identification with the company and about their desire to see the company to succeed. We predicted that consumer perceptions of a large company would be enhanced by the presence of an underdog brand biography.

A national sample of 295 participants was randomly assigned to one of four conditions in a 2 (small company vs. large company) × 2 (underdog brand biography vs. no brand biography) between-subjects design. In all conditions, subjects read about a hypothetical Company A. Participants in the *small* condition read: "Company A is relatively small in its industry with a very small market share and sales of less than $250,000 per year," and in the *large* condition read: "Company A is relatively large in its industry with a very large market share and sales of $1 billion per year." In addition to reading about the size of the company, participants in the *underdog biography* condition read: "The founders of Company A started in a garage with very few resources, but had a dream and struggled to succeed. They overcame the odds to bring their products to market." Participants in the *control biography* condition read no biography. After reading about Company A, participants were asked questions on their identification with the company, on a 1 to 7 scale where 1 indicated low levels of identification and 7 indicated high levels of identification.

Participants were also asked to predict their mood with an item that measured "If Company A succeeds I will be _____" with 1 indicating "sad" and 7 indicating "happy."

## Findings

Comparing the large company to the small company, without an underdog brand biography, consumers' level of identification was lower for the large company than for the small company ($M_{large} = 2.7$, $M_{small} = 3.8$, $t = 3.5$, $p = 0.001$) and consumers were less likely to want the company to succeed when it was large versus when it was small ($M_{large} = 4.5$, $M_{small} = 5.2$, $t = 3.0$, $p < 0.005$), highlighting the curse of success that accompanies a company or a brand achieving a large size. However, these negative effects were erased with the introduction of an underdog brand biography for both identification ($M_{large} = 4.2$, $M_{small} = 4.2$, $t = 0.04$, ns) and wanting the company to succeed ($M_{large} = 5.3$, $M_{small} = 5.4$, $t = 0.72$, NS). With an underdog brand biography the large company was able to enjoy the same level of consumer affinity as the small company. These results are graphically presented in Fig. 2.

Results showed a significant interaction between company size and brand biography in the predicted direction for identification ($F = 6.4$, $p < 0.05$). The underdog effect was stronger for the large company ($M_{underdog} = 4.2$, $M_{no\ biography} = 2.7$, $t = 4.85$, $p < 0.001$), whereas there was no significant effect for the small company ($M_{underdog} = 4.2$, $M_{no\ biography} = 3.8$, $t = 1.7$, NS). Results for the dependent variable "wanting Company A to succeed" were in the same direction and the interaction was marginally significant ($F = 3.3$, $p < 0.08$). The impact of the underdog biography on consumers wanting Company A to succeed was stronger for the large company ($M_{underdog} = 5.3$, $M_{no\ biography} = 4.5$, $t = 3.1$, $p < 0.01$), whereas for the small company it was not significant ($M_{underdog} = 5.4$, $M_{no\ biography} = 5.2$, $t = 0.77$, NS.). Finally, identification significantly mediated (via a Sobel test) the effect of communicating an underdog biography on wanting the company to succeed ($z = 3.7$, $p < 0.001$).

This study confirmed that underdog brand biographies can be strategically applied to large companies to reduce negative attributions associated with large size; participants identified more highly with big companies when they had an underdog biography and were happier when big companies succeeded when they came from underdog roots. An underdog brand

## Identification with the Company

| | Small Company | | Large Company | |
|---|---|---|---|---|
| | No Biography | Underdog Biography | No Biography | Underdog Biography |
| | 3.8 | 4.2 | 2.7 | 4.2 |

## Want to See the Company Succeed

| | Small Company | | Large Company | |
|---|---|---|---|---|
| | No Biography | Underdog Biography | No Biography | Underdog Biography |
| | 5.2 | 5.4 | 4.5 | 5.3 |

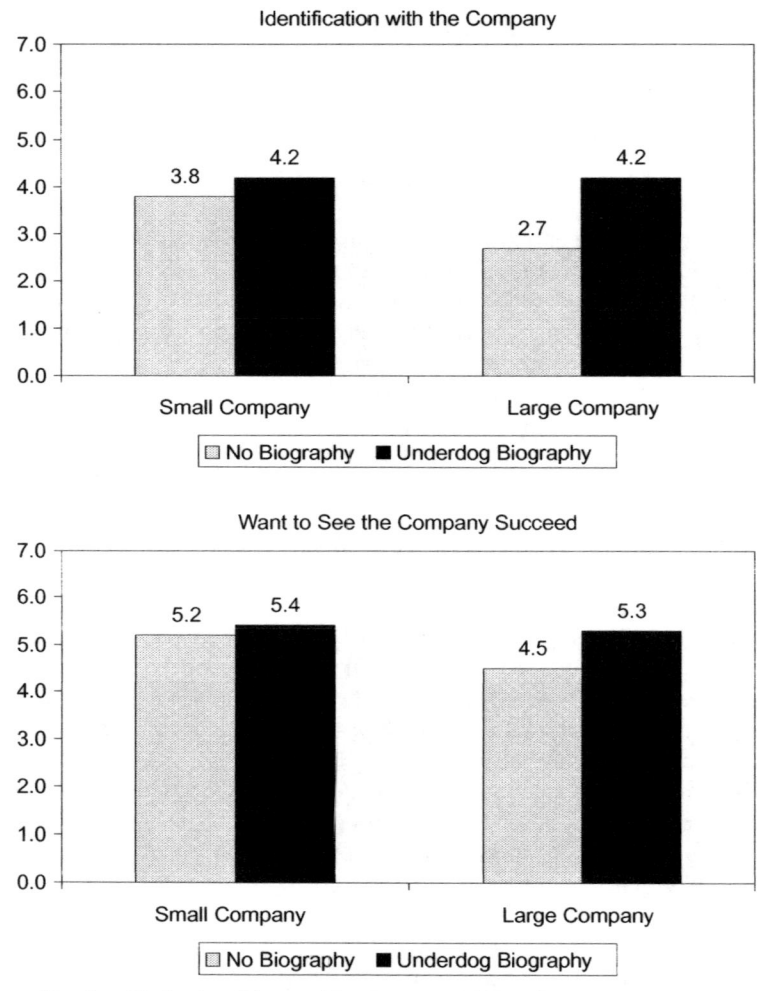

*Fig. 2.* Underdog Biographies Increase Liking for Big Companies.

biography, when strategically applied, can offset some of the negative stigma associated with becoming too big. People may have an easier time identifying with a large company when they understand the journey the company has had to endure along the way.

## DISCUSSION

Brand biographies offer tantalizing new ways to position brands in a dynamic market environment. Moving beyond the static construct of brand personality, managers can use dynamic brand biographies to reposition a mature brand to remind consumers of its roots and to show the development and maturity of the brand. Because a biography is a story of a lifetime, brand biographies can be continuously updated and refined as a brand changes over time. As selectively told stories, brand biographies can be woven to include narratives with which consumers can identify and which address cultural contradictions with which consumers are struggling.

Given the prevailing economic, political, social, and cultural trends, a particularly potent contemporary brand biography is the underdog brand biography that can be used to offset anticorporate sentiment. We show that firms can strategically use underdog brand biographies to weave compelling narratives about their brands that help protect them from negative consumer attitudes and actions. Emphasizing underdog roots may help consumers identify with struggles that the company and its founders overcame early on in the life of the brand, tempering negative feelings about its current position of market dominance and offsetting some of the negative implications of being too big.

Managers can leverage many existing narratives from the greater culture that resonate with consumers, beyond the underdog narrative explored here. Archetypal characters, such as the hero, the rebel, the prodigal son, the artisan, or the trickster, can be incorporated into brand biographies to make brands more familiar and identifiable to consumers. The founders of the company, the brand's employees, and the brand's customers can be mined for character development input. Archetypal conflicts and plot lines, such as the rebel's journey, the artisan's creative destruction, or the hero's tests, can be added to show dynamic conflicts, transitions, and developments in the life of the brand. The company's founding, the process by which the product is made, how consumers use the brand, and the brand's battles with its competitors can be mined for plot development. Brand biographies can be used strategically to strengthen the connection between consumers and a brand and/or to address areas of weakness that threaten consumer–brand bonds.

## REFERENCES

Aaker, D. A. (1991). *Managing brand equity: Capitalizing on the value of a brand name.* New York: The Free Press.

Aaker, J. L. (1997). Dimensions of brand personality. *Journal of Marketing Research, 34*(3), 347–356.
Aggarwal, P. (2004). The effects of brand relationship norms on consumer attitudes and behavior. *Journal of Consumer Research, 31*(1), 87–101.
Baron, R., & Kenny, D. A. (1986). The moderator-mediator variable distinction in social psychological research: Conceptual, strategic, and statistical considerations. *Journal of Personality and Social Psychology, 51*(6), 1173–1182.
Bauman, Z. (2000). A sociological theory of postmodernity. In: K. Nash (Ed.), *Readings in contemporary political sociology*. New York: Blackwell Publishing.
Beck, U. (1992). *Risk society: Towards a new modernity*. Thousand Oaks, CA: Sage.
Bowles, S., & Park, Y. (2005). Emulation, inequality, and work hours: Was Thorsten Veblen right? *The Economic Journal, 115*(507), F397–F412.
Brigham, N. L., Kelso, K. A., Jackson, M. A., & Smith, R. H. (1997). The roles of invidious comparisons and deservingness in sympathy and schadenfreude. *Basic and Applied Social Psychology, 19*(3), 363–380.
Cialdini, R. B., Borden, R. J., Thorne, A., Walker, M. R., Freeman, S., & Reynolds Sloan, L. (1976). Basking in reflected glory: Three (football) field studies. *Journal of Personality and Social Psychology, 34*(3), 366–375.
Deighton, J., Romer, D., & McQueen, J. (1989). Using drama to persuade. *Journal of Consumer Research, 16*(3), 335–343.
Fournier, S. (1998). Consumers and their brands: Developing relationship theory in consumer research. *Journal of Consumer Research, 24*(4), 343–373.
Giddens, A. (1991). *Modernity and self-Identity: Self and society in the late modern age*. Palo Alto, CA: Stanford University Press.
Green, M. C., & Brock, T. C. (2000). The role of transportation in the persuasiveness of public narratives. *Journal of Personality and Social Psychology, 79*(5), 701–721.
Holt, D. B. (2002). Why do brands cause trouble? A dialectical theory of consumer culture and branding. *Journal of Consumer Research, 29*(1), 70–90.
Holt, D. B. (2004). *How brands become icons: The principles of cultural branding*. Boston, MA: Harvard Business School Press.
Illouz, E. (2003). *Oprah Winfrey and the glamour of misery: An essay on popular culture*. New York: Columbia University Press.
Kapferer, J. (1992). *Strategic brand management: New approaches to creating and evaluating brand equity*. New York: The Free Press.
Keller, K. L. (1998). *Strategic brand management: Building, measuring, and managing brand equity*. Upper Saddle River, NJ: Prentice-Hall.
Leach, C. W., Spears, R., Branscombe, N. R., & Doosje, B. (2003). Malicious pleasure: Schadenfreude at the suffering of another group. *Journal of Personality and Social Psychology, 84*(5), 932–943.
Mick, D. G. (1987). Toward a semiotic of advertising story grammars. In: J. Umiker-Sebeok (Ed.), *Marketing and semiotics: New directions in the study of signs for sale* (pp. 249–278). Berlin: de Gruyter.
Mishel, L. R., Bernstein, J., & Allegretto, S. A. (2007). *The state of working America*. Ithaca, NY: Cornell ILR Press.
Paharia, N., Keinan, A., Avery, J., & Schor, J. B. (2011). The underdog effect: The marketing of disadvantage and determination through brand biography. *Journal of Consumer Research, 37*, February 2011.

Petty, R. E., & Cacioppo, J. T. (1981). *Attitudes and persuasion: Classic and contemporary approaches*. Dubuque, IA: Brown.

Puto, C. P., & Wells, W. D. (1984). Informational and transformational advertising: The differential effects of time. In: T. C. Kinnear (Ed.), *Advances in consumer research* (Vol. 11, pp. 638–643). Provo, UT: Association for Consumer Research.

Schor, J. B. (1992). *The overworked American: The unexpected decline of leisure*. New York: Basic Books.

Schor, J. B. (2007). In defense of consumer critique: Re-visiting the consumption debates of the 20th century. *The Annals of the American Academy of Political and Social Science, 611*(May), 16–30.

Schor, J. B., Slater, D., Zukin, S., & Zelizer, V. A. (2010). Critical and moral stances in consumer studies. *Journal of Consumer Culture, 10*(2), 274–291.

Smith, R. H., Turner, T. J., Garonzik, R., Leach, C. W., Urch-Druskat, V., & Weston, C. M. (1996). Envy and schadenfreude. *Personality and Social Psychology Bulletin, 22*(2), 158–168.

Stern, B. B. (1994). Classical and vignette television advertising dramas: Structural models, formal analysis, and consumer effects. *Journal of Consumer Research, 20*(4), 601–615.

Thompson, C. J., & Arsel, Z. (2004). The Starbucks brandscape and consumers' anticorporate experiences of globalization. *Journal of Consumer Research, 31*(3).

Thompson, C. J., & Coskuner-Balli, G. (2007). Enchanting ethical consumerism: The case of community supported agriculture. *Journal of Consumer Culture, 7*(3), 275–303.

Thompson, C. J., Rindfleisch, A., & Arsel, Z. (2006). Emotional branding and the strategic value of the Doppelganger Brand Image. *Journal of Marketing, 70*(1), 50–64.

Widmeyer Research and Polling (2004). "The New American Dream Poll" conducted for the Center for a New American Dream by *Widmeyer Communications*, Washington DC. Summary report available at www.newdream.org/about/pdfs/Finalpollreport.pdf.

# AUTHENTIC BRAND NARRATIVES: CO-CONSTRUCTED MEDITERRANEANESS FOR L'OCCITANE BRAND

Luca Massimiliano Visconti

## ABSTRACT

*Purpose* – *Stemming from extant literature on consumer brand narratives and the rising quest for consumption authenticity, the chapter aims at merging these two streams of knowledge. How can brand authenticity be defined and narrated? To what extent do companies and consumers interact? What are the consequences for branding?*

*Methodology* – *The chapter is case-based, and illustrates the branding strategy of l'Occitane en Provence, a company producing toiletries with a strong Mediterranean rooting. Data were collected through multisited ethnographic fieldwork in Paris and Manosque, Haute Provence. Depth and short interviews with customers and managers of l'Occitane were complemented by extensive observation and secondary data. The comprehensive dataset was analyzed consistently with interpretive research tenets.*

*Findings* – *Data document (i) five dimensions of brand authenticity contextualized to l'Occitane Mediterranean brand; (ii) the different branding strategies made possible to companies by the varied combination of these five dimensions; and (iii) the distinct profiles of brand consumers according to the specific authentic narrative each of them is more receptive to.*

Practical implications – *Implications for authentic brand narratives are drawn. I argue that when companies adopt a narrative approach to branding they can establish a stronger dialogue with customers and defend their competitive advantage more effectively. Actually, each brand narrative cannot be easily imitated by competitors since its imitation would turn out as a fake, unauthentic tale for the market.*

Originality of the chapter – *The chapter contributes to the fields of branding and authenticity, by extending the notion and understanding of consumption authenticity to brands.*

This chapter undertakes an emergent venue in branding. I observe the increasing relevance that scholars and companies attribute to brand narratives (Hirschman, 2010; Woodside, 2010) on the one hand, and authentic experiences (Grayson & Martinec, 2004), on the other. Brands are becoming conveyers of tales for their markets but these markets are also turning into hard to please audiences since they separate germane, authentic narratives from fake, unreliable ones.

Therefore, the convergence of these two trends asks for clarification. What does it mean for brand managers to generate an authentic brand narrative? What makes a narrative authentic? Can we envision alternative patterns of authentic narratives? Also, are consumers homogeneous in terms of the way they elaborate authenticity?

Ethnographic fieldwork on l'Occitane brand helps unpack these largely unknown points. Findings show that authentic brand narratives are generated by iterative interpretive processes involving the two sides of the market: companies and consumers. Companies have at their own disposal several levers to generate brand authenticity (cf. Beverland, 2009; Gilmore & Pine, 2007). Consumers are not all the same since they are differently receptive to brand narratives, and to authenticity in particular (cf. Beverland & Farrelly, 2010). As such, companies and consumers are involved in reciprocal dialogues, where the co-construction of authentic brand narratives emerges from ongoing confrontation, fine-tuning, and matches.

The following sections illustrate these points more deeply. In the first section, the theoretical frame is plotted by bonding together the literature on brand narratives and that on authenticity. The second section presents the case history of l'Occitane en Provence and briefly explains the methods for data collection and interpretation. In the third section, findings are extensively discussed by means of a music metaphor, which integrates the agentic behavior of managers and customers. Finally, the closing section draws managerial implications for branding and argues that the establishment and nurturing of authentic brand narratives constitutes a hardly imitable source of competitive advantage.

## DEFINING AUTHENTIC BRAND NARRATIVES

### Branding between Brand Architecture and Narratives

Brands are intangible resources for companies, and can represent one – if not "the" – most relevant asset for some of them, especially in consumer markets (Keller, 2009). Among others, Interbrand (www.interbrand.com), the worldwide leading consulting firm in brand management, states that brands are central for companies' strategies as much as they constitute marketable assets. For this reason, each year Interbrand ranks the best global brands and gives financial estimates of the market value for the top ones. Liz Moor (2007) notes that the booming of brands, which she defines as the institutionalization of branding or the affirmation of the branding discourse, has occurred over the last decade, and has largely appeared in parallel to its antithesis, brand contestation (Klein, 2000). Keller (2009) argues that the dominance of branding over other organizational priorities originates from the effect of successful brands on consumers: brands help consumers live "a little – or even a lot – better" (2009, p. 45). As such, consumers reward brands, and the companies that own those brands, in various ways, including loyalty, willingness to pay premium-prices, positive word-of-mouth and evangelization, brand communities, and the like. More radically, Lury (2004, pp. 149–150) postulates the "objectivity" of brands, that is, their relevance within the objects that structure our contemporary social life by means of relational practices.

In a valuable contribution appearing in *Marketing Science*, Keller and Lehmann (2006) draft the state of the art about the brand literature. The authors identify the key areas of knowledge acquired over years and contextually suggest new directions for future research. Overall, the representation of branding they offer is very much consistent with the dominating logic of the brand architecture. Brands result from the planned summation of various brand elements (e.g., marks, logos, symbols, slogans, and packaging), which have to empower and exploit the potential of a brand

(Kapferer, 2008; Keller, 2009). Such architecture, therefore, constitutes the skeleton of the brand where its single constituents find an organic, functional fit with the overall brand body, that is, its structure.

However more recently, an alternative approach to branding has been gaining increasing popularity within the so-called sociocultural branding literature (Diamond et al., 2009; Holt, 2004). The above-mentioned organicistic, traditional idea of brands has been actually reverted to the possibility of conceiving brands as cultural narrators (Hirschman, 2010; Woodside, 2010). Since the early times of McCracken's foundational model of cultural transfers (1986), it is acknowledged that meanings can be attached to products and brands via the fashion system and advertising. Elaborating upon this view, some scholars document the narrative essence of brands (Cayla & Arnould, 2008; Dalli & Romani, forthcoming), and raise them to the status of ideological carriers and storytellers. In other words, companies may no longer manage brands complying with Keller's (2008) brand-building vision (i.e., an architecture where managers are designers of the final building and its single components). Instead, brands engage customers and companies in an ongoing dialogical exchange, in which the company only partially controls the narrative while co-construction dynamics are welcomed. Thus, brand managers have to be part of a "multilogue" (Berthon, Holbrook, Hulbert, & Pitt, 2007) and "attend to, and leverage, a 'symphony' of old and new brand meanings" (Diamond et al., 2009, p. 119).

Examples of brand narratives in consumer research are countless. To quote but a few, Nike town in Chicago (Peñaloza, 1998), Disney (Boje, 1995), McDonald's (Ritzer, 1983), the Star Trek community (Kozinet, 2001), ESPN Zone restaurants (Sherry et al., 2004), Harley Davidson bikers (Schouten & McAlexander, 1995), the American Girl store in Chicago (Borghini et al., 2009), Weight Watchers (Moisio & Beruchashvili, 2010), Harry Potter (Brown & Patterson, 2010), and Camper (Dalli & Romani, forthcoming), all testify how consumers' interest can be captured by immersing them into veritable representations of brand cultures. A particular exemplar of brand narrative is emblematic for current discussion and is represented by Bryant Simon's recent book (2009) on Starbucks, provocatively titled *Everything but the Coffee*. The title underlines how much the product becomes marginal when confronted with the values, meanings, and stories that the brand brings to the market. Simon vividly documents how the worldwide success of Starbucks stems from the spread of its ideologies imbued with political, racial, and emotional flavor, the "taste" of which matters more than the taste of the coffee.

So much so, the best narrators are able to make their own brands become "lovemarks" (Roberts, 2006) and even "icons" (Holt, 2004). Brown suggests that such exceptional narrative skills originate from the construction of multilayered stories, given the numerousness and diversity of companies' audiences. Diamond et al. (2009) more disruptively demonstrate that the so-long established principle of integration and consistency across brand elements (Keller, 2008, 2009) may not be the most effective strategy. They contend that complementary narratives can outperform integrated and consistent brand elements since what matters are the synergies across the single constituents of what they call "brand gestalt."

In this chapter, I additionally show that, by incorporating a narrative perspective on branding, the rate of trustworthiness the story holds for its passionate listeners becomes an additional key issue. As a matter of fact, consumers fully enjoy brand narratives when these are perceived as germane, authentic tales of/for/from the market. For this reason, the following section overviews the work on authenticity and ties it to the so-far elaborated notion of brand narratives.

## Authenticity and Brand Narratives

As recently pointed out by the fathers of experience marketing (Pine & Gilmore, 1999), contemporary markets are characterized by the quest for authenticity. "People increasingly see the world in terms of real and fake, and want to buy something real from someone genuine, not a fake from some phony." (Gilmore & Pine, 2007, p. 1). The awakened attention for authenticity is due to a multiplicity of factors, such as the progressive globalization of markets (Askegaard & Kjeldgaard, 2002; Featherstone, 1990) that spurs reactions against market homogenenization (Thompson, Rindfleisch, & Arsel, 2006) and supports localisms as the Mediterranean consumer culture (Cova, 2005; Firat, 2005; Visconti, 2005); the nostalgic rooting as testified by retromarketing (Holbrook, 1993; Stern, 1992); and the numerous examples of consumer activism and resistance to inauthentic consumerism and materialism (Fischer, 2001; Kozinets & Handelman, 2004; Murray & Ozanne, 1991).

Authenticity constitutes a central tenet of modernity (Lowenthal, 1992) since what is said to be fake is often a source of derision for its holders (Gilmore & Pine, 2007, p. 107). Despite recent concern for this construct, the interest for authenticity – however conceived – is therefore not a new discovery. Actually, the debate around authenticity has originated since the early times of the Industrial Revolution (Orvell, 1989) but to date has been mostly kept in the background of the consumer literature. Among others, authenticity is synonymic of tradition in retromarketing research (Brown, 2001), constitutes the prerequisite to full-blown store and market experience (Peñaloza, 1998, 2001), or represents the outcome of offerings qualified on the basis of their country of origin (Ahmed, d'Astous, & El Adraoui, 1994; Hong & Wyer, 1989). In similar and other venues, however, it has never received focal attention.

Defining authenticity per se is controversial (Beverland & Farrelly, 2010). Grayson and Martinec (2004) recently comment on the paucity of systematic consumer research as much as the multiplicity of meanings attributed to authenticity. One major problem with the definition of the construct stems from the cross-cultural variance of the tenet. Jones (1990) demonstrates how the meaning of copying – and thus reproducing an authentic item – changes consistently across cultures, sometimes acquiring the valence of fake, sometimes becoming the emblem of realism. By focusing on the artistic production, he shows how the boundary between fake and authentic artworks cannot be easily traced, even within the same cultural milieu. For example, with reference to paintings he notes how the Western culture requires the personal involvement of the artist in the process of painting to attribute the status of authenticity to the canvas, whereas with marble or bronze sculpture it is not unusual that artists work solely on the idea, giving away the responsibility of producing their work to artisans.

More affirmatively, some contributions offer indications about the attributes authenticity should hold. Beverland and Farrelly (2010) list three main benefits that consumers look for in authentic objects (i.e., control, connection, and virtue) and tie them to the emergence of three equivalent sociocultural norms in the consumer culture (respectively, practicality, connectivity, and morality). Jones (1990) sets the principle of deception, meant as a form of fraud, and thus as unauthenticity. To him, deception does not result from the process of falsification, it is rather due to the concealment of falsification when falsification occurs. In the aforementioned case of bronze sculptures, buyers and spectators are conscious that the artist is often not part of the molding process. Thus, bronzes are authentic since everyone knows the distinction between the artist's and the artisan's role, and the possibility of having multiple copies of the same artwork. Analogously, Grayson and Martinec (2004) highlight that authenticity is strongly intertwined with the notions of genuineness and truth, and thus of trustworthiness, which however assume different interpretations according to the contexts of reference. More pragmatically, Gilmore and Pine (2007, pp. 96–97) identify two different dimensions to classify (un)authentic business offerings: (i) being true to own self, which constitutes a self-reflexive criterion; and (ii) being true to others, which envisions a relational criterion. By crossing the two dimensions, they obtain four ideal-types of artifacts: (i) real-fake; (ii) real-real; (iii) fake-fake; and (iv) fake-real. In particular, they observe how companies pursuing the real-real strategy expose themselves to constant external scrutiny and run the risk of being sanctioned should their offering be perceived as a fake. Differently, other companies disclose the process of falsification of their offering, and thus make it a "fauxthentic" (2007, p. 107) via transparency.

The above-mentioned discussion shows that the definition of authenticity has mainly to do with trust and information disclosure of producers with their markets. As commented by Beverland and Farrelly (2010, p. 839), the ultimate core meanings that authenticity maintains across this variety of approaches and works relate to "what is genuine, real, and/or true." At the same time, an even more central issue in the theoretical debate on authenticity questions its ontology. Do markets and consumer researchers hold an objective idea of authenticity or do they assume a constructivist view of it? Which are the branding implications in the two cases?

To answer these questions, the anthropological work on tourism is particularly beneficial. According to MacCannell (1976), the touristic experience shows the demarcation between realism and constructivism. The author observes how tourists generally receive a falsification of reality through forms of "staged" authenticity, which hides "real back stage" authenticity. Through the tourist market, places and people are commoditized complying with tourists' needs, stereotypes, and preferences. From a radically different perspective, Bruner (2005, p. 93) opposes that there are no originals since a single authentic culture does not exist. In his inquiry on the production and serving of the Maasai culture in Kenya (2005), he documents three different ways of authenticity construction for tourists: (i) the postcolonial approach of the Mayers site, now closed, in which colonial tourists were given a tribal representation of the Maasai; (ii) the postindependence site of Bomas ethnic theme park, which mostly targets domestic tourists and thus offers them a traditional view of the Maasai; and (iii) the postmodern strategy of the Sundowner site, in which contemporary tourists are immersed in hyperreal representations of colonial Kenya.

Generalizing from this literature, by endorsing realism and objectivity markets and researchers look for some "real" features that an artifact has to incorporate to make it authentic. As such, realistic authenticity – MacCannell's notion of back stage (1976) – deals with "true reality" and is grounded in the postpositivistic ontology, in which what is true and what is fake can be cleanly separated. Transferring it to branding, brands will be authentic if the goods they identify show real attachment to a place, history, craftsmanship, or uniqueness (Gilmore & Pine, 2007) which are part of the brand narratives. For example, LVMH French champagnes, Barilla Italian pasta, and Ralph Lauren exclusive clothes share similar bonds to "real" traditions, sites, and/or productive practices. Therefore, brands with stronger local ties, sounder historicity, or deeper social responsibility rank higher in the list of authentic icons.

Interpretive researchers and postmodern consumers also state that authenticity is part of a constructivist process, in which companies and markets agree upon some truly-false narratives (Graillot & Badot, 2006; Peñaloza, 2001). Umberto Eco (1986) comments that our society is receptive to the perfection of fakes and this fact witnesses our increasing obsession for simulacra and counterfeits. As such, consumers can willingly fall into hyperreal brand experiences qualified as pleasurable, trustable, and true. Disneyland immerses visitors in three-dimensional, interactive tales (Boje, 1995). Televiewers may even detect authenticity in the falsification of television reality shows (Rose & Wood, 2005). Additionally, by stepping in one of l'Occitane shops around the world, each customer can jump into Provencal colors and smells, and so enjoy forms of authentic escapism (Green & Brock, 2000).

On the ontological point, Grayson and Martinec (2004) elaborate upon the French semiotic tradition and classify two forms of authenticity, which they frame in terms of relations between the sign (here, the brand and goods) and the object (here, the tradition, the place, and/or the process of production implied by the sign). They distinguish between indexical and iconic authenticity, where indexicality postulates a cause–effect relationship between the sign and the object, while iconicity documents a form of cultural and symbolic construction of this relationship. As such, indexical authenticity is basically overlapping with the postpositivistic idea of objectivity and realism, where iconic authenticity mirrors the constructivist view on authenticity.

Focusing her attention on brands, Celia Lury points out that brands themselves are products of artificial sciences, including marketing, design, and economics. In this way, she (2004, p. 151) contends "the 'is' of a brand is also 'its may-be'; in its being – its objectivity – it has the potential to be otherwise, to become." Even though such brand flexibility occurs under limitations, Lury demonstrates that brands are co-constructed since they are an object of mediation constantly framed through consumer engagement and managers' actions. Adam Arvidsson (2007) extends this concept when he identifies the objective of brand management. Acknowledging Lury's idea of brands as platforms for consumer action, he argues that brand managers have to limit consumer agency in the interest of brands, and thus convey to the market brand structures able to guide consumer opposition and prevent the overthrowing of brand meanings.

From a managerial viewpoint, Gilmore and Pine (2007, pp. 49–50) overcome the ontological dispute about authenticity to illustrate five different dimensions companies can deploy to convey authenticity to their markets: (i) naturalness that is obtained by escaping brand/product contamination due to human intervention (e.g., organic crops); (ii) originality, which stems from brand/product's uniqueness in design (e.g., Alessi kitchen utensils); (iii) exceptionality granted by outstanding workmanship and craftsmanship (e.g., Dior tailor-made clothes); (iv) referentiality through which brands/goods are rooted in a given spatial and temporal tradition (e.g., Parmesan cheese); and (v) influentiality that results from the brand/product capability of moving people to purposeful action (e.g., Camper shoes invitation to under- and eco-consumption). Remarkably, authenticity is not achieved by jointly pursuing the five dimensions at one time. Each brand can build its narratives by tailoring these dimensions on the resources, personal history, and market objectives it has.

This chapter combines the emerging importance of brand narratives and authenticity by introducing the notion of "authentic brand narratives." I illustrate the relevance of authenticity in brand narratives as constructed by the interaction between a company and its markets. Theoretical considerations and managerial implications rely upon an extensive ethnographic case study (Visconti, 2010) on l'Occitane brand whose strong Provencal rooting is central both for the company's marketing strategies and the consumers' appraisal of the brand. After a brief description of the field, the following paragraphs extensively discuss: (i) the adaptation of Gilmore and Pine (2007) five dimensions of authenticity to l'Occitane brand; (ii) the various possibilities a firm has to leverage upon these dimensions for its branding strategy; and (iii) the various typologies of consumers that can be identified in the market with reference to their different ways of envisioning brand authenticity.

# THE FIELD: STAGING L'OCCITANE EN PROVENCE

### Narrating the Company

The empirical context of this research is constituted by one brand, in particular, l'Occitane en Provence. The company was founded in 1976 by the Provencal entrepreneur Olivier Baussan to produce body, face, and home toiletries compliant with the ingredients and traditional productive practices of Provencal artisans. From its establishment, the brand has been strongly rooted in Provence, a region located in the south-east of France, whose long history includes several dominations spanning from the Greek to the Ligures and Gauls, and from the Romans to the Germans. Provence is part of Occitania, a supranational area covering the south of France, Monaco, the north-east of Spain, and the Northern part of Italy. Occitania has never acquired any political or juridical recognition but constitutes a cultural district, in which heritage, common language (i.e., Occitan), and shared Mediterranean lifestyles (Cova, 2005) ground natives' sense of belongingness. Notably, Baussan drew from this body of values and meanings to label his company, which was originally branded "l'Occitane."

In its earlier years, l'Occitane was exclusively managed according to Provencal craftsmanship. The first factory was located in a disused soap plant in Manosque, a small village in Haute Provence, and the products – all obtained from the distillation of essential oils from local sweet herbs – were initially sold in local markets till the first mono-brand shop opened in 1978 in Volx, Provence. The first relevant turnaround occurred in the 1990s, when Baussan was dispossessed by the venture capitalists he had involved to support the expansion of his enterprise. The second turning point took place when the Austrian entrepreneur Reinold Geiger progressively acquired a stake of control in the company, called back Baussan to lead product innovation and creativity, and renamed the firm "l'Occitane en Provence" to further emphasize its cultural and geographical ties. To date, the company remains under the control of Geiger with a minority participation of the French group Clarins. It operates through exclusive stores in over 80 countries spread in the five continents with more than 1,500 shops, and has generated sales of around 540 million euro in 2009.

The branding strategy of l'Occitane en Provence is very consistent with its origins and focalized on the idea of product authenticity, as remarked in all the institutional communications and documented by the advertising pay off *"l'Occitane. Une histoire vraie [l'Occitane. A True Story]."* Taking into account the product, the main ingredients are mostly Mediterranean herbs and plants, including almond tree, anise, apricot, basil, calendula, chamomile, carrot, mint, fig tree, lavender, and lemon. These ingredients are strongly emphasized in the communication of the product, being the brand compliant with the principles of phytotherapy. On the company's web site (http://www.loccitane.com), for each ingredient a full description and additional information about the traditions, properties, and the products containing this ingredient are provided. The naturalness and craftsmanship

## Authentic Brand Narratives

of its products is enforced by the packs, which propose simple bottles and boxes, frequently aluminum-made, with images of the fresh ingredients, and sticky labels detailing the traceability of the content. The layout of shops is another key lever of authenticity. Stores are completely dominated by colors reminding of the sun and flowers of Provence, with deep yellow and blue lavender as dominant notes. Wood furniture displays products in pharmaceutical cabinets, which endorse the idea of tradition and effectiveness. Paintings, drawings, and photos portray Provence, while floor terracotta tiles recall the typical Mediterranean flooring of small streets and squares (Fig. 1).

Overall, and as reported on the company's web site, l'Occitane's branding strategies nurtures simple values, including "authenticity, respect,

*Fig. 1.* Visual Examples of l'Occitane Brand Narrative.

sensoriality and continual improvement. This is more than a philosophy: it is a commitment that, over the years, has driven many concrete actions. All of our actions and choices are guided by a twofold desire: to preserve and to pass on." The bridging between the past and the future goes hand in hand with the spatial bridging, which creates connections between Provence and the over 1,500 l'Occitane shops in the world. Each of them offers a hyperreal reconstruction of a piece of Provence, and so allows immersion in another place "out there" but enjoyable "here and now."

Relying on consumer field interviews, Gilmore and Pine (2007, p. 112) confirm the effectiveness of the company's branding strategy, since their informants include l'Occitane en Provence in the short list of brands perceived as exemplars of real-real offerings. This implies the company's capability of building a reputation of internal and external trustworthiness over time, which can be maintained only by means of restless commitment and high standards of performance. More minutely, Graillot and Badot (2006) leverage upon their French emic perspective (Berry, 1989) and question the ontology of l'Occitane brand authenticity. They carefully document the coexistence of indexical and iconic authenticity, since some "real" features (e.g., ingredients, the foundation of the company, and the transferred imaginary) accompany hyperreal elements (e.g., the derooting of l'Occitane shops in over 80 countries, the Austrian control over the company, and the fauxthentic packs and retailing furniture). In this light, l'Occitane en Provence represents a valuable brand to inspect authentic brand narratives since it offers a blurred, complex bundle of authentic constituents intentionally leveraged by its brand managers.

*Collecting and Documenting l'Occitane Narratives*

Data supporting the findings and implications illustrated hereafter were collected by means of extensive ethnographic fieldwork. Observation and depth and short interviews were conducted both in the market and within the company. With reference to the market, observation was led within two main l'Occitane shops, located in Manosque and Paris. Manosque was selected thanks to its indexical relation to Provence and being the site of the first and only productive plant of l'Occitane. On the other hand, Paris represents a cosmopolitan center, and l'Occitane shops here maintain an iconic connection to Provence. In detail, the Parisian shop under main, but not sole, investigation was the one located in Ile de Saint Louis, which is one of the earliest shops opened by the company and still preserved in its

**Table 1.** Consumer Informants.

| Name | City | Brand Associations | Age Range | Cosmetic Expertise Ranking[a] |
|---|---|---|---|---|
| Adèlie | Manosque | Excellent, pleasant, sweet | 55–64 | 14 |
| Amèlie | Paris | Traditional, perfumed, reassuring | 25–34 | 20 |
| Anne | Manosque | Simple, perfumed, reassuring | 45–54 | 15 |
| Annie | Paris | Ethic, fair, quality | 25–34 | 23 |
| Caroline | Manosque | Provencal, efficient, perfumed | 65–74 | 8 |
| Charlotte | Manosque | Fresh, pleasant, efficient | 65–74 | 15 |
| Elise | Paris | Natural, sweet, respectful | 15–24 | 28 |
| Elodie | Manosque | Quality, territory, authenticity | 35–44 | 12 |
| Emna | Paris | Authentic, French, warm | 25–34 | 28 |
| Frèdèrique | Manosque | Provencal, coloured | 45–54 | 21 |
| Sylvic | Manosque | Natural, Provencal, authentic | 25–34 | 17 |
| Vanessa | Paris | Authentic, natural, responsive | 35–44 | 13 |
| Vèronique | Manosque | Provencal, sensual, quality | 35–44 | 15 |
| Vicky | Paris | Freshness, serious, efficiency | 35–44 | 13 |
| Victoria | Paris | Natural, regional, pleasant | 45–54 | 25 |

[a]The cosmetic expertise ranking is provided by l'Occitane customer dataset.

original internal architecture, decoration, and commercial display. To confirm the foundational role of this shop, the virtual tour of l'Occitane stores provided on the company's web site reproduces the retailing experience of Ile de Saint Louis. Overall, 27 days of observation were carried out and documented by means of field notes and photos. Contextually, 15 in-depth interviews with customers were done, seven in Paris and eight in Manosque. Customers vary in terms of sex, age, expertise in the category of toiletries and cosmetics, and duration and frequency of their relationship with l'Occitane (Table 1).

Within the company, a research assistant conducted an ethnographic case study (Visconti, 2010), given his direct involvement as consultant in l'Occitane. The research project was presented to the European marketing management committee, which granted stable support in the process of data collection and in the validation of the findings. Again, observation and 16 depth interviews with managers were fulfilled. Professional informants vary in terms of age, sex, location (4 in Manosque and 12 in Paris), professional paths, seniority, and position (Table 2).

Interviews were electronically recorded and fully transcribed. Observation was documented by researcher's field notes and photographs. The complete dataset, which includes 493 single-spaced pages of transcriptions, was

**Table 2.** Company Informants.

| Name | Team | Task | Year of Hiring | Former Task at l'Occitane |
|---|---|---|---|---|
| Alexandre | Operational marketing | CWE operational marketing director | 2006 | – |
| Aline | Human resources | Internal communication director | 1988 | Export sales administrator manager; international logistics director |
| Armand | Sales | Boutique manager Paris Gare de Lyon | 1996 | Salesman; boutique security |
| Aurélie | Marketing development | Development product manager | 2005 | – |
| Aziz | Operational marketing | CWE merchandising project manager | 2000 | Boutique manager; salesman; salesman assistant |
| Daniel | Marketing | Project manager | 1997 | Boutique manager; CWE training director; international training director |
| Eloise | Marketing development | Development product manager | 2006 | CWE operational product manager |
| Jeanne | Sales | Boutique manager Paris Ile de St. Louis | 2004 | Salesman; salesman assistant |
| Karen | Human resources | Sustainable development director | 2004 | Internal training; communication director |
| Marine | Operational marketing | CWE merchandising senior manager | 1999 | Training manager; regional director; international merchandising director |
| Mathilde | Marketing development | Marketing assistant | 2002 | – |
| Morane | Operational marketing | CWE operational product manager | 2007 | – |
| Paulette | Sales administration | CWE inventory and stock flow manager | 2002 | Boutique manager; salesman; salesman assistant |
| Reinold | Marketing | Artistic director | 1993 | Boutique manager; CWE merchandising director; photographer |
| Simon | Operational marketing | CWE merchandising manager | 1998 | Senior district director; training manager; boutique manager |
| Yannick | B2B marketing | CWE B2B and franchising manager | 2005 | – |

codified and thematized consistently with conventional qualitative research standards (Arnould & Wallendorf, 1994; Hirschman, 1986; Lincoln & Guba, 1985).

## THE CO-CONSTRUCTION OF AUTHENTIC BRAND NARRATIVES

Empirical evidence confirms the convergence of indexicality and iconicity (Grayson & Martinec, 2004) in the construction of l'Occitane brand authenticity. While the overlapping between these two dimensions is present in the mind of managers, not all the customers are equally capable of perceiving the boundary between the two. In particular, metropolitan consumers do not have the cultural capital (Bourdieu, 1984) to help them identify the overcoming of realism in favor of hyperreality in the company's brand narratives. Natural ingredients and fauxthentic (Gilmore & Pine, 2007) store experiences are regarded as part of the same narrative, and do not hold different meanings for them. This evidence, which particularly emerges from the confrontation between Provencal and Parisian consumers, supports the conclusion that authenticity is constructed and originates from the interpretive processes of companies and customers altogether.

Consistent with the aforementioned conclusion, data document the co-construction of brand authenticity by l'Occitane managers and its customers. The interpretive model provided here develops around a music metaphor (Table 3). I assume that Gilmore's and Pine's five dimensions of authenticity constitute a stringed instrument. Each string resounds differently, and generates music both individually and together with other strings. In the same way, companies may convey authentic brand narratives to their markets by playing with a single dimension of authenticity or by integrating more dimensions at one time. For example, l'Occitane has been elaborating a sophisticated brand narrative, which basically involves all the five strings of authenticity in a multilayered tune. Additionally, when played together strings generate chords. If the company represents the player in the metaphor, these chords become the foundational principles of its brand strategy obtainable from the five dimensions of authenticity. Findings highlight three main chords that effectively generate an authentic music, including (i) sincerity and reliability; (ii) exhaustiveness; and (iii) pruning. Finally, I metaphorically portray consumers as an agentic audience, which is varied inside and expresses different types of requirements to the player.

*Table 3.* Modelling the Co-construction of Authentic Brand Narratives.

| Chords (Company's side) | +++ | + | +++ | +++ | ++ |
|---|---|---|---|---|---|
| | ? | ? | ? | ? | ? |
| | ? | ? | ? | ? | ? |
| Strings of authenticity (the shared playground) | *Naturalness* | *Originality* | *Exceptionality* | *Referentiality* | *Influentiality* |
| The sound of each string: associations | Link to nature | Uniqueness | Attention | Culture | Sustainability |
| | Ecology | Innovation | Care | Territory | Ecology |
| | Rusticity | Differentiation | Research | Traditions | Animalist |
| | Simplicity | Rarity | Craftsmanship | History | Fair trade |
| | Spontaneity | | Rarity | Longevity | Charity |
| | | | Preciousness | | |
| | | | Warmth | | |
| | | | Intimacy | | |
| | | | Respect | | |
| Authenticity listeners (consumer profiles) | +++ | + | ++ | +++ | + | Metropolitan |
| | ++ | + | +++ | +++ | + | Nostalgic |
| | ++ | + | +++ | ++ | + | Relational |
| | ++ | + | + | ++ | +++ | Ethical |
| | ++ | +++ | +++ | + | + | Elitist |

+, Low relevance of each string for a given chord or listener; ++, good relevance of each string for a given chord or listener; +++, greatest relevance of each string for a given chord or listener.

Empirical evidence supports the existence of five segments of audience: (i) metropolitan, (ii) nostalgic, (iii) relational, (iv) ethical, and (v) elitist listeners of authentic music. Detailed presentation of this conceptualization is, respectively, illustrated in the three following sections.

## The Five Strings of Authenticity: Play It Differently, Sam!

Aline, Internal Communication Director at l'Occitane, clearly acknowledges the centrality of authenticity to define the heart of the company's brand narrative:

> The past CEO of l'Occitane went on following the same trajectory since the very beginning. Thus, he maintained the same form of communication: 'It's a communication about authenticity!' (Aline, manager, Manosque)

Reinold, Artistic Director at l'Occitane, adds depth to the concept.

> In our field, authenticity is actually defined on the basis of the raw materials we use. It's the way we do things. It isn't authenticity any longer; it's just normality. Look at what we produce, look at what we do. ... We can't stick to pure authenticity now but we try to preserve the fundamental elements that reconnect us to our region [i.e., Provence]. (Reinold, manager, Paris)

In his words authenticity is presented as a strongly interiorized asset to the point of acquiring the spontaneous and daily flow of normality. This statement does not mean that authenticity is not salient to the mind of managers. Rather, it has become a structural constituent of brand identity and the steering compass of l'Occitane brand strategy. He also points out the historical evolution of l'Occitane's relationship with authenticity, which parallels its market expansion. Despite the constant effort of keeping its cultural heritage and the bond to Provence, he remarks that indexicality has been progressively coupled with iconicity.

Data also show the deployment of Gilmore's and Pine's five dimensions of authenticity (2007) in the branding policy of the company. However, these dimensions are inflated with Mediterraneaness (Cova, 2005; Firat, 2005; Visconti, 2005). The Mediterranean ground provides peculiar and rich stimuli to l'Occitane brand narratives since it comprises distinctive colors, flavors and smells, ingredients, locations and historical sites, but also cultural values such as eclecticism, openness, respect, slowness, and enjoyment of life (Cassano, 1996). Most of these traits have become part of the brand tales. Hereafter, I comment in detail each of these dimensions and the peculiar Mediterranean sound each of the strings utters.

*Naturalness*
As contended in Reinold's former excerpt, naturalness of ingredients is at the very heart of l'Occitane authentic narrative. Ingredients evoke the direct connection to a given place, and thus enforce indexicality and realism. At the same time, they are also symbolically elaborated by consumers. As a matter of fact, the use of Provencal raw materials is a physical tie to the land but also, and more relevantly, the expression of ecology, rusticity, simplicity, and spontaneity. Actually, the Mediterranean basin and Provence, in particular, are associated with positive images of sound rural life. As such, their connection to a place is also a connection to a point in time, and thus establishes a fluidity between the categories of time and space. Also, many of the plants and herbs distilled by l'Occitane are spontaneous (e.g., rosemary, lavender, mint, several fruits and berries, and flowers). This validates the narrative of naturalness since human involvement is limited to a few, basic activities. As Morane notices, it is not the simple use of natural ingredients that grants brand naturalness. Caudalìe, a competitor of l'Occitane, deploys natural materials obtained from grapes but, by emphasizing its technological and scientific outstanding results, cannot leverage upon its naturalness:

> Caudalie, of course, talks about grapes [...], but it is *so* technical, and brand communication is *so* focused on scientific results that you can't feel naturalness anymore. (Morane, CWE Operational Product Manager, Paris)

*Originality*
Original authenticity is defined as the brand's or product's capability of "being the first of its kind, never before seen by human eyes; not a copy or imitation." (Gilmore & Pine, 2007, p. 49) Voices are again eloquent in highlighting the point.

> Overall, authenticity is definable with reference to something else. What differentiates you from the others, this makes you authentic. (Armand, boutique manager, Paris, Gare de Lyon)

> Yeah, Lush, they are authentic! ... well, authentic means original, that they distinguish themselves from others. (Elise, consumer, Paris)

This trait of authenticity is particularly central for the current discussion on brand narratives since originality assures a company the advantage of the first mover and a hardly imitable source of competitive advantage. The managerial implications are going to be better discussed in the closing section but I here unpack the various meanings that managers and consumers attribute to originality. Informants describe this dimension of authenticity in terms of uniqueness, innovation, differentiation, and rarity of the tale. To a certain extent, l'Occitane is the sole company having a Provencal positioning. It is not unique for its use of natural ingredients (see Caudalie, Sisley, or The Body Shop) or rural tradition, but it is definitely alone in locating them within the geocultural basin of Provence.

*Exceptionality*
Exceptional authenticity results from the craftsmanship granted during the production and commercialization of the product. Despite its industrialized process, l'Occitane goes on preserving the illusion of manual work. Among others, some narrative linkages to past craftsmanship stem from the location of its plant, the product appearance, and the store layout. The plant has been maintained in Manosque, where the first productive site was established by the founder Olivier Baussan. More relevantly, the packaging and the shops play a terrific role in immersing consumers in the brand narrative. Emna and Elise admit their sensitivity towards the information reported on the label and the store atmosphere:

> I love the very handcraft gesture of sticking labels crosswise. It's genial! You've the impression they were stuck by hand. (...) I'm sure marketers studied it well. (Emna, consumer, Paris)

> I read that olives are harvested accurately by hand. (...) It may be unimportant to everyone, but there's some tenderness in this gesture. (Elise, consumer, Paris)

*Referentiality*
Long-established traditions, historical connection between a product and a place, well-known rituals participate in the construction of referentiality. In particular, l'Occitane builds its referential authenticity by explicitly mentioning its spatial and temporal ties with Provence. In this case, naturalness and referentiality appear strongly intertwined, and foundational for the company's brand strategy. As formerly recalled, after Reinold Geiger acquired the share of control in the company this position was further endorsed by incorporating the expression "en Provence" in the brand name. Empirical evidence documents the success of the company in pursuing the goal, since the brand is firmly associated with ideas of culture, territory, traditions, history, past, and longevity (Table 1).

> Well, there's a reason why we're not named l'Occitane but l'Occitane en Provence. (Karen, Sustainable Development Director, Manosque)

The decision of saying 'en Provence' [was the choice of] developing our identity on something everlasting, thus linkable to the brand. That's the case, apparently. (Aline, Internal Communication Director, Manosque)

*Influentiality*
Influential authenticity can be achieved when companies succeed in affecting and orienting the behavior of customers beyond the exchange transaction. This implies an extensive definition of the entrepreneurial activity, which is not confined to the market and the related profit-oriented dynamics, to include the social environment. On this level, l'Occitane evokes positive associations, including sustainability, respect for nature, animals, and humans, fair trade, and charity (Table 1).

The most important thing is being consistent communication. Summing up, if you say that l'Occitane respect nature, respect mankind, respect labour, that you produce in Burkina Faso because, well, you want to help underdeveloped countries, (...) that you use Braille inscriptions to respect your blind clients and make them independent, ... here you are! (Aziz, CWE Merchandising Project Manager, Manosque)

To wrap up, l'Occitane leverages upon most of Gilmore's and Pine's (2007) dimensions of authenticity. Nonetheless, it particularly elaborates upon naturalness, referentiality, and exceptionality, which best highlight its productive *savoir faire*, manual work, and history.

### The Chords of Authenticity: l'Occitane Authentically Narrates Itself

The field helps stretch the findings beyond the identification of the aforementioned dimensions of authenticity. Additionally, it helps complement Beverland and Farrelly (2010) discussion about the strategies that consumers pursue so as to build self-authenticity via authentic brands, products, and experiences. In their recent *JCR* article, they show that consumer authenticating strategies include placement, inference, and projection. My data illustrate how companies may play the five strings of authenticity to create chords so as to convey authentic brand narratives to their market.

Beyond controversies, former discussion demonstrates that authenticity implies trustworthiness of communications between the company and its audience. Not surprisingly, then, the three chords identified along my interpretive work allude to the drivers of companies' communicational choices. Communication is extensively intended here, since it does not only address linguistic contents provided by the company (e.g., ads, web communication, and brochures). It additionally covers marketing communication at large, and thus the paralinguistic contents embedded in brands, packaging, store layout, shopping assistants, and any other signifier a company uses to convey meanings to its market. L'Occitane case accounts for three principles guiding brand narratives, which are labeled (i) sincerity and informative reliability, (ii) informative exhaustiveness, and (iii) pruning.

*Sincerity and Informative Reliability*
This principle is qualitative in nature since it consists in the reliability, quality, and dependability of the company's communication.

> See, this is sincerity. It's what makes the difference between a good chef who cooks in person and a big chef who gives his name to frozen, ready-to-eat products. (Daniel, Project Manager, Paris)

> I know, for example, that the active principles they use are good, it is true. [It is true] that almond oil is good for the tonicity of the skin, (...) honey is good for hydration, etcetera. (Elise, consumer, Paris)

These voices reveal that sincerity originates pretty much from the rate of information disclosure operated by the company as well as from the trustworthiness of the disclosed information. By means of sincerity, authentic brand narratives become stronger since the narrator proves honesty, respectability, and loyalty towards its conversation partners. For l'Occitane – but, I would argue, for any company in general – sincerity is particularly requested for the core dimensions of its authenticity; in this case, with reference to the naturalness of the product, the craftsmanship of production, and the Provencal referentiality.

*Informative Exhaustiveness*
Exhaustiveness interrogates the completeness of the information sent to the market, and thus consists in the amount of details and indications customers receive more than the intrinsic quality of these messages. As such, it represents a quantitative criterion to orient brand narratives. Its connection to authenticity is more subtle, and stems from the consideration that customers can interpret incomplete information as a lack of reliability and a form of falsification, which lead to a loss of authenticity.

> When I buy them, I don't know where they are produced, I don't know what's in them, I don't know to what extent they devastated entire forests. Things like these. ... Leader Price brands [a chain of discount stores in France], to me, aren't authentic. (Reinold, Artistic Director, Paris)

Also and differently from sincerity, it is not possible to conclude that some dimensions of authenticity are more intensely tied to exhaustiveness. As better commented in the next paragraph, the required completeness of information on the five dimensions of authenticity will vary according to the specific typology of consumer to be targeted. For example, ethical consumers will be more interested in receiving full details about influentiality whereas nostalgic consumers are going to be more receptive in terms of referentiality of the brand.

*Pruning*
Finally, pruning indicates the company's capability of giving reliable (i.e., sincere) and satisfying (i.e., exhaustive) information while restraining the information load for its audience to the minimum. As proved by former research (Beverland & Farrelly, 2010; Chronis & Hampton, 2008), consumers seeking for authenticity keep their attention on a few indexical cues, which increase in number with the increase in personal involvement. As such, brand narratives are more effective when grounded on trustworthy and detailed information pertaining to the audience's priority cues.

> [...] It doesn't have to become a mess like The Body Shop, where you have lots of different stories about several different things, and it's right there that you lose authenticity. (Alexandre, CWE Operational Marketing Director, Paris)
>
> Something authentic is something simple, a starting point. (Aline, Internal Communication Director, Manosque)

### *Agentic Listeners: Consumers Co-Constructing Brand Narratives*

Beverland (2005, p. 460) argues that "brand managers are not the sole creators of brand meaning." Actually, brand narratives, and authentic brand narratives even more dramatically, require the adoption of these stories by the community of consumers. As mentioned earlier, Beverland and Farrelly (2010) identify three different strategies that consumers use to authenticate their consumption and, through that, authenticate themselves. This finding proves the agentic involvement of consumers and the existence of different ways for them to participate in the co-construction of brand authenticity. Similarly but more analytically, my data document the emergence of different segments of consumers with reference to their quest of brand authenticity. Reconnecting to the music metaphor, such segments represent diverse audiences looking for peculiar "listening experiences."

In detail, I discuss five consumer positions, including metropolitan, nostalgic, relational, ethical, and elitist listeners.

*Metropolitan Listeners*
Roughly speaking, around half of the world population lives in cities. Thus, metropolitan consumers constitute the largest segment of the five consumer positions illustrated here. If living in a city does not make a consumer metropolitan by definition, this correspondence has however been often confirmed in the data. These listeners are less knowledgeable and competent about "music." Their cultural capital (Bourdieu, 1984) does not support them in the critical evaluation of brand narratives. As such, they rely on simple cues and heuristics to judge the authenticity of the brand. Typically, the historical, geographical, and cultural rooting of products and brands attribute them a sense of exoticism that ultimately becomes the quintessence of authenticity.

> Green tea, jasmine from the Nile, (...) they bring you back a little bit further, passages that bring you a little further from Provence. [But it] remains authentic, in any case. Just the image of Provence is to me a little weaker than at the beginning, but it doesn't lose its sense of authenticity. (Mathilde, consumer, Paris)

As vividly expressed by Mathilde, authenticity has more to do with the sense of remoteness than with the real provenience of the product.

*Nostalgic Listeners*
Former studies on nostalgia (e.g., Brown, 2001; Holbrook, 1993; Stern, 1992) perfectly support the representation of these consumers who are past-oriented and conceptualize authenticity with reference to time and history. They treasure the craftsmanship of production, the adherence to tradition, the consumption of lost products, all of which frame a preindustrial scenario. They are also prone to associate change and transformation with corruption and waste, since the past appears to them an uncontaminated land of heritage asking for preservation. Overall, they show stronger cultural capital than metropolitan consumers, even though this capital is generally sounder when nostalgic listeners had been part of the past they regret, as in the case of elderly consumers.

> Authenticity is to succeed, be willing to succeed, having succeeded in keeping this heritage, *id est*, not having dilapidated it all. The saying 'the first generation builds the fortune; the second generation increases the fortune; the third dilapidates it', well, here, we're at the second generation. We're still in authenticity, which means we increased and

exploited profitably what the heritage left us. Next step shouldn't be made. (Daniel, Project Manager, Paris)

Daniel is even more optimistic than the average consumer. Still, he envisions the future as the jump into the devastating "third generation." He wishes l'Occitane brand could be stopped at the second stage of its evolution and, in so doing, gives voice to the nostalgic spectators.

*Relational Listeners*
These consumers construct authenticity within the relational ties the brand may offer to its market. To them, sociality appears as the really missing value in contemporary life. As such, the re-establishment of positive relationships between them and the company, especially by means of its sales force, activate connections with the past and ground authenticity. The Mediterranean values of sociality and interconnectedness (Cassano, 1996) are embraced by l'Occitane, and to these listeners become source of empathy, warmth, and bidirectionality.

> I am older. I think these young shop-girls ... they learn their script by heart and can't adapt to different customers. Sometimes, it seems they're just performing as in actor studios. With them, there's no passion, no human contact, no transmission of ..., nothing real! (Veronique, consumer, Manosque)

*Ethical Listeners*
To a certain extent, ethical listeners also look for relational ties so as to experience brand authenticity. Different from the relational consumers, however, the sociality they seek is disembodied. They do not establish one-to-one dialogues with the company's salesmen or other consumers. Rather, they wish the company could be a champion, a supporter of our society, leveraging upon its superior economic power and the capability of going beyond pure market interest. In this way, they conceive authenticity by means of abstracted closeness to humankind and with no personal involvement in the authentication process.

> Authenticity is the simplest relationship towards nature and mankind. (Karen, consumer, Manosque)

> A company can be authentic when it shows ability to bring forward some actions that individually couldn't be done, such as helping populations in need or preserving some ingredients, (...) This is also authenticity. (Aline, consumer, Manosque)

*Elitist Listeners*
Elitist consumers are at odds with relational and ethical ones. They privilege the most ephemeral part of authenticity, which they use to show off their wealth and refinement. As commented before, authentic goods can be expensive in their category and hard to identify, since a certain cultural capital is needed. As such, these goods can be used to mark social disjuncture rather than to establish embodied or disembodied sociality. Consumer informants did not openly disclose such feelings but several shop assistants and managers have agreed to include this segment of the market among the beholders of authenticity. Marine, Senior Merchandiser, demonstrates that l'Occitane takes into consideration also exclusivity when designing its offering:

> When I think of something authentic, I think of something unique, original, something rare and precious. (…) Well, something precious, rare, unique. … I don't know if it's a good description. ( … ) I don't like the Body Shop at all. There's someone who's going to hate me, but I think it's low profile, mass. To me, it doesn't look authentic at all because their packs aren't authentic, they aren't rare. (Marine, manager, Paris)

# DISCUSSION: THAT'S ALL FOLKS?

This chapter originates from the attempt of merging two increasingly dominating theoretical paradigms in branding: brand narrative (Cayla & Arnould, 2008; Woodside, 2010) and authenticity (Grayson & Martinec, 2004; Beverland & Farrelly, 2010). By founding the notion of authentic brand narratives, branding can be read as a powerful conveyer of meanings to the market, which involves consumers in the representation of the brand by active dialogues, personal and even conflictual confrontations, ethical tensions, and connections with imaginary places, times, and traditions. The established representation of brands as an integrated system of elements underestimates the true potential of branding, and limits its narrative power to simplistic stories. "In contrast to the great stories of humanity, brand stories are usually devoid of conflict, flaws, and intrigue," observes Michael Beverland (2009, p. 7). Instead, brands should comply with brand gestalt (Diamond et al., 2009), and thus attract the market into passionate, blurred, and open-ended tales.

The l'Occitane case documents how authenticity in brand narratives is constructed by the concurrent intervention of the company and its customers. However, with a few notable exceptions (Beverland, 2009), former studies on the topic have mainly focused only on one of the two sides of this dyad. The interpretive model (Table 3) provided here is holistic and relational, and shows how the dimensions and communicational principles of authenticity that companies may deploy have to match the various consumer profiles existing in the market.

By acknowledging the constructivist, interpretive nature of authenticity, the chapter deeply expounds the multivocality of the construct. Different companies can pursue authentication of their brands by leveraging upon different resources. Analogously, consumers are not equally receptive to authenticity nor do they agree upon the cues to infer brand authenticity. As such, authenticity is not conceived as a miraculous panacea for brand managers nor an additional product attribute (Beverland, 2009) but asks for vision and constant adaptation to the context, fine-tuning with the company's audiences, and definite neglect for standardized recipes.

This work leads to one major managerial implication. Strategic and marketing studies have always been concerned about the defendability of the company's competitive advantage. In particular, imitation constitutes the shortest way to erode competitors' advantage. The same applies to branding. The well-established approach to branding does not protect from imitation of a company's brand elements. Several companies in one industry may follow analogous strategies to compete in the market (the so-called "strategic groups"; Grant, 1991), and thus present similarities in terms of their brand elements. Think, for example, of Ferrari and Maserati, Coca Cola and Pepsi, or l'Oréal and Collistar, which show strict closeness in terms of pricing decisions, distribution channels, packaging, communication strategies, and even market positioning.

By holding a narrative perspective on branding imitation is almost excluded. In fact, each brand enjoys the advantage of the first mover. When telling a story, a brand creates its own distinctive universe of characters, settings, values, and narrative plots. The imitation of this narrative by other competitors would be easily detected by the market, and punished as an exemplar of unauthentic tale. The same occurs with kids any time a story they know is modified or distorted by someone. The typical reaction is to reject the fake that represents a pale, meaningless, and even offensive copy of the true narrative.

Trustable storytellers know their audiences, involve them, and give them unique tales. Consistent with that, l'Occitane is not mimicking the narrative of its frontal competitors, Lush and The Body Shop, and vice versa. Each of the three brands has elaborated a peculiar narrative rooted on a distinctive ground. Lush has introduced the idea of an edible beauty, where products seem to come out of the Brothers Grimm's fairy tale "Hänsel and Gretel."

The Body Shop has centered its stories around the defense of animals' rights, and thus acquired an ethical legitimacy in the market. L'Occitane has established a discontinuity in the tradition of international marketing by "thinking local and acting global" (Dalli & Romani, forthcoming). Actually, the Provencal tradition has been defended and celebrated, and made a global marketable concept. Not surprisingly, all these three brands feature in the list of authentic companies presented by Gilmore and Pine (2007). A story for each brand. A brand for each story.

## ACKNOWLEDGMENTS

The author wishes to thank Federico Bertulessi for his sound contribution during the phase of data collection, l'Occitane for the participation in the project, and the two anonymous reviewers for their precious support.

## REFERENCES

Ahmed, S. A., d'Astous, A., & El Adraoui, M. (1994). Country of origin effects on purchase managers' product perceptions. *Industrial Marketing Management, 23*(4), 323–332.
Arnould, E. G., & Wallendorf, M. (1994). Market-oriented ethnography: Interpretation building and marketing strategy formulation. *Journal of Marketing Research, 31*(4), 484–504.
Arvidsson, A. (2007). *Brands: Meaning and value in media culture*. Abingdon, Oxon: Routledge.
Askegaard, S., & Kjeldgaard, D. (2002). The water fish swim in? Relations between culture and marketing in the age of globalization. In: T. Knudsen, S. Askegaard & N. Jørgensen (Eds), *Perspectives on marketing relationship* (pp. 13–35). Copenhagen: Thomson.
Berry, J. W. (1989). Imposed etics-emics-derived etics: The operationalization of a compelling idea. *International Journal of Psychology, 24*(66), 721–735.
Berthon, P., Holbrook, M. B., Hulbert, J. M., & Pitt, L. F. (2007). Viewing brands in multiple dimensions. *MIT Sloan Management Review, 48*(Winter), 37–43.
Beverland, M. B. (2005). Brand management and the challenge of authenticity. *Journal of Product and Brand Management, 14*(7), 460–461.
Beverland, M. B. (2009). *Building brand authenticity*. New York: Palgrave Macmillan.
Beverland, M. B., & Farrelly, F. J. (2010). The quest for authenticity in consumption: Consumers' purposive choice of authentic cues to shape experienced outcomes. *Journal of Consumer Research, 36*(February), 838–856.
Boje, D. M. (1995). Stories of the storytelling organization: A postmodern analysis of Disney as "Tamara land". *The Academy of Management Journal, 38*(4), 997–1035.
Borghini, S., Diamond, N., Kozinets, R. V., McGrath, M. A., Muñiz, A., Jr., & Sherry, J. F., Jr. (2009). Why are themed brandstores so powerful? Retail brand ideology at American Girl Place. *Journal of Retailing, 85*(3), 363–375.

Bourdieu, P. (1984). *Distinction. A social critique of the judgment of taste.* Cambridge, MA: Harvard University Press.
Brown, S. (2001). *Marketing. The retro revolution.* Thousand Oaks, CA: Sage.
Brown, S., & Patterson, A. (2010). Selling story: Harry Potter and the marketing plot. *Psychology and Marketing, 27*(6), 541–556.
Bruner, E. M. (2005). *Culture on tour.* Chicago, IL: The University Chicago Press.
Cassano, F. (1996). *Il Pensiero Meridiano.* Romea-Bari, I: Gius. Laterza & Figli.
Cayla, J., & Arnould, E. J. (2008). A cultural approach to branding in the global marketplace. *Journal of International Marketing, 16*(4), 86–112.
Chronis, A., & Hampton, R. D. (2008). Consuming the authentic Gettysburg: How a tourist landscape becomes an authentic experience. *Journal of Consumer Behaviour, 7*(2), 111–126.
Cova, B. (2005). Thinking of marketing in Meridian terms. *Marketing Theory, 5*(2), 205–214.
Dalli, D., & Romani, S. (forthcoming). From rural Mediterranean to global markets. Realism and diversity in the Camper experience. In: Peñaloza, L., Toulouse, N., & Visconti, L. M. (Eds), *Marketing management: A cultural perspective.* London, UK: Routledge.
Diamond, N., Sherry, J. F., Jr., Muñiz, A. M., Jr., McGrath, M. A., Kozinets, R. V., & Borghini, S. (2009). American Girl and the brand gestalt: Closing the loop on sociocultural branding research. *Journal of Marketing, 73*(May), 118–134.
Eco, U. (1986). *Faith in fakes.* New York: Harcourt Brace and Company.
Featherstone, M. (Ed.) (1990). *Global culture: Nationalism, globalization and modernity.* London, UK: Sage.
Firat, F. A. (2005). Meridian thinking in marketing? A comment on Cova. *Marketing Theory, 5*(2), 215–219.
Fischer, E. (2001). Rethorics of resistance, discourses of discontent. *Advances in Consumer Research, 28*(1), 123–124.
Gilmore, J. H., & Pine, J. B., II. (2007). *Authenticity: What consumers really want.* Boston: Harvard Business School Press.
Graillot, L., & Badot, O. (2006). Marketing mediterraneo o marketing iperreale: un tentativo di chiarificazione a partire dal caso dei negozi "L'Occitane." In: Carù, A., & Cova, B. (Eds), *Marketing Mediterraneo: Tra Metafora e Territorio* (pp. 27–83). Milan: Egea.
Grant, R. M. (1991). *Contemporary strategy analysis. Concepts, techniques, application.* Oxford: Blackwell.
Grayson, K., & Martinec, R. (2004). Consumer perceptions of iconicity and indexicality and their influence on assessments of authentic market offerings. *Journal of Consumer Research, 31*(September), 296–312.
Green, M. C., & Brock, T. C. (2000). The role of transportation in the persuasiveness of public narratives. *Journal of Personality and Social Psychology, 79*(5), 701–721.
Hirschman, E. C. (1986). Humanistic inquiry in marketing research: Philosophy, method, and criteria. *Journal of Marketing Research, 23*(3), 236–249.
Hirschman, E. C. (2010). Evolutionary branding. *Psychology and Marketing, 27*(6), 568–583.
Holbrook, M. B. (1993). Nostalgia and consumption preferences: Some emerging patterns of consumer tastes. *Journal of Consumer Research, 20*(2), 245–256.
Holt, D. B. (2004). *How brands become icons: The principles of cultural branding.* Boston: Harvard Business School Press.
Hong, S. T., & Wyer, R. S., Jr. (1989). Effects of country of origin and product-attribute information on product evaluation: An information processing perspective. *Journal of Consumer Research, 16*(2), 175–187.

Jones, M. (Ed.) (1990). *Fake? The art of deception.* Berkeley, CA: The University of California Press.
Kapferer, J. N. (2008). *The new strategic brand management: Creating and sustaining brand equity long term.* London, UK: Kogan Page.
Keller, K. L. (2008). *Strategic brand management: Building, measuring, and managing brand equity.* Upper Saddle River, NJ: Pearson/Prentice Hall.
Keller, K. L. (2009). Five secrets to brand success. *Market Leader, 2*(March), 45–47.
Keller, K. L., & Lehmann, D. R. (2006). Brands and branding: Research findings and future priorities. *Marketing Science, 25*(6), 740–759.
Klein, N. (2000). *No logo.* New York: Knopf Canada.
Kozinet, R. V. (2001). Utopian enterprise: Articulating the meanings of Star Trek's culture of consumption. *Journal of Consumer Research, 28*(1), 67–88.
Kozinets, R., & Handelman, J. (2004). Adversaries of consumption: Consumer movements, activism, and ideology. *Journal of Consumer Research, 31*(3), 691–704.
Lincoln, Y. S., & Guba, E. G. (1985). *Naturalistic inquiry.* Beverly Hills, CA: Sage.
Lowenthal, D. (1992). Authenticity? The dogma of self-delusion. In: M. Jones (Ed.), *Why fakes matter: Essays on problems of authenticity* (pp. 184–192). London, UK: British Museum.
Lury, C. (2004). *Brands: The logos of the global economy.* Abingdon, Oxon: Routledge.
MacCannell, D. (1976). *The tourist: A new theory of the leisure class.* New York: Schocken Books.
McCracken, G. (1986). Culture and consumption: A theoretical account of the structure and movement of the cultural meaning of consumer goods. *Journal of Consumer Research, 13*(1), 71–84.
Moisio, R., & Beruchashvili, M. (2010). Questioning for well-being at weight watchers: The role of the spiritual-therapeutic model in a support group. *Journal of Consumer Research, 36*(February), 857–875.
Moor, L. (2007). *The rise of brands.* New York: Berg.
Murray, J. B., & Ozanne, J. L. (1991). The critical imagination: Emancipatory interests in consumer research. *Journal of Consumer Research, 18*(September), 129–144.
Orvell, M. (1989). *The real thing: Imitation and authenticity in American culture, 1880–1940.* Chapel Hill, CA: University of North Carolina Press.
Peñaloza, L. (1998). Just doing it: A visual ethnographic study of spectacular consumption behavior at Nike Town. *Consumption, Markets and Culture, 2*(4), 337–400.
Peñaloza, L. (2001). Consuming the West: Animating cultural meaning at a stock show and rodeo. *Journal of Consumer Research, 28*(December), 369–398.
Pine, J. B., & Gilmore, J. H. (1999). *The experience economy: Work is theatre & every business a stage.* Boston: Harvard Business School Press.
Ritzer, G. (1983). The McDonaldization of society. *Journal of American Culture, 6*(1), 100–107.
Roberts, K. (2006). *Lovemarks: The future beyond brands.* New York: PowerHouse Books.
Rose, R. L., & Wood, S. L. (2005). Paradox and the consumption of authenticity through reality television. *Journal of Consumer Research, 32*(September), 284–296.
Schouten, J. W., & McAlexander, J. H. (1995). Subcultures of consumption: An ethnography of the new bikers. *Journal of Consumer Research, 22*(June), 43–61.
Sherry, J. F., Jr., Kozinets, R. V., Duhachek, A., DeBerry-Spence, B., Nuttavuthisit, K., & Storm, D. (2004). Gendered behavior in a male preserve: Role playing at ESPN Zone Chicago. *Journal of Consumer Psychology, 14*(1 & 2), 151–158.
Simon, B. (2009). *Everything but the coffee: Learning America from Starbucks.* Berkeley, CA: University of California Press.

Stern, B. B. (1992). Historical and personal nostalgia in advertising text: The fin de siecle effect. *Journal of Advertising, 21*(4), 11–22.
Thompson, C. J., Rindfleisch, A., & Arsel, Z. (2006). Emotional branding and the strategic value of the Doppleganger brand image. *Journal of Marketing, 70*(1), 50–64.
Visconti, L. M. (2005). L'individualisme postmoderne et la pensée méditerranéenne: Oxymore et réconciliation par un approche de cultural-crossing. In: F. Silva, A. Carù & B. Cova (Eds), *Marketing méditerranée et postmodernité* (pp. 127–148). Marseille, F: Editions Euromed Marseille.
Visconti, L. M. (2010). Ethnographic case study (ECS): Abductive modeling of ethnography in business marketing research. *Industrial Marketing Management, 5*(39), 25–39.
Woodside, A. G. (2010). Brand-consumer storytelling theory and research: Introduction to a *Psychology & Marketing* special issue. *Psychology and Marketing, 27*(6), 531–540.

# Part II
# Creating Selves

# CONSUMING AUTHENTIC NEIGHBORHOOD: AN AUTOETHNOGRAPHY OF EXPERIENCING A NEIGHBORHOOD'S NEW BEGINNINGS AND ORIGINS WITHIN ITS SERVICESCAPES

Michelle Hall

## ABSTRACT

Purpose – *This chapter examines individual and collective quests for authenticity, as experienced through consumption activities within an urban neighborhood. It investigates the interplay between consumption experiences as authenticating acts and authoritative performances (Arnould & Price, 2000), and considers the implications with regard to Zukin's (2010) theories on urban authenticity, and how it may be experienced as new beginnings and origins.*

Methodology – *The chapter is based on autoethnographic research that explores how interaction and identity definition within servicescapes can work to construct place-based community.*

Findings – *It describes how a servicescape of new beginnings offered opportunities for individual authentication that also enabled personal identification with a specific cultural group. This authentication drew on the cultural capital embedded in such locations, including their association with gentrification. This is contrast with the collective identification offered by a servicescape operating as a place of exposure. This site of origins displayed the social practices of a different demographic, which worked to highlight a relational link between the authentication practices of the broader neighborhood. These sites also worked cumulatively, to highlight the inauthenticities within my identification practices and offer opportunities for redress. Through this interplay it was possible to establish an authentic sense of neighborhood that drew on its new beginnings and its origins, and was both individual and collective.*

Originality – *Through the combination of urban and consumption-based perspectives of authenticity, and an autoethnographic methodology, this chapter offers a different insight into the ways identification with, and attachment to, a neighborhood can develop through consumption experiences.*

# INTRODUCTION

The urban environment is a key site of identity definition for many individuals in contemporary society, and consequently consumption experiences and the urban places in which they occur are a fundamental aspect of contemporary urban living. Because of this, experiencing the urban environment is increasingly associated with consuming it, in that the identity of an urban area becomes an additional value that can be extracted through a consumption experience. Conversely then the urban experience is also created through its consumption, such that areas can take on identities associated with the consumption experiences available within them. For individual consumers this implies that urban identities can become yet another consumable, able to be adopted through everyday and lifestyle consumption experiences within urban servicescape.

This chapter explores this interplay between consumption and the urban environment within the context of neighborhood-based community. It shows the way in which personal processes of authentication may intersect with perceptions of urban authenticity, and in particular how those processes may relate to experiences of community. To do so it adopts Arnould and Price's

(2000) conceptualization of authenticating acts and authoritative performances, and considers the implications with regard to Zukin's (2010) recent theories on the ways that authenticity may be experienced within the urban environment, as new beginnings and origins. It draws on research that investigated the ways that individuals use the opportunities for interaction and identity definition offered by servicescapes for the purposes of constructing and reinforcing place-based community.

This chapter specifically focuses on the autoethnographic component of that project to explore how two neighborhood servicescapes worked as sites of my individual and collective authentication. It describes how these servicescapes worked to connect this authentication to the neighborhood's new beginnings and origins, by drawing on the cultural capital of the new urban middle class, and the traditional socializing practices of an older neighborhood-based demographic. It then also considers the ways that these sites worked cumulatively, to highlight the inauthenticities within my identification practices, which subsequently worked to authenticate a broader connection to the neighborhood. Firstly, however, a brief review of the literature of authentication is provided, with a focus on the work of Zukin (2010) with regard to the urban environment, and Arnould and Price (2000), in relation to consumer identity projects.

## AUTHENTICITY

Authenticity is associated with that which is genuine, real, true, or unique. The possibility of experiencing or expressing an authentic identity thus relies on the belief in a "true" inner core that exists apart from all outside influence (Taylor, 1991; Trilling, 1972). However, such claims of purity and separation are difficult to make in contemporary society, because the tools through which we seek to experience and express authenticity are provided by society (Taylor, 1991). These tools include the products and experiences provided by consumer culture.

Furthermore, authenticity is not only embedded within the social realm, but is also subjective. This is because assessments of the authenticity of objects or experiences are based on assumptions of perceived essence, rather than actual physical properties (Beverland & Farrelly, 2010). Thus the identity-defining outcome is not reliant on whether the experience is really authentic, but instead on whether the individual interprets it as being so (Arnould & Price, 2000; Beverland & Farrelly, 2010; Cohen, 1988). It is this subjective assessment that allows individuals to overlook or downplay the inauthentic elements in many consumption experiences; such as that which exists in the staged authenticity of museums, the contrived nature of reality television programs, and the fleeting connections of consumer communities (e.g., Goulding, 2000; Kozinets, 2002; Rose & Wood, 2005). That is, individuals willingly overlook the inauthentic aspects of an experience, in order to realize the identity benefits that authenticity is deemed to offer.

This chapter shows how these quests for authenticity may play out in, and through, the urban environment. For many people cities form the main physical and social context for their authentication practices. However, they are also environments that are themselves subject to assessments of authenticity. In particular, the positioning of the city as an experience to be consumed has implications for the manner in which authenticity can be used as a form of cultural power. This concern underlies Zukin's (2010) recent exploration of urban authenticity, which is summarized in the following section.

*Experiencing Authenticity in the Urban Environment*

The ways that quests for authenticity may be experienced within, and shape the urban environment, is the focus of Zukin's most recent book, *Naked City: The death and life of authentic urban places* (2010). In this work, she considers how understandings of authenticity as creativity or uniqueness, and as tradition or myth, may apply when authenticity is sought through the consumption of urban places and cultures. Drawing on the work of Said (1985), Zukin terms these two expressions of authenticity in the urban context as *new beginnings*, and *origins*. Urban authenticity experienced as *new beginnings* refers to the distinct features that each cultural group bring to the built and social environment; those that express their particular cultural distinctiveness or moment in time. Authenticity experienced as *origins* refers to features of city that seem to have always existed; its historical and mythical roots. This is authenticity that is acquired through age or patina. Whilst Zukin acknowledges that a city's constantly shifting identity draws on its origins and new beginnings, her concern is that claims of recognizing authenticity can be used as a form of moral superiority, with implications for the look and use of urban places.

In particular, when these claims of authenticity become claims of power, they can work to privilege the cultural capital of certain groups, and disadvantage others. As Zukin suggests, this process is most evident in gentrifying areas. Here, the social and cultural preferences that manifest as the new beginnings of the urban middle class are often presented as the model of an authentic urban experience, whilst the historical features of the built environment become an aestheticized version of the area's origins. This aestheticization implies distancing, which can depersonalize a neighborhood's origins, such that representations of traditional roots through historical buildings are valued over representation through demographic diversity. This aestheticization can also separate those making claims of authenticity from any commodifying or displacing consequences, because origins is still able to be experienced through the built form. Zukin's conclusion is that without the intervention of the state, through rent controls, land zoning, and financial incentives for small business, this aestheticization of origins will continue with significant implications for urban diversity, and for urban authenticity.

This chapter applies Zukin's categorizations on a more individual level. It investigates the identity-defining behaviors of the author as I attempted to use consumption experiences as a means of connecting to a neighborhood-based community. Zukin does not explicitly talk about community in her book. However, her concerns regarding the loss of diversity in neighborhoods, as new residents leverage their cultural capital to create new beginnings appears to hinge on an implied shift from collective identifications based on shared place of residence, to those based on shared lifestyle preferences. In this chapter, I am interested in the ways that my authentication practices may draw on new beginnings and origins, and if these experiences reflect Zukin's concerns regarding the use of cultural capital. Because this research is also interested in place-based community, the implications of Zukin's categorizations for the ways an individual may experience community are also a focus of this chapter. To do so, this chapter applies Arnould and Price's (2000) theorization of the ways authenticity manifests through both individual and collective processes. Their definitions of authenticating acts and authoritative performances are outlined in the following section.

*Experiencing Authenticity in Individual and Collective Ways*

The concepts of authenticity as new beginnings and origins were formulated by Zukin with specific reference to the contemporary urban environment. More broadly, however, Arnould and Price (2000) suggest that the quest for an authentic self in contemporary society occurs in two ways; as authenticating acts and as authoritative performances. These are individual and collective processes of authentication that utilize the tools of consumer culture as a means of challenging the destabilizing processes of postmodernity. This chapter applies these categorizations as a means of considering how authentication practices that draw on the new beginnings and origins of an urban neighborhood may work in individual and collective ways.

Authenticating acts are self-referential behaviors that construct or reinforce an individual's sense of self. Such authentication is often associated with experiences that induce flow, peak experience, or peak performance, such as white-water rafting or sky-diving (e.g., Arnould & Price, 1993; Celsi, Rose, & Leigh, 1993). However, Arnould and Price (2000) also suggest that authentication may result from an accumulation of experiences with more ordinary products, such as possessions that over time and through use, become intertwined with personal histories (see also Belk, 1988). In the same manner, Denzin (1992) argues that these epiphanic experiences need not only occur from a major upheaval. They can also be the result of an illuminative moment that highlights underlying existential structures; from a reflective moment where the consequences of change are realized; or from an accumulation of experiences which eventually force change. This suggests that ordinary experiences can also constitute that basis for authentication, provided they have not become routinized, typified, or fragmented to the extent they are unable to be disrupted by epiphanic events or synthesized into a broader life narrative (Arnould & Price, 2000).

This broader perspective of personal authentication is in line with that of Caru and Cova (2003, 2007) who argue for a more "humble" view of the consumption experience that recognizes the import of our everyday consumption activities in identity definition. It is also one that is particularly appropriate with regard to the urban environment, because whilst the city clearly offers opportunities for extraordinary experiences, our ordinary consumption activities also significantly shape our urban experiences, and thus our assessments of its authenticity.

Whilst authenticating acts are concerned with individual identity definition, authoritative performances are collective displays, such as festivals and rituals, which are aimed at constructing or reinforcing shared identity and traditions. These performances rely on "experiences-in-common," based around stylized invocations of tradition or ritual. In this respect, authoritative performances can be associated with the postmodern tribal aesthetic of "feeling emotions together" (Cova, 1997; Maffesoli, 1996). Neighborhood festivals and street parades are clear examples of these collective performances (e.g., Sherry, Kozinets, & Borghini, 2007). However the less extraordinary, but still staged authenticity of neighborhood farmers markets also provide opportunities for collective experiences that reinforce shared identity (e.g., McGrath, Sherry, & Heisley, 1993; Zukin, 2010).

As with authenticating acts, this chapter suggests that these acts of collective authentication can also be more ordinary. This possibility is illustrated through Anderson's (2006) concept of imagined community. This theory proposes that experiences of community are shaped by cognitive and symbolic structures that are not necessarily underpinned by lived social relations. That is, moments of collective identification can also be inspired by more everyday, but still symbolic actions and experiences, such as the simultaneous activity of people reading the same newspaper. Emphasizing this imagined element highlights an important aspect of authoritative performances, in that whilst they may be directed at reinforcing collective identity, they do not necessarily require the physical presence of that collective to be effective. This implies that the collective outcomes may depend as much on our ability to make those imaginative links, by overlooking inauthentic elements, as they do on the nature or visibility of the performance. This also suggests that assessments of urban authenticity as new beginnings or origins are dependent on which particular collective that imagined link connects one to.

Despite the power of this subjective and imaginative process, authenticating acts and authoritative performances are not interchangeable according to Arnould and Price (2000). That is, authenticating acts cannot successfully reinforce a community connection, nor can authoritative performances establish an individual's identity as separate from the collective. However, they can be complimentary; working in individual and cumulative ways to create a sense of identity (Arnould & Price, 2000). Thus in different ways, each process contributes to our narratives of identity that are both individual, and situated within a social space.

This chapter proposes that this accumulative potential is particularly relevant in an urban environment. This is because our identifications with and attachments to place are constructed over time, and through repeated interactions and experiences, that draw on a myriad of symbolic and cultural cues associated with that place. Of particular interest here is how this cumulative experiencing of authenticity may play out when it is being sought through the consumption of, and within, a specific neighborhood. Because a neighborhood is a space where individual and collective authentication and the experiences that construct it may be inextricably intertwined within the extraordinary and the ordinary consumption activities that an individual engages in. The focus of this chapter then is to explore how authenticating acts and authoritative performances may work individually and cumulatively when experienced through servicescapes that represent a neighborhood's new beginnings and origins. It will also consider the ways this may shape experiences of neighborhood-based community and assessments of urban authenticity.

## A SELF-NARRATIVE RESEARCH METHODOLOGY

To examine this process of individual and collective authentication through the urban environment, this chapter draws on an autoethnography conducted in a gentrifying suburb of Melbourne, Australia. This research followed the author's attempts to use its servicescapes to construct an experience of identification with that neighborhood's community. This project applied theories of postmodern consumer tribes (e.g., Cova, 1997; Cova, Kozinets, & Shaker, 2007; Maffesoli, 1996), proposing that fleeting relations and shared value that are experienced within servicescapes may work to construct an experience of community that is both ephemeral, and yet anchored within a shared identification with place.

The first phase of this research sought to explore this process from the perspective of the individual. It focused on the subjectivity inherent in the experiences of shared value and identity definition in servicescapes and the ways these may become linked as an experience of community. Investigating this subjectivity was deemed important to understand how individuals, businesses, and governing organizations may actively work to facilitate such connections. This is because subjective interpretation is inherent within both the symbolic and imagined aspects of community, and in the consumption experiences that are proposed here as a way of experiencing that shared identity. It is for this reason that an autoethnographic approach was adopted, recording the author's consumption experiences within the servicescapes of my new neighborhood for one year.

As a research methodology, autoethnography allows the experience of the individual to be used reflexively to illuminate certain aspects of broader social phenomena (L. Anderson, 2006a, 2006b; Ellis, 2004; Ellis & Bochner, 2000). In this research, it is applied as a means of connecting the personal experience of attempting to identify with a place-based community through consumption experiences, with broader cultural and theoretical ideas of what community represents. However because autoethnography is also embedded within the process of constructing a narrative of self-identity (Ellis, 2004; Ellis & Bochner, 2000), this project presents a unique opportunity to examine how authenticity may be experienced by an individual within the urban environment and in relation to place-based community. This is because I was not only interested in establishing an identity as part of a neighborhood-based community for research purposes, but as a new resident to Melbourne I also sought to establish a sense of my identity, utilizing the tools of the new physical and social space in which I found myself. That is, I was seeking to authenticate my sense of self, as well as experience that self in relation to the collective identity of my neighborhood.

## Data Collection and Analysis

Data collection took the form of extensive memo writing, as recommended by Ellis (2004), with over 150 pages of field notes recorded on just over 100 different servicescape-based consumption experiences, from September 2008 to September 2009. These memos focused on recording which servicescapes I frequented, and my actions within those locations. They also recorded the nature and general content of the conversations I had with staff and customers, and the way those interactions made me feel and act. A third focus of these memos was the assumptions and associations I made between servicescapes and people, both as individuals and collectively. That is, whilst the majority of my data records my actions within servicescapes, the places I did not go and the things I thought about but did not do were also an important component. Each memo can thus be thought of as an episode in the ongoing narrative of me trying to determine the neighborhood's identity, and my relation to it.

The data analysis has focused on the interplay between these servicescape-based interactions, my emotional responses, the experienced value, and the identity attributions recorded within my research notes. Statements about identity were considered from the perspective of whether I was making statements about my own identity or the identity of others (both people and places), and the means through which that identity was expressed. These identity statements were then categorized utilizing Richins (1997) descriptors of emotions experienced through consumption and Holbrook's (1999) consumer value typology. This allowed for the investigation of emotional responses in combination with value experiences, and the consideration of how they may combine during individual and collective consumption experiences. Whilst it may be expected that authentication would primarily result through value experiences that have positive emotional impacts, this analysis highlighted the relation between negative value experiences and emotional responses, and the tendency to overlook inauthenticity to achieve the desired identity benefits, as discussed within the literature review.

Statements that specifically related to people were also coded according to the type of interaction they most represented. To do so, Lofland's (1998) differentiation of the types of secondary relations that may occur in public space was applied. She defines these as fleeting, routinized, quasi-primary, and intimate-secondary, with shifts in the relational types occurring as information is exchanged between parties and emotional impact increases. In particular, quasi-primary relations describe the brief moments of shared experience of the tribal aesthetic, whereas intimate-secondary are the relations of acquaintances. It would be expected then that both relational types would feature within authentication processes, with the shift from quasi-primary to intimate-secondary reflecting a shift from collective to individual value experiences as relations become more personal. This manner of categorization allowed me to structure the data in ways so as to track these relational changes and then relate them to value experiences and emotional responses.

What this analysis has most clearly indicated is the extent to which personal and collective identification is intertwined, particularly when both are being acted out within a broader narrative of attempting to establish a place-based identity. It also highlighted the extent to which the desired outcomes guiding such interactions may only become apparent upon reflection, or when consumption experiences work as epiphanic moments that highlight hidden motives in past activities. In particular, the contrast between the emotions experienced across the two locations focused on here illustrated the extent to which experiences of inauthenticity inform future authentication practices. As these locations also represented the neighborhood's new beginnings and origins, this interplay between authentic and inauthentic experiences had implications for my broader assessments of the authenticity of my neighborhood. The particular features of these two locations are described in the following section.

*The Research Sites*

This chapter focuses on my experiences within two of the neighborhood's servicescapes, a bar, and the local shopping center. These sites were chosen because they are the key locations of my lifestyle and everyday consumption activities; they are also sites that I have identified to others as important to my developing place-based identity, as the following excerpt indicates.

[Acquaintance] asked me if I'd been hanging out at [the Plaza] doing fieldwork, if I still liked it. Which I said I did, "cause all the old folk hang out there, but really I'd been hanging out at [the Bar] doing fieldwork, meeting all the [neighborhood] weird people." He kind of laughed, in a way that implied he had a certain opinion of [the Bar], although I'm not sure what it is. He had mentioned the place to me before, I guess it could be seen as yuppie or exclusive in one way. And I had identified myself with it. (Research notes, February 8, 2009)

The Bar exemplifies Zukin's category of new beginnings, it also operates as a third place or anchoring place (Aubert-Gamet & Cova, 1999; Oldenburg, 1999). Here I interact with a neighborhood-based network of my sociocultural peers whilst also expressing and reinforcing personal identity preferences. The Plaza is the local shopping center, built in 1981 on an abandoned industrial site. This relatively ordinary space has been co-opted in ways that illustrate the neighborhood's origins, both as an ethnic, and lower socioeconomic area. The area's elderly residents in particular use its public spaces in the manner of a real plaza, or traditional main street. In this way, it also operates as a place of exposure (Aubert-Gamet & Cova, 1999) by displaying the diversity and social practices of a broader cross-section of the neighborhood's residents. In this respect the Plaza represents what Zukin describes as a social understanding of origins, in that it provides a place in which the neighborhood's historical roots are on display.

Both places have contributed to my understanding of the neighborhood's identity, and shaped the way that I relate to any communities that I associate with it. These sites thus play key roles in my perception and evaluation of the authenticity of the urban experience that my neighborhood offers. The following sections provide a brief description of these servicescapes and then describe my authenticating experiences within them. Each description firstly focuses on the relationship I developed with the servicescape, and then considers the ways this worked as a process of authentication. The final section considers how these separate places of authentication worked together to inform a broader identification with place and with neighborhood-based community.

# EXPERIENCING NEW BEGINNINGS IN THE BAR

The Bar opened in late 2007, in what was previously a shoe shop. They kept the name, and a photograph of the previous proprietor above the bar; however, beyond those limited nods to history, this small wine bar exemplifies the gentrifying new beginnings of the area. Whilst the Bar can be busy, it is rarely overwhelmingly so. Indeed it was initially described to me as a good venue to go with friends if you wanted to talk, rather than as a location in which to interact with strangers. The Bar is situated on the Main Street of the neighborhood, surrounded by cafes and restaurants, independent clothing stores, bookshops, and other bars. This street is the neighborhood's entertainment and lifestyle precinct, and its new beginnings writ large.

## The Bar as a Third Place

The Bar differentiates itself from the six other bars in the Main Street through music selection, service approach, product offering and servicescape layout, so as to target a specific niche of the larger resident demographic that could be described as new urban middle class. This value offering is built on a service gap identified by the owners based on their personal lifestyle preferences, which is a practice Zukin identifies as common with sites of new beginnings. The three owners maintain an obvious presence, with a least one of them working most nights. Their presence has a significant influence on the atmosphere and customer service approach of the bar. This was aptly summarized in the query of an acquaintance; "is that the bar where the bartenders are more interested in putting on records and dancing than they are in serving customers?" Ah, yes.

Whilst acknowledging the truth in that person's assessment, my defense of the bar owners and staff, "the service is better when they know you," illustrates my relationship with this servicescape; it has become my third place (Oldenburg, 1999). These are quasi-public spaces that allow for an experience of communal gathering that is inclusive and sociable, yet are not bound by the commitments of primary relations (Oldenburg, 1999). These sites are familiar in popular culture as the corner shop or local pub where "everybody knows your name," and as such third places are often presented as open, friendly places in which individuals can freely interact and connect. However, this assumption of openness simplifies the constraints that can surround secondary relations in public places, including social norms, and the physical elements of servicescape layout. Lofland (1998) in particular argues that such locations more often operate as parochial realms, where meaningful interaction is limited to those who are accepted as regulars or within specific social networks. In this more closed form, third places are similar to what Aubert-Gamet and Cova (1999) call anchoring places; servicescapes in which communities come together to reinforce their relationships and identity through ritualized and symbolic practices.

These physical and social constraints are evident within the Bar. It operates as an anchoring place for a neighborhood-based social network, which can co-opt certain sections of the servicescape in parochial ways. This potentially exclusionary practice is assisted by a layout that segments the venue, and can limit interaction between customers to brief encounters at the bar, or in the passage way. Like many bars, this means that the small seating area at the bar is the most conducive to secondary relations, and it was from this position that much of my interacting took place. One consequence of this seating arrangement is that much of my attention was directed towards the Bar's owners and staff. More generally this layout also limits the potential of the servicescape to operate as a site of collective identification. This is because sitting at the bar encourages a one-to-one focus, and separates those at the bar from the interaction occurring in the booths and passage way behind them. This seating arrangement had implications for the connections I was able to develop, as will be discussed in the following section.

### Constructing a Personal New Beginning in a Third Place

My third place relationship with the Bar has developed over time. I am what Katovich and Reese (1987) describe as an irregular regular; my patronage is infrequent, but I still have a regular's expectation of a certain level of interaction and recognition. This customer identity has developed as an initial identification with the excellence of product and the aesthetics of the servicescape design has grown over time into a deeper attachment to people and place. This shift has resulted from an accumulation of shared experiences and the value they represent. This includes the playful appreciation of music, and involvement in its selection; the status, esteem, and play experienced through personal greetings, meetings with other regulars, and shared conversations over the bar. That is, value experiences based on materiality were superseded by those with relational value, as the routinized and quasi-primary relations between me and the Bar's owners, staff, and other regular customers evolved into intimate-secondary relations. The beginning of this shift is evident in the following excerpt:

> Much happier with [the Bar] lately, I was there on Thursday, and again tonight, and staff ... they've been attentive, on Thu night definitely. Well I felt like they could see my pain and they kept on checking on the volume of wine in my glass. And he [owner 1] said goodbye to me when I left, and he said goodbye to me again tonight, which is just is one of those things I've been watching out for. And this evening I went for a glass and stayed for three because actually I was quite liking it. I was just reading the paper and randomly

looking about and talking a little bit to the dude who was sitting next to me and to the bar staff. And I guess that was the first time I've chatted with them generally. And [owner 1] gave me some olives, as a freebie, which I guess is perhaps the first sign of some level of recognition of being some – local, regular. ... So I'll need to definitely go to [the Bar] a lot more now. It's becoming more what I thought it should be. (Research notes, December 6, 2008)

However, the development of my relationship with the Bar and the people associated with has not been as easy Oldenburg (1999, p. 35) recommendation that "one simply keeps reappearing and tries not to be obnoxious" would suggest. My expectations of recognition and the emotional value I came to attach to this servicescape, did not always match my experiences within it. For example, it took another four visits spread over seven weeks before I managed to learn Owner 1's name, after eventually asking another customer. It then took another two visits over four weeks before I was able to tell them mine. Whilst the time frame is not surprising given the infrequency of my patronage, the extent of my emotional investment in this simple act of introduction was. Indeed my research notes over this period suggest that discontent, embarrassment and feelings of being ignored or out of place, are as much a feature of my reflections of my interactions in that place as are joy, excitement, and a feeling of connection, as the following excerpt suggests.

Thinking about tonight and [owner 2] and [staff member] and introductions and realizing I feel a bit let down/disappointed about the lack of something from them. But I realize also that is because I am wanting something more from them than the superficial I keep on going on about. I want recognition, as a person worth knowing. And that is perhaps where the thing of doing it by yourself falls down. I have an emotional investment in it. (Research notes, February 2, 2009)

The intensity of this emotional response can be linked to confusion between authenticating and authoritative aims. In fact, whilst I originally viewed the Bar as a means of establishing connections to a neighborhood-based collective, my research notes illustrate that much of my energy was directed to establishing more personal connections to the owners and staff. These aims are not mutually exclusive; previous research has highlighted that owners and staff play important roles as gatekeepers and bridging ties to the social networks that operate within their servicescapes (e.g., Rosenbaum, 2007; Spradley & Mann, 1975). However, my desire for personal authentication and the personal emotional conflict it caused would seem to be somewhat at odds with the mythology of the third place as a place of easy sociality. This is because whilst my experiences in the Bar were clearly social, they were rarely collective. They instead hinged on one-to-one interactions that were directed at affirming my membership of a cultural group with whom such consumption practices and locations are associated. That is, I was using my third place identification with the Bar as a means of authenticating my personal new beginning.

It is worth noting that only two weeks later a brief stop for a glass of wine turned into a long revelatory evening in the company of the two owners referenced in these quotes. That is, my uncertainty was soon relieved by an experience that reinforced my status as a "person worth knowing." However, this subsequent experience of authentication did not significantly alter the underlying secondary nature of my relationship with the Bar owners, and had little bearing on my relations with other regular customers. Nor did it prevent future moments of self-doubt. Indeed my research notes, and experiences, continue to reinforce the superficial nature of this authenticating act and its need for ongoing reinforcement. This reinforcement is necessary to overcome the conflict between my desire to identify the Bar as a site of collective identification, and the personal focus of my authenticating practices.

## (In)Authenticities and New Beginnings

The Bar then not only exemplifies the new beginnings of the neighborhood, but also my personal new beginning. I used the symbolic value embedded within the Bar, its association with the neighborhood's new beginnings, and with a specific cultural group, as tools within that authentication process. Essentially I was drawing on the cultural capital invested in the types of consumption practices and spaces the urban middle class use to authenticate claims of new beginnings to establish my membership of that cultural group. As part of this process I also sought to establish intimate-secondary relations with the Bar's owners and staff, in an attempt to embed myself within a social network, and as means of performing that broader collective identification. Thus whilst this bar now operates as my third place, a location in which I have constructed, and reinforce the intimate-secondary relations that are anchored there, it only became so once I was able to establish for myself an authentic sense of who I was within that place. My attachment to and identification with the Bar, and the people with whom I interact when within it, primarily serves to reinforce my belief in my neighborhood as a place in which I can express that authentic self.

To do so however, I must overlook a number of inauthentic aspects of my construction of the Bar as a third place. This includes the contradiction between the positive mythology of the third place, and the many negative aspects of my relational practices. In particular, my emotional need for personal recognition through intimate-secondary relations undermined the possibility that this site may work to connect me to a broader neighborhood-based collective. Instead as I authenticate my personal new beginning, by becoming friends with the Bar owners, I also reinforce the collective use of this cultural capital of new beginnings as a means of representing a certain model urban authenticity. In this respect, my experiences of authentication within the Bar would appear to support Zukin's conceptualization of new beginnings, suggesting that they are primarily about individual authentication through the cultural capital of the new urban middle classes. However, the moments of disruption that my negative experiences represent also highlight the limitations of this authentication within a neighborhood context. This is because when I am questioning my own identifications, I am also recognizing that these new beginnings offer only a partial expression of both the identity of my neighborhood, and of my identification with it. This partial expression is made more apparent when my experiences in the Bar are in contrast with those in the Plaza, which is described in the following section.

# EXPERIENCING ORIGINS IN THE PLAZA

The second site of interest here is the local shopping center, the Plaza, built in 1981 on an old industrial site. This shopping center primarily services neighborhood residents for everyday shopping purposes. It is not a destination mall. It contains two supermarkets, a discount department store, and a full range of other food and retail stores including bakeries, chemists, a newsagent, butcher, health food store, travel agent, pet shop, takeaway food outlets, electronics store, plus some low cost clothing and homewares stores, and generic "$2" junk shops. Some of these stores are major retail brands. Many are nondescript small businesses, that are not identifiably independent or locally owned. They are ordinary shops.

The Plaza is well patronized; on Saturdays, or when it is raining, cold, or hot, the center is bustling, often in stark contrast to the quiet Main Street just beyond it. For this pulling power the Plaza is often disparaged; by the new beginnings Main Street traders, or individuals who appear to subscribe to an ethic of supporting small business and primarily associate the Plaza with the supermarkets that anchor it. As is common with shopping centers, it does appear to have impacted on the retail offerings of the Main Street, concentrating everyday shopping amenities within its walls, and essentially creating a separation between the ordinary and lifestyle shopping areas of the neighborhood.

## The Plaza as an Exposure Place

In line with this separation, the Plaza is a site in which I mainly engage in mundane or everyday shopping activities, such as buying groceries. I also use it as a short cut on my way to the Main Street; it thus forms a part of my neighborhood "round." For me, the value offered by the Plaza is mostly one of efficiency. It offers convenient access to a broad range of essential products and services that I use to supplement my ethical preferences of supporting small business. It also offers a climate-controlled route from my house to the lifestyle areas of the suburb and beyond.

However, as an ordinary shopping space, the Plaza is also the most diverse servicescape within the neighborhood, offering a range of products and services that appeal to, or at least would be required by, most residents within the area. It is effectively a place in which everyone ends up at some stage, and thus presents opportunities for what might be called ordinary authoritative performances, through quasi-primary encounters with other residents. My growing awareness of this potential is evident within my research notes. I moved from references to the Plaza as a "non-place" (Auge, 1995), with no real identity-defining value for me, to the recognition of its social role in the lives of other residents, and an increased expectation that it may offer me similar experiences. This shifting perception and its impact with regard to my sense of neighborhood-based identity is illustrated in the following research note excerpt.

> I don't really see [the Plaza] as a place of sociality – for me. I see lots of other people engaging in interaction there, particularly the old Greek men, but also people running into each other, and I have even seen [neighbour] and [hairdresser] there once. But in reality I don't expect to see people or have the potential for recognition experiences there, despite the fact it is the most certain place where people will be eventually and also most likely to mark a person as being from the local area. I just don't expect it from a shopping mall – with relation to my demographic.
>
> But today I saw both [resident familiar from the Bar] and the guy from [cafe staff member]. Neither of them recognized me. ... Neither of those experiences where particularly exciting, and didn't do anything for the "being recognized thing" but did make me think about, have I been here long enough that I'm starting to run into people in the supermarket? Maybe I am becoming local after all? (Research notes, March 4, 2009)

Unlike the Bar however, the hope of intimate-secondary interaction is not the key driver of my authentication practices in the Plaza. Instead it is primarily a place in which I observe and appreciate the consumption practices and associated sociality of other neighborhood residents, in particular an older generation of men and women who use the shopping center's public spaces as their third place. As with my consumption experiences within the Bar, this appreciation draws on a range of experienced value to which meaning is attributed in a comparative and accumulative process. This appreciation takes on spiritual qualities; it is intrinsic, reactive and other-oriented, and overrides my more generalized dislike for shopping centers as a whole. As Zukin suggests, I also use my appreciation of the Plaza to affirm my moral or ethical superiority over those who disparage its ordinariness. Significantly though these claims are directed at those within my cultural group whom I see as being unable to look beyond the mundane nature of the shops and mass market implications of the supermarket, to appreciate the ways that Plaza's spaces appeal to a broad range of neighborhood residents. This ethical stance is reinforced through occasional playful quasi-primary interactions with some of the Plaza regulars, which further serves to reinforce my impression of its open and inclusive sociality.

Most significantly however, I use my appreciation of the Plaza as a social space to affirm my identification with the broader neighborhood community. That is, my exposure to the anchoring practices of a different cultural group works in the manner of the simultaneous actions of an imagined community. In seeing others act out what I strive so hard to achieve in the Bar; I recognize the possibility of a shared link. Thus my experiences in the Plaza are in some ways epiphanic, highlighting the extent to which my experiences in the Bar are primarily aimed at self-authentication, whilst suggesting a different pathway to collective identification.

## Attachment and Authentication at the Plaza

The combination of efficiency, play, my spiritual and ethical response to the Plaza's social value for others, and the recognition of the shared authentication practices that are bound up in that sociality, has worked to create a sense of attachment to my local shopping center. This is clearly indicated in the research note excerpt below.

> [The Plaza] is clearly a contributor to the place-identity of [suburb] – in as much because some people dislike it and thus react against it ... But it also contributes to my identity within this place. My appreciation for what [the Plaza] offers some people is an example of that, given I would have previously put myself in the anti-shopping center box. I kind of like [the Plaza], and seeing all the old guys use it the way they do makes me smile.

I shop there and am not ashamed by it. Certainly I maintain the same usage patterns regarding the supermarket – but I can separate what [the Plaza] is as a place from what Coles is. I think if I did move down the hill, so that [the Plaza] was no longer on my path to other places, that I would miss it a little bit. Miss seeing its sociality anyway. (Research notes, March 26, 2009)

This sense of attachment to the Plaza, and in particular to its role as an exposure place, illustrates the ways that authenticating acts and authoritative performances can work in complimentary and cumulative ways. My assessments of its value have moved from being of no identity-defining value, to a hope of the possibility of meaningful interaction, to authenticating statements, to concern at the potential loss of it as a place in which to regularly witness and engage in authoritative performances. Furthermore, it was the realization of the potential for interaction with members of my cultural group, reinforced through an authenticating appreciation of the sociality of others, which illustrated the potential of broader authenticating performances. That is, ones that linked me to neighborhood residents outside the limited cultural group with whom I interact in the Bar and other places of new beginnings. Significantly this recognition of a shared identification with a broader demographic worked to further highlight the inauthenticities in the identity of new beginnings I authenticate within the Bar. That is, I have used my identification with a Plaza-based collective as a way to differentiate myself from assumed cultural practices of a more restricted sociocultural based collective. In my appreciation of the Plaza I individuate myself from those I sought to identify with when in the Bar, as a means of remedying some of the insecurities I experience in that location.

## *Distancing and Exposure in a Site of Origins*

The Plaza's role as a space of exposure is fundamental to this comparative process. As an exposure site it displays the neighborhood's roots through the ordinary shopping practices of a broad range of residents. In this way the Plaza works as a leveling place, reducing cultural and demographic differences to one of shared geography and shopping practices. Whilst this effectively reduces the strength of the potential link between individuals, because rituals and traditions need to be broadly recognizable, it increases its potential breadth, ensuring these aspects of the neighborhood's history continue to be performed. In this case, the relational practices of the older residents who are co-opting the Plaza's spaces highlights the extent to which my new beginning, expressing authenticity through social interaction in third places, is merely the continuation of the practices of original residents. Thus my collective authentication within the Plaza draws on my individual authentication within the Bar, to reinforce the authenticity of my neighborhood, as a place in which traditions can be continued, across different servicescapes, and demographics.

However, whilst my appreciation of the social opportunities the Plaza offers diverse residents may have value to me in confirming a connection to the area's broader community, it also involves an element of distancing against which Zukin warns in her discussion of the aestheticization of authenticity as origins. The appreciative stance I adopt toward the sociality of others is taken from the safety of my ordinary shopping practices, which offer me a position from which to observe, but only superficially engage with others. This distancing though is in effect a requirement of the function of an exposure place, and I suggest that it is this element of distancing that allows me to compare my experiences of authenticity and consider their cumulative impact. This is because this distancing reduces the emotional impact of my relational activities in the Plaza, and thus leaves me more open to experiencing the collective identification of a neighborhood-based community.

What is significant with regard to Zukin's concerns however is that this emotional distancing does not prevent the development of attachment. Indeed, I would suggest it played a key role in facilitating it. This may in part be a response to the social ways in which origins are expressed in this location, that is, the Plaza's is more than a physical expression of the neighborhood's history. However, this attachment goes beyond an appreciation of social practices, it is embedded within the Plaza's physical spaces. It shapes my usage patterns and my adoption of it as site of authentication. Furthermore, despite the distancing, and the claims of recognizing authenticity that can accompany it, my attachment to this ordinary shopping space works as a representation of my attachment to my neighborhood. Indeed it is mostly through this ordinary space that my attachment to and identification with my neighborhood is expressed.

## INDIVIDUAL AND COLLECTIVE AUTHENTICATION THROUGH NEW BEGINNINGS AND ORIGINS

At the heart of the research that inspired this chapter is a concern regarding the interplay between consumption practices and neighborhood-based community. This is also a key concern in Zukin's recent work on authenticity within the urban environment. In effect we are both interested in the ways that the consumption spaces of the urban environment can offer individuals a means through which to effectively express their desire for individuality and for collective identification. This chapter considered these concerns through the rubric of authenticating acts and authoritative performances as defined by Arnould and Price, by drawing on autoethnographic data of my experiences within two neighborhood servicescapes; the Bar and the Plaza.

The Bar, is a place of new beginnings for both the neighborhood and myself. Whilst it operates as a third place for me, and an anchoring place for others, it is primarily a place in which I authenticate my personal new beginnings by associating them with the consumption preferences and social practices of a specific cultural group. The Plaza meanwhile has been co-opted by older residents as a social space that displays the neighborhood's diversity and origins. It works as an anchoring place for this cultural group; however, for me it takes on the role of a place of exposure. Here I can observe, and engage with that community's authoritative performances from the safety of my ordinary shopping behaviors. The Plaza also works as a place where some of the insecurity suggested in my struggles for recognition within the Bar, are remedied. I use my appreciation of its value as an anchoring place for others, as a means to reassert my moral credibility to myself, with reference to what I see as the less appreciative attitudes of my peers. That is, my desire for individual authentication in one highlights the possibility for collective authentication in the other.

This interplay of identity definition across these two servicescapes highlights the cumulative nature of authentication practices and the complicated ways they can work together in the construction of a place-based identity. I only began to see the identity-defining value of the Plaza, when I recognized the value it offered others. Furthermore, my attachment to the Plaza that developed out of this recognition of value worked to highlight the narrowness of my authentications in the Bar. In both locations I must overlook inauthenticities so as to achieve the individual or collective authentication I desire, such as my failed attempts at personal recognition in the Bar, and the aesthetic distancing that prevents my complete collective engagement in the Plaza. However when considered cumulatively these locations also offer opportunities to remedy these inauthenticities through their complementary nature; the Bar offers opportunities to establish my identity with reference to a cultural group, and the Plaza allows me to experience a less emotionally taxing collective authentication. Importantly these separate individual and collective experiences also work to authenticate a broader identification with my neighborhood that is reinforced through the link of our shared social practices, whether lived out in sites of new beginnings or origins.

The interplay between my authenticating practices in these two locations and the relational activities also speaks of aspects of the postmodern approach to place-based community that underlies this research. If sites of new beginnings work primarily to reinforce individual identity by operating as third places, and sites of origins work as exposure places to demonstrate broader connections to a collective, then it could be suggested that the latter are more significant with regard to constructing a place-based postmodern community. However, the rituals being performed in the Plaza take on much of their collective meaning when they are contrasted to the more individual identification practices of the Bar. That is, the Plaza's exposure role only became apparent in contrast to my attempts to anchor within the Bar. This reinforces the importance of both anchoring and exposure sites within neighborhoods, and the opportunities for individual and collective authentication that they offer. It also suggests the importance of sites of origins taking on that exposure role, because they are by their nature more inclusive than the anchoring sites of new beginnings.

In effect this conclusion returns to Zukin's concerns regarding urban authenticity, suggesting that the loss of a social understanding of origins, and spaces in which this can be experienced, can limit our understanding of urban authenticity overall. However, it also illustrates how individual authentication within sites of new beginnings provides an important contrast against which this experience of origins can be defined. Whilst this reconfirms that urban identities cannot be reduced to individual experiences in servicescapes, my experience also suggests that individual authentication practices will also not tolerate such narrow urban identifications. Whilst authenticating acts that are anchored in sites of new beginnings and draw on the cultural capital of the new urban middle class are unlikely to lead to social change, I would also argue that this authenticating potential relies on comparative experiences, such as offered by sites of origins. This chapter also suggests that the exposure places that can provide a space for such experiences do not necessarily need to be themselves a representation of those origins. Instead they may be ordinary shopping spaces that allow for traditions and rituals to be performed in tandem with everyday practices. This final point may be significant in gentrifying neighborhoods, because despite their tendency toward lifestyle consumption spaces, they generally retain their more ordinary offerings, such as supermarkets and local shopping centers. Thus whilst Zukin proposes that the pervasive nature of experienced-based consumer culture means that only state intervention can address this inevitability, I am more hopeful for the potential of individuals to affect change through their consumption practices.

# REFERENCES

Anderson, B. (2006). *Imagined communities: Reflections on the origin and spread of nationalism* (Rev. ed.). London: Verso.

Anderson, L. (2006). Analytic autoethnography. *Journal of Contemporary Ethnography, 35*(4), 373–395.

Arnould, E. J., & Price, L. (1993). River magic: Extraordinary experience and the extended service encounter. *Journal of Consumer Research, 20*(June), 24–45.

Arnould, E. J., & Price, L. (2000). Authenticating acts and authoritative performances: Questing for self and community. In: C. Huffman (Ed.), *The why of consumption: Contemporary perspectives on consumer motives, goals, and desires* (pp. 140–163). London: Routledge.

Aubert-Gamet, V., & Cova, B. (1999). Servicescapes: From modern non-places to postmodern common places. *Journal of Business Research, 44*, 37–45.

Auge, M. (1995). *Non-places: Introduction to an anthropology of supermodernity*. London: Verso.

Belk, R. (1988). Possessions and the extended self. *Journal of Consumer Research, 15*(September), 139–168.

Beverland, M. B., & Farrelly, F. J. (2010). The quest for authenticity in consumption: Consumers' purposive choice of authentic cues to shape experienced outcomes. *Journal of Consumer Research, 36*(February), 838–856.

Caru, A., & Cova, B. (2003). Revisiting consumption experience: A more humble but complete view of the concept. *Marketing Theory, 3*(2), 267–286.

Caru, A., & Cova, B. (2007). Consuming experiences: An introduction. In: A. Caru & B. Cova (Eds), *Consuming experience* (pp. 3–16). London: Routledge.

Celsi, R. L., Rose, R. L., & Leigh, T. W. (1993). An exploration of high-risk leisure consumption through skydiving. *Journal of Consumer Research, 20*(June), 1–23.

Cohen, E. (1988). Authenticity and commodization in tourism. *Annals of Tourism Research, 15*, 371–386.

Cova, B. (1997). Community and consumption: Towards a definition of the "linking value" of products or services. *European Journal of Marketing, 31*(3/4), 297–316.

Cova, B., Kozinets, R. V., & Shankar, A. (Eds). (2007). *Consumer tribes*. Oxford: Butterworth-Heinemann.

Denzin, N. (1992). *Symbolic interactionism and cultural studies: The politics of interpretation*. Cambridge: Blackwell.

Ellis, C. S. (2004). *The ethnographic I: A methodological novel about teaching and doing autoethnography*. Walnut Creek, CA: Altamira.

Ellis, C. S., & Bochner, A. P. (2000). Autoethnography, personal narrative, reflexivity: Researcher as subject. In: N. K. Denzin & Y. S. Lincoln (Eds), *Handbook of qualitative research* (pp. 733–768). Thousand Oaks: Sage.

Goulding, C. (2000). The commodification of the past, postmodern pastiche, and the search for authentic experiences at contemporary heritage attractions. *European Journal of Marketing, 34*(7), 835–853.

Holbrook, M. B. (1999). Introduction to consumer value. In: M. B. Holbrook (Ed.), *Consumer value: A framework for analysis and research* (pp. 1–28). London: Routledge.

Katovich, M. A., & Reese, W. A. I. (1987). The regular: Full-time identities and memberships in an urban bar. *Journal of Contemporary Ethnography, 16*(3), 308–343.

Kozinets, R. V. (2002). Can consumers escape the market? Emancipatory illuminations from burning man. *Journal of Consumer Research, 29*(June), 20–38.

Lofland, L. H. (1998). *The public realm: Exploring the city's quintessential social territory.* Hawthorne, NY: Aldine De Gruyter.

Maffesoli, M. (1996). *The times of the tribes: The decline of individualism in mass society.* (Smith, D., Trans.). London: Sage.

McGrath, M. A., Sherry, J. F., Jr., & Heisley, D. (1993). An ethnographic study of an urban periodic marketplace: Lessons from the Midville farmers' market. *Journal of Retailing, 69*(3), 280–319.

Oldenburg, R. (1999). *The great good place: Cafes, coffee shops, bookstores, bars, hair salons and other hangouts at the heart of a community.* New York: Marlowe and Company.

Richins, M. L. (1997). Measuring emotions in the consumption experience. *Journal of Consumer Research, 24*(September), 127–146.

Rose, R. L., & Wood, S. L. (2005). Paradox and the consumption of authenticity through reality television. *Journal of Consumer Research, 32*(September), 284–296.

Rosenbaum, M. S. (2007). A cup of coffee with a dash of love – An investigation of commercial social support and third-place attachment. *Journal of Service Research, 10*, 43–59.

Said, E. (1985). *Beginnings.* New York: Columbia University Press.

Sherry, J. F., Jr., Kozinets, R. V., & Borghini, S. (2007). Agents in paradise: Experiential co-creation through emplacement, ritualization, and community. In: A. Caru & B. Cova (Eds), *Consuming experience* (pp. 17–33). London: Routledge.

Spradley, J. P., & Mann, B. J. (1975). *The cocktail waitress: Woman's work in a man's world.* New York: Alfred A Knopf.

Taylor, C. (1991). *The ethics of authenticity.* Cambridge: Harvard University Press.

Trilling, L. (1972). *Sincerity and authenticity.* London: Oxford University Press.

Zukin, S. (2010). *Naked city: The death and life of authentic urban places.* New York: Oxford University Press.

# BETTER UNDERSTANDING CONSTRUCTION OF THE SELF IN DAILY CONTINGENCIES: AN INVESTIGATION OF THE MATERIALITY OF CONSUMPTION EXPERIENCES IN ONLINE DISCUSSION FORUMS

Alexandre Schwob and Kristine de Valck

## ABSTRACT

Purpose – *The first purpose of this chapter is to better understand, and to propose a means to understand the ways selves are constructed in daily contingencies during consumption experiences. To do so, the second purpose, which aims to bring an additional contribution, is to investigate the materiality of consumer experiences in a technological context.*

Methodology/approach – *We have investigated materiality (as conceptualized by Miller) of experiences in online discussion forums in a community of video games enthusiasts. Grounded theory is elaborated from an ethnography mixing interviews and nonparticipative online observation. The focus is on consumers' perceptions of their constructions as subjects in relationship to the various objects and practices they face.*

Findings – *The process through which subjects are contingently constructed follows three intertwined logics. Each of these logics, namely (1) finding a position, (2) building "appropriation logics" and accomplishing practices, and (3) enacting meaning empowerments, is detailed in its specific contingencies and modalities.*

Research limitations/implications – *Contribution of this research relies mostly on findings from one online community.*

Practical implications – *This research opens new ways to understand technological consumption experiences as they are lived by consumers, and it allows for an understanding of structuration in experiences characterized beforehand by their indeterminacy.*

Originality/value of chapter – *This chapter belongs to the few ones that propose a methodological approach to tackle with the construction of the self in daily contingencies and with dynamic materiality. It also opens new ways to de-essentialize ordinary consumption activities.*

# INTRODUCTION

In 2002, Reed states that very little consumer research has drawn on the perspective of social identities of selves in social interactions where people categorize and act toward each other in ways based on their understanding of social roles, rules, and symbols (Backman, 1988; McCall & Simmons, 1978; Stone, 1962). Almost 10 years later, this statement remains widely true. The growing literature in consumer research about the variety of consumer cultures (e.g., tribes, virtual communities, brand communities …) has not led to a similar development of literature focusing on the development of selves in interactional contexts. Undertaking this development requires taking into account appropriate consumption sites that fit with the sociological definition of consumption experience. Moreover, we believe that it requires a different conceptualization about the construction of the self than is currently used in most CCT research. Hence, we want to achieve two aims with this chapter. First, we justify the previous claims by bringing to the fore a research agenda that aims to better understand how social identities are formed in consumption experiences characterized by interactional contexts. Second, we offer an empirical investigation to advance this research agenda.

## THEORETICAL FRAMEWORK

### *The Dominant Research Paradigm about the Self and Its Limitations*

In consumer research, "self" can be conceived as a sense of who and what we are, and as such it is an organizing construct through which everyday activities can be understood (Kleine, Schulz Kleine, & Kernan, 1993). This vision of self as an object of introspection (Reed, 2002) has given birth to different concepts describing broad activities of this organizing construct: extended self (Belk, 1988), saturated self (Gergen, 1991), malleable self (Aaker, 1999), transformation of self (Schouten & McAlexander, 1995), and self-realization (Hemetsberger, 2005). With this focus on the self as an object of introspection, other conceptualizations of the self have been underdeveloped. As argued by Reed (2002), this underdevelopment is especially strong regarding the self, social relationships, and the social identity paradigm. This conceptualization, however, is at the premise of a sociological view of consumption. As such, it is very relevant for CCT as one of this paradigm's main goals is to unravel social and cultural meanings of consumption (Arnould & Thompson, 2005). We argue that the subjective experiences of product consumptions that substantially contribute to the consumer's structuring of social reality, self-concept, and behavior have only received indirect attention in interactional contexts. Reed's claim that social identity may be a useful perspective for self-concept-based consumer research is at the origin of our research.

While Arnould and Thompson (2005) claim that understanding consumption implies viewing people as cultural producers, and not only as cultural bearers, we believe that the dominant research about identities in consumption contexts is based on the concept of the extended self (Belk, 1988), which originally relies on anthropological and philosophical literature that establishes people as cultural bearers. This conceptualization, which also presupposes control over resources (Borgerson, 2005), does not take into account social identities as they may be recognized outside of the domain of the subject's possessions. More fundamentally, we agree with Bettany (2007) who states that consumer research literature that follows this dominant paradigm has not really taken into account contingencies of everyday activities. Nevertheless, we believe that as "we are what we have is perhaps the most basic and powerful fact of consumer behavior" (Belk, 1988, p. 139), it is all the more important to understand the limits of this conceptualization for our understanding of how consumers constitute their social reality by daily consumption experiences.

## A Structuration Approach to Study Ordinary Consumption

Dealing with contingencies in consumer activities implies an understanding of agency and structure. In this chapter, therefore, we adopt a structuration approach. This approach has been developed as an attempt to resolve a fundamental division within the social sciences between those researchers who consider social phenomena as the product of the actions of human agents that comes forth out of their subjective interpretation of the world, and others who see these phenomena as caused by the influence of objective, exogenous social structures (Jones, 1999). Holt and Thompson (2004) belong to the few CCT researchers who have used structuration. Relying on an investigation into the construction of masculinities, these authors propose that in given social frames, variation of consumption practices among individuals help them to negotiate their identities. We would like to advance this attempt to conceptualize structuration in consumption research by adopting a sociological view of consumption. In the sociology literature, processes have been investigated in contexts like education (Bourdieu, 1990) or politics (Giddens & Held, 1982). As we want to apply structuration to consumption contexts, we adopt a sociological definition of consumption. We rely on Warde's (2005, p. 137) definition of consumption, which states that consumption is "a process whereby agents engage in appropriation and appreciation, whether for utilitarian, expressive or contemplative purposes, of goods, services, performances, information, or ambience, whether purchased or not, over which the agent has some degree of discretion."

This sociological definition of consumption allows for a strong focus on the consumption experience. Carù and Cova (2003) state that research on consumption experiences has focused on a limited conception of experience. According to these authors, this limitation "tends to consider every experience as extraordinary" (p. 267), which results in lack of taking into account daily contingencies. Joining these authors, we notice that this limitation establishes an ideological view of consumption which does not conceptualize ordinary consumption as a cultural practice, and as such, denies its potentially enlightening theoretical roots in traditions of sociology (especially the structuration theory of Giddens, 1984). This potential of taking into account ordinary consumption experiences is especially valid in the field of technology. Kozinets (1999), for example, studies consumer activities in virtual communities of consumption. Ten years later, he studies consumer narratives about consumption of technologies (Kozinets, 2008), thus shifting from an investigation of consumer (and extraordinary) experiences to consumption (and more ordinary) experiences. Schau and Gilly (2003) make a clear statement about their approach of consumption: they take up a sociocultural approach of consumption, and focus on consumers' transformation of goods into possessions and symbols into personal expressions (Strathern, 1994). Schau and Gilly (2003) show that on personal websites, consumers use brands and hyperlinks to create multiple nonlinear cyber self-representations without necessarily sacrificing the idea of an integrated self. We believe that, as consumer researchers investigate more and more domains that were previously not considered as consumption-related (such as experiences and use of technology), we need more than ever to be clear about the approach of consumption that is adopted, including the definition of consumption and the methodological orientation that are taken. We believe that this recommendation is especially valid in investigations about the role of technology in the emergence of autonomous consumer movements (Kozinets, Hemetsberger, & Schau, 2008). Given the structuration potential (De Sanctis & Poole, 1994) of technology, investigation of the rise of these movements may emphasize structures as enabling and constraining factors, and, thus, give insight into the conditions of self-emergence in a collective environment.

# METHODOLOGICAL APPROACH

In this part of the chapter, we propose a methodological approach to fill the theoretical gaps we have previously identified about the conceptualization of the construction of the self in ordinary consumption experiences. A discussion about methodology is necessary given the difficulties some researchers have outlined regarding the application of structuration theory to empirical settings (e.g., Gregson, 1989). We believe that we propose a promising way to unravel structuration in ordinary consumption experiences that could be helpful to understand construction of the self in fields of growing importance. Whereas previous approaches that claimed to depict structuration in a consumption context did not really rely on structuration theories (e.g., Allen, 2002; Holt, 1997, 1998; Peñaloza, 1994; Thompson, 1996) or started with a minimal level of knowledge about the social schemes that delineated the existence of social structures (like cultural models of masculinity in the case of Holt & Thompson, 2004), in our approach, structuration may appear through empirical investigation, and without any preexisting knowledge about what it could gather in terms of structuring elements and processes. This approach seems particularly adapted to fit with contexts for which daily contingencies are not well known.

We have chosen materiality as the lead structuring principle. Materiality as a structuring process is illustrated in the following quote from Miller (1995, p. 54): "A theory of materiality parallels a dialectical perspective that understands the link between emerging differentiation or specificity and new forms of totalization and generality." Materiality is an interesting concept, because it presents the possibility to understand structuration aspects in a field in which it is not necessary to consider the existence of any social structure before the empirical investigation. In its broad definition, materiality refers to assumptions about the way relations work between subjects and objects. Thus, materiality investigates object and subject formations and interrelations (Borgerson, 2005). Miller (1995) emphasizes the idea that, through ethnography, we can find potential means to understand the role that the material environment plays in creating us as subjects. Our aim is to propose one means among several possible others to address the conceptualization of daily contingencies pervading self-emergence in the context of socializing consumption experiences in online communities. In the remainder of this section, we first depict the theory of materiality as an interesting lens through which conditions of self-emergence, and, more broadly, structuring elements and/or processes should appear in a clearer way. Then, we describe our field site, and discuss our data collection and analysis.

*From Materialism to Theories of Materiality*

Referring to Borgerson (2005), and given the preceding explanations about the dominant paradigm of self in consumer research, we aim here to demonstrate that the concept of materiality as depicted by Miller could be a promising approach to understand conditions of self-emergence. Borgerson (2005) states that consumer research has mostly dealt with materialism, defined as "the role of material objects in affecting terminal goals such as life satisfaction, happiness, and social progress" (Claxton & Murray, 1994). This definition does not conceptualize the influence of objects, subjects, and practices on who we are. Indeed, Borgerson (2005, p. 439) wonders: "What do consumer researchers mean when they claim that consumer selves are "transformed," "created," "expressed," or "emancipated" in relation to objects and contexts in consumer culture? Recent attempts to address this issue can be divided into two research streams. The first stream of studies has addressed materiality implicitly, and, in general, through concepts like extended self (Belk, 1988), possession attachment (Schultz Kleine & Menzel Baker, 2004), or object-meanings (Richins, 1994). Despite the fact that Miller's theory of consumption has attracted considerable attention, to the best of our knowledge, only Kedzior (2009) has explicitly adopted his theory of materiality (applied to SecondLife in a static approach of materiality). The second stream of research consists of studies aimed at overcoming the duality of objects and subjects (Bettany, 2007; Epp & Price, 2010; Zwick & Dholakia, 2006). These studies show the importance of object agency, and the implications for object-centered socialities. However, focus is on collective meanings of consumption, without taking into account either duration or socializing effects on individuals. Moreover, their key message is about the agency given to objects. Thus, daily contingencies and constructions of selves are not well conceptualized.

## *Jeuxvideo.com, the Site for our Ethnography*

We have chosen to investigate an online community of video games enthusiasts that was established in 1997 and is the second most frequented online community in France. Given the high number of forums in this community, we believe it is an appropriate site to conceptualize existing consumer cultures in online communities in general. Jeuxvideo.com (also called JVC) gathers mostly youngsters (aged 15–25) and males. This limitation regarding the scope of our investigation has been addressed through explicitly including some older and some female community members among our informants, and also by questioning our sample of informants about their frequenting of other online communities. Informants' membership length ranged from 1 to 10 years.

By means of 19 in-depth interviews and four focus groups, we wanted to gain insight into the following main research question: How do consumers lastingly build themselves as subjects in relationship to various objects in the context of online discussion forums? We interviewed our informants about their trajectories in the community from year to year. We were interested in gaining insight into how consumers perceive the way they have built relationships to others, or to the various kinds of objects they could face in online discussion forums (video games, avatars, pseudonyms, objects more or less central to online conversations ...). More precisely, we aimed at following a rigorous sociological way of investigation by questioning how consumers appropriated online discussion forums considered as the most important part of consumers' activities in Jeuxvideo.com, and in other communities frequented by them. Individual interviews lasted between one and two hours, and focus groups lasted between two and half and four hours. We followed a systematic approach to qualitative research as defended by Glaser and Strauss (1967) under the grounded theory concept. A first round of interviews and focus groups were first analyzed and coded separately, and then reinterpreted in a comparative manner to others (Spiggle, 1994). Subsequent interviews were analyzed in the light of previous interviews.

Our informants' narratives and discussions have allowed us to understand how they lived socializing consumption experiences in online communities, and how they became autonomous subjects facing different kinds of objects. Eventually, we could formulate an account of key processes and mechanisms related to the social constructions of consumers as subjects in online communities. The result is a grounded theory bringing answer to the following subquestions: (1) What elements and processes constitute consumers as subjects?; (2) How is consumer experience structured in the course of forum appropriation, and how can the co-construction of subjects and objects be conceptualized?; and (3) What meanings do these overall processes establish at the subjective and at the collective level?

## FINDINGS

Our data analysis reveals that material arrangements, objects, practices, and site boundaries are very important contingencies that both enable and constrain consumers in developing their subject positions lastingly. We show that all the types of objects are used in different ways by consumers. We explain that, as such, a myriad of collective, individual, and social identities can be realized, and we discuss to what extent these constructions configure the social life online and offline. The answers to our three subquestions represent intertwined logics of a single process of co-construction of subjects and objects. First, in their constitutions as consuming subjects, consumers are guided by the forum's structural imperatives to take position and to position themselves. Second, their affiliation needs lead them to adopt one (possibly shifting) "appropriation logic," characterized by a strongly embedded co-construction of subjects and objects, and an accomplishment of practices. Third, the forum and its related objects are a means for the subject to create and to recreate meanings online and offline in an environment in which he is socialized and empowered. We show how these three stages are strongly intertwined, and how consumers, throughout their experiences, accomplish the three stages in different ways.

### The Positioning Logic as the First Structural Imperative of Online Consumption Experience

Consumers are not born as forumers, but they get to be forumers. If this sentence about acquisition of social behaviors is true for a wide range of roles and identities in our contemporary world, the interesting aspect about forumers is that consumers' constitutions as subjects can be appreciated through a widely intelligible environment. This environment is characterized by consumption as a practice located at the junction of specific situations and imperatives provided by the structure, that is, online forums, and its related objects. Consuming online forums requires consumers to position themselves first, and to position them thereafter in the social stage. These positioning activities guided by the forum as an object establish what we can label the positioning logic. As revealed by states lived during the online activities, and between sessions in which consumers connect to the forums, we show that this logic, which is more or less reflexive, is rather invasive throughout the consumption experiences. This may result in consumers displaying various strategies and being more or less reluctant to play this "game."

### When Online Consuming Subjects are Constituted in Relation with Situational Factors

When questioned about giving a definition of online forums, our informants reflect on the forum as a complex and tumultuous site. Forums are ambivalent places that are connoted positively and negatively, and are sometimes even considered inadequate and useless. The two following members clearly show this ambivalence in their perceptions of the forum when they are asked which animal it could be.

> *Lucas* (18, 4 years on JVC): a sea urchin because it has a rather rounded shape, it does not really have any form, and inside it both very good and disgusting things are next to each other.

> *Jerôme* (21, 7 years on JVC): a penguin because it goes awry (laugh); simply penguins go awry, and open often their beaks without any reason

Nevertheless, when they go to the forum, consumers believe they have the discretionary power to go there, even if some of them are not so much at ease when discussing their online experiences, and avoid speaking about it to their friends. This personal valorization makes sense, because forums are seen as a place of freedom compared to other activities that are considered as compulsory. Our informants have all said they go on forums in order to relax, and to rest from daily life obligations, like work or other (often social) constraints. Sometimes they say they go on the forum because they have nothing special to do in their lives and they are simply bored, but, once again, when they connect, we can consider they are in a consumption experience, because they feel they do something they like.

> *Olivier* (15, 4 years on JVC): During this period I became withdrawn, and I looked for alternatives and for a way to communicate with people. I had been there (on forums) accidentally, and I found a forum for youngsters under 15, and a forum for 15–18, and I saw that in that second forum there was an atmosphere that I appreciated. Now, I spend so much time on forums that I think that if it was not this activity, it would be replaced by something else.

> *Lucas* (18, 4 years on JVC): My evolution on the forum was conditioned by that ... When a new game interested me strongly, which implied that I was looking for information each week, and I was expecting the release of the game, I went automatically on forums to speak and exchange, to get information, to know what I could expect, and to know finally if I would buy the game or not.

## *The Immanent Necessity to Take Position*

The analysis above establishes the importance of situational factors in the possibility of emergence of a consuming subject through online forums. Although consumers may have an initial motivation to join the community, they have to observe the community for some time to understand its rules and norms, before they actually dare to participate. By deciding to post a message, to create a topic, to develop an avatar, or to think up a pseudonym, members are required to position themselves in the community. Some claim they prefer to be original, and really feel enabling power through, for example, their choice of pseudonym.

> *Olivier* (15, 4 years on JVC): I have not been like the one who has 200 pseudonyms. I have probably had around twenty pseudos, but with some of them, I have surfed few days, and I have been banished. Generally, when I change my pseudo, it is because of a jabber on something, which relates to a book, a film ...

> *Florent* (16, 4 years on JVC): I have hundreds of pseudonyms. These are two of the pseudonyms that I have had; today, people recognize me through these pseudonyms.

I tell myself that some topics that I have created with dedicated pseudonyms were a bit special. When I look at these topics today, I feel it is rather pathetic.

The positioning logic is fostered by the fact that consumers face a form of acculturation in the community that strongly incites them to follow some rules commonly shared, like writing with no mistakes and posting in the good sections and threads. This mechanism and the enabling and constraining power of pseudonyms and forums as a whole, are commonly shared impressions that are mentioned by nearly all of our informants. Sébastien puts it in words as follows;

Sébastien (29, 7 years on JVC): We have to show that we have our ideas, our personality. We have to show we are who we are. We arrive in a forum in which many people discuss, and we want to show our point of view, and that we are not all the same, even if we have some points in common. Some things gather us, and others differentiate us, and we want to make them known. And so, in a way or another we have to impose our presence to others. It is like that, and all the more since the Internet is virtual, and we are invited to let go and post. I see people in their forties who behave like that on France Television forums.

*Choosing an Appropriation Logic and Accomplishing Practices*

Constituted as subjects according to situational factors and structural imperatives that dictate them to position themselves, consumers have to face the complexity of the social environment. Thus, beyond being situationally constituted, subjects are also socially constructed. The social construction, which is embedded in the online structures, is done through idiosyncratic but identifiable appropriation logics and practices. To put the appropriation logic in perspective with the positioning logic, it is important to state that positioning practices imply the exchange of ideas and words with other consumers; so positionings have to be recognized or they could possibly be legitimized by others' acceptance. In a foruming context, positioning, thus, implies the use of a set of available tools that are mostly linked to cognitive artifacts around the exchanged texts. We focus here on the diversity of available tools, that is, objects used by consumers, and we show that there are key differences among consumers in the ways they use it. These differences give them different identities. It is especially interesting to see how social identities arise and develop, all the more since most of them are explicitly given and affirmed in online forums.

*Entering into an Appropriation Logic*
Community members deal with the constraining aspects of positioning themselves by adopting routines of making use of the community. Hence, all

informants generally visit only a limited number of forums, and they develop routinized behaviors regarding the moments at which they connect, their length of connection, which threads they read, whether they create messages, what they write and how they position themselves. Finding one's position may be difficult, at least at the beginning and especially in the threads that are characterized by the rapidity of exchanged posts. Many informants have trouble posting and positioning themselves given this fast rhythm. Lucas explains us his difficulty to appreciate specific kinds of forums for these technical reasons. On the other hand, Maxime explains that he appreciates the intense activity in these forums, because through an embedded structure he finds communita with people that he gets to know well.

> *Lucas* (18, 4 years on JVC): No, on Jeuxvideo.com, I really stay on the forum dedicated to the game I am interested in. I don't go to general forums, and only for a simple and technical reason: on Jeuxvideo.com, there is a system that makes topics go at the upper part of the page, so that on Blabla sessions, there is so much traffic, that in one minute, a given topic can go to the second page.

> *Maxime* (20, 9 years on JVC): I find the same people more or less every evening, at the same hours. If nobody is here we leave and do something else. Generally on Blabla 15–18 (general forum), we have a community, we build a topic. There is one that will get 300,000 posts, and we post there. It will become our Blabla, our place, and behind that, some new discussions are sometimes created. Opinion polls can appear, but there are necessarily people that are serious and discuss, and others that will post trolls.

In communities characterized by the rapidity of exchanges, positioning is all the more difficult since there are implicit rules and a jargon, which makes people who are invested comfortable and socialized in their environment. In fact, when members are parts of these subcommunities and once they have settled their boundaries (or embedded structures), consumers' subject positions evolve around a limited perimeter of actions. They get accustomed to their "regime of materiality," for example, the speed with which co-construction between subjects and objects is done, and this allows them to take part and further develop the emanating practices and jargons. These fundamental differences among behaviors depending on context of the subcommunity has brought us to consider that there are different appropriation logics. By appropriation logics, we mean a set of coherent routinized behaviors matching with a specific technological environment, and producing sense-making and structuration principles for a given consumer. These appropriation logics have different effects; the properties of the context, and the "regime of materiality" tend to make that collective, mental and physical structures, including practices, last.

Based on our interviews, we have established four appropriation logics that are ideal types built on a set of coherently determined behaviors. Some consumers are more interested in looking for information or delivering information to others, whereas others are more interested in having fun. These different motivations, which materialize in log-in sessions that are marked by particular social behaviors, should be completed by key manifestations of the "temporal component" of appropriations. This includes the difference among consumers in the frequency with which they post, and the special status they enjoy (e.g., being a moderator). This co-construction of subjects and objects has resulted in a typology of four consumer profiles according to the ways they built subject–object relationships, the temporal component, and the special status they enjoy. The first type are "consumers"; they are infrequent posters, or "newbees" who did not have the possibility yet to get structured in their online forum experience. The second type are "experts," who are mostly concerned by informational aspects and driven by external materiality. By external (and conversely internal) materiality, we mean that the objects of interest that structure their experience are mostly objects out of (vs. in) the forums. The third type are the "players," who are mostly concerned with fun, and interaction with members in the community. They are driven by internal materiality. Finally, we have the "social actors." These include moderators who are driven by both internal and external materialities.

The concept of appropriation logic makes the link between structural imperatives that dictate the positioning logic, and self-development. It justifies the idea that not all consumers are driven by the same regimes of materiality, even if some of them manage to follow and to be at ease with different appropriation logics. The complex nature of materiality in online contexts, and the construction of subjects is also explained by the fact that these kinds of configurations in which people are finally more at ease to socialize are also strongly characterized by more or less explicit reliance on various sets of cognitive artifacts that could be considered as the objects they relate to. The collective use of these objects is linked to practices.

*Social Practices and Competing Goals for a Wide Set of Identities*
When they have passed the stage of feeling at home in the forums they frequent, community members are guided by appropriation logics to accomplish practices. These practices differ regarding the depth of their social roots. Practices could be considered as more or less anchored to the social roots or to the objects, and as such they may be considered as quasi objects (Latour, 1993; Serres & Latour, 1995), that is, neither purely natural

facts (in a transcendental sense of being a thing-in-itself) nor completely socially constructed. We could state that some practices are in fact "quasi practices." Indeed, informing other consumers, and boosting one's number of posts are both practices, even if we can consider that the first is more socially anchored than the second.

Accomplishments of practices are widely tied to consumer perceptions of the constraining and liberatory powers of material elements, objects, and other more embedded practices. Appropriation logics guide consumers to a certain extent in their willingness and ability to accomplish practices, because each practice can be considered as more or less central to a given appropriation logic. Some consumers admit they have to accomplish practices to "follow the movement," but they do not feel obliged to, all the more since the existence of practices reproduces a given culture in a forum, including the part in which practices are not at stake. Thus, in online discussion forums, practices are often clustered in specific topics dedicated to them. Cedric who seems to be at ease with two kinds of appropriation logics (experts and players logics) shows us the kinds of small trade-offs members (both him and others) may make during their appropriation logics.

> *Cédric* (19, 6 years on JVC): It happens to me to say stupid things, but in an appropriate post; these are posts that could be considered as trash, in which fun is at stake. In some posts, it annoys me to see some answers that are completely off topic.
>
> *Interviewer:* And what do you call posts in which fun is at stake?
>
> *Cédric:* It is what we call flooding topics, little games. It happens often to make games on series. Each of us posts a word, and next to each other we post a word that has a relationship with the previous one.
>
> *Interviewer:* And do you do this ?
>
> *Cédric:* Yes it happens to me simply to follow the movement and have fun. Sometimes I laugh when I see people's answers.

## *Located Social and Personal Identities and Their Constructions*

Identities are elaborated in the socialized environment through different relationships that consumers have with cognitive artifacts that are bundles of subjects and objects. Some of these artifacts and examples of related identities that come from them could be given: video games or consoles (e.g., "pro-Sony," "pro-Microsoft"), practices (e.g., trolls), appropriation logics in consumers' minds (e.g., core members, moderators), smileys ("noëlistes"). Each of these identity constructions is built, and more or less recognized in relationship to others in the communities in which consumers evolve.

This explains why some respondents do not know "noëlists" identity, because it is widely inscribed in a given forum of the community. Originally, "noëlists" are consumers who frequent "Blabla 15–18" session that use the smiley of Santa Claus in their posts, and who usually adopt a very ironical tone. "Blabla 15–18" is the most important Blabla session of the forum dedicated to youngsters between 15 and 18 years old. Here is an extract of a focus group conversation showing agreement among informants to underline the multiplicity of social identity that is located, or even embedded, in Jeuxvideo.com, and also in other online communities. The conversation also shows that the sense of belonging of participants who go to the same forums is not precisely identical; each of them puts boundaries around which his or her identity constructions are performed.

*Mathieu* (16, 7 years on JVC): I find it interesting that 15–18 is really a community, and we really have the impression to belong to something more than a forum.

*Axel* (15, 4 years on JVC): Something more, I would precise that if you only go to 15–18, you will feel that you really belong to 15–18, and not to Jeuxvideo.com

*Maxime* (21, 10 years on JVC): Even on 15–18, what I find striking is the fact that even in a forum you could have several communities. So, for the 15–18, a good example is to see all the guys claiming they are Noëlists or Happists. They will make their topic and be five to post about it. I go to the 15–18 and I have a community, but I don't associate to 15–18.

*Sébastien* (29, 7 years on JVC): The oldest communal spirit I have seen on Jeuxvideo.com, when I arrived, was the war between the pro N, the pro M, the pro S, and it is a very old war. When I was younger than you, it was pro Sega against pro Nintendo.

*Rémi* (16, 5 years on JVC): On the forum called « guerre des consoles » ( = war of consoles), we could still find that.

*Sébastien:* In fact, I realize more and more that people need to aggregate with others. They don't go there with the idea it is me against me among others, but it is me and I go in the direction of others who have the same opinion as I. We will be together and approve what the others say, something like "what you have said is interesting." This is not only on Jeuxvideo.com, as I said. I participated to political debates for regional elections, and it is the same, there are the guys, ecologists, everybody gathers, and sometimes even on points of disagreement. Some people don't take part to the debate.

Social identities appear to be located in contexts, time, space, and also in relationship to reflexive or, conversely, collective visions. Given the non-exact overlap between appropriation logics among consumers, many of them tend to disregard some other consumers who they believe to have an inadequate behavior. At the same time, this behavior tends to valorize their own identity. This behavior is at the origin of classifications of members and their related social identities. Romain who is completely invested in forums in which consumers are only interested by video games, and who consequently adopts the "expert logic," makes a conscious subjective classification of members based on his own practices.

> *Romain* (20, 6 years on JVC): If it was only my opinion, it would be the ones who bring ideas, and are motivated but who don't have necessarily an analytic point of view. Some really try to analyze games, and think about them. I always have a very literary approach on things, and I really try to think and analyze, whereas some others are only going to help others. Nevertheless, helping others remains essential.

### *The third logic: being socialized and empowered by objects*

Even if positioning and appropriation logics are means to accomplish experience and to build consumer's identity, it is important to state that these logics do not catch all the richness of the ways experience has built consumers as subjects in their own point of view. It appears that the essence of consumers' appreciation of their online experience comes from their ability to feel empowered by things provided by the forum and their related objects in what we call the "empowerment logic." Like in the modalities bound to becoming a subject through the positioning logic, situational factors play a key role in the appreciation consumers have of their experiences and of its discrete constitutive acts.

*Online Creation and Recreation of Meanings and Their Related Mechanisms*
Our study has revealed that objects of all kinds have a much more developed enabling power for the constructions of subjects than merely providing locally situated identities: they also create and recreate meanings. These processes could go beyond the online discussions toward the boundaries of the community. Focusing on online discussions, we have distinguished three complementary, and often intertwined, mechanisms through which these creations of meanings are achieved: "search for authenticity," "disambiguation of ambiguous objects," and "experiencing the frontiers of morality."

The search for authenticity is a widespread behavior that appears most of the time in reaction to behaviors of other members who are considered to use the online forums in improper ways. Consumers reflexively inscribe their online behavior and their appropriation logic as more authentic than those of others. Humor may be considered as an important means to overcome problems, or even online conflicts between consumers.

*Interviewer:* How do you classify people you could find online? What could be your criteria?

*Cedric* (19, 6 years on JVC): People that have a little bit the same opinions as me, who go to the forums with a feeling of pleasure, who use it very seriously, but with pleasure as a main motivation, people who will make constructive debates, and who will post in a clever way and with humor of course. After that, there are more occasional categories. (...) It is a form of cowardice not to show really what we want and to take a role; I don't say that irony is cowardice, on the contrary, I enjoy using it, but it is true that some people hide behind Internet to feel more powerful, instead of explaining themselves.

Disambiguation of ambiguous objects has to do with discussions about artifacts that have received a special treatment in the community because they have been widely discussed. These discussions result in consumers taking position, often with humor. There are many marks of humor in discussion forums, and these marks could also concern consumers themselves, who for example fail to create a topic that generated many posts. Forumers have invented expressions to tackle with these possible difficulties. We could consider the marks of humor as a means to collectively perpetuate meanings about key practices of the forums. Humor can also be widely diffused to sustain or, conversely, to criticize smileys that have received special status in Jeuxvideo.com. In fact, the smiley that represents Santa Claus has not only resulted in the located social identity of participants ("noëlistes") in the forum "Blabla 15–18," but also in a myriad of stories in which this smiley, or Noëlists themselves, is implicated. We could state that this located social identity provided a means of expression for concerned consumers, but also that it generated debates about the utility of this identity. When coming to real-life contingencies, these aspects could give meaning and empowerment in related actions and to the world in general. For example, Pauline explains she has been hounded by Noëlists because she was one of the very few active girls in a forum.

*Pauline:* This happened indeed one year ago. It was from January 2009 to May 2009, it was the worst period because people came to hack me all the time. Everybody knew me and sent me messages, and some people came into my college with a Christmas hat. They wanted to fight me. I was there telling myself "what is this shit ? This was just because I was a one of the very few active girls in a forum."

Ambiguity could also come from practices themselves. In fact, the judgments consumers have in the dialogic relationships with cognitive artifacts that they meet online, are often Manichean. Following collective manifestations of positioning and appropriation logics, consumers tend to excessively appreciate some types of behaviors, and discredit others. Gatherings are indeed made primarily on the basis of very located appraisals of things or artifacts, and the prevalence of the positioning logic could drive some consumers to have intent to deceive others. Moreover attempts to singularize or position may lead some consumers to adopt behaviors that could be considered as immoral by others, like sending pornographic or pedophile links. This kind of behavior is a manifestation of what we have called the experience of frontiers of morality. The behaviors we have mentioned are generally despised by our informants, not only because they have been personally shocked by these kinds of posts, but also because they feel empathy regarding other younger forumers who may be facing these problems and be deeply traumatized.

> *Olivier* (15, 4 years on JVC): There are mad people that post these kinds of links and want to show it to others. These video should be erased. And I especially think about children of 8 years old.
>
> *Interviewer:* do children of 8 go to the forum ?
>
> *Olivier:* absolutely! I have discovered pornography because of the Blabla 15–18. And I blame myself, pornography is disgusting.

As established by conversations among the informants in our focus groups, this kind of behavior remains, however, very localized to some parts of the forums, and even to some moments in which moderators are not present. This explains why some forumers had never heard about this kind of problems. Given these kinds of experiences, some consumers intend on fighting against behaviors of others who are considered as incorrect. These militating consumers experience the frontiers of morality, especially when they are widely involved in the foruming activity. We speak about experiencing the frontiers of morality because their condemnations are active, and the consumers at the origins of them may steal the online identities of the people they condemn, through practices like computers' hacking. These actions and others like criticizing or gossiping on more or less famous people, who could possibly create online "buzz," deeply divide consumers. For example, whereas some consumers strongly oppose computer hacking, others encourage such behaviors.

## *From Online to Offline Activities*

Many informants report that their online consumption experience allowed them to accomplish new consumption activities that they had not initially expected. For example, some consumers have become moderators in the course of their online lives, which is a form of consumption-driven empowerment. Others speak about events in which they participated, which were planned online, but occurred in real life. Real-life events could also be addressed in online discussions, and bring forumers to take part in these events. Interesting is the case of "meeting IRL," (IRL = In Real Life) which is shared in the community as a common practice, and sometimes bound to video games, sometimes not.

Liminal states, that are interstructural situations that often enlighten consumption phenomena (e.g., Thompson & Hirschman, 1995; Thompson & Troester, 2002), are lived by consumers between or during their connexions to online forums. During these states, consumers recognize that forums have given them interesting possibilities to socialize, and they become more self-confident. This reality is reflected in the concept of "claimed aspects of selves," which could be formally defined as the broad array of competencies or personality traits consumers believe they have, and that appears clearly in their minds given the consumption experience they have lived. Because of this, and their evolving social competencies and expectations, some consumers go from one forum to another, or from one community to another. Nevertheless, some consumers do not acknowledge that this gain of maturity is an effect that should be attributed to their activities in forums. They believe they have just grown up, and the gain of maturity may be unrelated to their online consumption experiences.

Online consumption experiences could even result in consumers feeling guilty, or to have feelings that they have lived a transitory and useless experience that obliges them to return in the real world. This motivation to go offline "by the negativity" of the experience is often the consequence of what consumers may consider as a certain addiction or a state close to addiction. Nevertheless, this feeling and motivation is also situationally constructed, as informants generally realize that this perception of uselessness appeared at one moment of their experience, and, consequently, was not immanent to it. Some of our informants show that there is a complex overlap between forum life and real life. Pauline's account of her first impression of online forums is very illustrative of this complexity.

> *Pauline* (17, 3 years on JVC): It has made me feel good. I have the impression to have learned a lot of things, and to be less annoying to my mother, because I had, online, other people to annoy. It occupied me, and allowed me to see other people than the people of my college that I could not bear. But, as a girl, people asked me my photo, I have become more or less famous in the community. This is more annoying, because it takes a lot of time, and all the stories about the forum take time in real life. When I go out with other girls or Jeremy (a good friend Pauline met in the forum), I knew all the stories of moderators, and of the most boring people of the forum, and my pseudo had been regularly hacked by these people. Some days I received mails, 700 mails to insult me. I was there and complained "I haven't done anything, and it is not even real life. Why do people come to annoy me?"

## DISCUSSION AND CONCLUSION

Our research has investigated the materiality of consumption experiences in online discussion forums, and as such it has brought interesting insights to appreciate daily contingencies in construction of the self and to initiate a more systematized thinking about structuration in consumption-related domains. In the following sections, we will further discuss our contributions.

### An Empirical Application of Miller's Materiality

The core of our contribution is an empirical investigation of Miller's materiality. Materiality has not been a very common topic of investigation in consumer research, because as established by Borgerson (2005), this discipline has tended to deal with cultural manifestations of materialism, which is "the role of material objects in affecting terminal goals such as life satisfaction, happiness, and social progress" (Claxton & Murray, 1994) much more than with manifestations of materiality. In this perspective, our research has brought two kinds of contribution. The first is a methodological approach: we have proposed a way to apply Miller's materiality to understand the construction of the self. We have then implemented a sociological approach for which we justified that some choices had to be made (point of view, stance, stability/instability of the object of investigation ...). In this perspective, given our research goals, our choices have led us to focus on the consumers' points of view in an ethnography of consumption experiences and to adopt a positive stance in a consumption "system" considered as stable.

The second contribution is a theoretical one: our ethnography has given an account of three intertwined "logics" in which subjects and objects are co-constructed. The logics are important ways through which consumers build themselves as subjects, and which provide them a wide range of actions and representations. Taken in isolation, each logic is not sufficient to fully build subjects who regularly meet additional needs that could be addressed by another logic. We have referred to the three mechanisms of co-construction as positioning logic, appropriation logic, and empowerment logic.

In their constructions as consuming subjects, consumers are extensively led by forums' structural imperatives to position themselves and to take position. We have called this process the "positioning logic." In "appropriation logic," consumers' affiliation needs bring them nevertheless to come into one (possibly shifting) or several way(s) to feel at home (i.e., to appropriate) forums. This logic and the four ideal types of appropriation logics we have identified ("consumer," "expert,, "player," and "social actor") are characterized by strongly embedded co-construction of subjects and objects and the accomplishment of practices. Forum and its related objects are however necessarily a means for the subject to create and to recreate meanings online and offline through the "empowerment logic" in an environment in which he has been socialized. These meanings are often elaborated at liminal states between online and offline experiences. We have shown how these three stages are strongly intertwined, and how throughout their experiences consumers accomplish the three stages in different ways. These behaviors have some important consequences like perpetuating collectivity and practices, and constructing "located" individual and social identities.

*Daily Contingencies in the Construction of the Self in Ordinary Consumption Contexts*

Our research shows that contingencies pervade consumers' everyday actions since the very beginning of their experience, in which they are constituted as subjects in online context, to the liminal states they could experience at the online/offline junctions while escaping forums. We have shown that these contingencies could be gathered around logics that are guiding principles that consumers may at least partially consciously realize. These logics, called positioning, appropriation and empowerment logics, are dedicated to competing needs like self-affirmation, affiliation, and understanding. In each of these logics, with a more or less quick rhythm that depends on situational factors and on the material properties of the context in which they evolve, consumers meet contingencies bound to the presence of others and various kinds of objects. These entities could be considered as cognitive artifacts and impose consumers to be structured in their behaviors and reasoning in transient ways. The diversity of behaviors and contexts observed in our research site has allowed us to draw some conclusions about structuration principles in online communities, among which the idea that through the variety of appropriation logics, experiences are the realm of expression of located social identities, and often of free accomplishment of practices and "quasi practices" like trolling and boosting. Despite the enlightening of these guiding principles, and their reliance on material objects in order to build themselves as subjects, the "power" of consumer agency comes from the latitude they have throughout their experiences. We have noticed that as they escape from the online context, consumers could also enjoy more freedom in establishing boundaries in which meanings can be created and recreated. Nevertheless at these liminal states, agency and structure are also intertwined because we have identified three mechanisms liminal to consumption experiences ("search for authenticity," "disambiguation of ambiguous objects," and "experiencing the frontiers of morality") that could be considered as structures through which meanings are elaborated.

*Toward a Better Theorization of Structuration Various Social Contexts?*
Through the adoption of the sociological definition of consumption and a sociological approach of studying consumption experience, we believe we have opened a research avenue to investigate structuration in consumption activities and even in broader social contexts in general. We remind the reader that by structuration we mean "an attempt to resolve a fundamental division within the social sciences between those researchers who consider social phenomena as product of the action of human agents, in the light of their subjective interpretation of the world, and others who see them as caused by the influence of objective, exogenous social structures" (Jones, 1999, p. 104). It is important to acknowledge that some previous attempts had already been made to adopt a more constitutive vision of consumption activities, and these attempts brought interesting insights about structuration in consumption. We could cite studies analyzing the types of actions present in consumption as a practice (Holt, 1995), but also studies depicting the interplay between existing social structures and consumption practices (e.g., Holt & Thompson, 2004), or even research that has adopted concepts like social practices in brand communities (e.g., Schau, Munizet, & Arnould, 2009). The practice concept is interesting, because it is a way to deepen knowledge about structuration by giving a solution to solve the fundamental division that Jones mentions while defining structuration. Nevertheless, we believe that all these studies have not elaborated a research agenda which can bring potential cumulative advances in order to better deal with structuration issues.

The agenda we call for is all the more important that, as shown by our research, today's consumer socialities take place in online communities whose systematic influence on individuals could be intelligible. But these findings call for research about structuration in other kinds of consumption experiences both online and in real contexts. To what extent could structuration in these other contexts be intelligible? We believe investigation on structuration could be done in a lot of ordinary contexts, which could be technological or non technological. It could address other kinds of online sites like social network sites, virtual worlds…. But this kind of investigation seems also adapted to understanding of behaviors taking place in real world's sites in which agents keep some degree of discretion and have already been assimilated as consumption contexts by researchers. It is the case of services encounters, and more or less long term consumption experiences like tourism, leisure, vacation ... We believe it could be interesting to try to see whether the three logics we have developed could also be relevant in very different kinds of social sites. We also believe that despite we have relied on Miller's materiality as a theory to conceptualize structuration, other possible sociological theories could be helpful to conceptualize the systematic influences collectivities and objects have on consumers. For example, we could consider socialization theories or Resource Based View, as interesting guidelines to contribute to our research agenda. Despite these approaches have been underdeveloped in consumer research, they could indeed be beneficial to conceptualize structuration in ordinary consumption experiences. We believe indeed that just like Gidden's (1984) structuration theory encompasses various forms of structures (structures of signification, of domination, and of legitimation, see Jones, 1999, p. 105), we could enlighten various forms of structuring theories to interpret consumption and ultimately social activities in different kinds of contexts.

# REFERENCE

Aaker, J. L. (1999). The malleable self: The role of self expression in persuasion. *Journal of Marketing Research, 36*, 45–57.

Allen, D. (2002). Toward a theory of consumer choice as sociohistorically shaped practical experience: The Fits-Like-a-Glove (FLAG) framework. *Journal of Consumer Research, 28*(4), 515–532.

Arnould, E. J., & Thompson, C. J. (2005). Consumer culture theory (CCT): Twenty years of research. *Journal of Consumer Research, 31*(4), 868–882.

Backman, C. W. (1988). The self: A dialectical approach. In: L. Berkowitz, et al. (Eds), *Advances in experimental social psychology. Vol. 21: Social psychological studies of the self: Perspectives and programs* (pp. 229–260). San Diego, CA: Academic Press.

Belk, R. W. (1988). Possessions and the extended self. *Journal of Consumer Research, 15*(2), 139–168.

Bettany, S. (2007). The material semiotics of consumption or where (and what) are the objects in consumer culture theory. In: R. W. Belk, & J. F. Sherry (Eds), *Research in consumer behavior. Vol. 11. Consumer culture theory* (pp. 41–56). Bingley, UK: Emerald.

Borgerson, J. (2005). Materiality, agency, and the constitution of consuming subjects: Insights for consumer research. *Advances in Consumer Research, 32*, 439–443.

Bourdieu, P. (1990). *Reproduction: In education, society and culture*. London: Sage.

Carù, A., & Cova, B. (2003). Revisiting consumption experience. A more humble but complete view of the concept. *Marketing Theory, 3*(2), 267–286.

Claxton, R. P., & Murray, J. B. (1994). Object-subject interchangeability: A symbolic interactionist model of materialism. In: C. T. Allen & D. R. John (Eds), *Advance in consumer research* (Vol. 21, pp. 422–426). Provo, UT: Association for Consumer Research.

De Sanctis, G., & Poole, M. S. (1994). Capturing the complexity in advanced technology use: Adaptive structuration theory. *Organization Science, 5*(2), 121–147.

Epp, A. M., & Price, L. L. (2010). The storied life of singularized objects: Forces of agency and network transformation. *Journal of Consumer Research, 36*(5), 820–837.

Gergen, K. J. (1991). *The saturated self dilemmas of identity in contemporary life.* New York: Basic Books.

Giddens, A. (1984). *The constitution of society: Outline of the theory of structuration.* University of California Press.

Giddens, A., & Held, D. (1982). *Classes, power, and conflict: Classical and contemporary debates.* University of California Press.

Glaser, B. G., & Strauss, A. L. (1967). *The discovery of grounded theory: Strategies for qualitative research.* Hawthorne, NY: Aldine de Gruyter.

Gregson, N. (1989). On the (ir)relevance of structuration theory to empirical research. In: D. Held & J. B. Thompson (Eds), *Social theory of modern societies: Anthony Giddens and his critics.* Cambridge: Cambridge University Press.

Hemetsberger, A. (2005). Creative cyborgs: How consumers use the internet for self-realization. *Advances in Consumer Research, 32,* 653–660.

Holt, D. B. (1995). How consumers consume: A typology of consumption practices. *Journal of Consumer Research, 22*(1), 1–16.

Holt, D. B. (1997). Poststructuralist lifestyle analysis: Conceptualizing the social patterning of consumption. *Journal of Consumer Research, 23*(4), 326–350.

Holt, D. B. (1998). Does cultural capital structure American consumption? *Journal of Consumer Research, 25*(1), 1–25.

Holt, D. B., & Thompson, C. J. (2004). Man-of-action heroes: The pursuit of heroic masculinity in everyday consumption. *Journal of Consumer Research, 31*(2), 425–440.

Jones, M. (1999). Structuration theory. In: W. Currie, & R. Galliers (Eds), *Rethinking management information systems: An interdisciplinary perspective* (pp. 103–135). New York: Oxford University Press.

Kedzior, R. (2009). Mapping out digital materiality-insights for consumer research. *Advances in Consumer Research, 36,* 22–23.

Kleine, R. E., Schulz Kleine, S., & Kernan, J. B. (1993). Mundane consumption and the self: A social-identity perspective. *Journal of Consumer Psychology, 2*(3), 209–235.

Kozinets, R. V. (1999). E-tribalized marketing?: The strategic implications of virtual communities of consumption. *European Management Journal, 17*(3), 252–264.

Kozinets, R. V. (2008). Technology/ideology: How ideological fields influence consumers' technology narratives. *Journal of Consumer Research, 34*(4), 865–881.

Kozinets, R. V., Hemetsberger, A., & Schau, H. J. (2008). The wisdom of crowds: Collective innovation in the age of networked marketing. *Journal of Macromarketing, 28*(4), 339–354.

Latour, B. (1993). *We have never been modern.* Cambridge, MA: Harvard University Press.

McCall, G. J., & Simmons, J. L. (1978). *Identities and interactions* (Rev. ed.). New York: Free Press.

Miller, D. (1995). *Acknowledging consumption.* London: Routledge.

Peñaloza, L. (1994). Atravesando fronteras/border crossings: A critical ethnographic exploration of the consumer acculturation of Mexican immigrants. *Journal of Consumer Research, 21*(1), 32–54.

Reed, A. (2002). Social identity as a useful perspective for self-concept–based consumer research. *Psychology & Marketing, 19*(3), 235–266.

Richins, M. L. (1994). Valuing things: The public and private meanings of possessions. *Journal of Consumer Research, 21*(3), 504–521.

Schau, H. J., & Gilly, M. C. (2003). We are what we post? Self-presentation in personal web space. *Journal of Consumer Research, 30*(3), 385–404.

Schau, H. J., Munizet, A. M., & Arnould, E. J. (2009). How brand community practices create value. *Journal of Marketing, 73*(5), 30–51.

Schouten, J. W., & McAlexander, J. H. (1995). Subcultures of consumption: An ethnography of the new bikers. *Journal of Consumer Research, 22*(1), 43–61.

Schultz Kleine, S., & Menzel Baker, S. (2004). An integrative review of material possession attachment. *Academy of Marketing Science Review, 1,* 1–35.

Serres, M., & Latour, B. (1995). *Conversations on science, culture, and time.* Ann Arbor: University of Michigan Press.

Spiggle, S. (1994). Analysis and interpretation of qualitative data in consumer research. *Journal of Consumer Research, 21*(3), 194–203.

Stone, G. P. (1962). Appearance and the self. In: A. M. Rose (Ed.), *Human behavior and social processes.* Boston: Houghton Mifflin.

Strathern, M. (1994). Forward: The mirror of technology. In: R. Silverstone & E. Hirsch (Eds), *Consuming technologies: Media and information in domestic spaces* (pp. 7–13). London: Routledge.

Thompson, C. J. (1996). Caring consumers: Gender consumption meanings and the juggling lifestyle. *Journal of Consumer Research, 22*(4), 388–407.

Thompson, C. J., & Hirschman, E. C. (1995). Understanding the socialized body: A poststructuralist analysis of consumers' self-conceptions, body images, and self-care practices. *Journal of Consumer Research, 22*(2), 139–153.

Thompson, C. J., & Troester, M. (2002). Consumer value systems in the age of postmodern fragmentation: The case of the natural health microculture. *Journal of Consumer Research, 28*(4), 550–571.

Warde, A. (2005). Consumption and theories of practice. *Journal of Consumer Culture, 5*(2), 131–153.

Zwick, D., & Dholakia, N. (2006). The epistemic consumption object and postsocial consumption: Expanding consumer-object theory in consumer research. *Consumption, Markets and Culture, 9,* 17–43.

# "PIXELIZE ME!": DIGITAL STORYTELLING AND THE CREATION OF ARCHETYPAL MYTHS THROUGH EXPLICIT AND IMPLICIT SELF-BRAND ASSOCIATION IN FASHION AND LUXURY BLOGS

Gachoucha Kretz and Kristine de Valck

## ABSTRACT

*Purpose* – *The purpose of our study was to better understand how bloggers organize branded storytelling in fashion and luxury blogs using explicit and implicit self-brand association.*

*Methodology/approach* – *We have carried out a Netnography on a sample of 60 fashion and luxury blogs. Data analysis relied on a visual denotational and connotational analysis. We have also conducted hermeneutic interviews of influential fashion bloggers and readers to validate our findings.*

*Findings* – *Bloggers differently combine explicit and implicit textual and visual branded stimuli depending on their character types. The most influential blogs combine textual implicitness and visual explicitness, regardless of their character types. Other influential bloggers combine visual and textual elements of the story more or less explicitly depending on the archetypes they have constructed. Bloggers reintermediate the relationship between brands and consumers and serve as a "lens" through which readers may select a brand and decide on purchase. The quality of the relationship between the bloggers and the readers relies on the initial reading contract, the evolving presence of the advertised brands in the blog's content, and the amount of privacy shared by the bloggers with their audience.*

Research limitations/implications – *Our sample is very limited and includes very influential and professionalized blogs.*

Practical implications – *Our study should help brand managers in selecting fashion blogs as a new relay for advertisement or sponsored content.*

Originality/value of paper – *Our study provides a framework to brand managers by highlighting recognizable storytelling patterns.*

Blogs are "the Social Media equivalent of personal web pages and can come in a multitude of different variations, from personal diaries describing the author's life to summaries of all relevant information in one specific content area. Blogs are usually managed by one person only, but provide the possibility of interaction with others through the addition of comments" (Kaplan & Haenlein, 2010). They offer consumers an almost unlimited space for self-expression on the Internet (Kozinets, 2006) with an access to a large audience. Bloggers thus benefit from considerable space for storytelling about products and brands on their blogs that brand managers cannot fully control.

"Brand-consumer storytelling" (Woodside, 2010; Woodside, Sood, & Miller, 2008) relates to narratives arranged by consumers where brands and products play a role in the stories told. Existing research on brand-consumer storytelling has reported that consumers create identities through branded storytelling (Edson Escalas, 2004; Holt, 2004) and that consumers' narratives enact myth production in their lives (Adaval and Wyer Jr., 1998; Shankar, Elliott, & Goulding, 2001; Woodside et al., 2008; Woodside, 2010). Studies of online narratives show that consumers digitally associate with brands on personal web spaces to construct identities (Jensen Schau & Gilly, 2003) and that consumers' narratives follow "archetypal patterns" (Kozinets, De Valck, Wojnicki, & Wilner, 2010) depending on the character type aimed at. However, little account has been made of how consumers arrange branded storytelling in online personal spaces such as fashion blogs and what possible characters and myths may be pursued.

In this chapter, we focus on influential fashion bloggers as opinion leaders (Katz & Lazarsfeld, 2008). We assume that these opinion leaders use their blogs as spaces for self-stories about fashion consumption practices thus offering fashion and luxury brands access to "character narratives" (Kozinets et al., 2010) about fashion and luxury brands and products. We postulate that character narratives either comprise textual self-stories with brands and products or pictorial forms such as paintings, photographs, or illustrations staging branded products on blogs' pages.

Drawing on the literature about brand-consumer storytelling and self-brand association, we try to unravel how fashion bloggers arrange branded digital storytelling on their blogs, taking into consideration the pressure from the blogs' audiences and from the brands as advertisers on these blogs.

Findings highlight self-brand association patterns pertaining to explicit or implicit visual and textual self-brand association processes, depending on the bloggers' character types. In addition, we found that character types, depending on their self-presentation motivation, will associate with brands as objects of desire, brands as performers, and brands as partners.

## CONCEPTUAL FRAMEWORK

### Digital Storytelling

Consumer storytelling theory has been very much addressed by scholars (for a thorough review, see Woodside et al., 2008 or Cooper, Schembri, & Miller, 2010). Consumers' stories about their consumption experiences of brands and products have been reported to assign roles to brands (Fournier, 1998) and to enact archetypal myths (Holt, 2003; Woodside et al., 2008; Kozinets et al., 2010). Although providing access to insights about symbolic relationships to brands, those consumers' narratives are "introspection produced and used for research purposes" (Pace, 2008) and therefore lack spontaneity. Muniz and Schau (2005) and Schau and Muniz (2006) state that communities help generate spontaneous storytelling about brands, and Pace (2008), Jensen Schau and Gilly (2003), and Kozinets et al. (2010) suggest that personal websites offer new space for the study of unleashed consumers' narratives. However, little research has addressed how consumers arrange personal branded narratives depending on the character type and myth they want to construct on their personal online spaces. Jensen Schau and Gilly (2003) have concluded that consumers digitally associate with brands to construct identities but suggest further investigation about the "types of digital stimuli" and "how they communicate brand associations and enact consumer–brand relationships." Fashion blogs present branded storytelling combining visual and textual branded stimuli and therefore provide a field to study how consumers spontaneously arrange branded digital stimuli through stories. In addition, Kozinets et al. (2010) have found that consumers' narratives follow "archetypal patterns" and report narrative strategies adopted by bloggers after a "seeding" campaign. However, we do not know much about spontaneous narrative strategies when bloggers' branded stories are developed regardless of a seeding campaign.

The present research aims at adding to the existing findings on consumer–brand storytelling and particularly on digital storytelling in fashion blogs by exploring how fashion bloggers combine textual and visual branded stimuli to generate stories and myths. Building on a preceding chapter, we investigate digital storytelling through visual and textual brand association depending on three character types highlighted in that previous research: Real Life (RL) Facsimile, Stereotypes, and Fiction. RL Facsimile are the most professionalized fashion blogs where bloggers perform as fashion professionals and associate with exclusive fashion and luxury brands that they carefully select. Stereotypes are blogs where specific features are made salient by the blogger (the Trendy Mom, the Fashion addict, The Rebel): brands are thus selected to stress that feature or stereotype. Finally, the Fiction blogs are the most creative and aesthetic blogs, displaying artistic talent and associating very scarcely and/or very implicitly with carefully selected brands. As a consequence, bloggers seem to differ in how they self-associate with brands and particularly in how they visually and textually stage the brands. The stories and myths thus generated should also differ depending on the bloggers' character types. In this chapter, we focus on consumer–brand storytelling and particularly on the combination of textual and visual branded digital stimuli spontaneously organized by bloggers to create stories.

## METHOD

We carried out a Netnography on 60 fashion blogs, selected from a famous fashion platform until saturation was reached. The selected blogs aged from one year at least to four years' existence time. We assumed fashion blogs to offer a rich ground for branded storytelling as blogs report particular consumption habits and brands narratives (Kozinets, 2006) and that narratives create or enhance self-brand connection (Edson Escalas, 2004).

Data collection followed two phases: a first study analyzed how bloggers self-presented visually and reported three character types (RL Facsimile, Stereotype, and Fiction). The second phase focused on brand narratives with particular attention on how each character types visually and textually self-associate with brands. Influence strength was defined by the width of the audience (number of visits), the number of comments, the number of posts and archives, and the blog's media coverage.

We carried out a longitudinal visual analysis of all the visual branded digital elements appearing on each blog to understand visual online self-brand association. Following Barthes, (1961 and 1964) and Penn (2000) we inventoried denotational, that is, "raw," visual elements and then analyzed how they combined to form connotation and mythical and ideological meaning. We also carried out a longitudinal textual semiotic analysis, following Greimas (1966) narrative scheme. Actants, that is, roles taken up by the characters in the story were highlighted to better understand what actantial role patterns emerged in each blog for the mentioned brands. Parallel to that visual and textual semiotic analysis, we interviewed the 13 selected bloggers and analyzed each blog's content, to validate our findings and to add perspective and richness to our interpretation. Finally, since the bloggers' success highly depends on their audience, we reviewed the readers' comments both on the blog and on external fashion forums to add insight or clarify self-brand association issues including the audience's reactions.

We found that bloggers combine two kinds of self-brand association processes that we have called explicit and implicit digital self-brand association processes. The balance of explicit and implicit self-brand association elements depends on the character types aimed at and their motivations in holding a blog. However, the most influential blogs regardless of the character types turn out to combine all explicit visual and implicit textual brand association and place brands in the plot as characters. Besides, we discovered that the branded storytelling organized by bloggers undergo great pressure from the brands as advertisers on their blogs and from the readers as warrants of the bloggers' influence. Finally, discussion about digital storytelling and consumer–brand theory is advanced; particularly from the audience standpoint and recommendations for brand managers are suggested.

# FINDINGS

## Explicit and Implicit Self-Brand Association Processes

Fashion bloggers organize branded storytelling by visually and textually combining explicit and implicit self-brand association. Indeed, bloggers generate branded stories by mentioning, featuring, and mimicking brands and brands' identities (Kapferer, 2008) or by assigning roles to brands.

### Explicit Self-Brand Association

We have defined explicit self-brand association as the process of intentionally inserting readily recognizable visual or textual brands on the blog page. Brands are "denoted," that is, featured "as they are" in the reality, like a "codeless message" (Barthes, 1961, 1964). Brands are clearly cited or staged through active links, names, and logos. We have excluded visual and textual elements that do not belong to the blog's editorial line, that is, on which the blogger has no upper hand, such as banners, blocks, and advertising links.

Visual explicit branded elements mainly pertain to clear featuring of the brand logo in illustrations or photographs. For example, the model carries a Chanel bag, easily recognizable thanks to its famous "quilted stitch" and logo (http://www.garancedore.fr/2009/10/07/chanel-lhypershow) or a fashion drawing features an outfit with clear appearance of the brand logo (http://www.garancedore.fr/2008/10/28/xoxo-gossip-girl). Culturally embedded products like the 2.55 Chanel bag are so famous that visually featuring them – even without explicitly showing the logo – also pertains to visual explicitness (http://www.thecherryblossomgirl.com/page/4/?s = chanel).

Branded textual elements either appear as active external links or are dropped in the story, either accompanying a picture or by themselves. Where the textual branded element is inserted depends on the blogger's purpose. If they want to inform their audience and detail the outfit, brands will appear close to the photograph as in any fashion magazine. If they want to tell a story including the brand, textual branded elements will be "dropped" in the story and pictures will serve as pretexts to write about the mentioned brands. Sometimes, brands are not linked to a picture and are mentioned for narrative purposes where they play a role for the plot.

*Implicit Self-Brand Association*
We have defined implicit self-brand association as featuring visual indices of a brand or as textually assigning roles to brands in the branded narrative.

Implicit visual self-brand association consists in borrowing the visual codes used by a brand and in transferring to the blog's visual identity the salient identity features of a brand. For example, we often noticed that the bloggers would self-picture inspiring from luxury brands' press ad campaigns like the Dior Addict fragrance campaign (http://www.thecherryblossomgirl.com/bling-bling-slot-machine/7521). It can also relate to featuring "it" products in pictures or illustrations that only fashion experts and addicts are to recognize. For example, one of the fashion bloggers we have monitored often draws illustrations featuring products that only fashion addicts and experts are able to recognize. One striking example was a Yves Saint Laurent "Tribute" pair of shoes left on a Baroque sofa and that only fashion addicts would spot in the comments (http://www.garancedore.fr/2009/04/16/mix-match).

We found actantial patterns in each blogger's branded storytelling. Indeed, bloggers assign implicit roles to brands in their narratives, as performers, objects of desire, or construction partner.

*Brands as Performers*
Some bloggers behave as "senders" or "judging senders" (Greimas, 1966). Indeed, they assign tasks to brands and then evaluate how they performed:

> When I have received an invitation to discover Maison Martin Margiela's new fragrance [...] I was really curious to face what one of my favourite designers had been able to create with the mighty L'Oréal. And what I have seen has upset me a little. [...] What's inside the bottle bothers me the most [...] the fragrance smells too intoxicating to me. [...] And probably that, despite of its feminine positioning, it would better suit a dude. And yet, not any dude. (Café Mode, post, January 12, 2010)

These bloggers are willing to sound as experts. Some of them are really influential and were appointed journalists in famous fashion magazines. In that implicit self-brand association the brand does not have the upper hand. The blogger expects to be persuaded through efficient demonstration and arguments to issue their evaluation.

## Brands as Objects of Desire

For some bloggers, brands are "objects" and therefore, possessing a product of their favourite brand is the ultimate quest. The brand is considered an object of desire. Narratives about brands as objects of desire are overwhelmingly enthusiastic and sometimes even hysterical and voice emergency to possess.

> The first time I have seen that Vuitton bag on Sofia Coppola, I fell over backwards. Yes, I agree, I AGREE!!! Some material things down here still make totally hysterical. [...] You probably never wondered what happens in a girl's head when she falls totally in love with apparel, the big crush, huh? Here is the raw truth: the music of ultimate happiness. As simple as that. (Garance Doré, post, June 4, 2009)

Bloggers who consider branded products as objects of desire usually behave as fans and worshippers of the brand. Therefore, the brand serves as an "elevator" for the self in the self-brand association and contributes to the construction of an Ideal Self. Some bloggers also present branded objects as objects of desire, not for themselves but for others. In that case, they behave as senders: they demand the audience to consider the brand as a desired product and thus, to become addicts of that brand. Senders reveal high influence to their loyal audience who often follow purchase instructions:

> You can trigger genuine moves [by promoting a product on your blog]: fifteen girls will ask you where you found it, in what H&M shop, what the collection was and "hurry up, hurry up, I am buying it"! The skirt I showed in one of the looks I have shot ... well. I had bought it weeks ago, so when Punky [another blogger] linked my look picture to her blog, it was out of stock almost everywhere. Since more than ten thousand people visit her blog a day, I think I have generated A LOT of frustration, that day, if I believe what has been said in the comments. (Mode Opératoire, interview)

## Brands as Identity Construction Partners

Brands can also act as identity construction and transformation tools. The bloggers already possess one or many products of a brand and talk about them as "helpers" or partners that help them construct archetypes. The story relies on a transformation from a beginning state to a final better different state generated by the use of the brand. The blogger only mentions briefly the brand and proves the "metamorphosis" thanks to the branded products through a series of pictures of the final stage. The result of the transformation is then left to the audience's evaluation.

Interestingly enough, brands may be implicitly associated to "opponents" or evils that encourage shopping crimes. In that case, bloggers claim they want to keep away from the sinful branded product:

> I had abstained from coming any closer than twenty meters to any Sofia Coppola for Louis Vuitton handbag in case I could not resist. I passed by a Louis Vuitton boutique ... I could not help it. I asked a sales attendant to grab it for me so that I could examine it a little bit closer. The blue one. Suede leather. More than three thousand dollars. I now need a four hectares safety zone. (Garance Doré, post, April 10, 2009)

The opponent brand in that case plays the role of what Jensen Schau and Gilly (2003) called "digital association": the blogger self-presents and constructs an identity thanks to products they do not physically own but that are able to express a potentially ideal self.

We have discovered that bloggers use visual and textual explicit and implicit self-brand associations to generate branded stories. However, we also found that the self-brand associations underlying the bloggers' storytelling also differ across the character types constructed.

### Constructing Characters and Archetypal Narratives by Combining Explicit and Implicit Self-Brand Association

Fashion bloggers digitally associate with brands they chose but do not always possess as a way to create wanted online identities (Jensen Schau & Gilly, 2003). Therefore, it has come as no surprise that self-brand associations differ across blogs depending on the identities the bloggers want to put forward. Particularly, findings show that bloggers rely on different combinations of visual and textual implicitness and explicitness in the way they make branded stories depending on the archetype and myths they want to create.

### Real Life Facsimile Characters Mainly Rely on Textual Explicitness

RL Facsimile chiefly combine implicit visual and explicit textual elements and assign brands the role of performers. Narratives usually rely on textual facts and figures, critical analyses, experts' stories about fashion, textually displayed knowledge about brands, and recommendations about brands and purchases; visual elements are scarce and aim at illustrating the blog and making the textual less "staunch." Indeed, RL Facsimile analyze and criticize brands or praise them spontaneously.

And yet, those bloggers are often subject to the pressure of brands as advertisers and thus as money providers and to the pressure of the audience who seek genuine and independent content and acts as a strong counter-power as the influence of the bloggers totally depends on the number of readers that can drastically disappear if they do not trust them anymore. Therefore, RL Facsimile need to balance criticism and analysis with visual elements. They also need to soften criticism so as not to scare the brands they work for.

*Stereotypes Stress Explicitness Whether Visually or Textually*
Stereotypes mainly combine visual and textual explicit brand association. Stereotypes want to construct stereotyped characters relying on salient personalities like "the good friend," "the fashion rebel," "the trendy Mom." The branded stories they generate aim at reinforcing the related myths. For example, the "fashion rebel" will only mention unknown or sharp designers' brands, give a rock flavor to her blog, and create stories stressing the blogger's rebel attitude. Stereotypes also assign brands the role of objects of desire: brands are therefore explicitly praised and presented as a "must have." As a consequence, texts and pictures explicitly feature and mention brands related to the stereotype the bloggers want to create.

However, Stereotypes are subject to pressures from the brands that advertise or want to or their space and from the readers. Indeed, influential Stereotypes have a loyal and large audience and therefore attract advertisers: they must therefore screen them so as to avoid unwanted or unrelated advertising on their blogs. In addition, the readers usually read Stereotypes' blogs for the personality and salient features and brands they stage and push forward. Therefore, they have to remain consistent in the way they tell branded stories and need to respect the initial reading contract they have set up in launching their blogs.

*Fiction Blogs Stress Implicitness Whether Visually or Textually*
Fiction blogs usually combine visual implicit and textual implicit brand associations. Brands are assigned the role of construction and transformation partners. Indeed, Fiction bloggers aim at creating characters based on famous myths like Cinderella or the "Femme Fatale." Therefore, creating a personal universe and reinforcing the targeted myth through the visual and textual storytelling are the main motivation. As a consequence, explicit brand praising is not appreciated as it is supposed to ruin the magic and to bring some vulgarity to the aesthetics of the blog. Fiction blogs thus rely on creativity and artistic mastery and mimic the brands they love: luxury or sharp fashion designers' brands.

Fiction usually live on their blogs as they are fashion designers, photographers, or consultants. They thus depend on financial or content resources allocated by fashion and luxury brands. And yet, they resent to advertise explicitly and may scare the brands that will not consider them as potential advertising platforms. In addition, Fiction readers like their creativity, the aesthetics of the blog, and the fact that advertising and product placement are absent or scarce. Thus, branded storytelling needs to remain implicit to maintain the audience.

Finally, digital storytelling in fashion blogs depends on both the character types and the archetypal myths sought for. The bloggers seeking for "digital likeness" (Jensen Schau & Gilly, 2003) and trustworthiness like RL Facsimile stress argumentative and factual textual storytelling. Stereotypes who aim at pushing forward a salient domain of expertise and who need to please their audience as a person arrange digital storytelling in order to maintain the blog's initial personality and reading contract. Fiction bloggers who privilege artistic creation and aesthetics but who are dependent on the brands for the financial and material resources (gifts, products, press releases, and bloggers' events) provide combined implicit visual and textual elements to create branded stories preserving the magic of their blogs.

However, when taking a closer look at the most influential blogs in our sample, we discovered that blogs combining textual implicitness and visual explicitness and placing brands in the plots as character – regardless of any character type or actantial role – were the most influential ones. We labeled those blogs "Brands' artists-fans." In order to better understand why such blogs are more influential, we studied the case of Garance Doré, one of the most famous fashion bloggers in the world, more deeply.

## Brands' Artists-Fans: Balancing Brands' Expectations and the Audience's Demands

Brands' artists-fans are bloggers who practice "DIY cultivation" (Holt, 2002) and want to stress personal and creative branded content. Indeed, artists-fans like Garance Doré magnify products by making beautiful and genuine pictures or illustrations, by creating a very personal story about the products or the brands. Personal, genuine, and creative digital storytelling able to magnify the brands as advertisers and content providers and the audience as entertainment and sensation seekers is the key.

### Pleasing the Audience: Balancing Verisimilitude and Dream

Garance Doré started her blog in June 2006. She is now considered one of the most influential key fashion figures in the world with almost 30,000 unique visitors per day (December 2009). Garance Doré was an illustrator and had no connection with the fashion world except her passion for fashion in general, outfits, and for the Vogue magazine. She left her southern province to come to work in Paris and get closer to the City of Fashion. She finally joined the Vogue.com team as a fashion journalist in October 2008. From that point, she has become one the most influential women in the world of fashion and sits at the front row of the most prestigious catwalks of every Fashion Week.

What her readers love about her blog is the rags to riches tale and the Cinderella myth Garance Doré represents: she could be anybody and any of her readers. She was just luckier than anyone else. In addition, her readers like the fact that she has remained simple and close to them and that she keeps on reporting her encounters in the glittering fashion world with enthusiasm. Indeed, readers are eager for information and insights about the fashion world, and are therefore looking for genuineness and verisimilitude. They want to know more about Garance Doré, her life, her joys and griefs, and some private details.

> I love Garance because she is so fresh and accessible and nice. And I love to come to her blog and discover what happened to her, in her life, how it is going on with Scott and in her job ... She remains simple and she shares things about herself. Alix (another blogger) ... she just irritates me. She is so cold! She never shares anything about herself, her life, who she is. It is boring now! (Stephanie, blog reader, April, 2010).

However, readers like Garance Doré's life for it is exceptional and sounds like a fairy tale. Thus, having readers dream is essential as part of the entertainment. Therefore, Garance Doré is expected to report exclusive information, insights, stories, or even gossips about the exclusive fashion environment she now belongs to. For that reason, name dropping and exclusive brands' mentioning is necessary. However, some readers accuse her of being sold out to the brands she writes about and doubt her trustworthiness. As a consequence, branded storytelling needs to balance the audience's expectation of extraordinary stories about exclusive designers' and luxury brands and the audience's reluctance about sponsored content.

To manage perceived neutrality, Garance Doré arranges explicit visual branded associations and implicit textual branded associations. Indeed, her reputation is one of making pictures and illustrations of branded products and telling nice, fun, and entertaining stories about the products that she visually stages. The text usually does not explicitly mention brands per se: brands are always placed in the plot as characters, which reduces the risk of being accused of writing sponsored posts.

*Satisfying the Brands as Advertisers and Customers: Magnifying and Creating a Personal Vision of the Branded Content Provided by the Brand Managers*
Garance Doré progressively got exclusive access to information, insights, and content about designers' and luxury brands. Brand managers offer her gifts or lend her products and branded content to feed her blog. Therefore, while a "regular" blogger strives to have access to branded content, she can add value to the branded content and products she was lent by addressing it in a personal and creative way. Brands now expect bloggers to show talent and to give a personal interpretation of what the brands are, see, to magnify them. Fashion bloggers like Garance are expected to generate both creative and personal genuine content and also to reintermediate the consumer–brand relationship as a "filter" or a "lens" through which the readers might consider the brands as a part of the relationship they have with the blogger.

## DISCUSSION

*Digital Storytelling and Self-Brand Association*

Conclusions that bloggers arrange digital storytelling depending on targeted archetypes is consistent with previous research on consumer–brand storytelling and myths: bloggers as storytellers experience myths reflecting archetypes (Holt, Thompson, & Iacobucci, 2004; Holt, 2004; Woodside et al., 2008). Our findings provide further detail about how bloggers combine visual and textual digital branded stimuli to balance both the brand managers' and the audience's expectations, that is, brand magnifying and authenticity and trustworthiness. We particularly suggest that depending on the character type, either textual or visual explicitness or implicitness are stressed. More surprising at first is the fact that the most influential blogs combine explicit visual and implicit textual brand association regardless of the archetype sought for. Closer examination leads to the hypothesis that fashion bloggers are advertising literate and mimic advertising techniques where textual claims are allusive and visual promises are explicit. Interestingly, bloggers seem to have reversed brand communication: advertising used to stage consumers to appeal to consumers whereas bloggers as consumers create and stage brands or branded content in a "mise-en-scène" to both appeal to brands and consumers.

*Reintermediation of the Relationship between Brands and Consumers*

The study of digital storytelling has drawn our attention on the fact that bloggers reintermediate the consumer–brand relationships. Indeed, bloggers serve as filters who propose selected branded content to a dedicated and familiar audience. Our study of fashion bloggers show that bloggers have great influence on their audience and that such an influence relies on the quality of the relationship held between the blogger and the readers. The quality of that relationship seems to depend and the initial reading contract settled by the blogger, on the perceived genuineness and trustworthiness of the blogger and the informative and entertaining aspects of the stories told. Indeed, as for TV shows, stories, or soap operas, readers integrate the stories told in the blogs they read to update and evaluate their personal lives (Livingstone, 1988; Livingstone, 1998). Therefore, people might read blogs because the ups and downs of their favorite bloggers help them live their own lives.

*Why Read Fashion Blogs?*

The question then arises: why do people read blogs? Preliminary results show that people read blogs to grab information or recommendations about brand and products, for fun, to better understand the world they live in and also to consume insights, secrets, gossips, and some of the bloggers' privacy. Kapferer (1990) suggests that people are eager to consume rumors and gossips: bloggers who tell stories about themselves and their favorite brands are finally perceived as "friends" for many readers because of a parasocial interaction process. Readers we have met indeed have yielded that they like bloggers who share intimate and juicy anecdotes about themselves or celebs they meet.

## MANAGERIAL IMPLICATIONS

Our study provides a framework for managers when addressing fashion bloggers to advertise their brands. First, managers should distinguish the famous and very influential bloggers from the other influential ones. Very influential bloggers are the most courted and the most demanding ones: they can afford to choose the brands they want to advertise or to write stories about. Carefully studying what brands are explicitly magnified in pictures or illustrations may provide insights on their favorite brands. Besides, pointing out what brands are implicitly placed in the stories may help understand what brands they are ready to advertise. Moreover, brand managers should not expect to advertise through banners or links on very influential blogs. Second, brand managers should pinpoint influential blogs and distinguish the character types and myths pursued: whereas RL Facsimile value argumentation and proof, Stereotype carefully select brands that fit their personality and Fiction avoid explicit mentioning of the brands and use creative and artistic branded content. That said, brand managers may think that the fit between a brand's identity (Kapferer, 2008) and the blogger's personal brand represents the main criterion to select blogs as advertising platforms. However, brand managers should also take into account the audience's expectations. Indeed, it seems like readers will not have it when the brand interferes in the relationship they hold with the blogger by bringing in advertising if the initial reading contract was totally freed for ads or if they consider the brand is not "like the blogger." Brand managers therefore need to reintermediate their relationships with the end consumers but also to understand each blogger's audience and their expectations.

## LIMITATIONS AND FUTURE RESEARCH

Our findings are drawn from a very small corpus of influential bloggers and should not be generalized. In addition, we have selected influential and famous bloggers on purpose. However, our findings may not apply to less influential ones in that such blogs do not undergo the pressure of advertising and monetization. Finally, further research on the bloggers' readership is needed to better understand the quality of the relationship held by the bloggers and their audience.

## ACKNOWLEDGMENT

The authors thank Professor Marc Vanhuele and HEC Paris School of Management for their funding. They also want to express their gratitude to Professor Jean-Noël Kapferer, Marketing professor at HEC Paris School of Management for his insightful comments and much appreciated help.

# REFERENCES

Adaval, R., & Wyer, R., Jr. (1998). The role of narratives in consumer information processing. *Journal of Consumer Psychology, 7*, 207–245.

Barthes, R. (1961). Le message photographique. *Communications, 1*, 127–138.

Barthes, R. (1964). Rhétorique de l'Image. *Communications, 4*, 40–51.

Cooper, H., Schembri, S., & Miller, D. (2010). Brand-self identity narratives in the James Bond movies. *Psychology and Marketing, 27*, 557–567.

Edson Escalas, J. (2004). Narrative processing: Building consumer connections to brands. *Journal of Consumer Psychology, 14*, 168–180.

Fournier, S. (1998). Consumers and their brands: Developing relationship theory in consumer research. *Journal of Consumer Research, 24*, 343–353.

Greimas, A. J. (1966). *Sémantique structurale*. Paris: Larousse.

Holt, D. (2002). Why do brands cause trouble? A dialectical theory of consumer culture and branding. *Journal of Consumer Research, 29*, 70–90.

Holt, D. (2003). What becomes an icon most? *Harvard Business Review, 81*, 43–49.

Holt, D. (2004). *How brands become icons: The principles of cultural branding*. Harvard Business Press.

Holt, D., Thompson, C., & Iacobucci, D. (2004). Man-of-action heroes: The pursuit of heroic masculinity in everyday consumption. *Journal of Consumer Research, 31*, 425–440.

Jensen Schau, H., & Gilly, M. C. (2003). We are what we post? Self-presentation in personal web space. *Journal of Consumer Research, 30*, 385–404.

Kapferer, J. N. (1990). *Rumors*. New Brunswick: Transaction Editions.

Kapferer, J. N. (2008). *The new strategic brand management: Creating and sustaining brand equity long term*. Kogan Page.

Kaplan, A., & Haenlein, M. (2010). Users of the world, unite! The challenges and opportunities of social media. *Business Horizons, 53*, 59–68.

Katz, E., & Lazarsfeld, P.-L. (2008). *Influence personnelle: ce que les gens font des médias*. Paris: Armand Colin.

Kozinets, R., De Valck, K., Wojnicki, A., & Wilner, S. (2010). Networked narratives: Understanding word-of-mouth marketing in online communities. *Journal of Marketing, 74*, 71–89.

Kozinets, R. V. (2006). Netnography 2.0. In: R. W. Belk (Ed.), *Handbook of qualitative research methods in marketing*. Northampton, MA: Edward Elgar Publishing Inc.

Livingstone, S. (1988). Why people watch soap opera: An analysis of the explanations of British viewers. *European Journal of Communication, 3*, 55.

Livingstone, S. (1998). *Making sense of television: The psychology of audience interpretation*. Routledge.

Muniz, A., & Schau, H. J. (2005). Religiosity in the abandoned Apple Newton brand community. *Journal of Consumer Research: An Interdisciplinary Quarterly, 31*, 737–747.

Pace, S. (2008). YouTube: An opportunity for consumer narrative analysis? *Qualitative Market Research: An International Journal, 11*, 213–226.

Penn, G. (2000). *Semiotic analysis of still images*. London: Sage.

Schau, H., & Muniz, A. (2006). A tale of tales: The Apple Newton narratives. *Journal of Strategic Marketing, 14*, 19–33.

Shankar, A., Elliott, R., & Goulding, C. (2001). Understanding consumption: Contributions from a narrative perspective. *Journal of Marketing Management, 17*, 429–453.
Woodside, A. (2010). Brand-consumer storytelling theory and research: Introduction to a Psychology & Marketing special issue. *Psychology and Marketing, 27*, 531–540.
Woodside, A., Sood, S., & Miller, K. (2008). When consumers and brands talk: Storytelling theory and research in psychology and marketing. *Psychology and Marketing, 25*, 97–145.